Women, Gender, *and* Human Rights

A Global Perspective

Edited by MARJORIE AGOSÍN

RUTGERS UNIVERSITY PRESS

WOMEN,

GENDER,

and HUMAN

RIGHTS

NEW BRUNSWICK, NEW JERSEY, AND LONDON

Library of Congress Cataloging-in-Publication Data

Women, gender, and human rights : a global perspective / edited by Marjorie
Agosín.
      p. cm.
   Includes bibliographical references and index.
   ISBN 0-8135-2982-4 (alk. paper)—ISBN 0-8135-2983-2 (pbk. : alk. paper)
   1. Women's rights. 2. Human rights. I. Agosín, Marjorie.

   HQ1236 .W5852 2001
   305.42—dc21   2001019296

British Cataloging-in-Publication data for this book is available from the British
Library

Manufactured in the United States of America

To the Mothers of the Disappeared in Latin America
To Violeta Morales

Contents

Acknowledgments

Ever since I left Chile as an adolescent, human rights activism and writing have been a way of life as well as a tool for surviving my own exile and sense of displacement and for coping with the brutal reality of my homeland during the years of the Pinochet dictatorship. I thank the Mothers of the Disappeared all through Latin America, human rights activists who struggled to achieve a democratic society. Their constant efforts and belief in my work have made this book possible. I thank in particular Violeta Morales and Doris Maniconi.

In the United States many friends continue to inspire me in the pursuit of justice. My thanks go to Christopher Merrill, Robert Bonazzi, Paul Roth, Ruth Behar, Liliana Wilson, Emma Sepulveda and Isabel Alvarez Borland, Florinda Russo, Temma Kaplan, and Felice Gaer.

At home I am nurtured by the love of my family, especially my husband and our two children, who continually inspire me, as well as by my dear friends Paul and Laura Nakazawa, whose dialogue encourages and challenges me.

As always, I thank Leslie Mitchner, editor and friend, whose vision to publish books on issues of gender and human rights is at the core of her work; Brigitte Goldstein for her guidance, encouragement, and belief in my work; Theresa Liu for her careful editorial support; and Jessica Hornik for her skillful copyediting.

Finally, at Wellesley College I thank my student Sabrina de Melo for her technical brilliance and sense of humor.

Women, Gender, *and* Human Rights

Introduction

Marjorie Agosín

∞ IN the 1970s most Latin American countries were ruled by military dictatorships. All forms of civil disobedience were met with arrests, torture, or even death. The bodies of the victims often simply disappeared. The vanished body, deprived of identity, of physical and spiritual space, of social as well as historical memory, brings to mind the nearly universal condition of women pushed to the margins of official and recorded history, uneducated, illiterate, and powerless. The story of the disappeared represents a startling parallel to the worldwide struggle by women for visibility and for human rights and justice. Human rights, and particularly women's rights, must also be defined as being seen and treated as equal in the political and ideological as well as domestic and private arenas. The participation of women in the political and the social realm allows for delegitimizing discrimination against women—and achieving genuine equality—not only under the law. It also affects individual cultures that previously denied women the possibility of an education and confined them to a world of silence.

The Universal Declaration of Human Rights, created in 1948 as an international body of laws, was meant to protect the integrity and dignity of human beings. Those laws, together with the 1979 Convention for the Elimination of All Forms of Discrimination Against Women, have been pivotal in the affirmation and implementation of human rights. At the same time, these instruments have been used to prove the continued existence of violations of rights in both public and private spheres.

Conventional international human rights must also be understood as a way of truly living and participating in the world without physical or psychological coercion.

In war, women are often trophies and targets. Thus, human rights violations against women must be recognized not only as features of the developing world but as a continuum that cuts across cultures, races, and ideologies. In economically developed societies such as the United States and many European nations, domestic violence is rampant. In the United States, political leadership is often invisible or subsumed by the male-dominated system. Evidence from numerous studies of public schools suggests that girls are being shortchanged in the study of the sciences. On a worldwide scale, the most appalling rights violations occur in Afghanistan, where the Taliban, a radical Islamic movement, came to power in 1994. Girls and women are denied education, health, and employment outside the home; once again, under the requirement that they wear the *burqua,* they have become veiled ghosts deprived of even the most basic of human rights.

The image of a veiled body in fundamentalist societies has become a familiar one on Western television. Feminist thinkers, including Charlotte Bunch, have pointed out that the central debate on human rights seems to concern the body itself: a body that is coerced into obedience and veiled, that is raped as a trophy of war, that is mutilated and systematically violated, and, ultimately, a body that disappears from the public sphere of life.

Trafficking in child prostitutes, women being beaten in the suburbs, clitoridectomies with broken glass, the arrest of women searching for their husbands and children—such are the almost endemic violations of human rights tolerated by society at large and by policemen, teachers, and religious leaders, the supposed keepers of law and order.

The tenacity and persistence of rights violations, throughout history but especially in the twentieth century, which has been called the century of genocide, have generated a substantial body of work by activists, grassroots leaders, writers, and thinkers. The purpose of these writings has been to bring international attention to the gender-based abuses that cut across cultural, social, and political lines. Many of these violations discriminate against status as equal partners and citizens. Widow burnings and honor killings are just two of the most extreme examples.

As one begins to grasp the central issue of and human rights, it is important to realize that most governments as well as nongovernmental organizations (NGOs) define human rights in terms of male models and patterns of thinking. For example, they fail to take issues of health and reproductive freedom, which are often a matter of life and death, into separate account. In the late twentieth century, gender rarely played a role in decisions over the granting of asylum. Gender-based discrimination in times of war or peace has been systematically violated, from rape to being barred from holding high office.

This anthology continues the work begun by scholars, activists, writers, and health professionals in the pluralistic field of human rights and aims to contribute to its growing literature. The essays collected here demonstrate that the human rights of women form part of a global landscape in which oppression figures regardless of culture, religion, or levels of education; they show how rights can reflect a systematic and universal pattern of abuse. Although there are multiple cultural differences among women and the societies in which they live, there is also a strong commonality that goes beyond national, economic, and social boundaries. This commonality is the anthology's unifying theme, and its definition of human rights recognizes the rights of women both in the public as well as in the private sphere. Such a definition revises and expands the traditional view of human rights, which has focused on actions such as state-sponsored terrorism, and arrives at a more inclusive understanding of human rights.

It is in the spirit of inclusiveness that this anthology was created. The participants, scholars, artists, and human rights activists, were asked to contribute essays exploring human rights from the point of view of their own disciplines, but also to explore the universality and commonality that are inherently a part of women's lives. From an international perspective, this collection explores issues marked by a regional point of view as well as those that are universal and tries to shed light on the common traits of so many lives. The essays address the centrality of bodies as objects of punishment, either as trophies of war or as victims in abusive domestic relationships that force women into invisibility, silence, and psychological punishment.

This collection brings together the works of distinguished authors, most of whom wrote these essays expressly for this anthology. The first three essays address the historical development of human rights as well as the international movement of activists working for change in NGOs and grassroots organizations. The first of these is Arvonne Fraser's "Becoming Human: The Origins and Development of Human Rights," in which the author traces the history of human rights from the perspective of education. She explores the extent to which women were exposed to a world outside the confining and invisible communities in which many of them have lived. Reading, thinking, and teaching lead to participation in the world and become essential tools for the implementation of rights. Fraser elucidates the development of access to knowledge and power, from the writings of Christine de Pizan six centuries ago to international human rights activism on behalf of women in the modern world. The essay provides a textured understanding of human rights, which must begin with the right to knowledge and culminate in the right to public leadership.

The second essay, by Sheila Dauer, director of Amnesty International Women's programs, addresses developments in the pursuit of human rights and equality for all women since 1979, a year of pivotal importance. That year saw the creation of the United Nations convention calling upon governments to eradicate discrimination against women; it also marked the height of the human rights movement, a period of intense activity that undoubtedly had a great impact on the convention. Dauer's essay explores forms of discrimination women and girls face in both Western and non-Western countries, and the ways in which governments often ignore these abuses, by way of two examples: abuse of the rights of women inmates in the United States, and "honor" killings of women in Pakistan along with other abuses faced by Pakistani women. This essay also highlights the important role of the international legal and NGO community in increasing awareness of these violations and in implementing change. Relying on documentation gathered by AI and other sources, she exposes continuing government-sponsored violations of women's human rights, in developed as well as developing countries, as well as women's legacy of invisibility.

In "Women, Violence, and the Human Rights System," the anthropologist Sally Engle Merry traces the historical, political, and social development of human rights laws within the framework of the Universal Declaration of Human Rights. Merry addresses the dramatic changes in the concept of human rights since 1948, and specifically in the context of women's rights, in particular relating to private and public violence. She shows how global circumstances constantly affect articulations of the human rights system. Her essay also explores the evolution of the concept of gender violence and the ways in which countries around the world have failed to meet international obligations to uphold laws against such violations of human rights.

Merry discusses the complexities of gender violence, such as the genital mutilation practiced in some parts of Africa, in its intricate connection to cultural practices and customs. Her essay shows the ways in which local groups and NGOs have lent unprecedented support to a redefinition of rights that maintains respect for cultural practices; yet changing these practices inevitably challenges certain cultural norms. "There is an inevitable collision," she writes, "between protecting women and preserving marriages." In the difficulties posed by such a collision lie the particular challenges of global women's human rights. The conceptualization of human rights violence vis-à-vis cultural practices, especially where vulnerability to violence is deeply entwined with sociocultural practices pertaining to sexuality and marriage, is, as Merry shows, an ongoing process within the human rights field.

In her essay, "Mainstreaming a Concern for the Human Rights of Women: Beyond Theory," Felice Gaer writes of the work that international human rights organizations have undertaken specifically to address women's human rights concerns. An important concept that has emerged in these efforts is "gender mainstreaming": the term signifies that policies must be examined as to their implications for women and men. Just as certain human rights abuses affect only women or women more than men, women have specific human rights needs. Thus gender, Gaer argues, must be linked with human rights issues—whether violence, health care, or access to power—and gender issues must be brought to the attention of the United Nations and other international bodies. Gaer discusses abuses of women's human rights in Afghanistan and how the international community has responded to them. Many governments and aid organizations take the least challenging path in implementing human rights policy and delivering aid—that is, rather than withhold aid on the grounds that Afghan women are denied the most basic of human rights, the UN and other bodies offer the aid in the hopes of changing the country from within in a slow and perhaps invisible way. The terrible risk is that the changes may come too late and fall far short of what is needed. The longer women are invisible, the more ground is lost in the struggle to make human rights apply equally to men and women. Gaer stresses the need for practical models of change so that obstacles to women's advancement, whether deriving from a country' laws and customs or practical barriers, be lifted around the world.

The second section of this volume addresses issues related to women's health. Sandra P. Levison, a physician, and Julie H. Levison, at the time of writing a student at Harvard's School of Medicine, contribute a significant essay on the subject. Not only the pursuit of health and access to health care but the pursuit of dignity and personal freedom are the authors' themes. They describe the extent of access to and types of health care in several countries and the cultural concepts of health care in different societies. A dramatic example is the limits imposed on Afghani women by the Taliban. In the United States, issues such as accessibility of contraception and violence against women are discussed from the dual perspective of human rights and health.

As serious as are the problems of women prevented from obtaining medical care, the situation of children, especially girls, is of even graver concern. Julia Chill and Susan Kilbourne, in "The Rights of the Girl Child," observe that "horrible things happen to children every day in every corner of the world. Boys and girls alike face unimaginable abuses, exploitative labor, forced military recruitment, exposure to fatal disease and denial of fundamental human rights. For girls, the human rights violations are compounded by gender bias, physical limitations, and traditional social roles." Girls suffer from a range of abuses: female children are more likely to be the victims of infanticide; girls are more likely than boys to be denied access to education; and girls are the victims in a vast network of prostitution, pornography, and sexual exploitation. These are the conditions that millions of children live under, yet, as the authors lament, the world remains indifferent. Chill and Kilbourne outline the international legal framework for the protection of the girl child and discuss ways to implement such laws.

Carola Suárez-Orozco's article, "Psychocultural Factors in the Adaptation of Immigrant Youth: Gendered Responses," explores the many factors that influence how well immigrants adapt to their host cultures. She offers a wide context of issues that face immigrants and refugees, from the trauma of border crossings to family destabilization to the challenges of learning a new language and functioning in school and the workplace. Special challenges face the children of immigrants, who must learn to become bicultural in order to survive and thrive. Noting the paucity of research on the specific experiences of girls, she presents findings in the field that lay the groundwork for further research. The lives of young immigrant girls and their mothers must be brought into the light so as to ensure that both girls and boys can make strides in their new cultures.

The third section of the volume deals with women as activists fighting for social change. Miep Gies, the Dutchwoman who hid Anne Frank's family in the secret annex in Amsterdam, has been asked about the courage it took to hide the Franks. Her reply is to state simply that "of course it takes courage to do one's duty as a human being." Why do people ask such a question in the first place? Why do so many hesitate when their turn comes to help their fellow human beings? Miep's powerful yet simple remark exemplifies the spirit of Temma Kaplan's essay, "Women's Rights as Human Rights." Kaplan sets out the ways in which activism, mobilization, and the international struggle for social justice are integral parts of human rights.

Temma Kaplan presents the ways in which women in the international community and at the grassroots level have redefined human rights, the notion of community, and the relationship of human rights to civil and political rights. She notes that a new concept of human rights has developed that encompasses certain rights often negated by governments, such as the right to food, water, and shelter. This new revision and expansion of rights has made civil society a subject attended to by the United Nations; the general nature of women's rights, as well as the relationship between survival and the way in which political institutions affect women's survival, have also become subjects of international discussion. Recounting the story of a Chilean woman activist now living in New York, Kaplan portrays the collective power of grassroots activism and demonstrates the importance of linking international concerns with local initiatives.

In "The Forgotten Minority," Jean Trounstine, who worked extensively in the prison system in Framingham, Massachusetts, explores the experiences of women behind bars. She treats specifically the issue of institutionalized violence against women, the mistreatment of their bodies, the erosion of their sense of identity and dignity, and the particular health issues faced by women in prison. Trounstine shows that the experience of incarcerated women is radically different from that of incarcerated men; the particular needs of women are consistently overlooked, their sexuality constantly humiliated. Once again the issue of invisibility arises, in this case with all the stigmas and stereotypes that surround incarceration.

Jane Stapleton Deziel's "Degrees of Separation" addresses the ways in which rape and domestic violence occur in our midst in places often overlooked, under a veil of silence and indifference. Campus rapes and violence against women are rampant, Stapleton Deziel argues, though ignored by the media and public officials, who view rape strictly as assault by a stranger and fail to recognize that the most common form of rape is acquaintance rape. She establishes a connection between hidden, unrecognized, domestic violence and worldwide violence against women by men. Women's bodies and their territories of apparent safety, their homes and private spaces, are subject daily to assault, conditions that challenge their very survival. Stapleton Deziel stresses the connections between all women, whether enduring extreme loss of human rights in nations like Afghanistan, where women's status is virtually that of nonpersons, or suffering from abuses such as rape that are cloaked in silence.

Mahnaz Afkhami's perceptive essay, "Gender Apartheid, Cultural Relativism, and Women's Human Rights in Muslim Societies," addresses women's human rights within the diverse communities of the Muslim world. For a Muslim woman living under a fundamentalist regime, certain central human rights questions are constantly at issue: Why cannot a Muslim woman have the right to determine and organize her own life? What gives another person, simply by virtue of being born a man, the right to intervene in a woman's life? Why is it that a Muslim cleric has the right to place a woman within preordained, prescribed boundaries? Afkhami rejects the notion that he derives this authority from God, from a text, or from a tradition. Further, she argues that the relativist discourse on human rights, essentially a Western approach entailing the concept of universal rights, has been manipulated by Islamists to appear as a form of cultural imperialism. By arguing that universal rights do not exist—that rights derive only from the body of Islamic "experts" and cannot be imposed by external notions or movements—Islamic societies have been able to perpetuate the oppression of women.

The pursuit of equal rights, justice, and freedom for and by women across the globe has been carried out through an alliance of governments, NGOs, and grassroots movements. Mary Geske and Susan Bourque, in "Grassroots Organizations and Women's Human Rights," show the links that have been established between local and global human rights bodies. The authors showcase Latin American groups such as the Mothers of Plaza de Mayo in Argentina who, in pursuit of a fair civil society, have defied their governments and reigns of political terror. Such women have devised strategies to defy government oppression and have thereby fostered new political imaginations to fight for democratic values and a more democratic concept of human rights for Argentina and the rest of Latin America. Other case studies explored are women's groups in Brazil and Peru that have challenged repression on a national scale from the perspective of gender.

The fourth and final section, "Beyond the Mirror: Women and the Cultures of Displacement," begins with Barbara Harlow's essay, " 'What Was She Doing There?': Women as 'Legitimate Targets,' " which examines the murders of two women in South Africa. Amy Biehl, an American, and Ruth First, a South African, were human rights activists, both engaging in tactics for achieving peace in a society torn by conflict. Biehl happened to be at the wrong place at the wrong time, targeted for being white. First was an anti-apartheid activist, murdered by South African security forces when she opened an envelope containing explosives. Not only the women themselves but the human rights struggle they were engaged in were the victims of violence. "What was she doing there?" The question—one that blames the victim—provokes another: Did these women have the right to be engaged in the work they believed in?

Harlow discusses the South African Truth and Reconciliation Commission, which granted amnesty to the killers of Biehl, and has yet to make a decision on whether First's killers should also go unpunished. As Harlow explains, the main criterion for amnesty was whether the victim was a "legitimate target" on political grounds. Harlow's article examines the issue of acknowledgment, justice, and historical memory. She weighs the historical and moral role of the victims against that of the perpetrators and prods us to wonder whether it is possible to feel forgiveness for the perpetrators, acknowledging that forgiveness is a way of transforming civil society. For the exile, participating in a civil society—first and foremost through acquiring a new language—is essential in order to create a culture of belonging and to construct a new sense of self. It is important to consider the components of exile, of exile identity, as part of the larger vision of human rights.

The novelist Agate Nesaule, in her elegant and moving piece, "How Long Does Exile Last?," presents an incident at a Latvian church social hour as a defining moment in her self-definition as a perpetual exile. The theme of inner exile and displacement runs through the images she presents of exiled women from a European war. Their eyes have witnessed death and suffering, and it is their eyes that betray the estrangement they feel as they become "other" in a new land and yet are unable to forget the traumas of war. Beneath their façades, the exiles have deep wounds. They are filled with a sense of being forced into pain, haunted by what they have seen and experienced. The exile strives to show a positive attitude while mourning for lost loved ones, destroyed homes, and devastated countries. In the unlikely event of an exile's return, it is only to discover she no longer belongs there, just as she does not really belong here.

The alliances between literature and human rights, as well as the multifaceted ways in which literary expression becomes a voice for dissent and struggle, are explored by Joseph Slaughter and Jennifer Wenzel in their essay, "Letters of the Law." They discuss three short stories that make use of the private realm of letters, often associated with "female writings," to address issues of human rights. In letters women writers struggle with the dichotomy of private and public, negotiating between the secretive realm of the private self and the external face on the public self. As Slaughter and Wenzel point out, human rights documents also are marked by the duality of private and public, involving as they do relationships among individuals, families, communities, and nations. In stories by the Colombian Helena Araujo, the Zimbabwean Tsitsi Dangarembga, and the Australian Janette Turner Hospital, we see how women from the secret and guarded spaces of the private can disturb and eventually change the order of the public sphere.

Christopher Merrill's provocative essay, "Before the Mirror," which closes the volume, is a series of portraits of women—an architect, a poet, and others—who decided to endure by remaining in the besieged cities of the Balkan war. His spare evocations of their lives and personalities shows the power of human resilience amidst the horror of war and ethnic hatred. Often such monumental resilience was achieved on a small scale: "Women went to great lengths during the siege to keep up their appearances. Beauty parlors thrived, and with little water the Sarajevans prided themselves on wearing clean clothes whenever possible." As one of the women interviewed remarked, "I would like to go to concerts and travel again. For this someone has to be alive." Thus does Merrill allow us to understand that the will to live itself—the desire to pursue simple human pleasures, to engage in activities others can take for granted—is a human rights issue.

At the beginning of this new century, we stand in possession of accelerated information and communications. The global society with its global citizens has indeed democratized the landscape of the Western world and much of the non-Western world as well. We have become world citizens, with travel and telecommunications becoming easier and more affordable. As we go out to see the world, the world also comes to us. Refugees, immigrants, and uncertain travelers all seem to interact in a transnational and transcultural world. In the domain of academia there has been a move toward internationalism, especially in the study of literature and in the conviction that Western superiority can no longer be taken for granted. Yet nationalistic identities persist, and along with nationalism a worldview that does not embrace pluralism and globalization. Fundamentalist religions believe that this new global society contradicts their system of beliefs. The concept of an inclusive and diverse world, and of a more free and open society, presents challenges and, in many cases, tensions.

Even as the world converges into a global society, much work remains to be done to improve the condition of women and to support their attempts to achieve justice and equal citizenship rights. Revisions of and additions to international law calling for the elimination of discrimination against women and children show a willingness to achieve a more just society. And yet, in countless ethnic wars waged during the twentieth century, in Europe, Latin America, and elsewhere, women were massacred, raped, and tortured; they were the victims of honor killings in many parts of the Middle East and of genital mutilation in many countries in Africa. Nations have attempted to control their culture and their national identity by controlling women's bodies and their access to power, knowledge, and public life.

The purpose of this collection is then to focus on the universality of women's invisibility and the ways we can engage in a human rights movement that will create a new vision and response to issues of women, violence, and their legitimacy in civil societies. These essays lend new visibility to women's human rights. Where solutions to ever-pressing problems are elusive, still the authors make plain that to focus awareness on the ways in which the state and the cultural patriarchy treat the rights of women, from reproductive freedom to the right to education, asylum, and refuge, is one path toward the goal of human rights for all.

The affirmation of the dignity of all human beings resides at the center of the Universal Declaration of Human Rights. Yet people everywhere continue to be deprived of their human rights. The uniqueness of this collection lies in its naming and honoring the numerous voices that have articulated what human rights have been through history, but especially in the twentieth century. The resilience of women all over the world, as well as their commitment to their communities, has profoundly changed the meaning of human rights and of women's rights. Grassroots movements, in many cases mobilized by mothers, have been a powerful lobby to pressure the United Nations and governmental institutions. The search for missing loved ones in Argentina, South Africa, and Rwanda has ultimately come to symbolize the search for truth and peace in societies where human life often takes the form of human remnants, of traces of a life that are reconstructed through acts of defiance and courage.

The Chilean feminist and sociologist Julieta Kirkwood was one of the first to establish a correlation between peace within the home and peace in the nation. Domestic violence in the United States bears profound similarities with abuse of women worldwide. It is always the body that is tortured, abused, and punished in wars fought between countries, sects, or partners. If women's bodies rest at the center of the complex debate over women's rights, we must endorse and strive for the body's preservation and protection. We must remake the world so that women and girls can be free and equal, so that the integrity of the female body is recognized in the national and cultural realms. So too the integrity of the voice: not succumbing to silence—using one's voice to resist oppression, to reconcile history's wrongs—is an essential theme of this volume. Having witnessed that which is beyond language's power to represent, women continue to search for the meaning of hope. Their resistance to silence bespeaks the desire to to remain whole and human.

I: THEORETICAL

VISIONS

Becoming Human

THE ORIGINS AND DEVELOPMENT
OF WOMEN'S HUMAN RIGHTS

Arvonne S. Fraser

∞ WHEN the Taliban took power in Afghanistan in 1994, one of its first edicts removed girls from school, forbade women from employment outside the home, and required women to wear garments totally covering themselves when they appeared in public. This measure was a clear abrogation of the principles set forth in the Universal Declaration of Human Rights, adopted in 1948, and the Convention on the Elimination of All Forms of Discrimination Against Women, adopted in 1979. It struck at the most basic of women's human rights, depriving them of economic, physical, and intellectual independence, and overturned what women internationally had been struggling to achieve for more than five centuries.

As John Stuart Mill argued in 1869 in his essay *The Subjection of Women,* the question is whether women must be forced to follow what is perceived as their "natural vocation," that is, home and family—often called the private sphere—or should be seen, in private and public life, as the equal partners of men. While the division of spheres, based on sex and known as patriarchy, may have been justified as a necessary division of labor in the early evolution of the human species, the system long ago outlived its functionality and has been challenged by women, and a few men, since at least the fifteenth century.

This essay traces the evolution of thought and activism over the centuries aimed at defining women's human rights and implementing the idea that women and men are equal members of society. Three caveats are necessary. First, because women's history has been deliberately ignored

over the centuries as a means of keeping women subordinate and is only
now beginning to be recaptured, this is primarily a northern story until
the twentieth century. Second, because of this ignorance—that is, because
so much is still unknown—any argument that the struggle to attain rights
for women is only a northern or western effort is without foundation.
Simply not enough available records exist detailing women's struggles or
achievements in the southern or eastern parts of the world. The few
records available to northern writers attest that women in other parts of
the world were not content with their status. Third, the oft-heard argument that feminism (read the struggle for women's equality) is a struggle
pursued primarily by elite women is simply another example of the traditional demeaning of women. Although history is replete with examples of
"elite" male leaders, few have been so branded.

This essay aims to stimulate historians and human rights activists to
delve deeper into the history of women's human rights throughout the
world and further develop this neglected half of history. Such historical
research would be a contribution to promoting women's human rights because it is from history, whether written or oral, that role models and traditions are created.

The historian Gerda Lerner has written:

> The fact that women were denied knowledge of the existence of Women's
> History decisively and negatively affected their intellectual development as a
> group. Women who did not know that others like them had made intellectual
> contributions to knowledge and to creative thought were overwhelmed by the
> sense of their own inferiority or, conversely, the sense of the dangers of their
> daring to be different. . . . Every thinking woman had to argue with the
> "great man" in her head, instead of being strengthened and encouraged by
> her foremothers.[1]

The Debate over Women's Rights

The original contributors to women's human rights were those who first
taught women to read and thus to explore the world outside the home and
immediate community. The idea of women's human rights is often cited as
beginning in 1792 with Mary Wollstonecraft's book, *Vindication of the
Rights of Women,* published in response to the promulgation of the natural-
rights-of-man theory. Historical research, however, has revealed a much
longer gestation period, beginning at least in the early fifteenth century
with the 1405 publication of *Le livre de la cité des dames* (*The Book of the
City of Ladies*) by Christine de Pizan. This work stimulated what French

feminists call the *querelle des femmes* (debate about women), which continues to the present.[2]

Because human life has so many facets, this long debate has been broad and wide-ranging. Much of the debate has involved the traditional demeaning of women. Over time, demeaning an individual or group—a common, often subconscious, technique used by one group seeking to maintain power over another—results in stereotyping and the denial of recognition of that group's accomplishments or contributions to society. As the demeaning becomes customary, discrimination results, establishing a rationale for differential treatment of groups and the individuals within the particular group. With discrimination, the less powerful are deprived of their history, their self-confidence, and, eventually, their legal ability to function as full citizens or members of the larger group. The great irony is that women have been charged with—and have often found security in—maintaining customs and tradition, thus institutionalizing the discrimination against them through the education and socialization of children.

Breaking tradition, defying custom, and overcoming discrimination require courage and leadership. Leaders bent on effecting change must develop a new vision of the world, articulate the problems of the status quo and a new theory of social and political order, and, over time, mobilize a critical mass of supporters who share the new vision and new articulation of the problems. For women, taking leadership was a double-edged problem, a contradiction in terms. For most women, especially before safe and effective birth control was available, marriage, home, and family were their means of economic survival and social acceptance. Girls were groomed for marriage, for reproduction and nurturance of the human species. While lauded in the abstract, and often romanticized, marriage and reproduction also have been demeaned throughout history. As Menander said two or three centuries before the birth of Christ, "marriage, if one will face the truth, is an evil, but a necessary evil."

As the Taliban so clearly understand, the prerequisites for development and implementation of women's human rights are education; the means and ability to make a living beyond childbearing, homemaking, and caring for families; freedom of movement; and a measure of respect as individual human beings, not prisoners of their sex.

Education involves the ability to receive, create, and disseminate knowledge. Knowledge is power, the foundation of intellectual and political development. It is gained through experience, education, and association with knowledgeable others. Expanded literacy among women allowed those who could not escape the confines of home to learn about the outside world and, through writing, to recount their experiences and express their ideas. Freedom to move in public and to travel independently, even within a limited area, allows both for gaining more experience and for exchanging experiences with others, increasing both knowledge and education. It took centuries for women to gain the right to education and the opportunity to find employment outside the home; it was only after women were afforded these opportunities that they could communicate their experiences inside and outside the home. The resulting education offered new opportunities for women, such as the ability, for sexually active women, to limit childbearing.

The beginning of women's education began with literacy. As literacy rates increased, women began to articulate their view of the world. Many wrote anonymously at first in order to have their work accepted for publication. The Industrial Revolution and the concomitant advances in science and technology contributed immensely to women's emancipation. Not only did more women find employment outside the home, travel and communication too became easier and cheaper. A major breakthrough was the development of safe, effective, and legal means of birth control. The fact that distribution of birth control information and devices was illegal in most countries until the early twentieth century, and that the term "family planning" became a substitute for birth control, is additional testimony to the dilemma Mill identified—men's belief that, for women to engage in their natural vocation, that of bearing and raising children and maintaining homes, they must be controlled by men.

With advances in health, sanitation, and medicine, an increasing number of women lived beyond their childbearing years, and more children lived into adulthood. Men's fear that women would not reproduce and that their progeny would not survive lessened, and the ability of women to participate in economic and political life increased.

By the time the United Nations was formed in the mid-twentieth century, internationally, a critical mass of women had been educated, were employed outside the home, and had obtained enough legal and social freedom to participate in public life, even at the international level. Numerous international women's organizations had fifty years of experience behind them. As a result of lobbying by these organizations, and with support from female delegates, the phrase "equal rights of men and women" was inserted in the UN Charter. When the Universal Declaration of Human Rights (UDHR) was drafted, the word "everyone" rather than the male personal pronoun was used in most, but not all, of its articles. When the Commission on Human Rights failed to recognize women's aspirations adequately, women delegates and the nongovernmental organizations (NGOs) supporting them were politically powerful and astute enough to obtain a freestanding Commission on the Status of Women (CSW).[3] By

1979 the CSW, with the support of women delegates and NGOs and a new wave of feminism under way, had drafted and successfully lobbied the adoption of the Convention on the Elimination of All Forms of Discrimination Against Women.

The Convention wove together all the ideas discussed during the preceding five centuries of debate and placed a strong emphasis on the concept of equality in family matters. The Convention covered civil and political rights as well as economic and social rights, and in 1980, with the requisite number of ratifications obtained, it became the international women's human rights treaty. At the 1993 world conference on human rights, NGOs focused on women's human rights brought the previously hidden issue of violence against women to international attention. "Women's rights are human rights" became the cry. Although the debate, begun in 1405, continues, and the Taliban's edict illustrates that women's position in society can deteriorate, there is now worldwide recognition that the term "women's human rights" is not a redundancy.

The drive to define women's human rights and eliminate discrimination against them can be seen as part of the worldwide democratization effort. The question at the beginning of the twenty-first century is whether women will exercise their political muscle sufficiently at national, local, and international levels to assure universal implementation of the women's human rights treaty. This depends on whether women, in partnership with men, can effectively rationalize the relationships between the private and public spheres—between work, family, and public life. An important related question is whether women in all countries will redeem their history and use it to validate and support their struggle for equality and justice or, as in the past, new women's movements will have to be organized every few generations to account for the lack of women's history and the shortcomings in traditional education and socialization of girls.

The Origins: Defining the Issues

Christine de Pizan's *Le livre de la cité des dames* was published partially in response to Giovanni Boccaccio's work of 1361, *Concerning Famous Women,* which described exceptional women of history who had acquired "manly spirit" and other male attributes such as "keen intelligence . . . and remarkable fortitude"[4] and who dared to undertake difficult deeds. Boccaccio believed the histories of these women should be recorded just as the histories of male leaders were recorded. De Pizan, a widow supporting her family by writing, responded to Boccaccio and other male writers of her day, not only by creating her own list of important women of the past, but also by encouraging women of all classes to look to their own experience and resist being limited and demeaned by men. (The word "demeaning" was used frequently before "discrimination" was popularized.) De Pizan argued for women's right to be educated, to be able to live and work independently, to participate in public life, and be masters of their own fate. As Marina Warner noted in her foreword to *The Book of the City of Ladies* (1982), de Pizan was one of the leading intellectuals of her day, and her extensive published works demonstrate that she was an astute political observer as well as a theorist.

The feminist historian Gerda Lerner credits de Pizan with the first deliberate effort to raise women's consciousness but laments the fact that, although numerous women later published lists of famous women, few used de Pizan as a reference—an example of how the lack of knowledge of women's history impedes intellectual development.[5] Joan Kelly, another feminist historian, argues that de Pizan opened the debate about women by establishing the basic postulates of feminism.[6] (*Feminism* is used throughout this essay in its original meaning: the theory of, and the struggle for, equality for women.) Kelly also asserts that de Pizan and her European successors focused on what is now called "gender"—the concept that the opposition to women is not simply biologically based but culturally based as well.

Four points are important about de Pizan and her work. The first is obvious but merits stating: she could not have written her book if she had been illiterate. Like many who followed her, she used the printed word and publication of her ideas to describe the situation of women. She not only contributed to the historical record, she analyzed life from a woman's perspective, basing her conclusions not only on her own life but also on the lives of her predecessors. The ability to gain and disseminate knowledge, to record history, and to express new ideas and life experiences in printed form is, as has been noted, a prerequisite for challenging social and political norms. De Pizan used her education and experiences as a basis for independent thought, a process that Wollstonecraft would later argue was a necessity for girls. The ability to analyze one's circumstances and derive wisdom from that analysis is an important intellectual exercise, especially when the individual, her group, and her work are demeaned by the wider world.

Second, de Pizan directly challenged the confinement of women to the private sphere of home and family. She placed herself in the public sphere and demonstrated that women could provide for themselves economically, as many women, particularly widows, had done before her.

Third, de Pizan began a tradition of women writing for publication not only to express their ideas but to offer economic support for themselves and their families. Finally, she understood that history, whether oral or written, is a political tool used to maintain power, to reinforce the dominant culture, and to record actions that affect the public sphere. History is not merely a record of leadership; it provides role models. As Cicero said, history provides guidance in daily life.

De Pizan understood that denying a group its history and suppressing its record of leadership results in disempowerment of the group. She knew that the record of actions by those who challenge existing power structures is often deliberately suppressed and that, unless that group is successful and becomes a new political force, the history is lost. History, as a record of male leadership, has been used, perhaps subconsciously, to reinforce the idea that women are insignificant and subordinate and therefore belong to the private sphere. Especially in societies where literacy is low and women's organizations are apolitical, male-dominated history and tradition maintain the existing social and political order. De Pizan and many of her successors have been omitted from recorded history, thus prolonging the struggle for women to achieve their human rights.

The Drive for Education and Independence

Throughout the sixteenth and seventeenth centuries, increasing numbers of girls, primarily in royal and wealthy families, were educated. More and more women began writing for publication, although often anonymously for fear of being seen as "intruding" on the public sphere. During the seventeenth century numerous women writers, including Marie de Gournay of France, in her *Egalité des hommes et des femmes* (1641), argued for the education of girls and women, citing the lack of education as a major cause of women's inferior status. In 1659 Anna Maria van Schurman's *The Learned Maid; or, Whether a Maid May Be a Scholar* appeared in English translation (from the Dutch), echoing de Gournay. (A modern translation of the title is *Whether a Christian Woman Should Be Educated.*) In 1670 Aphra Behn, said to be the first Englishwoman to make her living by writing, had her play *The Forc'd Marriage, or the Jealous Bridegroom* performed in London. While satirizing male behavior, Behn argued in her play for women's education and responded to public criticism of her lack of Greek and Latin by noting that Shakespeare had not known the classical languages either. She was one of the first—and still too rare—feminists who used humor and public entertainment to make her point. A generation later, in 1694, the Englishwoman Mary Astell, in *A Serious Proposal to the Ladies, for the Advancement of Their True and Greatest Interest,* called for institutions of higher learning for women.

De Gournay, Behn, Astell, and others, some still unknown in history, followed in de Pizan's tradition by using their own experiences and skills to

expose the folly of women's position in society and to dramatize male condemnation of any deviation from that norm. Behn, a popular playwright
and novelist who argued for a woman's right to choose to marry or to remain single, was publicly scorned and her work ignored after her death.
Dale Spender, a historian of the intellectual progress of women, makes the
point that discrimination and sexual harassment are new in name only.[7]
She notes that the demeaning of women—not only of women of achievement but of all women—took a virulent form in print and in person.

Spender argues that it was Astell who defined patriarchy and its attributes by attacking marriage as an institution that served to keep women
subordinate. Astell was succeeded in this line of attack by Lady Mary
Wortley Montagu. Spender credits Lady Montagu with being the first
Englishwoman directly to enter the political arena by publishing a period-
ical entitled *The Nonsense of Common Sense.* It is assumed she was also the
author of a series signed "Sophia, a Person of Quality." In the series and in
her *Letters,* published a year after her death in 1762, Lady Montagu introduced numerous topics attributed to later feminists, including the
rights to education and construction of knowledge based on their own experiences; she also discussed the legal and social constraints of marriage
and the influence of custom and its confusion with nature.[8]

During the eighteenth century educated women who argued for women's
intellectual equality and promoted expanded educational opportunities for
women became known as "bluestockings." The Englishwoman Hannah
More and others throughout Europe not only argued for women's and
girls' education but also organized women to establish schools. Even the
more conservative women argued that education of girls was important because it meant that they would be better wives and mothers.

Organizing women to promote girls' education became socially acceptable, as did writing for publication. As Anne Hutchinson's experience in
the colony of Massachusetts dramatically demonstrated, however, organizing for more political purposes was dangerous. In 1637 Hutchinson was
charged with heresy for daring to question the religious-political authorities of the colony. Though Hutchinson left no personal written record, the
proceedings of her trial for heresy were published.[9] Hutchinson and her
husband had emigrated from England as members of a dissident religious
community. A midwife and lay medical practitioner, she organized a series
of women's meetings in her home, where she expressed the belief that individuals had the right to determine their own beliefs, to read the Bible
and talk directly to God, and not to be subject to the explications and interpretations of religious authorities. This open assertion of freedom of
conscience and of speech was anathema to the colony's religious and political leaders, who asserted that only they had the right to interpret God's

word. Hutchinson and her merchant husband also hosted discussions in their home about the decisions of the political leaders on business matters in the colony.

Interestingly, at trial Hutchinson was allowed to testify on her own behalf, a practice that was later abolished in many jurisdictions, leaving representation of women to their husbands or other male relatives. During her trial, Hutchinson refused to be demeaned. She held her own in intellectual sparring with Governor John Winthrop, who served as both judge and prosecutor. Her hosting of meetings was considered "a thing not tolerable nor comely in the sight of God nor fitting for [her] sex."[10] Hutchinson was excommunicated for troubling the church and for drawing people away from the church.[11] Although she and her family were banished from the colony and moved to Rhode Island, her assertion of her human rights became legendary. In the twentieth century American schoolchildren, in their study of early American history, would learn about Anne Hutchinson as a champion of religious freedom.

Wollstonecraft and the Rights of Women

By 1792, when Wollstonecraft published *A Vindication of the Rights of Women,* she only reiterated what numerous women, and a few men, before her had already written. Wollstonecraft had previously written *Thoughts on the Education of Daughters* (1787) as well as an autobiographical novel entitled *Mary* (1788) based on her own experiences as the daughter of a violent father and as a governess and teacher. In her *Thoughts on the Education of Daughters,* Wollstonecraft urged that girls be taught to think and their curiosity stimulated, revolutionary ideas for her time. She also responded to Edmund Burke's *Reflections on the French Revolution* (1790) with her own pamphlet entitled *Vindication of the Rights of Men* (1791), in which she ridiculed his oversight of poverty in England, an issue that other female writers would discuss in the nineteenth century. Drawing attention to other less powerful groups and analogizing their situations to those of women was a path numerous leaders would later follow.

As a political commentator and translator working for Joseph Johnson and his *Analytical Review,* Wollstonecraft was familiar with the intellectual currents of Europe and was a friend of the American revolutionary writer Thomas Paine. She was undoubtedly familiar with the work of Madame de Genlis, who promoted girls' education, and that of Olympe de Gouges, a well-known pamphleteer on behalf of women's political rights and equality in law. Whether she knew of Condorcet's *Sur l'admission des femmes aux endroits de la Cité,* published in 1790, or of the German legal scholar von Hippel's revised views on women that called for political, educational, and professional rights for women is unknown, but both von Hippel and Wollstonecraft acknowledged Catharine Macaulay's earlier work on women's education.[12] A well-known English historian and an early bluestocking, Macaulay was a correspondent of George Washington and an advocate of the American experiment. Her reputation as a historian was tarnished when her *Letters,* in which she bemoaned women's lack of political rights and particularly the lack of married women's legal rights, were published.[13] Both Wollstonecraft and Macaulay lived their beliefs be undertaking unconventional marriages or choosing not to marry at all. Yet while Wollstonecraft's reputation among feminists survived, Macaulay's did not—despite Wollstonecraft's acknowledgment of her debt to her.

Feminist historians argue that what distinguishes Wollstonecraft is that she was the first to put her theories in the context of a broader liberationist modern human rights theory. In addition, she wrote in a more modern style, defining and describing women's limitations in public and private life in short, declarative sentences full of fury at both men and women. Wollstonecraft seems to ask female readers, Have you no integrity, no sense of self? as she rails against their coquetry and submissiveness to men and their general irresponsibility toward themselves, their children, and society.

Another Wollstonecraft contribution was her emphasis on women's health, promoting exercise of body and mind. Her predecessors made similar arguments for women's education, against the legal disabilities of marriage, and against women's lack of participation in politics, but only Wollstonecraft argued that women should be more active physically and more knowledgeable about health, anatomy, and medicine. Her work was also a precursor to the discussion of violence against women. In this area she was almost two centuries ahead of her time: "The being who patiently endures injustice, and silently bears insults, will soon become unjust, or unable to discern right from wrong. . . . Nature never dictated such insincerity—and, though prudence of this sort be termed a virtue, morality becomes vague when any part is supposed to rest on falsehood."[14]

Although Wollstonecraft agreed with Rousseau on his rights-of-man theory, she was incensed by his views on women. Hobbes and Locke had argued that the rights-of-man theory encompassed woman. Rousseau, on the other hand, followed the traditional, paternalistic line of thought: "In the family, it is clear, for several reasons which lie in its very nature, that the father ought to command."[15] Later, in his book *Emile,* he forcefully asserted the common view that woman's purpose in life was to serve and entertain men. Wollstonecraft devoted an entire chapter to Rousseau's idea that the education of women should be always relative to . . . men. To please, to be useful to [them], . . . to educate [them] when young, and take care of [them] when grown up, to advise, to console [them], to render [their] lives easy and agreeable: these are the duties of women at all times."[16] Wollstonecraft dismissed Rousseau's views as nonsense while strongly criticizing women who upheld such views and taught them to their daughters.

Meanwhile, in America, Abigail Adams was expressing similar ideas. A respectable married woman and wife of the second president of the United States, Adams is portrayed indulgently by historians for her "don't forget the ladies" letter to husband John while he was off helping draft the new country's constitution:

> Do not put such unlimited power in the hands of the husbands. Remember all men would be tyrants if they could. If particular care and attention is not paid to the ladies we are determine [sic] to foment a rebellion, and will not hold ourselves bound by any law in which we have had no voice, or representation.[17]

These are distinctly personal political sentiments based on women's experience. What most historians ignore is that this letter was only one example of her outspoken irritation at the legal constraints on women. In other letters Adams lamented the fact that, although she managed the farm and other family enterprises while her husband was off on political ventures, she could not make contracts or sell any of their property without his signature. Adams was also concerned about women's education, lamenting her own lack thereof, and she inquired about Macaulay in correspondence with an English cousin.[18]

The pleas of Abigail Adams and other women did not move male political leaders. Women were not considered citizens in the new U.S. Constitution. On the European continent, the Allgemeines Landrecht of 1794 and the Napoleonic legal code of 1804 declared married women legally subordinate. Yet in 1808 in France, Charles Fourier, whom some have called the inventor of feminism, asserted: "As a general thesis: Social progress and historic changes occur by virtue of the progress of women toward liberty, and decadence of the social order occurs as the result of a decrease in the liberty of women. . . . The extension of women's privileges is the general principle for all social progress."[19] Fourier's ideas found few adherents. In 1832 the English Reform Act, in extending voting rights, limited those rights to "male persons."

However, by the end of the eighteenth century, strong feminist arguments were being made on both sides of the Atlantic, although no major social or political women's organization existed to promote feminist views except that of education. Before organizing for political purposes, women articulated their experience and ideas through published writings and only gradually broke the tradition that good women did not address public audiences. A new political movement, the abolition of slavery, gave women experience in organizing and moved them into the political arena and onto public platforms.

Marriage and Children

While women's rights in the public arena received some attention, it was discrimination in the private sphere that was the more compelling issue. In the 1830s the Caroline Norton case in England captured public attention.[20] A member of the well-placed Sheridan family, Caroline married George Norton, a lawyer and member of Parliament, only to find that he was a brutal drunk who expected her earnings to support the new family. A writer and magazine editor whose income, under law, belonged to her husband, Norton refused to be quiet, as women of her time were expected to do, about her frequent beatings at his hands. While abjuring feminism and using her social contacts, Caroline Norton nevertheless argued for justice in marriage, putting her case before the public when the couple separated and her husband filed for divorce and took the children. The case generated immense publicity because of the Nortons' social standing. Like all other English women, she could neither legally appear in court nor be represented. A jury disallowed the divorce but, under law, Norton's husband retained custody of the children. This drove Caroline to a study of English law and cases similar to hers. She not only wrote and distributed a pamphlet, *The Separation of Mother and Child by the Law of Custody of Infants Considered,* in 1837 to members of Parliament and to the public; she also got the attention of a young barrister interested in child custody cases. As a result, in 1839 Parliament passed an infant custody reform bill allowing children under seven years of age to remain with their mother if she was of good character and the Lord Chancellor agreed.

This, however, was not the end of the matter for Caroline. George next sued for access to her trust monies and other inheritances to pay his debts. She contracted with him, assuring him an allowance if he gave her a legal separation, forgetting that as a woman she had no legal right to contract. Although she was allowed in court as a witness this time, she lost the case. Again, her response was to go public, achieving immense notoriety. In 1854 she published *English Laws for Women in the Nineteenth Century.* In a private letter, Norton, while disavowing feminism, admitted that she was seen "as a cross 'between a barn actress and a Mary Wollstonecraft.'"[21] At this point an avowed feminist, Barbara Leigh-Smith (a.k.a. Barbara Bodichon), brought out her own pamphlet on women and the law in England and circulated a women's petition drive for reform of the laws regarding married women, obtaining more than twenty thousand signatures.

In 1857 the British Parliament passed an omnibus bill that allowed wives directly to inherit and bequeath property; permitted a wife who had been deserted by her husband to keep her earnings; empowered courts to direct payments for separate maintenance; and gave a separated wife the right to sue, be sued, and make contracts.[22] Only in 1882, with the Married Women's Property Act, did married women achieve the same rights as unmarried women.

Almost as if to prove the point that women—and especially married women—had little power either in the public sphere or in the home, it took a distinguished Englishman and member of Parliament, John Stuart Mill, to put the question of marriage on the international map. His 1869 essay, *The Subjection of Women,* drew tremendous attention in England and was almost immediately translated and distributed throughout Europe and the United States. Susan Bell and Karen Offen argue that Mill's essay "forced thinkers to grapple with fundamental issues of political and social theory."[23] Mill argued that men took contradictory positions by believing that women's "natural vocation" is that of wife and mother, while also believing that women must be controlled by men and forced by them to engage in this natural vocation. If natural, why was force necessary? Mill thought too many men were afraid of equality in marriage. In that case, he argued, men should never have allowed women "to receive a literary education. Women who read, much more women who write, are, in the existing constitution of things, a contradiction and a disturbing element."[24]

Mill argued that marriage should be thought of as a voluntary association, a contract between equals similar to any business partnership. The partners could be assumed to settle issues of control amicably, each assuming those responsibilities which they could perform most efficiently. He also argued that it was in the interests of children and of society that equal rights within the family be the basis of marriage; otherwise the family would become

> a school of despotism [when it ought to be] the real school of the virtues of freedom. . . . The moral regeneration of mankind will only really commence, when the most fundamental of the social relations is placed under the rule of equal justice, and when human beings learn to cultivate their strongest sympathy with an equal in rights and in cultivation.[25]

Mill's arguments were exactly what an incipient international women's movement needed. As Bell and Offen point out, Mill's essay, and the ferment it caused, were significant in mobilizing women to push for legal, economic, educational, and political rights in virtually every country in Europe. Yet it was not until 1923 that English women gained equal rights in divorce, and it took fifty more years, until 1973, for Parliament to give English mothers equal standing with fathers in the matter of legal custody of children.

The Contribution of Nineteenth-Century Women Writers

Denied direct access to the world of politics by custom—it was unseemly for women to speak in public—and subordinate under law, many English, French, and American women took to writing literature and political commentary as a means of intruding on the public sphere and, not incidentally, like de Pizan and Wollstonecraft, as a means of economic independence. During the nineteenth century, numerous women writers became noted literary figures, often using the novel to express political sentiments. According to Ellen Moers in *Literary Women* (1976), these writers gave voice, directly and indirectly, to the feelings and aspirations of women. They pitted the conservative, traditional woman against the feminist through literature and indirectly encouraged feminist views in many of their readers. Like Wollstonecraft before them, they became spokeswomen for the underprivileged, whether slaves, factory workers, the poor, or women.

Among the late-eighteenth- and nineteenth-century novels written by women concerning women's role in society, the best known are those of Jane Austen (1775–1817) and Charlotte Brontë (1816–1855). Fanny Burney (1752–1840) of England and Madame de Staël (1766–1817) of France were also notable popular writers who described the world from a woman's perspective. Much more famous and widely read in the nineteenth century was a novel not about women but about slavery. Harriet Beecher Stowe's *Uncle Tom's Cabin* (1852) brought her to international attention. The millions of copies sold not only helped her family survive economically but influenced public policy during the U.S. Civil War. Stowe's influence on the novelist George Eliot (1819–1880), some of whose works portrayed the stifling conditions of girls' and women's lives, is perhaps not well known. Moved by Stowe's portrayal of slavery, Eliot wrote in a letter to Stowe that she "felt urged to treat Jews with such sympathy and understanding as my nature and knowledge could attain to,"[26] a sentiment that resulted in Eliot's 1876 novel, *Daniel Deronda*.

Mary Barton (1848), by Elizabeth Gaskell (1810–1865), is the most notable early novel about factory workers, but, as Moers points out, it was not the first written by a woman on this subject. That distinction belongs to Caroline Norton, who, left in penury by her dissolute and violent husband, published *A Voice from the Factories* in 1836 and *The Child of the Islands* on child labor in 1845.

The English author Harriet Martineau (1802–1876) was well known for her writings on political economy and one of many European women, such as Frances Wright and Frances Trollope, Anthony Trollope's mother, to tour the United States and write about conditions there. During the 1820s and 1830s, Frances Wright became notorious for espousing women's and worker's rights, antislavery sentiments, free thought, and public education for both girls and boys. An intimate of General Lafayette of France, Wright's personal life and radical ideas made her persona non grata, like many other women before and after her whose nontraditional personal lives have been denigrated in an attempt to lessen the impact of their ideas on the public mind. One of the things that interested Wright, as it did de Tocqueville in his 1838 work, *Democracy in America,* was the position of American women as pragmatic, thinking beings, who knew, or learned, how to organize—a requirement for survival on the frontier.

The French writer George Sand (1804–1876) achieved international fame not only for the proletarian political views expressed in her numerous novels but also for her life of political activism and defiance of social mores. Sand is often remembered as a woman who dressed in men's clothing in order to move more freely around Paris. Widely recognized as the Muse of the 1848 Revolution, she lived out her beliefs. Defying convention, she separated from and divorced her husband; lived with a series of notable men without marrying them; demanded custody of her children, inheritance, and property; earned her living by writing while expressing revolutionary thoughts; and became a role model—albeit, a highly controversial one—for women as well as men. She also became one of her generation's most popular and prolific writers, gaining praise from contemporaries such as Dostoyevsky, Turgenev, Henry James, Walt Whitman, and, not incidentally, John Stuart Mill.[27]

Perhaps as important, in terms of women's human rights, as the writings and ideas of these noted women is the interaction between the writers and female activists. In today's parlance, this would be called "networking across international borders." Sand was at times besieged by visitors. Margaret Fuller, the American journalist and author of *Woman in the Nineteenth Century* (1845), en route to Italy to cover its independence movement, was only one of many who called upon Sand. By this time, more women were traveling internationally. Flora Tristan, Sand's contemporary, went to Peru in an attempt to claim her father's inheritance, and then came home to write *Pérégrinations d'une paria 1833–34,* followed by

Promenades de Londres in 1840, and in 1846, *L'Emancipation de la femme ou le testament de la paria.*[28]

Networking among women who had attracted public attention was taking place not only across international boundaries but within borders too. According to Moers:

> George Eliot knew Barbara Leigh-Smith (founder of the Association for Promoting the Employment of Women); Mrs. Gaskell knew Bessie Parkes; and Charlotte Brontë knew Mary Taylor (early settler and businesswoman of New Zealand), who wrote home, denouncing the author of *Shirley* as "coward" and "traitor" for the hesitant ambivalence [Miss Taylor] sensed in Charlotte Brontë's attitude toward work for women.[29]

Ernestine Rose is a prime example of the networking that took place between nineteenth-century European and American women who became women's rights activists. Rose, like many others, became interested and active in a variety of progressive movements and the object of a great deal of publicity in her day. Born in Poland, she escaped an arranged marriage and in court defended her inheritance claim. She later emigrated to Germany, where she supported herself by selling her own invention, a household deodorant; moved to Paris during the 1830 revolution; and subsequently moved to England, where she became associated with Robert Owen and other reformers. By 1840 she and her English husband had moved to the United States, where Rose lobbied for passage of a married women's property act in New York. The legislative act allowed women to hold property in their own names and be legal guardians of their children. A forceful orator and leader in the numerous state and national women's rights conventions held in the eastern United States between 1850 and the onset of the U.S. Civil War, Rose kept in touch with European women working on women's rights issues. She often used the term "human rights" in her speeches and in at least one instance sponsored a resolution stating that "by human rights we mean natural rights."[30]

Women leaders on both sides of the Atlantic were not deterred by resistance to their ideas. At the 1853 New York City Women's Rights Convention, Lucretia Mott (discussed below) introduced Mathilde Francesca Anneke, editor of *Die Frauenzeitung,* who fled Germany when her husband was tried for treason after supporting the 1848 revolutionary movement. Rose was Anneke's translator, although translation services were not needed when an unruly mob entered the hall and brought the meeting to a halt—not an uncommon event for women's rights meetings. Before the meeting was disrupted, however, the convention had adopted a resolution that stated that their movement was "not of America only" and had formed a committee to communicate with women of "Great Britain and the Continent of Europe." Rose, who was made a member of the committee, was also active in peace, free-thought, and social reform movements and kept in touch with European feminists, reading letters and other communications from them at other women's rights conventions.[31]

Although little of women's writings or their leadership in eastern and southern nations during the nineteenth century was common knowledge in the Western world, in 1905, "Sultana's Dream," a patently feminist story, was published in the *Indian Ladies Magazine* by Rokeya Sakhawat Hossain.[32] It described, in good humor, a world in which men's and women's positions were reversed and noted the lack of women's education and the strictures of the veil.

Organizing for Political Action: From Antislavery to Women's Rights

While Europe produced most of the writers who depicted women's experiences, organizing for political purposes was the major contribution of American women to the development of women's human rights. Organizing, as pointed out by de Tocqueville, was a necessity in America. Pioneers in the new land had to organize to survive, especially those who settled the northern sections of the United States where the winters are severe. It was the abolition of slavery—and later the civil rights movement—that provided the impetus for American women to organize to eliminate discrimination and promote women's rights just as the French and American revolutions had contributed to Wollstonecraft's and Abigail Adams's thinking.

Two sisters from the slave-owning South of the United States turned their experiences with slavery first into anti-slavery advocacy and then to advocacy for women's rights. Sarah Grimke, daughter of a leading South Carolina judge and political activist, became deeply frustrated by her family's refusal to allow her to study law with her brother. She had hated slavery from childhood, having been severely reprimanded for secretly teaching her own slave servant-companion to read, an illegal act. Refusing marriage and the traditional life of a Southern lady, she moved to Philadelphia after her father's death and later was joined by her younger sister Angelina. Both found a measure of personal freedom in Quaker society but soon found even the Quakers and male abolitionists too conservative. As agents for the American Anti-Slavery Society, they were placed in charge of organizing women. Later, Angelina's 1836 antislavery pamphlet, *An Appeal to the Christian Women of the South,*[33] brought her to national attention. Angelina frequently spoke in public on the abolition of slavery and was often heckled by unruly mobs; at one such speech, a mob burned the new Philadelphia hall in which she spoke to the ground.

According to Gerda Lerner, "the Grimké sisters [came] to represent in the public mind the fusion of abolition and woman's rights . . . [and] precipitated an ideological crisis among reformers."[34] Like Anne Hutchinson before them, Sarah and Angelina refused to be demeaned by religious leaders who resented their interference with doctrine, their organizing of women parishioners, and their daring to speak to audiences of both sexes. Sarah Grimké's incisive *Letters on the Equality of the Sexes*,[35] issued in response to a pastoral letter to congregational churches, referred to Cotton Mather and witchcraft, a nod toward Hutchinson's fate; demanded equality in education and equal pay for equal work; and drew analogies between women's lives and those of the slaves. An intellectual far ahead of her time, Sarah Grimké in an essay on marriage used language similar to that used in the 1993 world conference on human rights: "Human rights are *not* based upon sex, color, capacity or condition. They are universal, inalienable and eternal, and none but despots will deny to woman that supreme sovereignty over her own person and conduct which Law concedes to man."[36]

Action at the 1840 World Anti-Slavery Conference in London spurred two women to organize. Lucretia Mott, a Pennsylvania Quaker, who reputedly kept a copy of Wollstonecraft's book at the foot of her babies' cradle, was an organizer of the Philadelphia Female Anti-Slavery Society, consisting of black and white members. Mott, with her husband, attended the 1840 World Anti-Slavery Conference in London, as did the newly married Elizabeth Cady Stanton. Upon reaching London, they discovered they were barred from participating in the conference despite all their antislavery organizing at home—women at the World Anti-Slavery Conference were only allowed to listen from behind a balcony curtain. Although some male delegates—not including Mrs. Stanton's new husband—argued in favor of women's participation, the ban remained.

This manifest discrimination in a cause dedicated to freeing individuals from bondage shocked Mott and Stanton into action. Earlier, as a school teacher, Mott had protested against male and female pay differentials to no avail, while Stanton had complained to her father, a lawyer and judge, about women's legal subordination. While in London the younger Stanton, a rebel by nature, found Mott "a suitable female role model and a willing mentor"; Mott told Stanton "of Mary Wollstonecraft, her social theories, and her demands of equality for women."[37] In London the two women decided to organize a women's rights meeting when they returned to America. It took eight years before their idea came to fruition. Family duties, abolition activities, Stanton's childbearing, and limited means of travel constrained both women, although they remained in correspondence. In 1848, when Mott was visiting upstate New York, Stanton and Mott called their now historic Seneca Falls meeting.

By 1848 a strong foundation of thought and advocacy for women's rights had been built, but it had not won public favor. Most of the principles that would appear a hundred years later in the Universal Declaration and the Women's Convention—the rights to education; to employment outside the home with wages paid directly to the woman; to custody of their children; to hold and inherit property; to contract and be represented in court; and to participate in the world of public affairs—already had been espoused. What was required was to put these concepts in a theoretical framework. The framework, in addition to demanding the right to vote, organizing women, and giving women a different vision of the world, was Stanton's contribution. She had spent the eight years between meeting Mott and calling the 1848 convention reading and studying while raising her children.

In the Declaration of Sentiments that Stanton wrote for the 1848 meeting, she expressed strong resentment of the fact that, throughout history, men had established "an absolute tyranny" over women. Women were required to abide by laws they had no hand in making, and were thereby deprived, viewed "if married, in the eye of the law, [as] civilly dead." Stanton wrote that, without rights to property or to the wages they earned, women become "morally irresponsible in marriage, can be chastised by the husband, are discriminated against in the laws of divorce and, if single and the owner of property, taxed to support a government which recognizes her only when her property can be made profitable [for the government]." Kept from most profitable employment and professions such as law and medicine, she is paid low wages when employed at all, and denied good education, with colleges not open to her. Thus, her confidence is destroyed, her self-respect lessened, and she is subject to a different code of morals, all of which, Stanton continued, made her willing to lead a dependent and abject life, depriving her of her citizenship. She concluded with a prophecy and call to action: "We shall employ agents, circulate tracts, petition the State and National legislatures, and endeavor to enlist the pulpit and the press in our behalf [and] hope this Convention will be followed by a series of Conventions embracing every party of the country."[38]

The resolutions adopted at this historic meeting echoed sentiments expressed by earlier feminists and were reminiscent of Olympe de Gouges's 1791 Declaration of the Rights of Woman and Citizen.[39] Whether Stanton, a well-read intellectual, knew of de Gouges's work is unclear. What is known is that the 1848 meeting was attended by many of the nation's leading reformers—black and white—and received extensive, primarily negative, publicity.

Although her resolution on women's suffrage—the only resolution not passed unanimously—has attracted the most attention from historians, feminist and nonfeminist alike, its significance is sometimes overestimated. As some feminists have observed, the right to vote accomplishes little if male power within the home is absolute. In its time, however, the call for the right to vote was for the legal right to participate in the public sphere. Suffrage was the metaphor for equality in public life, for full citizenship. Public discussion of the husband's right to chastise or beat his wife, perhaps, had greater contemporary impact, although it was not discussed widely or used as an organizing tool until the late twentieth century, when violence against women became an international organizing effort and united women of all classes and nationalities.

What was important in 1848 and retains its importance is the full legal and de facto capacity of women to act as free, independent, equally empowered citizens in both the private and public spheres. It was this 1848 call to action on all fronts—public and private—that spurred women's organizing nationally and then internationally, and that ultimately led not only to women achieving the right to vote but to their increasing political activity. A widely publicized series of state and national women's rights conventions, interrupted by the Civil War, gathered converts to every issue in the Declaration and, after intense organizational efforts, ultimately led to American women's finally achieving the vote in 1920 in the form of the Nineteenth Amendment to the Constitution. These early conventions could be called a first wave of organized consciousness-raising, because they brought a wide range of women's issues to public attention and spurred individuals and groups of women to action on many fronts.

Another important step was the struggle of women to enter acknowledged professions such as law, medicine, and science. Among the most notable early trailblazers were Elizabeth Blackwell of the United States and Florence Nightingale of England, who both broke barriers for women in medicine. Blackwell is recognized for her fight to enter medical school and become the first certified female doctor, while Nightingale is remembered not only for her pioneering efforts in modern nursing but also for her research and advocacy in the field of public health. In the same period, women also broke the college entrance barrier. Lucy Stone, the first American woman to attend college, is known for her leadership in the suffrage movement as well as her insistence on keeping her own name upon marriage and her strong advocacy of education of girls and women.

The resistance to women's participation in public life as professionals in the United States is illustrated by an 1870 decision of the State of Illinois Supreme Court refusing Myra Bradwell admission to the bar on the grounds that "God designed the sexes to occupy different spheres of action, and that it belonged to men to make, apply and execute the laws. . . . This step, if taken by us, would mean that . . . every civil office in this State may be filled by women . . . governors, judges and sheriffs. This we are not yet prepared to hold."[40] However, in 1874 the Illinois legislature passed legislation preventing discrimination in bar admissions on the basis of sex, and in 1879 the U.S. Supreme Court allowed Belva Lockwood to appear before it. In spite of these victories, it was not until 1973, when the U.S. Congress adopted Title IX of the Education Amendments—among other things designed to eliminate discrimination against women in education—that U.S. law schools were opened to more than a small quota of women and schoolgirls were encouraged to participate in sports.

Organizing Internationally

Women's organizing was not limited to the United States, nor were women's suffrage leaders the only leaders organizing women for political action. Although the Women's Christian Temperance Union (WCTU) is remembered, often jokingly, for its crusade against the evils of alcohol, its primary emphasis, under the leadership of Frances Willard, was local political action in the name of motherhood and home. Willard's "do everything" policy for local WCTU units encouraged women to improve their communities. Many units established kindergartens, libraries, and other community institutions. This local activity brought new recruits to the suffrage movement. Later, Willard formed an international WCTU with units in other countries, including Japan.[41]

In March 1888, forty years after the Seneca Falls meeting, an International Council of Women meeting, organized by Stanton and her friend and colleague, Susan B. Anthony, was held in Washington, D.C. Anthony had been active in the temperance movement and proved herself to be the consummate organizer, while Stanton was a theoretical politician. The International Council of Women meeting was cosponsored by the WCTU. In addition to delegates from England, France, Norway, Finland, Denmark, India, and Canada, representatives from over fifty U.S. women's organizations attended. This meeting was not the first international organization of women; by 1888, Marie Goegg of Switzerland had formed an International Association of Women, an International Women's Rights Conference had been held in Paris, and the World Young Women's Christian Association (WYWCA) and the World WCTU had been formed. In the early part of the twentieth century, the International Conference of

Socialist Women was formed under the leadership of Klara Zetkin. This group proposed what later became International Women's Day. Also, in Russia, Alexandra Kollontai, who concentrated on organizing employed women, built upon and defined the feminist movement.[42]

With headquarters in Zurich, the International Council of Women promoted the formation of national councils to work on social and economic questions. Although Anthony and Willard were extremely pleased that more conservative women were joining the women's rights movement, Stanton and others had a broader, more liberal or progressive vision. By this time, Stanton was spending more and more time in Europe, primarily England and France. Although suffrage remained a primary issue for her, in perhaps the most significant speech of her life, made before the U.S. Senate Committee on Woman Suffrage, she called on women to be self-reliant, independent beings whose birthright was "self-sovereignty."[43] At the age of seventy-six, Stanton argued the essential basis for women's human rights, the sovereignty of the individual:

> No matter how much women prefer to lean, to be protected and supported, nor how much men prefer to have them do so, they must make the voyage of life alone. . . . The strongest reason why we ask for woman a voice in the government under which she lives; in the religion she is asked to believe; equality in social life, where she is the chief factor; a place in the trades and professions, where she may earn her bread, is because of her birthright to self-sovereignty; because, as an individual, she must rely on herself.[44]

Achieving that birthright required organizing internationally. Women's suffrage, at the end of the nineteenth century and the beginning of the twentieth, like the violence against women issue at the end of the twentieth century, became the most visible issue in the feminist movement. Less visible were other issues supported by a variety of women's organizations, ranging from those concentrating on meeting short-term social welfare needs to the more political organizations that were demanding the right to vote.

In 1902 delegates from ten countries—the United States, England, Russia, Norway, Germany, Sweden, Turkey, Australia, Chile, and Canada—attended an International Woman Suffrage Conference held in Washington, D.C. as part of the National American Women Suffrage Association's annual convention.[45] By this time, New Zealand and Australia had given women the vote. In 1904, meeting in Berlin, women active in national suffrage campaigns formed the International Woman Suffrage Alliance (IWSA) and elected as president Carrie Chapman Catt, a second-generation U.S. suffragist whose talent was organization. Although suffrage was its original focus, the group understood the importance of setting end goals and developing means to achieve them. Suffrage was a means, not an end. Effecting changes in law and policy required lobbying formal political bodies, garnering political support, and continually educating both women and men about women's concerns.

The principles on which IWSA was established were precursors to ideas that would later find their way into the Convention:

1. That men and women are born equally free and independent members of the human race; equally endowed with intelligence and ability, and equally entitled to the free exercise of their individual rights and liberty.
2. That the natural relation of the sexes is that of interdependence and cooperation, and that the repression of the rights and liberty of one sex inevitably works injury to the other . . .
3. That in all lands, those laws, creeds, and customs which have tended to restrict women to a position of dependence; to discourage their education; to impede the development of their natural gifts, and to subordinate their individuality, have been based on false theories, and have produced an artificial and unjust relation of the sexes. . . .
4. That self-government in the home and the State is the inalienable right of every normal adult, and the refusal of this right to women has resulted in social, legal, and economic injustice to them, and has also intensified the existing economic disturbances throughout the world.
5. That governments which impose taxes and laws upon their women citizens without giving them the right of consent or dissent . . . exercise a tyranny inconsistent with just government.
6. That the ballot is the only legal and permanent means of defending the rights to the "life, liberty and pursuit of happiness" pronounced inalienable by the American Declaration of Independence, and accepted as inalienable by all civilized nations. In any representative form of government, therefore, women should be vested with all political rights and privileges of electors.[46]

These principles clearly hark back to Wollstonecraft and the rights-of-man theory. The reference to the home is significant as are the terms "laws, creeds, and customs." These women were out to revolutionize relations between men and women and were determined that women should be full citizens. They had no intention of remaining subordinate and knew that marriage and the home were among the legal, as well as customary, means of maintaining women's subordination. In short, they were taking on the responsibilities of citizenship before they were legally equal citizens, concentrating on civil and political, as well as economic and social, rights.

By 1904, when these principles were adopted at their Berlin conference, increasing numbers of women were employed outside the home as clerks and secretaries in offices and in industrial production. By the 1913 conference in Budapest, where twenty-four countries were represented, IWSA board members had traveled to all continents to survey the status of women. During the conference the Alliance decided to admit to membership women from countries where suffrage was an impossible or impractical idea, but where a "woman's movement" was either necessary or under way. The Alliance also adopted its first nonsuffrage resolution on the problem of "white slave traffic" (trafficking in women).[47] Interest in the "white slavery" issue continued and would occupy the minds of CSW members, eventually finding its way into the Women's Convention in the article on prostitution as well as in the section on marriage and family law requiring consent to marriage.

The alliance was neither the first nor the only organization to address this issue. In Britain, Harriet Martineau had written on the subject in 1862, and Josephine Butler, president of the North of England Council for the Higher Education of Women from 1868 to 1873, was asked by male doctors to lead opposition to the cruel provisions regarding prostitutes in England's Contagious Diseases Act. Under this legislation, prostitutes and women suspected of prostitution were required to submit to medical examinations for venereal disease to protect the health of soldiers and sailors.[48]

During World War I women's participation in the paid labor force increased exponentially, and because the war prevented travel and diverted organized women to the war effort, most international women's activities ceased. However, in 1915 an International Congress of Women was held at the Hague in an effort to promote peace among the warring nations. Jane Addams of Hull House in Chicago, notable for her work in urban reform and a supporter of the suffrage movement, was chosen as president of the Hague conference. In 1919 the International League for Peace and Freedom was organized, reflecting many women's concerns for peace.[49] When the 1919 Paris Peace Conference was called, a French women's suffrage union invited a small group of feminist activists to Paris to discuss women's participation in the peace process. The group proposed to Wilson and Clemenceau that women's interests be heard at the peace conference and that women be allowed to participate as both delegates and employees of the League of Nations. The first to hear the group's views was the labor commission, before which the women proposed a forty-four-hour work week, a minimum wage, and equal pay for women. Another presentation to the Commission of the League of Nations covered women's education, suffrage, trafficking in women, and improvement in marriage laws.[50]

As a result of this lobbying, the League's Charter included provisions that League positions be open equally to women and men and workers have fair and humane employment conditions; also, the charter mentioned the issue of trafficking in women and children.[51] Later IWSA members urged the British War Office to send women police to Germany to assure that German girls were not abused by the occupying troops.

Postwar activity resulted in the adoption by the IWSA of a charter of women's rights at its 1920 conference that covered, in order of priority, political rights, personal rights, domestic rights, educational and economic rights, and moral rights.[52] Political rights included not only suffrage but equal recognition in legislative and administrative bodies, both nationally and internationally. Personal rights covered protection under laws against slavery and rights of married women to retain or change their nationality. Domestic rights revolved around marriage, with a married woman having the right to "the use and disposal of her own earnings and property, and that she should not be under the tutelage of her husband. . . . [The married mother should have the same rights over her children as the father." Domestic rights also supported the concept that, as widows, women should be accorded guardianship of their children and "the right to maintenance by the State." The final section stated that "a child born out of wedlock . . . should have the same right to maintenance and education from the father . . . as a legitimate child, and that an unmarried mother, during the period when she is incapacitated, should . . . have the right of being maintained by the father of her child."[53] The new charter of women's rights called for "no special regulations for women's work, different from regulations for men. . . . [and] that laws relative to women as mothers should be so framed as not to handicap them in their economic position."[54] This was a harbinger of the argument over the protection of women workers that would continue into the 1980s.

All of the provisions would eventually find their way into CSW resolutions and into the Women's Convention, though it would take over fifty years of advocacy and lengthy discussions within the CSW and the United Nations. Resolutions at the 1920 IWSA Geneva conference also called for an annual League of Nations women's conference and attention to the problems of venereal disease and prostitution. By this time, twenty-five countries had granted women suffrage, but forward-looking women were already beyond suffrage and onto a broader women's agenda. Too many historians, male and female alike, have overlooked the broader agenda.

Birth Control, Family Planning, and Women's Health

What was not the subject of resolutions at the 1920 IWSA conference was birth control, which was presumably an issue too hot to handle publicly, though, it can be assumed, it was certainly discussed in private conversations at the convention. Birth control is at the very heart of male-female relationships, and of any society's future; few other facets of life have the same emotional depth, as John Stuart Mill and others understood so well. Safe and effective birth control and related information, including information on abortion, threatens a system as old as human life. Just as suffrage was a metaphor for women's equality in public life, birth control meant a measure of equality in private life for sexually active women.

Because of the deep emotions wrought by the issue of birth control and the few radicals, like Emma Goldman, who publicly discussed birth control, it is understandable why birth control was not an issue on the 1920 IWSA agenda. It would take courage, leadership, time, and a great deal of organizing before birth control would become legal and its use widespread. As with so many other new issues, it was the radicals, those who first dare to speak out on an issue, who put this new issue into the realm of public discourse. Radicals serve an important political function. They make those who follow them, including traditional organizations that may take up the new cause, look more respectable. However, too often it is the traditional groups that are recorded in history for accomplishments in a particular area or on a specific issue, when it was the radicals who first brought the matter to public attention.

Europeans led the way in developing birth control devices and making the discussion and promotion of their use legal. Although the condom is thought to have originated in Egypt centuries ago, it was named only in the seventeenth century for an English doctor who provided sheaths made from sheep organs to members of the court of King Charles II of England as protection against venereal disease. In nineteenth-century England, Annie Besant and Charles Bradlaugh won a landmark case involving the right to write, publish, and discuss birth control publicly.[55] Later, in the 1880s, the diaphragm was developed in Germany. Information about it and its use spread quickly, although not without strong opposition.

In 1873 the U.S. Congress passed the Comstock Act, which equated birth control information with pornography and made it illegal to mail, transport, or import into the United States any kind of birth control devices or information. However, the dissemination of information of such importance to women could not be stopped. Emma Goldman, a Russian-born immigrant to the United States and sometime midwife, who was active in the labor movement, took up the cause. A brilliant lecturer, she was unafraid to speak about the issue and argued that women had to free themselves from within, not simply through suffrage.[56] It was in the labor movement that Margaret Sanger, the preeminent name associated with the U.S. birth control movement, met Goldman, who opened Sanger's mind to the impact birth control could have on women. The fact that Goldman also preached "free love"—love and sexual intercourse without marriage—made her, and the birth control movement, anathema to many. In 1916 Goldman, called "Red Emma" by much of the press, was arrested for lecturing on birth control in New York City and spent fifteen days in jail as a consequence.[57]

Sanger's main concern was women's health and sexuality. She felt passionately that women, especially poor women, needed birth control information and devices for their own health and for that of their children. She had watched her mother die of tuberculosis after bearing eleven children, not uncommon for the time. As a nurse-midwife and labor movement activist, Sanger saw too many poor women at the mercy of their sexuality. In 1912 she began writing a series of articles on female sexuality and on venereal disease in a socialist weekly, but soon became distressed at the reaction of male labor leaders who did not share her passion.

After traveling to Europe with her first husband and learning more about birth control, Sanger returned to the United States in 1914 and later that year published a small magazine called "The Woman Rebel" in which she "intended to challenge Comstock's prohibition of information about sexuality and contraception."[58] That same year, Goldman was doing a lecture tour around the United States and sold Sanger's magazine on her tour. Prohibited by law from using the mails to distribute her magazine, it being considered too radical even by left-wingers, Sanger distributed it herself around New York. In August of that year she was arrested for writing and distributing her magazine. Instead of preparing for trial, though, she wrote a pamphlet called *Family Limitation,* with specific birth control information, and then escaped to Europe, where she met and became the lover of Havelock Ellis.[59] In England, Sanger lectured before the Fabian Society and became acquainted with the ideas of Olive Schreiner, the South African novelist and activist, and Ellen Key of Sweden, both of whom promoted birth control and women's liberation, although neither were active suffragists.

After visiting England and the Netherlands to learn more about contraception, Sanger opened a birth control advice center in New York that was promptly closed by the police. Despite her radical beginnings, the generation of enormous publicity regarding her activities eventually attracted wealthy women and medical doctors to her cause. Sanger and her supporters smuggled diaphragms into the United States, successfully challenged the Comstock Act and other restrictive laws in court, and established the American Birth Control League, the predecessor of Planned Parenthood Federation of America. Sanger later became involved in the international birth control movement and lived to see the U.S. Supreme Court, in *Griswold vs. Connecticut,* uphold contraception for married couples.

Sanger was by no means alone in the campaign for birth control rights and recognition of women's health issues. In the Dominican Republic, Evangelina Rodriguez, an African-Dominican, became that country's first woman doctor after obtaining her medical degree in Paris in 1909. Upon returning to her native country, she combined a medical career with feminist activism, including assistance to poor children, support of women's suffrage, and promotion of birth control. In Sweden, Elise Otteson-Jensen founded the Swedish Association for Sex Education, promoted family planning, and later worked with Sanger on an international birth control conference. In Egypt, educator Zahia Marzouk helped organize a conference on population issues sponsored by the Egyptian medical association. At the conference, she defied tradition by delivering her own paper on the population issue at a time when women were prevented from speaking in public. Twehida Ben Sheik, a Tunisian woman, went to medical school in Paris and later started a family planning clinic in a Tunisian hospital and worked to make abortion legal in that country. As Perdita Huston has noted in her book, *Motherhood by Choice,* these pioneers in the birth control movement came from a variety of backgrounds, but, "regardless of their social standing, they were insulted and threatened for speaking out, for mentioning human sexuality and advocating the right to voluntary motherhood. . . . They were an easy target for those who opposed change or women's rights. Theirs was a constant struggle to maintain honor and courage."[60]

Each of these women followed the pattern of earlier feminists by becoming educated, defying tradition, organizing and informing their communities, and speaking out publicly. In short, they exercised leadership in the public sphere, helping to put women's health and reproductive issues on the international agenda. Between 1929 and 1935, the All India Women's Conference took up the birth control issue, and in 1935 "went on record in support of artificial contraception, making it the largest group in the world to have done so at the time."[61] In 1940 Eleanor Roosevelt, soon to be chair of the Human Rights Commission, declared herself publicly in favor of birth control. In spite of these gains, however, there were still setbacks. As late as 1959, President Dwight Eisenhower rejected the Draper report that addressed the necessity of population planning in foreign aid. It took Helvi Sipila of Finland and other strong-minded CSW delegates, including those from India, to put birth control on the UN agenda in the 1960s under the rubric of family planning. The abortion issue continues to raise strong objections in many quarters.

The United Nations and Its Commission on the Status of Women

By the time the United Nations was formed in 1945, women were deeply involved in the public sphere, primarily in nongovernmental organizations, but a number of countries had women among their delegations. The suffrage movement had been successful in thirty-one countries. Women's participation in the paid labor force during both world wars had been massive and never returned to prewar levels. Employed women in Europe and the United States had organized and were part of the international labor movement. The number of women's organizations had increased; these organizations advocated issues ranging from study and self-improvement to social welfare to suffrage, and many employed a variety of measures to draw attention to the causes.[62] Women from many countries also had gained extensive experience in lobbying government officials locally, nationally, and even internationally. The International Federation of Working Women (IFWW), for example, had lobbied the International Labor Organization (ILO) and achieved adoption of the 1919 conventions on maternity protection and night work for women.[63] An area where the women's organizations had not been successful, however, was in convincing the League of Nations, the predecessor to the United Nations, to take up the question of the nationality of married women.

The work of women's organizations internationally came to fruition with the establishment of the United Nations.[64] Led by South American delegates, notably women from Brazil, Mexico, and the Dominican Republic, and with support from Indian and North American NGOs, the linkage between women's rights and human rights was effectively made in the UN Charter in its introduction and in four separate articles. The equal rights of men and women clause in the UN Charter established a legal basis for the international struggle to affirm women's human rights.

Although only eleven of the fifty-one nations represented in the 1946 UN General Assembly had women on their delegations, with the support of women's NGOs, women made their presence known. Early in 1946 Marie-Hélène LeFaucheux of France introduced an agenda item on the participation of women in UN conferences, which was adopted. Brazil proposed establishing a status of women commission, but the proposal was strongly opposed by the U.S. delegate, Virginia Gildersleeve, a founder of the International Federation of University Women. She argued the U.S. position that such a commission would be discriminatory and that the human rights commission was able to deal with women's questions.

Minerva Bernardino of the Dominican Republic (one of four women who signed the UN Charter in 1945) suggested that a committee of the Commission on Human Rights be established to work on women's rights. The New Zealand chair of the Economic and Social Council (ECOSOC) Organization Committee took up the suggestion, and soon thereafter a Human Rights Sub-Commission on the Status of Women was established. Eleanor Roosevelt, the widow of President Franklin Roosevelt, who was named chair of the Human Rights Commission, is commonly reputed to be the impetus for the establishment of the CSW. This is a historical error. She actually shared the American view, articulated by Gildersleeve, that the Human Rights Commission and its Sub-Commission on Women could be trusted to deal effectively with women's issues. She had, however, been a signatory, along with Jan McKenzie of New Zealand, Evdokia Uralova of the Soviet Union, and Ellen Wilkinson of Britain, to an "Open Letter to the Women of the World" calling on women to take a more active role in politics and government.[65]

Mrs. Roosevelt's position against a separate women's commission was not sustained. Within a year, the Sub-Commission became a freestanding commission, the current Commission on the Status of Women (CSW). Support for a full commission was led by the chair and vice-chair of the Sub-Commission as well as Bodil Begtrup of Denmark, Minerva Bernardino of the Dominican Republic, and Marie-Helen LeFaucheux of France. Bernardino had chaired the Inter-American Commission on Women; Begtrup had been active with the League of Nations on women's issues; and LeFaucheux had been a part of the French resistance movement.[66] These women knew how to organize and strategize, and they realized that a full commission was the only sure way to get their recommendations on women's rights directly to ECOSOC and the General Assembly.

The Sub-Commission had proposed "four immediate tasks. . . . (1) the creation of a U. N. Secretariat office headed by a competent woman; (2) the conclusion of the worldwide survey of laws on women [originated under the League of Nations]; (3) the promotion of equal educational opportunity; and (4) a [world] women's conference."[67] Dropping the idea of a world conference, the women succeeded in obtaining Roosevelt's support, and on 21 June 1946 ECOSOC authorized a freestanding Commission on the Status of Women and requested the Commission report back in 1947.

The purpose of the full commission was to promote women's rights in all fields of human endeavor. The object was to elevate the equal rights and human rights status of women, irrespective of nationality, race, language, or religion, in order to achieve equality with men in all fields of human enterprise and to eliminate all discrimination against women in statutory law, legal maxims or rules, or in interpretations of customary law.[68]

Meanwhile, the UDHR was being drafted, and it is worth noting that the Council of Women and the YWCA were among the twenty-two NGOs who urged the United Nations to draft such a declaration. Commission members and female delegates were concerned that terms such as the "rights of man" would not be interpreted specifically to include women. Bodil Begtrup, CSW chair, stated in one meeting that the drafting of the UDHR "was of fundamental importance for women," and pointed out that because "sex equality was a right which had been acquired but recently, it would be necessary to emphasize it explicitly in certain Articles."[69] Later, she suggested the term "human beings" be substituted for the word "men." Five days later, on 12 December, the wording about women was still an issue. Mrs. Mehta of India objected to the words "all men" and "brothers," fearing that "they might be interpreted to exclude women, and were out of date." The working group drafting the Declaration adopted the idea of a footnote to Article 1 indicating that the word "men" referred to all human beings. This legislative history clearly shows that the subject was debated and that the women in the drafting group made their point known. Ultimately, the ungendered term "everyone" was used extensively in the UDHR.

The CSW reflected the work on women's rights that had gone on before in the United Nations and earlier within various international bodies and women's organizations. In 1951, as a result of a Commission initiative, the ILO adopted the Convention and Recommendation Concerning Equal Remuneration for Men and Women Workers for Work of Equal Value and later issued recommendations on women's right to employment opportunities, pensions, retirement, and social insurance.[70] By 1952 the CSW succeeded in having the Convention on Political Rights of Women adopted—a direct result of the suffrage movement. Reflecting centuries of concern about the position of women in marriage, the Convention on the Nationality of Married Women was drafted and adopted by the General Assembly in 1957, supplementing Article 15 of the UDHR. In 1962 the Commission's Convention on the Consent to Marriage, Minimum Age for Marriage and the Registration of Marriages was adopted. CSW also worked with UNESCO on an equal education convention, adopted in 1960, and made recommendations on political and civic education, women's right to inherit property, a contentious issue that would surface again and again, and to equal treatment before the law.

A Declaration on Eliminating Discrimination against Women

Although the British Federation of Business and Professional Women had suggested to UN General Assembly President Spaak in 1946 that a UN convention on discrimination against women would be in order, it was not until 1963 that the first, tentative steps toward such a convention were undertaken.[71] In that year a series of events put a new focus on women in the United Nations. A General Assembly resolution was adopted, introduced by developing and Soviet-bloc countries, calling for the CSW to draft a declaration on eliminating discrimination against women. The resolution invited member states and "appropriate non-governmental organizations" to submit comments and proposals on principles that might be included in such a declaration. Also, 1963 was the first year that the CSW formally considered birth control, albeit under the guise of the term "family planning," and agreed to study the issue. (The two terms are quite different: birth control refers to the means the individual takes to prevent contraception, whereas family planning refers to a couple's decision making.) Helvi Sipila of Finland, a longtime commission member, was appointed Special Rapporteur on the question of family planning and subsequently produced a landmark document entitled "Study on the Interrelationship of the Status of Women and Family Planning." Sipila was typical of many CSW members—she was a professional woman who brought her long experience in the nongovernmental world to the UN system. Before working with the United Nations, Sipila served as president of the Finnish Girl Guides and the International Federation of Women Lawyers; as a lawyer her primary interest had been family law.

Also in 1963, a new UN Report on the World Social Situation, dealing with housing, population, health, nutrition, education, and social services—all traditional concerns of women—was before ECOSOC. The year also marked the fifteenth anniversary of the Universal Declaration of Human Rights and saw the Human Rights Commission complete a series of regional seminars on the status of women in family law. In the same year the General Assembly adopted an ECOSOC resolution on women in development, which had originally been submitted by Chile and cosponsored by numerous other delegations. The resolution reflected the contents of the World Report and the new emphasis within the United Nations on development. The resolution called on all UN member states, specialized agencies, and nongovernmental organizations to appoint women "to bodies responsible for the preparation of national development plans" and drew attention to the "importance of training women so as to enable them to participate fully in all phases of . . . national development programs."[72]

During the discussion of these resolutions, the CSW was congratulated for its work on the legal status of women and essentially told to consider economic and social development as well. The question became one of priorities: were programmatic efforts to improve women's current circumstances the priority, or was changing laws and policies to improve women's long-term legal and political capacity more important? Within the CSW and ECOSOC, some European and developing country representatives tended to favor the more programmatic, social welfare approach, while others took the more legalistic approach. This division continues. The more simplistic want to know what women want; the answer is both, and everything, as Frances Willard advised the WCTU years before. The ultimate desire, then and now, is for women to be considered human, a diverse, multifaceted group with both common and conflicting interests.

Although CSW members were representatives of governments, most also had experience in national or international women's organizations, and, unlike the mainstream human rights organizations, the CSW never reflected strong distinctions between political and civil rights and economic and social rights. Women's experiences tending home and family and as participants in the economic, social, and cultural life of their communities blurred these distinctions. Also, the basic rights to education, employment, and health fall under the economic and social rights rubric.

Against this background, work on a declaration eliminating discrimination against women began. By 1965, thirty governments, fifteen women's NGOs, and four UN specialized agencies had submitted comments on the proposed declaration. Not surprisingly, education was a high priority among the submissions, as was the view that marriage and family law, reinforced by tradition and custom, was at the heart of much discrimination. Interestingly, Afghanistan's reply at that time stated that eliminating discrimination required the "combating of traditions, customs and usages which thwart the advancement of women" and noted that this would require an intensive public education campaign. The idea that public opinion had to be changed was reiterated by numerous governments and NGOs. Afghanistan also suggested that "amends must be made to women by granting them certain privileges," which suggestion was a precursor of the idea of affirmative action, later called "temporary special measures" by the United Nations.

The same point was also made in the International Social Democratic Women's comments, which concentrated on employment rights. There was strong support from Eastern Europe and the Soviet bloc for the declaration with suggestions that the problems of mothers, including employed and unmarried mothers, be taken into account, a clear indication that Alexandra Kollontai's influence survived. St. Joan's Alliance, an international Catholic women's organization, suggested that resolutions adopted at their 1964 Antwerp meeting covering inheritance, ritual operations (a very early reference to female genital mutilation), and equal pay be considered for inclusion in the declaration. Other replies mentioned penal code reform, and many referred back to the UDHR, indicating that numerous respondents understood that women's rights were human rights.

With these comments, a draft declaration submitted by Poland, and working papers submitted by Ghana and the Mexican delegate, CSW chair Maria Lavalle Urbina, the CSW began drafting a declaration at its 1965 meeting in Teheran. A drafting committee brought forward an eleven-article text that began with a definition and condemnation of discrimination, covered virtually all the areas mentioned in the responses submitted, and concluded with an article calling on women's organizations to educate the public about the declaration's principles. This draft was sent out for comments, an exercise in public education as well as a test of political sentiment. At the 1966 CSW session, the major debate concerned protection of women workers. Many argued that protection perpetuated and reinforced discrimination, while others took the more conventional view that women needed protection because of their maternal function.

When the CSW draft of a declaration came before ECOSOC's Third Committee, an article calling for the abolition of discriminatory customs and traditions and raising the issue of protection of women workers created a furor. Some Third Committee delegates had suggested women be protected from "arduous work." NGOs responded with vehemence that protecting women from arduous work was ridiculous because women worldwide did such work. Nursing, tea picking, child care, and household work were arduous, they insisted, and customary family law simply reinforced women's subordinate status. By the end of their 1967 session, after some astute political maneuvering, the commission unanimously adopted its draft, and with the support of women delegates to ECOSOC's Third Committee an eleven-article Declaration was adopted by the General Assembly on 7 November 1967.[73] It covered the issues women had been working on for centuries.

Meanwhile, a second wave of an openly feminist international women's movement was becoming evident in the late 1960s. Small, informal consciousness-raising groups, public demonstrations on a variety of issues, and the exchange of information via informal newsletters and privately published studies and reports characterized this movement on local and national levels. It was essentially an underground movement with primarily negative and disparaging media attention. The emphasis of the new movement was on examining the pervasiveness of sex discrimination at all levels of society, and strategizing as to the most effective means to overcome it. Ad hoc caucuses were organized within professional organizations to examine discrimination within the professions and academia. Integrating women into all facets of public life and at higher levels became one theme of the movement, but first the age-old concerns about women's education, health, birth control and abortion, and employment discrimination were analyzed by small groups and gradually brought to public attention. Within the United States during the 1970s, the new feminists and main-line, or traditional, women's organizations collaborated to have the U.S. Congress pass numerous new antidiscrimination laws, including Title IX of the Education Amendments, which required all educational institutions receiving federal funds to eliminate discrimination against women and girls. This eventually brought about exponential increases in the numbers of women studying law, medicine, and science and initiated more sports and physical education programs for girls. All of the activity drew increased media attention. Although often demeaning, the attention was still useful in raising consciousness and expectations among women, not only in the United States, but in the United Nations as well. Like all political and social movements, publicity about the feminist movement attracted attention, motivated people to ponder their own situation and make comparisons, and inevitably resulted in increased numbers joining the movement. As a learned sociologist friend of the author's once said, political movements are like snowballs rolling downhill, they gather momentum and get bigger. While the new U.S. feminist groups paid no attention to CSW and little to international affairs in the early 1970s, traditional NGOs who lobbied the commission were influenced by this new movement, and with the increased dominance of the U.S. press, the new movement gave momentum to, and reinforced, CSW's work.

Following the UN custom of moving from a declaration to a convention, the Polish CSW delegate proposed the move shortly after the Declaration was adopted in 1967. Yet it was not until 1972 that the commission had a secretary general's report on the existing status of women's conventions, their relationships to the Declaration, and responses from governments on the idea of a convention. Also, in 1972 the UN General Assembly approved what had been a dream of some female delegates when the United Nations was formed—the holding of a world women's conference. Moreover, 1975 was designated as International Women's Year. Mexico City was selected as the site for the Conference and Helvi Sipila, a CSW representative since 1960, was chosen as Assistant Secretary General for Social Development and Humanitarian Affairs in charge of the year and the conference. Equality, development, and peace were selected as the themes of the conference—a clear, if unacknowledged, tribute to the 1926 Conference of the International Alliance of Women, which had first used the term "woman's movement" and asserted that the goals of this movement were "Equality, International Understanding and Peace."[74]

Sipila set to work, traveling the globe, urging governments to support the conference and to set up "national machineries," the UN term for women's bureaus or commissions. Sipila also understood that a symbol of the year was needed, one that transcended language barriers. The instantly popular result still symbolizes the international women's movement—a stylized dove, representing peace, with the women's and equality signs embedded in the body of the dove.

Preparations for International Women's Year dominated CSW's agenda, but a special working group, appointed at the suggestion of the Soviet Union, Tunisia, and the United Kingdom and composed of experienced CSW workers, was created to begin work on a possible convention. The Philippines' delegate presented a draft text, noting that it implied no commitment on the part of the Philippine government. CSW leaders from the Dominican Republic, Hungary, and Egypt became the working group's officers. Taking up the Philippines' delegate's strategy of drafting with no commitment from their governments, the group decided not to attribute positions taken on specific articles or language to a particular delegate, thus allowing free discussion among the members. This created what later feminist historians called a "free space" for UN women who believed a legally binding convention was the desired goal.[75]

The World Women's Conferences

The 1975 International Women's Year Conference attracted five thousand representatives, from all branches of the new women's movement, to Mexico City and to the NGO Tribune held in conjunction with the official UN Conference. In both the tribune and the governmental conference, contentious divisions between developing and industrialized countries surfaced and were energetically reported by the world's media. Developing country representatives argued that development would bring equality; new feminists from industrialized countries vehemently opposed that idea, citing innumerable areas of discrimination in their countries. The atmosphere in Mexico City appeared more tense than it actually was, fed not only by the media but also by many male delegates who thought the whole idea of a world women's conference was unnecessary, but who used it to test the political waters on such questions as development, the new international economic order (NIECI), and the influence of colonialism on developing countries, many of them newly independent. Soviet and American delegates sparred over cold war issues in the plenary sessions, while in the drafting committee meetings for the World Plan of Action women came together around common interests.[76]

A new international women's movement was in the making. In some countries the formation of in-country women's commissions or the "national machineries" that Sipila had encouraged followed a strong feminist approach. In others new, avowedly feminist NGOs were formed. In all countries the symbol adopted by CSW for International Women's Year became visible.[77] These events and the symbol served to bring women together at local and national levels around common concerns and to raise awareness about sex discrimination and equality, as well as women's place in the development process.

The World Plan of Action adopted at the Conference gave credit in its introduction to the work of CSW and to the numerous women's rights conventions already adopted.[78] The plan noted that the promotion and protection of human rights for all was one of the fundamental principles of the UN Charter and that "history has attested to the active role which women played . . . in accelerating the material and spiritual progress of peoples." It predicted that, "in our times, women's role will increasingly emerge as a powerful revolutionary social force." An overly optimistic fourteen-point list of five-year minimum goals was set forth, including:

a. Marked increase in literacy and civic education of women . . . ;
g. Encouragement of a greater participation of women in policy-making . . . ;
h. Increased provision for . . . health education and services . . . ;
i. Provision for parity in the exercise of civil, social and political rights such as those pertaining to marriage, citizenship and commerce;
j. Recognition of the economic value of women's work in the home in domestic food production and marketing and voluntary activities . . . ;
i. The promotion of women's organizations . . . ;
m. The development of modern rural technology . . . to help reduce the heavy work load of women . . . ; [and]
n. The establishment of interdisciplinary and multisectoral machinery within the government for accelerating the achievement of equal opportunities for women and their full integration into national life.

The plan called for the "active involvement of non-governmental women's organizations [to achieve] the goals of the ten-year World Plan of Action." In the global action section, the plan called on the United Nations to proclaim 1975 to 1985 the UN Decade for Women; also, it called for the drafting and adoption of a convention on eliminating discrimination against women. In another section, the plan stated that the theory and practice of inequality begins in the family and called for more equal sharing of family responsibilities between men and women. Without the latter, the plan stated, women could not be fully integrated in society or achieve equal rights. Also, without more data and information on women, development could not proceed.

The United Nations and women's organizations around the world responded to the outpouring of interest generated by the IWY Conference. The Decade for Women was established by the UN General Assembly with the subthemes of education, employment, and health, the three issues that women leaders and women's organizations had been discussing for centuries. During the decade there was an explosive growth in the number, style, and content of women's organizations. Many were not organizations in the precise meaning of that term but informal groups operating often on an ad hoc, as needed basis. New international organizations were also formed. One of the most notable was the International Women's Tribune Center, devoted to exchanging information worldwide and concentrating on providing readily accessible information to women in developing countries. Although its emphasis was on development and on rural women, women's rights were not ignored.

The resurgence of a second-wave women's movement was believed to be concentrated in the United States and Europe—and the majority of the 1975 NGO Tribune's participants were from the industrialized countries—but by 1976 there was enough activity to warrant and support three international publications: WIN NEWS, established in 1975; *Isis,* a magazine published by a new collective based in Geneva; and the newsletters of the International Women's Tribune Center, focusing on women's activities in developing countries. The Tribune Center's materials were distinguished by simple graphics and easy-to-read content aimed at women with low-level reading skills. WIN NEWS emphasized UN activities (in 1975 it published a 300-page directory of women's development organizations, from the Afghan Women's Society to the World Feminist Commission), while *Isis* emphasized the more radical new women's groups in developing countries and Europe. WIN NEWS and *Isis* represented the two different wings of the new movement—*Isis* the "liberationists" who wanted to free women from traditional constraints of all kinds, and WIN NEWS the "legalists" who aimed to change law and policy to guarantee more equality for women.

Also, by the mid-1970s foreign-aid donor nations had responded to the new international women's movement and UN development initiatives by establishing women-in-development (WID) offices. Ester Boserup's landmark book, *Women in Economic Development,* published in 1969, had persuasively documented the role women played in agricultural production in developing nations. Although the expressed purpose of these WID programs was to assist the male-dominated donor agencies in integrating women as both beneficiaries and agents of economic development, the momentum of the new feminist movements in industrialized countries and the World Women's Conferences influenced how WID funds were allocated. Data collection and income—generating projects was given high priority by most donors, but some, such as Swedish SIDA, supported the new women's bureaus in developing countries while others supported legal literacy and other projects devised by indigenous organizations. In terms of women's human rights, the support of legal literacy programs, including an early one in Nepal, was extremely important.

Among many of the WID officers in donor countries, a primarily long-term, albeit unadvertised, objective was improving the status of women within their own agencies and within developing countries. Leaders of women's groups, researchers, and new networks were identified and supported in both developing and industrialized countries. Family planning organizations, most notably International Planned Parenthood Federation (IPPF), also identified and trained women leaders through their projects in developing countries; IPPF was noted as being one of the most effective NGOs focusing on the CSW.

Before the 1980 mid-decade conference, an international consortium of WID offices was established under the OECD/DAC umbrella. Primarily a research, data, and information-exchange mechanism, one result of the consortium was that millions of dollars were allocated by the donor nations to support the 1980 UN World Women's Conference held in Copenhagen, Denmark. Funds went not only to support the UN Conference and the parallel NGO Forum but to support NGO workshops, tremendous numbers of publications, and the attendance of hundreds of developing country participants. While the media focused on the Israeli-Palestinian and other political confrontations at the Copenhagen conference, the emphasis in the NGO Forum was on networking among women and the importance of women's organizations.

Unnoticed by the media was the solidarity among women in recognizing discrimination even across lines of intense political disparities. Males headed virtually every government delegation, even in the preparatory conferences. Interested primarily in the political issues and protecting their country's point of view, they left their chairs to female delegation members unless a political issue was on the agenda; then the blue suits, white shirts, and ties would emerge en masse into the meeting hall. Women would turn around and look at each other knowingly as they relinquished their seats. Finally, in one preparatory meeting when the men emerged from the outer hall, a swell of spontaneous laughter greeted them. By 1985 many women led delegations and the political officers were more discreet.

The Copenhagen Programme of Action, while building on the Mexico City Plan, moved economic considerations to the fore. However, it emphasized that development was not only economic, but covered political, social, and cultural realms as well and that economic development projects often disadvantaged women, depriving them of their traditional forms of livelihood.[79] For the first time, as a result of WID studies, attention was directed to male-headed households, although the term "women who alone are responsible for families" was used, after considerable debate, because some delegations insisted only men could head households.

Extended debate was also had over the Programme's historical perspective section on the "roots of inequality." Western industrialized countries argued that the cause of inequality was the division of labor between men and women—justified by many on the basis of a woman's distinct child-bearing function; developing countries argued that "mass poverty" resulting from colonialism and unjust international economic relations was the cause, while the Soviet bloc argued that the predominant economic analyses of labor and capital (capitalism, that is) ignored women's work as producers and reproducers. Consensus was reached that discrimination was the result, no matter what view of history was taken. The Programme of Action stated that, while women were half the population of the world, they performed two-thirds of the world's work while only receiving one-tenth of world income and owning less than 1 percent of world property.

From Declaration to Convention to Women's Human Rights Treaty

Following the IWY Conference and establishment of the UN Decade for Women, the CSW undertook a three-part program: drafting the Convention; monitoring the status of women, including women in development efforts; and preparing for the second and third world conferences. In 1976 CSW took up the draft convention prepared by the special working group with the objective of having a convention ready for the 1980 Conference in Copenhagen. Articles on access to health services, including family planning, and on rural women were added, the latter clearly a product of women in development efforts. Articles 15 and 16, with very specific provisions for equality under the law and in marriage, were highly contentious because they conflicted with national legal systems. The implementation article also proved difficult: should CSW or an expert group be the implementation monitoring body?[80]

In early December 1979, the Third Committee took up the proposed convention. Time was running out if the convention was to be ready for signatures at the 1980 World Conference. The Swedish proposal for a monitoring body of twenty-three experts, which would report to the UN General Assembly through ECOSOC, was finally adopted. Then Mexico proposed giving governments another year to consider such a formidable document. In an astute parliamentary move, the Netherlands delegate succeeded in convincing the committee that the Mexican proposal was not germane. The convention would not be delayed. On 19 December 1979 the General Assembly adopted the Convention on the Elimination of All Forms of Discrimination Against Women, but not without strong debate on the political preamble; on paragraph 2 of Article 9, concerning the right of women to convey nationality to their children; and on Article 16, concerning marriage and family law.[81] The ideas John Stuart Mill had described in 1869 were still alive and well in a number of countries.

During the opening ceremony of the 1980 conference, the convention was presented to national governments for signature. Fifty-seven nations signed the document, and by December 1981 the convention had acquired the twenty ratifications necessary to give it force as a treaty. The result was a momentous victory, but most of the newer women's groups were now concentrating on women in development or single issues, such as health care or employment, and other programmatic efforts to improve women's current circumstances. On the whole, the convention received little attention.

By 1985, when the Third World Women's Conference was held in Nairobi, Kenya, the twenty-three-member expert Committee on the Elimination of Discrimination Against Women (CEDAW), which was to receive reports from governments on convention implementation, had begun its work, albeit rather slowly. The Nairobi Conference, with its approximately fifteen thousand attendees at the NGO Forum held on the University of Nairobi campus, demonstrated to the world through extensive media coverage that the new international women's movement was extremely diverse. Again, WID offices and international donor agencies were joined by national and international foundations in providing support for the conference, yet thousands of women still paid their own way. Attendees ranged from fresh-eyed recruits to sophisticated scholars to parliamentarians. The twelve hundred forum workshops on a wide array of topics reflected the diversity of women and their interests.[82] One multinational group mounted a workshop series on the convention. As with most NGO workshops, a standing-room-only crowd gathered each day to learn about the convention, exchange information, and report on ratification efforts in their own countries. Out of this workshop series, a group called the International Women's Rights' Action Watch (IWRAW) was formed to publicize and monitor the convention and its implementation.

During the NGO Forum, the violence against women issue finally came out of the world's closet and forced itself into the public attention. Innumerable workshops on the topic were held and thousands of publications distributed. Crowds gathered daily at the Peace Tent on the Nairobi campus to discuss the links between violence in the home, violence in society, and violence between nations. The Forward Looking Strategies (FLS) document, adopted by the UN Conference in Nairobi, called for constitutional and legal reform in accordance with the convention and for equality in social and political participation. In the peace section, the violence against women issue warranted two long paragraphs and was referenced numerous times in other sections. As in the Mexico City and Copenhagen documents, education was the priority. In the FLS it was called "the basis for the full promotion and improvement of the status of women" and the "basic tool that should be given to women in order to fulfill their role as full members of society."[83] Christine de Pizan had said the same thing centuries earlier, but by 1985 education was not merely about literacy; it encompassed concern about scholarships, stereotyped curricula, access to the highest levels of education, vocational training, and political and legal education.

Women's Rights as Human Rights

In the twenty-year period from 1975 to 1995, masses of women moved from portraying themselves as victims at the mercy of male rulers in the private and public sectors to taking leadership roles in demanding their human rights. The three world conferences allowed an ever-growing mass of activist women to exchange experiences across national boundaries and form new international networks around common interests. The electronic and print media as well as governments responded. Women gradually became a new political constituency.

Although IWRAW, through its quarterly newsletter, *Women's Watch,* and other publications focusing on the convention and the work of CEDAW, tried to draw international attention to the convention, the majority of women's organizations continued to focus on their more particular issues. It was the violence against women issue, especially domestic violence, that finally drew wide international attention to the idea that women's rights are human rights. The issue transcended race, class, and cultures and united women worldwide in a common cause. It dramatically illustrated women's subordinate position as no other issue had. Activity around the violence issue at local and national levels brought thousands of new recruits into the international movement and moved increasing numbers of women into the political arena.

Although the women's convention did not address violence specifically, in its 1989 session the CEDAW adopted General Recommendation No. 12, describing how violence against women was covered by the convention. At its 1992 session, CEDAW expanded on this in General Recommendation No. 19, which stated that gender-based violence is discrimination; that such discrimination violates women's human rights; that the convention covers both public and private acts; and that governments should take legal and other measures to prevent such violence and, in reporting under the convention, indicate the measures taken. Earlier, the Asian and Pacific Development Centre in Kuala Lumpur, Malaysia, had introduced the violence issue in a book on women's health, and in 1986 the UN Division for the Advancement of Women convened an expert group to identify implementation measures for the FLS section on violence against women.[84] During the late 1980s and early 1990s, women's organizations, governments, and the United Nations produced well-researched publications on the issue that were widely distributed.[85] Local and national organizations did the same. The United Nations' *Violence Against Women in the Family* is one of the most comprehensive of these publications. It pointed out the obvious, that violence within the home "has long existed . . . hidden by family privacy, guilt and embarrassment and, to a certain extent, traditional customs and culture."[86]

While some organizations, especially local ones, concentrated on treating the victims of such violence, others worked to bring the issue to public attention. The momentum behind the issue made women's human rights the most dramatic agenda item at the 1993 World Conference on Human Rights held in Vienna, Austria. Virtually every government at the conference felt compelled to give at least lip service to the violence issue and to women's human rights. The parallel NGO Forum was inundated with materials and activists on both the violence issue and on women's human rights generally. Highlighting the issue, a dramatic tribunal organized by the Global Campaign for Women's Human Rights was carried live on TV monitors throughout the conference hall. As a result, the Vienna Declaration and Programme of Action contained an extensive section on women's human rights with additional references throughout the document. It declared that "[t]he human rights of women and of the girl-child are an inalienable, integral and indivisible part of universal human rights" and that women's human rights "should form an integral part of the United Nations human rights' activities."[87] Traditional human rights groups that had long concentrated on human rights abrogations by governments against their citizens began to accept the fact that violations of rights by citizens against each other were equally valid human rights abrogations. The private and public spheres began to merge in human rights theory and practice.

The 1995 UN World Conference on Women held in Beijing, China, and the regional preparatory meetings for that conference reaffirmed the conclusions of the Vienna Conference and put women's human rights even more firmly on the world agenda. Among the critical areas of concern for the Beijing conference were, in order of priority: the burden of poverty on women; unequal access to education and training; health care; violence against women; the problems of armed conflict; economic inequalities; inequality of power and decision making; insufficient mechanisms to promote the advancement of women; lack of respect and protection of women's human rights; stereotyping of women and inequality in communications, especially the media; and the environment. Discrimination against and violations of the rights of the girl-child was added at the behest of African women who, at their 1995 regional preparatory meeting in Senegal and also at their 1985 Arusha conference, argued what Wollstonecraft and de Pizan had articulated centuries earlier: if attention is not paid to girls and their education, and if girls are not thought of as equal potential citizens, the situation of women will never change. This was a recognition of history and a determination not to repeat it.

Conclusions

The history of the drive for women's human rights indicates that only when women are literate, when they can articulate their view of life in publications and before audiences, when they can organize and demand equality, when girls are educated and socialized to think of themselves as citizens as well as wives and mothers, and when men take more responsibility for care of children and the home, can women be full and equal citizens able to enjoy human rights.

The question of shared responsibility for, and the valuing of, the care of children and the home goes to the heart of the implementation of the women's human rights. The Taliban edicts are only an extreme example of the resistance to this idea. Resistance is found even among educated women who accept the double burden of being wholly or partially responsible for both the economic support and physical care of children and the home. Numerous articles in the Convention on the Elimination of All Forms of Discrimination against Women deal with this problem. Article 5 seeks to eliminate stereotyped roles for men and women and to ensure that family education teaches that both men and women share a common role in raising children. Article 10, dealing with education, reiterates the same idea. Article 11 calls for maternity leave and "social services to enable parents to combine family obligations with work responsibilities."[88]

As John Stuart Mill put it in 1869, marriage should be thought of as a partnership of equals analogous to a business partnership, and the family not "a school of despotism" but "the real school of the virtues of freedom."[89] Article 16 of the Women's Convention lays out the legal framework for such a partnership, but the legal and de facto situations vary because of age-old customs and traditions. Over the centuries tremendous progress has been made in defining, demanding, and implementing women's human rights. Women have moved from the private sphere of home and family into the public sphere as citizens and workers. In many respects and in many countries, women are now considered equal humans, legally if not socially or economically. Yet reconciling family obligations with political and economic responsibilities remains a challenge for most women of the world. It is a formidable problem in the most industrialized nations and in the poorest families of all nations. The challenge for the twenty-first century is to find ways to reconcile these responsibilities so that women can exercise their human rights and become full citizens in all respects. It may take a new wave of an international women's movement to accomplish this task.

Meanwhile, however, the Women's Convention, now popularly called the women's human rights treaty, has been ratified or acceded to by 163 nations[90] and has become a formidable weapon in the struggle for worldwide implementation of women's human rights. Women's groups around the world are using the principles set forth in the convention to promote women's rights observance through court cases; as the basis for advocacy in changing national laws and policies; and for highlighting abrogations of women's human rights before international committees. Increasing numbers of women's organizations are developing "shadow reports" on implementation of the treaty in countries coming up for review by the CEDAW committee, which in turn is becoming more aggressive in challenging governments on conformance with the treaty. Christine de Pizan would be delighted to know that Mary Robinson of Ireland became the United Nations High Commissioner for Human Rights, but early-nineteenth-century women writers, such as Jane Austen, would also recognize the fear that compels women living in the Gulf nations to write anonymously or to use pseudonyms. Although women's rights are now recognized as human rights, recognition does not mean implementation. Much work still needs to be done to achieve human rights for all.

NOTES

1. Gerda Lerner, *The Creation of Feminist Consciousness: From the Middle Ages to 1870* (1993), p. 12.

2. See Joan Kelly, *Women, History and Theory* (1984), pp. 65–66.

3. See Arvonne S. Fraser, *Looking to the Future: Equal Partnership Between Men and Women in the 21st Century* (1983).

4. Guido A. Guarino, Introduction to *Concerning Famous Women* [1361] by Giovanni Boccacio (1963), p. xxxviii.

5. Lerner (1993).

6. Kelly (1984).

7. See Dale Spender, *Women of Ideas (and What Men Have Done to Them)* (1982).

8. See Natalie Zemon Davis and Arlette Fargo, eds., *A History of Women in the West: Renaissance and Enlightenment Paradoxes,* vol. 3, general editors Georges Duby and Michelle Perrot (1993); Ellen Moers, *Literary Women* (1976); Bonnie S. Anderson and Judith P. Zinsser, *A History of Their Own: Women in Europe from Prehistory to the Present* (1988); and Lerner (1993).

9. See Amy Schrager Lang, *Prophetic Woman: Anne Hutchinson and the Problem of Dissent in the Literature of New England* (1987); and Selma R. Williams, *Divine Rebel: The Life of Anne Marbury Hutchinson* (1981).

10. Williams, *Divine Rebel* (1981), p. 149 (quoting Governor Winthrop's opening statement against Hutchinson at her trial).

11. See Williams, *Divine Rebel* (1981), citing *A Report of the Trial of Mrs. Anne Hutchinson Before the Church in Boston, 1638.*

12. See Susan Groag Bell and Karen M. Offen, *Women, the Family and Freedom: The Debate Documents* (1983), pp. 97–118.

13. See Anderson and Zinsser, *A History of Their Own* (1988), pp. 345, 352.

14. Wollstonecraft, *Vindication of the Rights of Women* [1792] (1971), p. 105.

15. Jean-Jacques Rousseau, "A Discourse on Political Economy," in *The Social Contract and Discourses,* translated by G.D.H. Cole (1913), reprinted in part in *History of Ideas on Woman: A Source Book,* edited by Rosemary Agonito (1977), pp. 117, 119.

16. Wollstonecraft, *Vindication* (1971), p. 101, citing Jean-Jacques Rousseau, *Emitius: A Treatise of Education* (1768), p. 181.

17. See Alice Rossi, *The Feminist Papers: From Adams to de Beauvoir* (1973), pp. 10–11; and Sally Smith Booth, *Women of '76,* (1973) p. 89.

18. Phyllis Lee Levin, *Abigail Adams: A Biography* (1987).

19. Bell and Offen, *Women, the Family and Freedom* (1983), p. 41.

20. See Margaret Forster, *Significant Sisters: The Grassroots of Active Feminism 1839–1939,* (1984), pp. 15–52.

21. See Forster, *Significant Sisters* (1984), p. 46.

22. See, e.g., Forster, *Significant Sisters,* pp. 47, 48, 51; Bell and Offen, *Women, the Family and Freedom,* p. 22 (highlighting the Divorce Act of 1857, the Married Women's Property Act of 1870, and its successor act of 1882, three acts that changed the legal position of married women in England); Genevieve Fraisse and Michelle Perrot, eds., *A History of Women in the West: Emerging Feminism from Revolution to World War,* vol. 4, general eds. Georges Duby and Michelle Perrot (1993), 97–113.

23. Bell and Offen, *Women, the Family and Freedom* (1983), p. 392.

24. Mill, *The Subjection of Women,* reprinted in part in Agonito, *History of Ideas on Woman* (1977), pp. 225, 243.

25. Bell and Offen, *Women, the Family and Freedom* (1983), pp. 398–399.

26. Moers, *Literary Women* (1976), p. 39 (quoting Eliot).

27. Joseph Barry, *Infamous Woman: The Life of George Sand,* (1978), p. xiv.

28. See Moers, *Literary Women* (1976), pp. 20–22. For a list of Flora Tristan's publications, see Moers, pp. 316–317.

29. Moers, *Literary Women* (1976), p. 19.

30. Yuri Suhl, *Ernestine L. Rose and the Battle for Human Rights* (1959), p. 149.

31. Suhl, *Ernestine L. Rose* (1959), pp. 145–148.

32. Rokeya Sakhawat Hossain, *Sultana's Dream and Selections from "The Secluded Ones"* [1905 and 1928–1930], edited and translated by Roushan Jahan (1988).

33. Angelina E. Grimke, *An Appeal to the Christian Women of the South* [1836] (1969). See Gerda Lerner, *The Grimke Sisters from South Carolina* (1967).

34. See Lerner, *The Grimke Sisters* (1967), p. 183.

35. Sarah M. Grimke, *Letters on the Equality of the Sexes and Other Essays,* edited by Elizabeth Ann Bartlett (1988).

36. Sarah M. Grimke, *Marriage,* reprinted in part in Gerda Lerner, *The Female Experience: An American Documentary* (1977).

37. Elisabeth Griffith, *In Her Own Right: The Life of Elizabeth Cady Stanton* (1984), p. 38.

38. Mari Jo Buhle and Paul Buhle, *The Concise History of Woman Suffrage* (1978), p. 94, reprinting Stanton's Declaration of Sentiments *in toto.*

39. Bell and Offen, *Women, the Family and Freedom* (1983), pp. 98, 104–109.

40. Eleanor Flexner, *Century of Struggle: The Woman's Rights Movement in the United States* (1974), pp. 120–121.

41. Ruth Bordin, *Frances Willard: A Biography* (1986).

42. See Margaret E. Galey, "Forerunners in Women's Quest for Partnership," in *Women, Politics, and the United Nations* 1, edited by Anne Winslow (1995); Richard Stites, *The Women's Liberation Movement in Russia* (1978).

43. Griffith, *In Her Own Right* (1984), pp. 203, 204.

44. The full text of the speech, "The Solitude of Self," can be found in Elizabeth Cady Stanton et al., eds., *The History of Woman Suffrage [1881]* (1985), pp. 189–191.

45. See Arnold Whittick, *Woman into Citizen* (1979), pp. 22, 31.

46. Whittick, *Woman into Citizen* (1979), pp. 31–32.

47. See Whittick, *Woman into Citizen* (1979), p. 60. The Alliance was not the only organization that developed an interest in ending white slave traffic (trafficking in women). Following World War 1, the Union Française pour le Suffrage des Femmes invited women from Allied countries to help lobby against trafficking in women at the Paris Peace Conference. (See Whittick, pp. 70–71.) Resolutions on "the moral, political and educational aspects of women's life" were presented to various commissions of the League of Nations. (Whittick, p. 71). The resolutions on moral status included the following objectives:

1. "To suppress the sale of women and children."
2. "To respect and apply the principle of woman's liberty to dispose of herself in marriage."
3. "To suppress the traffic in women, girls, and children of both sexes, and its corollary, the licensed house of ill fame."

See also Natalie Kaufman Hevener, *International Law and the Status of Women* (1983), pp. 10–12, 78–102 (providing cites for international conventions relating to trafficking in women).

48. Forster, *Significant Sisters* (1984), pp. 169–171.

49. See Edward T. James, ed., *Notable American Women 1607–1950,* vol. 1 (1971), p. 20 (providing section on Addams).

50. See Whittick, *Woman into Citizen* (1979), pp. 70–71.

51. See Whittick, *Woman into Citizen* (1979), p. 72 (stating that Article 7(3) of the Covenant states that "all positions under or in connection with the League, including the secretariat, shall be open equally to men and women"; while Article 23(a) is concerned "with fair and humane conditions of labour for men, women

and children" and 23(c) with "the supervision over the execution of agreements with regard to the traffic in women and children").

52. See Whittick, *Woman into Citizen* (1979), pp. 75–76 (reprinting the charter).

53. Whittick, *Woman into Citizen* (1979), p. 75.

54. Whittick, *Woman into Citizen* (1979), p. 76.

55. See Margaret Sanger, *Margaret Sanger: An Autobiography* (1938), pp. 127–128. For information on Besant, *See also Birth Control Review* 13, 106 (1929).

56. See Ellen Chesler, *Woman of Valor: Margaret Sanger and the Birth Control Movement In America* (1992), pp. 85–86.

57. See Barbara Sicherman et al., eds., *Notable American Women: The Modern Period: A Biographical Dictionary* (1980), pp. 623–627; Marian J. Morton, *Emma Goldman and the American Left: "Nowhere at Home"* (1992); Candace Falk, *Love, Anarchy and Emma Goldman* (1984); E.T. James et al., eds., *Notable American Women: A Biographical Dictionary* 2 (1971), pp. 57–59.

58. Chesler, *Woman of Valor* (1992), p. 97.

59. Margaret Sanger, *Family Limitation,* 5th rev. ed. (1914), microformed on *History of Women,* Reel 962, No. 9989 (Research Publications).

60. See Perdita Huston, *Motherhood by Choice: Pioneers in Women's Health and Family Planning* (1992), pp. 95–106.

61. Chesler, *Woman of Valor* (1992), p. 357.

62. In the United States, a women's club movement, primarily dedicated to self-education and social welfare, had expanded across the country. See Theodora Penny Martin, *The Sound of Our Own Voices: Women's Study Clubs, 1860–1910* (1987); Anne Firor Scott, *Natural Allies: Women's Associations in American History* (1991). Social reformers such as Jane Addams, of Hull House in Chicago, had invented social work; Addams later became a force in urban affairs. See Allen F. Davis, *American Heroine: The Life and Legend of Jane Addams* (1973); Jane Addams, *Jane Addams: A Centennial Reader* (1960); Jane Addams, *Twenty Years at Hull-House* (1914). U.S. suffrage leaders ranged from the organizationally minded Susan B. Anthony and Carrie Chapman Catt to the more militant Alice Paul, all of whom were also active internationally. A similar range could be found in England, including the militant Pankhursts. See Ellen Carol Dubois, *Feminism and Suffrage: The Emergence of an Independent Women's Movement in America 1848–1869* (1978); Carrie Chapman Catt and Nettie Rogers Shuler, *Woman Suffrage and Politics: The Inner Story of the Suffrage Movement* (1970); Inez Hayes Gillmore, *Story of Alice Paul and the National Woman's Party* (1977); Antonia Raesurn, *The Suffragette View* (1976) (providing information on Pankhurst).

63. See Hevener, *International Law and the Status of Women* (1983), pp. 119, 67–77 (discussing the maternity convention and night work convention respectively).

64. Margaret E. Galey, "Women Find a Place," in *Women, Politics, and the United Nations,* edited by Anne Winslow (1995), p. 11.

65. See Galey, in *Women, Politics, and the United Nations,* ed. Winslow (1995), pp. 11–12.

66. Interview with Margaret E. Galey (23 June 1997).

67. Galey, in *Women, Politics, and the United Nations,* ed. Winslow (1995), p. 13.

68. Margaret E. Galey, "Promoting Nondiscrimination Against Women: The

UN Commission on the Status of Women," *International Studies Quarterly* 23 (1979): 276.

69. Working Group on the Declaration of Human Rights, *Summary Record of the Second Meeting,* UN ESCOR, Commission on Human Rights, 2nd Session, UN Doc. E/CN.4/AC-2/SR.2 (1947). See also Johannes Morsink, "Women's Rights in the Universal Declaration," *Human Rights Quarterly* 13 (1991): 229, 234.

70. See Hevener, *International Law and the Status of Women* (1983).

71. See Hevener, *International Law and the Status of Women* (1983), pp.165–176; Galey, "Promoting Nondiscrimination," (1979), p. 278.

72. See Galey, "Women Find a Place," in *Women, Politics, and the United Nations, ed.* Winslow (1995), p. 12.

73. See Arvonne S. Fraser, "The Convention on the Elimination of All Forms of Discrimination Against Women (The Women's Convention)," in *Women, Politics, and the United Nations,* ed. Winslow (1995), p. 77.

74. Whittick, *Woman into Citizen* (1979), pp. 92.

75. See Sara M. Evans and Harry C. Boyte, *Free Spaces: The Sources of Democratic Change in America* (1986), p. vii (discussing the definition of the "free spaces" idea).

76. See Arvonne S. Fraser, *The UN Decade for Women: Documents and Dialogue* (1987), pp. 17–54.

77. The author of this article, then U.S. Agency for International Development coordinator of the Office of Women in Development, received reports from mission directors who saw the symbol posted across remote corners of the developing world.

78. United Nations, *Report of the World Conference of the International Women's Year* (World Plan of Action), reprinted in *Women and World Development,* edited by Irene Tinker and Michele Bo Bramsen (1976), pp. 185–218.

79. For more on the Copenhagen conference, including the NGO Forum, see Fraser, *The UN Decade for Women* (1987); Jane S. Jaquette, "Losing the Battle, Winning the War: International Politics, Women's Issues, and the 1980 Mid-Decade Conference," in *Women, Politics, and the United Nations,* ed. Winslow (1995), p. 45.

80. For a fuller discussion of the drafting and adoption of the Convention, see Fraser, "The Convention," in *Women, Politics, and the United Nations,* ed. Winslow (1995), p. 81.

81. Ibid.

82. For the first time, a number of reports on the NGO conference were published. *FORUM '85: Final Report, Nairobi, Kenya* was commissioned by the NGO Planning Group for the Forum while *Images of Nairobi* and Caroline Pezzullo's For the Record . . . Forum '85 were both published by the International Women's Tribune Center in 1986. See also Fraser, *The UN Decade for Women* (1987), p. 199.

83. This document was officially known as the United Nations Report of the *World Conference to Review and Appraise the Achievements of the United Nations Decade for Women: Equality, Development and Peace, Nairobi, 15–26 July 1985,* UN Doc. A/ CONFA 16/27/Rev.1, UN Sales No. E.85.IV.1 0 (1986). It was subtitled *The Nairobi Forward-Looking Strategies for the Advancement of Women.*

84. This expert group meeting was only one result of ECOSOC Resolution 1984/14 of 24 May 1984 on violence against women that allowed the Branch for the Advancement of Women to expand work on the subject. *Violence in the Family,* E.S.C. Res. 1984/14, UN ESCOR, 19 plenary meeting (1984).

85. See *Women's Watch* (the quarterly newsletter of the International Women's Rights Action Watch) for a sampling of these publications.

86. UN Center for Social Development and Humanitarian Affairs, *Violence Against Women in the Family,* UN Doc. ST/CSDHA/2, UN Sales No. E.89.IV.5 (1989).

87. Vienna Declaration and Programme of Action, UN GAOR, World Conference on Human Rights, 48th Session, 22d plenary meeting, UN Doc. AICONF.157/24 (1993).

88. Convention on the Elimination of All Forms of Discrimination against Women (CEDAW), adopted 18 Dec. 1979, G.A. Res. 34/180, UN GAOR, 34th Sess., Supp. No. 46, UN Doc. A/34/46 (1980) (entered into force 3 Sept. 1981), reprinted in 19 I.L.M. 33 (1980).

89. Bell and Offen, *Women, the Family and Freedom* (1983), p. 398.

90. Sadly, the United States is not one of the ratifying countries. Although Presidents Carter and Clinton both submitted the treaty for ratification to the U.S. Senate, the Senate has yet to act, and U.S. women's organizations have not made ratification a priority item.

Indivisible or Invisible

WOMEN'S HUMAN RIGHTS IN THE
PUBLIC AND PRIVATE SPHERE

Sheila Dauer

∞ THE last century saw a great leap forward in the struggle for women's human rights. In many countries women won the right to vote and take part in government, though in some, such as Kuwait, they did not. Many women acquired an economic independence and social status unthinkable a hundred years earlier. A few countries have adopted constitutions or legislation banning discrimination on grounds of gender. But women are still treated as second-class citizens all over the world. By the end of the twentieth century, women comprised two-thirds of the world's one million illiterate people. Women continue to bear the double burden of work and childcare, to own and earn less than men, and to be excluded from making decisions that affect the way society is organized, even decisions over their own bodies. Women are struggling to help their families and communities survive poverty and armed conflict. And in many countries they still contend with violence in the family, in the community, and from the government.[1]

This essay examines two kinds of violence against women in relation to the human rights treaties and agreements to protect women that came into existence in the second half of the twentieth century. It also examines issues surrounding government accountability to implement these agreements and present recommendations for government action.

One of the great milestones in the protection of women's human rights was the adoption by the United Nations General Assembly in December 1979 of the UN Convention to Eliminate All Forms of Discrimination against Women (CEDAW). The convention laid the foundation and universal standard for women's equal enjoyment without discrimination of civil, political, economic, social, and cultural rights. Subsequent approval of new UN treaties, declarations, and mechanisms has advanced the recognition and protection of women's human rights. Since 1979 many organizations have emerged throughout the United States and around the globe to promote awareness of women's human rights and to advocate for their defense.

However, throughout the world governments resist taking action. Many lack the political will to prevent and punish human rights violations against women and girls committed by their own agents and employees. Countless women in many parts of the world are raped and subjected to other forms of abuse and sexual violence by the very authorities that have a duty to protect them. For example, on separate days in early March 1999, two young Kurdish women—sixteen-year-old high school student N.C.S. and nineteen-year-old student Fatma Deniz Polattas—were arrested by police authorities and detained at the Anti-Terror Branch of police headquarters in Iskenderun, Turkey, for seven and five days respectively. The young women claim to have been tortured—including beatings, rape and rape threats, forced "virginity tests" by doctors who did not report that they had been tortured, and other acts of assault—and forced to give false confessions while in police custody. In recent years Amnesty International has documented several cases of rape and sexual assault committed by Turkish security force members. The experiences of N.C.S. and Fatma Deniz Polatta demonstrate the continuing vulnerability of children and women to violence in Turkish police stations and prisons.[2]

Governments also ignore or sanction abuses of women and girls committed by private actors. For example, in some countries women cannot make independent decisions about their lives without placing themselves at risk of violent retaliation. In certain parts of Bangladesh, many young women have been disfigured in acid attacks after they rejected suitors or were involved in dowry disputes. Ajuka Khatum was asleep when her rejected suitor threw acid into her face, blinding her permanently. Responsibility for these abuses rests with the government, which has systematically failed to bring these attackers to justice and neglected its obligations to protect women against this form of violence. The increase in such attacks highlights the government's failure to take adequate measures to protect women and address underlying gender discrimination.[3]

In spite of these problems, signs of growth are evident in the awareness of human rights issues at the governmental level. Since 1979 increasingly more countries have ratified CEDAW. They have officially subscribed to the goals of subsequent declarations and agreements aimed at eradicating public and private abuses against women and ensuring equal protection of the law. Governments around the world have been forced to admit that violence against women is an integral part of both state practice and so-called private relationships, and that they can be held accountable to take serious steps to eradicate both of these kinds of violence against women.

The Women's Convention

Article 1 of the Universal Declaration of Human Rights (UDHR), adopted by the UN in 1948, states that: "All human beings are born free and equal in dignity and rights." In Article 2 it states that "everyone is entitled to all the rights and freedoms set forth in this Declaration, without distinction of any kind, such as race, colour, sex, language." However, these words proved, for women, to provide a false hope even when subsequent treaties were approved, such as the International Covenants on Civil and Political Rights (1966) and on Social, Economic, and Cultural Rights (1966), which were intended to translate the UDHR into international human rights law. Government agents and private actors still discriminated against them and either carried out or tacitly condoned violence against them.

CEDAW seeks to advance women's human rights protection by applying a gender perspective to principles enunciated in the UDHR. CEDAW was the first international human rights treaty to define discrimination against women. Its first sixteen articles call on governments to ensure the eradication of such abuses in practically all walks of life. In Article 5, CEDAW also holds governments responsible for taking steps to modify practices based on stereotypes about women's role as well as beliefs about women's inferiority. The implication of this article is that discriminatory cultural, traditional, or religious practices may be harmful to women and girls and that government is responsible to take steps to modify or eliminate them.

In the decade that followed, the committee that monitors government compliance with CEDAW (also called CEDAW) recognized that widespread gender-based violence often prevents women from enjoying their fundamental human rights. In 1992 the CEDAW Committee issued Recommendation 19, in which states were asked to include information about violence against women and measures introduced to deal with it. The recommendation stated that the women's convention covers public and private acts and that states should take effective measures to overcome all forms of gender-based violence, whether by public or private actors. Finally, the committee recommended that the question of the equal enjoyment of human rights by women be fully reflected in the agenda of the Second World Conference on Human Rights in Vienna in June 1993.[4]

The Second World Conference on Human Rights in Vienna

By the 1980s and 1990s, the women's human rights community began to present a critique of male bias in the prioritization and interpretation of human rights at the UN, especially its Human Rights Commission. Until that time the International Covenant on Civil and Political Rights was considered the primary human rights treaty, with its definition of human rights violations focusing entirely on state actors. "This approach to human rights, which gives priority to protecting citizens from certain types of direct state coercion, also facilitates the 'protection' of male-defined cultural, family or religious rights often at the expense of the human rights of women."[5]

Governments around the world often rationalized discriminatory or violent practices against women as culturally authentic and pleaded a perverse interpretation of cultural relativity as a justification for their refusal to end and redress these practices. To counteract the invisibility of abuses against women at the Second World Conference on Human Rights in Vienna, the Global Campaign for Women's Human Rights was organized to influence the outcome of this historic meeting. The Center for Women's Global Leadership (based at Rutgers University's Douglass College campus in New Brunswick, New Jersey) collaborated with women's organizations around the world to launch and coordinate the campaign.[6]

The campaign goal was to give visibility to forms of violence against women that the UN experts in human rights and governments had failed to include as part of human rights, especially those occurring in the community, family, and private sphere, and to demand government accountability for eradicating them. To do this, the global campaign organized a series of tribunals around the world, culminating in the Vienna Tribunal for Women's Human Rights, in which thirty-three women testified to first-hand experience of violence in the family, war crimes against women, violations of bodily integrity, socioeconomic violations, and political persecution and discrimination. The testimonies were heard by an audience of nongovernmental organizations (NGOs) and country delegates to the official conference and judged by a distinguished panel. The judges concluded that widespread failure to recognize abuses against women and to protect their human rights was pervasive and required urgent attention. The reasons for this general failure, they stated, were "(1) lack of understanding of the systematic nature of subordination of women, and the social, political and economic structures which perpetuate such subordination; (2) a failure to recognize the subordination of women, particularly in the private sphere, as a violation of their human rights; and (3) an appalling failure or neglect by the state to condemn and provide redress for discrimination and other violations against women."[7]

The judges recommended (1) strengthening enforcement of CEDAW by universal ratification and withdrawal of reservations, (2) development of an Optional Protocol to CEDAW as a mechanism by which women denied access to justice in their own countries could bring complaints to CEDAW, (3) appointment of a Special Rapporteur on Violence Against Women at the UN Human Rights Commission, (4) General Assembly approval of a UN Declaration on the Elimination of Violence against Women, and (5) recognition of war crimes against women in an international criminal court.

The strength and effectiveness of the Global Campaign can be seen in the adoption of many of these recommendations in the Vienna Declaration, the conference's final document and later by the United Nations. The Declaration to Eliminate Violence Against Women was approved by the General Assembly in December 1993. The UN Human Rights Commission did approve a Special Rapporteur on Violence against Women, appointing Radhika Coomaraswamy, who still holds this position. The Optional Protocol to CEDAW was approved by the UN General Assembly in December 1999 and went into force in 2000. An International Criminal Court was established in December 1999 that includes rape and other forms of sexual violence—including enforced prostitution, forced pregnancy, and sexual slavery—as crimes against humanity, and as war crimes when committed in the context of international or internal armed conflict.

Armed with these new agreements, with a rapporteur inside the Human Rights Commission, and with an all-out effort at the United Nations to integrate and mainstream a gender perspective in all its institutions, human rights organizations have been able to work more closely with women's organizations to bring urgent issues of violence against women into the mainstream of human rights practice.

What follows are examples of Amnesty International's work on two kinds of violence against women: government-perpetrated (rape of female inmates) and violence perpetrated by private actors in the community and the family ("honor" killings). In each case, AI worked closely with women's human rights groups in the country, seeking their documented evidence and advice on campaign goals and tactics. In each case, AI holds government accountable to apply due diligence to eradicating these human rights violations whether government-sponsored or carried out by private actors.

Government-Sponsored Violence against Women

Women are tortured, imprisoned, and killed for raising their voices against brutal governments and for defending women's rights. Government-perpetrated, gender-based violence against women in custody includes rape (a form of torture) and other forms of cruel, inhuman, and degrading punishments such as flogging or stoning to death. AI has reported for many years that women in custody are at risk of rape and other sexual torture and ill-treatment. Rape, threats of rape, and sexual humiliation are often used to elicit information or a confession during interrogation, or to humiliate and intimidate women, thus weakening their resistance to interrogation, and to punish them for their activism or for perceived transgressions of social roles and mores. Often police and jailers rape women in their custody because they know they can get away with it. Rape and sexual abuse by state agents continue to be a global problem. In 1991 and again in 1992, AI published reports about gender-specific human rights violations against women that identified rape in custody as a form of torture.[8] But it was not until 1992 that rape was explicitly mentioned at the UN Human Rights Commission as a form of torture.[9]

Persistence of this form of torture is due in large part to the impunity with which these acts are carried out. Governments rarely take these acts of brutality seriously. In most cases investigations are not carried out and those responsible, if they are punished at all, suffer only minor disciplinary sanctions.[10]

Sexual Abuse of Female Inmates in United States Prisons and Jails

Until recently the idea that torture occurs in the United States was unheard of. But AI and other human rights organizations have reported on torture in United States prisons and jails.[11] As the female prisoner population exploded in the 1980s and 1990s, the problem of abuse of women inmates in United States prisons and jails became acute. For example, California's female prison population alone rose by 450 percent between 1980 and 1993. In the space of fifteen years, the number of women in prison in the United States has almost quadrupled, reaching 148,200. Overcrowding in women's facilities has them running between 60 percent to 100 percent over capacity, making human rights violations all the more difficult to report and almost impossible to remedy. Strained resources make it close to impossible to supervise male guards' activities and encourage the gross medical neglect of the women in detention. Responding to the growing proportions of the problem, in March 1999 AI published a report, "USA: Not Part of My Sentence: Violations of the Human Rights of Women in Custody," accompanying it with an international campaign.

The common profile of the United States female inmate is a young single mother with few marketable skills, a high school dropout who lives below the poverty level. Seventy-five percent are between the ages of 25 and 34, and an estimated 90 percent have an alcohol or drug related history. An estimated 59 percent suffer from mental illness. Seventy-eight percent of women in prison are mothers with dependent children. According to various studies, somewhere between 50 percent and 80 percent of all female inmates experienced sexual abuse and/or domestic violence in their lives before coming to prison.

Women of color are disproportionately represented in United States prisons and jails. Over 46 percent of the women in prison in California, for example, are African-American and over 30 percent are Latina. Although a greater number of European-American women than women of color are arrested, African-American women are eight times more likely than white women to be sent to prison.

Most significantly, the percentage of violent offenders has decreased steadily since the 1980s while the incarceration rate has increased dramatically. In fact, 92 percent of women in prison are nonviolent offenders, and more than 60 percent of the women in prison in the United States are first-time offenders.[12]

Many women in prisons are victims of rape and other sexual misconduct by staff. This misconduct may take various forms, including sexually offensive language and groping inmates' breasts and genitals during pat-frisk searches. Often male staff will coerce inmates to trade sex for necessities such as soap, shampoo, desired work assignments, or being allowed to visit their children.

Contrary to international standards (Rule 53 of the UN Standard Minimums for the Treatment of Prisoners), prisons in the United States employ men to guard women and place relatively few restrictions on the duties of male staff. For example, male guards are able to watch female inmates in their living spaces when they shower and undress. Other countries are able to control access of male corrections officials to female inmates. In the Canadian federal prison system, only 9 percent of those who guard women are male; in the United States federal prison system, 70 percent of the guards of female inmates are male.

Many of the lack-of-privacy abuses that women experience as humiliating are permitted by law. For example, Susan Shinn, held at Albion Prison in New York State, is paralyzed below the waist and requires a wheelchair. She claims, along with five other women, that for over five years they suffered "legalized sexual molestation." A lawsuit filed by the women against prison authorities describes their sexual abuse by male guards. One of Shinn's co-plaintiffs reports that during a pat-frisk, a male officer rubbed his penis against her, grabbed and squeezed her breasts, then propositioned her. When she cursed at him, he wrote a misbehavior report against her for "harassing an officer." This cruel and degrading treatment, she later reported, contributed to her subsequent suicide attempt.[13]

When an officer's conduct violates institutional rules (for example, prohibiting any staff-inmate sexual contact), or criminal laws (rape and other sexual assault), the victim often makes no complaint because she fears retaliation. This is a realistic fear. In March 1998 the Federal Bureau of Prisons agreed to pay three African-American women who had been held in isolation in the male prison at Dublin, a federal facility in California, a total of $500,000 to settle a lawsuit in which they reported that guards had taken money from male inmates in exchange for allowing them to enter the women's cells so they could rape them. No one was ever charged or tried for these crimes. The women complained about this sexual abuse at that time. They also reported that there were European-American female prisoners who were also being sexually abused at the same time. The European-American prisoners were moved immediately after a complaint was made. The African-American women were not moved for another ten days, a delay which permitted violent retaliation. Four guards entered the cell of one of the women, beat and sodomized her and urinated on her, calling her a "snitch." Although there was a monetary settlement, the perpetrators of this brutal act have not been tried and convicted.

A second reason female inmates hesitate to make complaints about sexual misconduct is that when it comes down to their word against that of the corrections official, they are rarely believed. In Washington State, an inmate who had been imprisoned since 1985 became pregnant. The inmate alleged she was raped, but prosecution authorities did not charge the officer because he claimed the sex was consensual. When the child was born, DNA testing confirmed that the officer was indeed the father. Because the inmate could not prove coercion, and because at that time Washington State had no law criminalizing all sexual contact between staff and inmates, no charges could be brought.

AIUSA, the U.S. section of AI, and other human rights and prison service organizations have found this to be a widespread problem. AI has found that sexual relations between staff and inmates are inherently abusive and can never be truly consensual simply because of the considerable difference in power between the parties. The environment created by male guards' continuing access to women's private living spaces and their carrying out of cross-gender pat-frisks contributes to male staff's feeling they can rape and sexually coerce female inmates with impunity.

AI and other human rights and prison service organizations concluded that female inmates need legislative protection against widespread sexual misconduct by correction officials. AI and other organizations have worked together for legislation that makes it a matter of professional duty for corrections officials not to enter into sexual contact with inmates. Under this legislation, consent of the inmate may not be used as a defense.

In 1999 AI launched an international campaign on human rights violations in the United States. As part of the campaign, the organization published "Not Part of My Sentence" on human rights violations against women in U.S. prisons. AIUSA local chapters lobbied for passage of legislation to protect female inmates from sexual misconduct by corrections officers. Such legislation has been passed in Washington, Virginia, Massachusetts, Nebraska, West Virginia, and Pennsylvania. AIUSA continues to campaign to obtain this legislation, to amend or repeal laws that criminalize the female inmate when sexual misconduct occurs, and to ensure that such legislation is implemented.

AI recommends that corrections authorities publicly recognize that rape and other sexual abuse constitutes torture, or cruel, inhuman, or degrading treatment or punishment, and take the following measures to combat it:

1. Female inmates should be guarded only by female officers and male staff who provide professional services in female facilities should always be accompanied by female officers.
2. Sexual abuse of inmates by staff should be expressly prohibited.
3. Sexual abuse should be widely defined to include sexual assault, threatened sexual assault, sexual contact and sexually explicit language and gestures.
4. Correctional staff who rape and sexually assault female inmates should be prosecuted under the state's rape laws.
5. Male staff must be banned by law from entering into sexual relations with female inmates under any circumstances and prosecuted under such laws.
6. Inmates and staff who make these complaints must be protected against retaliation by guards and disciplinary and/or legal action should be taken against any staff member who seeks to deter inmates and staff from reporting this abuse or to punish or intimidate those who already have done so.
7. Staff must be fully trained concerning the legal limits on their behavior.

Private-Actor Violence against Women

Acts of violence against women and girls carried out by private actors are often ignored or sanctioned by governments in the name of culture or religion, including abuses such as wife beating, acid throwing, honor killing, bride burning, forced prostitution, and female genital mutilation.

An International Planned Parenthood Federation report, "The Facts about Gender-Based Violence," cites studies by the World Health Organization (WHO) indicating that gender-based violence is one of the leading causes of female injuries. Those studies indicate that between 16 percent and 52 percent of women worldwide are assaulted physically by an intimate partner at least once in their lives. WHO also reports that domestic violence accounts for more deaths and disabling injuries among women aged 15 to 44 than cancer, malaria, traffic injuries, and war put together. The global magnitude of gender-based violence is manifest in the following statistics:[14]

1. In Africa, it is estimated that over 130 million girls and women have undergone some form of female genital mutilation. Each year in Africa, about two million girls are at risk of being subjected to this practice. Other studies suggest about one-third of all women in Africa will be a victim of rape in their lifetimes.
2. Domestic violence data gathering in some Asian countries suggest that rape is rampant. A large percentage of women report being physically abused by their husbands. Over one million children in Asia are reported to provide regular sexual services for adults.
3. Studies conducted in several Latin American countries reveal that over 50 percent of women can expect to be victims of private violence at some stage in their lives.
4. Some European studies show that nearly 25 percent of women in an intimate relationship can expect to be abused physically. Most of the abuse suffered by these women is at the hands of their husbands.
5. Another report indicates that, in the United States, wife battering is believed to be the most common cause of female injuries, accounting for more personal trauma than all the rapes, muggings, and traffic accidents combined.[15]

These shocking statistics reveal the serious, continuing shortcomings in worldwide governmental efforts to protect women from private acts of violence.

The great contribution of the December 1993 UN Declaration to Eliminate Violence Against Women was its clear definition of violence against women (as occurring in the home, the community, and sponsored by governments) and the fact that it held government accountable to "refrain from engaging in violence against women" and to "exercise due diligence to prevent, investigate and in accordance with national legislation, punish acts of violence against women, whether those acts are perpetrated by the State or by private persons." This declaration reinforces the commitments of the Vienna Declaration not to allow governments to justify committing or condoning human rights violations using cultural, religious, or historical circumstances as a rationalization.

Pakistan: "Honor Killings"

In September 1999, AI published a report, "Pakistan: Violence against Women in the Name of Honor." The lives of millions of women in Pakistan are circumscribed by traditions that enforce extreme seclusion and submission to men. Traditional perceptions of honor severely limit some of the most basic rights of women in Pakistan. Every year in Pakistan hundreds of women, of all ages and in all parts of the country, are reported killed in the name of honor. Many more cases go unreported. Almost all go unpunished.

The number of such killings appears to be steadily increasing as the perception of what constitutes honor widens. The flimsiest of suspicions, such as a rumor spread in a village, or in one extreme case, a man's dream of his wife's adultery, is enough to elicit lethal violence. Women are not even given a chance to resolve possible misunderstandings. Tradition decrees only one method to restore honor—to kill the offending woman.

Some awareness of rights has seeped into the secluded world of women in Pakistan. Tragically, women's tentative steps to assert these rights—by choosing a spouse or divorcing an abusive husband—are increasingly seen to undermine honor as well. The backlash has been both harsh and swift, resulting in an increase of so-called honor killings in Pakistan.

Originally a custom of the Baloch and Pashtun tribes, residents of Pakistan, Afghanistan, and other countries in the region, honor killings derive from the twin concepts of honor and commodification of women. Women are married off for a bride price paid to the father. If this commodity is "damaged," the proprietor, the father or husband, has a right to compensation. If a husband kills his wife for alleged sexual misbehavior and her alleged "lover" escapes, the latter must pay the husband compensation, for the wife that was lost and for his own life which was spared. Often the dead woman's alleged "lover" hands over a sister to the husband, in addition to a large amount of money.

Arranged marriages, a common practice in Pakistan, may lead to a woman's defying her parents' wishes. She may not wish to marry the man chosen for her. When she does agree, after some time he may prove to be a batterer from whom she wishes a divorce. Satta-watta marriages, which involve exchange of siblings across generations, place an additional burden on women to abide by their fathers' marriage arrangement. Often women choosing another spouse are targeted by their relatives.

Standards of honor and chastity are not equally applied to men and women in Pakistan, though the honor code applies to both equally. In surveys conducted in the NWFP (North West Frontier Province) and Balochistan, men were found going unpunished for "illicit relationships," whereas women were killed on the merest rumor of "impropriety."

According to the Human Rights Commission of Pakistan (HRCP), 888 women were murdered in Punjab alone. Of these, 595 killings were carried out by relatives and 286 were reportedly for reasons of honor. The Sindh Graduates Association said that in the first three months of 1999 alone, 132 honor killings had been reported there.[16]

The law of Qisas and Diyat (having to do with physical injury, manslaughter, and murder) allows the heirs of the victim of an honor killing to decide whether to report such crimes and whether to prosecute the offender. Hence, the practice condones the family's forgiveness of the "honor" killer and signals that men murdering their wives will not be punished in the same manner as other murderers.

Police have upheld this custom both by apprehending condemned women instead of protecting them, and by accepting bribes either to turn them over to their families or the tribe, or not to register complaints against perpetrators. When an honor killing gets into the courts, the judiciary often responds with extraordinary leniency. The law offers loopholes for murderers who act in the name of honor, so tradition remains unbroken. In fact, more and more killings committed for other motives take on the guise of honor killings on the correct assumption that they are rarely punished. These practices deny women their right to equal protection and treatment before the law, rights that Pakistan must accord to them under the Universal Declaration of Human Rights.

In a hideous twist, women victims of rape are judged as defilers of their male relatives' honor. Sixteen-year-old Jamilla, for example, was repeatedly raped by a junior clerk of the local agriculture department in her province. Jamilla's uncle filed a complaint with the police, but the police arrested Jamilla and turned her over to her tribe. She was shot dead in March 1999 after a tribal council of elders decided that she had brought shame to her tribe and that honor could be restored only by her death. Police detained the rapist for "his own protection" when tribesmen demanded that he be handed over to them for execution. His current whereabouts are not known.

The case of Samia Sarwar not only illustrates government's ignoring murder committed in the name of "honor," it also shows the danger facing women human rights defenders working for justice. Since marriage is often arranged between families, it represents family honor. Even seeking divorce from a physically abusive husband can trigger a deadly attack in an arranged marriage. Twenty-nine-year old Samia Sarwar was shot dead in her lawyer's office in Lahore on April 6, 1999. Her parents instigated the murder, feeling that Samia had brought shame on the family by seeking divorce after ten years of marital abuse. Although the perpetrators can be easily identified, only one of them has been indicted. Her lawyer, Hina Jilani, and her colleague and sister, Asma Jahangir, have been publicly condemned and received death threats. The government has failed to bring those responsible for this harassment to justice. In July 1999 the upper house of Pakistan's Parliament failed to approve even a greatly weakened version of a resolution condemning honor killing.

Action by Pakistan's Women's and Human Rights Advocates

Women's human rights NGOs in Pakistan that have been working for an end to violence against women, including honor killings, know there is a need for a cultural strategy. For even if the laws are revised, or new laws passed, this may not change women's reality. Along with the changes in law that will protect dissenters from traditional gender roles, there must be recognition that the concept of women's equality already exists in Pakistan. Such laws and values must be disseminated in areas where the concept may be weak in such a way that it strikes a responsive chord in public consciousness throughout civil society.

Legal literacy and training is one of their strategies. In Pakistan the research organization Shirkat Gah carried out a study describing customary legal practice and comparing it with statutory law.[17] This resulted in a training manual in Urdu, Sindhi, and English, which gives women practical ways to use this information. The authors, who are lawyers, social workers, and development activists, explicitly recognize that both statutory and customary law is constantly evolving, reflecting change in contemporary Pakistan.

They have a two-pronged strategy. First, they fight in government and other decision-making arenas; second, they work to educate poor and working urban women as well as women in rural areas about their international human rights. To accomplish this, women's organizations have forged alliances with other forces struggling for change in their society, such as with those working for protection of minority religious groups and with trade unions. Before the military coup in October 1999, these alliances allowed the women's movement to stop a law making purdah (strict seclusion of women in their households) compulsory, and a law handing over jurisdiction of all family affairs to Islamic Shariat courts. Finally, when the economic crisis pushed the government to sell Pakistan's only women's bank, they were able to persuade parliament to maintain the bank's original purpose (microcredit for women) as part of the charter no matter who the owner.

State Responsibility

Having ratified the UN Women's Convention (CEDAW) and under its own constitution, Pakistan is obliged to treat women equally and to protect their fundamental human rights. Pakistan has also ratified the UN Convention on the Rights of the Child, yet it systematically fails to prevent, investigate, and punish violence against women and girls, and has taken no measures against discriminatory laws or customs.

Recognizing that women's NGOs and human rights activists work at considerable personal risk, AI designed its report and campaign to support their efforts. AI's recommendations focus on changes the government should make in three areas in order to demonstrate application of due diligence to prevent honor killings, and to investigate and punish the perpetrators:[18]

Legal measures:

1. Review criminal laws and revise them to ensure equality before the law and equal protection of law to women and girls, including the Zina Ordinance and the Law of Qisas and Diyat.
2. Make the sale or giving of women and girls in marriage against financial consideration in lieu of a fine or imprisonment, a criminal offense.
3. Adopt legislation that makes all types of domestic violence a criminal offense and ensure that law enforcement and judicial officials are made aware of their obligation to enforce it.
4. Ensure that provincial governments investigate all reports of honor killings and that perpetrators are brought to justice. Police should promptly and without bias register and investigate all complaints of honor killings.
5. Withdraw Pakistan's reservations to the UN Women's Convention and ratify the Optional Protocol, and report on implementation of it and the Convention of the Rights of the Child.
6. Abolish the death penalty.

Preventive measures:

1. Undertake wide-ranging public awareness programs through the media, the education system, and public announcements to inform both men and women of women's equal rights under CEDAW.
2. Provide gender sensitization training to law enforcement and judicial personnel.

3. Ensure that data and statistics are collected in a manner that ensures the problem of honor killings is made visible.

Protective measures:

1. Ensure that human rights activists, lawyers, and women's rights groups can pursue their legitimate activities without harassment or fear.
2. Expand victim support services, both state and NGO, including the establishment of safe refuges, readily accessible counseling, and rehabilitation and support services for women and girls at risk of honor-related violence.

Some defenders of honor killings claim that these are the authentic customs and traditions of Pakistan's tribal cultures and may not be subjected to scrutiny from the perspective of human rights treaties. However, such views fail to recognize that cultural practices are sometimes both the context of human rights violations and a justification for them. More important, cultures are not static. They change and evolve in response to the needs of society, interactions with other cultures, and the demands of modern living. Traditions can be and are reshaped or discarded by the new realities of today's world. And one of those realities is the global acceptance of the universality of international human rights standards for the protection of women's human rights. Until Pakistan's government takes seriously its obligations under CEDAW, which obliges states to "modify the social and cultural patterns of conduct of men and women" to eliminate prejudice and discriminatory customs, the women of Pakistan will continue to pay the price of their families' "honor" with their freedom and their lives.

So it was with great hope that the women's and human rights community welcomed General Pervez Musharraf's announcement in mid-March 2000 that he will introduce legislation to make honor killings a recognized crime in Pakistan and will set up burn centers in hospitals around the country to deal with this form of domestic violence.[19] This announcement illustrates the effectiveness of campaigning both by domestic and international women's and human rights organizations. At the time of writing, however, the legislation had not passed, funds had not yet been allocated, and concrete plans had yet to be completed.

Conclusion

The cases presented above reveal patterns of violence committed against women both by public and private actors. Such abuses continue today for several reasons. First, public institutions have failed to act to prohibit these abuses and to detain and punish perpetrators. Acts of violence, whether by private people or by government agents, will continue so long as perpetrators are not punished. Government action to stop them will not occur unless there is a demand for justice inside the country supported by the international community.

Second, government agencies have condoned practices dangerous to women on the basis of protecting a country's customs or culture. Underlying these practices are discrimination against women, placing them in a subordinate status, and disempowering them. Governments not only fail to protect women who are victims of these acts; they also fail to protect women working domestically for the defense of women's human rights. Private acts of violence against women will continue so long as governments ignore the fact that these acts violate not only international treaties they have ratified but also the principles and articles in their own constitutions. This lack of political will is what impells human rights and women's organizations to continue campaigning domestically and internationally.

NOTES

1. "Women's Rights Are Human Rights," AI International Newsletter Focus: AI Women's Day Leaflet 30, no. 2 (March 2000).

2. "Women's Rights Are Human Rights: The Struggle Persists—Women's Day Action 2000," AI Index AFR 54/01/00.

3. "Women's Rights Are Human Rights," AI International Newsletter Focus: AI Women's Day Leaflet 30, no. 2 (March 2000).

4. CEDAW General Recommendation 19, January 1992, stated that "gender-based violence is a form of discrimination that seriously inhibits women's ability to enjoy rights and freedoms on a basis of equality with men, including, (a) the right to life, (b) the right not to be tortured, (c) the right to equal protection in times of armed conflict, (d) the right to liberty and security of person, (e) the right to equal protection under the law, (f) the right to equality in the family, (g) the right to the highest standard attainable of physical and mental health, and (h) the right to just and favorable conditions of work. The Convention applies to violence perpetrated by public authorities and private actors." Forms of gender-based violence may breach the Convention's provisions regardless of whether the text expressly mentions violence. *International Human Rights of Women: Instruments of Change*. Carol Lockwood et al., eds. American Bar Association (1998), 352–358. See also *Women and Human Rights: The Basic Documents,* Center for the Study of Human Rights, Columbia University (New York, 1996).

5. Charlotte Bunch and Niamh Reilly, "Demanding Accountability: The Global Campaign and Vienna Tribunal for Women's Human Rights," Center for Women's Global Leadership and UNIFEM (New Jersey), 1994, p. 3.

6. The Coordinating Committee for the Global Campaign of 1993 included Asma Abdel Halim (WiLDAF, Sudan); Marion Bethel (CAFRA, Bahamas); Flo-

rence Butegwa (WiLDAF, Zimbabwe); Roxanna Carrillo (UNIFEM); Winde Even-huis (HOM, Netherlands); Alda Facio (ILANUD, Costa Rica); Hina Jilani (AGHS Legal Aid, Pakistan); Nelia Sancho Liao (Asian Women's Human Rights Council, Philippines); Rosa Logar (Austrian Women Shelter network); Annette Pypops (Match International Centre, Canada); Ana Sisnett (Fund for a Compassionate Society); Maria Suarez (FIRE, Costa Rica); and Anne Walker (IWTC). Organizational sponsors included the Asia and Pacific Forum on Women, Law and Development; the Family Violence Prevention Fund in San Francisco; and the International Solidarity Network of Women Living Under Muslim Laws (WLUML).

7. Bunch and Reilly, p. 84. The judges for the Global Tribunal in Vienna were Gertrude Mongella, Secretary-General of the UN Fourth World Conference on Women and former Tanzanian High Commissioner to India; Justice P. N. Bhagwati, former Chief Justice of the Supreme Court of India and Chair of the Asian human rights NGO, AWARE; Ed Broadbent, former Canadian Member of Parliament and President of the International Centre for Human Rights and Democratic Development in Montreal; and Elizabeth Odio, Minister of Justice from Costa Rica and a member of the UN Committee Against Torture. The judges worked on their individual and collective recommendations with an advisory committee of women lawyers from different regions: Rebecca Cook (University of Toronto Law School, Canada); Alda Facio (ILANUD, Costa Rica); Ratna Kapur (Legal Advocate, India); Mona Zulficar (Shalakany Law Office, Egypt).

8. "Women in the Front Line," Amnesty International (London, 1981); "Rape and Sexual Abuse as Torture," Amnesty International (1992).

9. "The Special Rapporteur on Torture has characterized methods of torture involving sexual abuse as 'essentially gender based.' He has explicitly recognized that rape or other forms of sexual assault against women in detention constitutes torture." Donna Sullivan, "Promoting Accountability for Women's Human Rights: Working with the Thematic Special Mechanisms of the Commission on Human Rights," UNIFEM (1993), p. 21.

10. "Human Rights Are Women's Right," Amnesty International (1995).

11. "All Too Familiar: Sexual Abuse of Women in U.S. State Prisons," Human Rights Watch (New York, Dec. 1996); "Nowhere to Hide: Retaliation Against Women in Michigan State Prisons," Human Rights Watch (New York, Sept. 1998); Brenda Smith, "An End to Silence: Women Prisoners' Handbook on Identifying and Addressing Sexual Misconduct" (Washington, D.C., National Women's Law Center, 1998).

12. Christine Doyle, AIUSA staff, unpublished ms., Oct. 1998.

13. "USA: Breaking the Chain: The Human Rights of Women Prisoners," Amnesty International, United States Campaign Document (London, March 1999).

14. "The Facts about Gender-Based Violence," International Planned Parenthood Federation (1998). Available at www.ippf.org/resource.

15. Naomi Neft and Ann D. Levine, *Where Women Stand: An International Report on the Status of Women in 140 Countries (1997–1998)* (New York, 1997). See also Rebecca J. Cook, *Human Rights of Women: National and International Perspectives* (Philadelphia, 1994).

16. "Pakistan: Violence Against Women in the Name of Honor," Amnesty International (1999). See also "Pakistan: Time to Take Human Rights Seriously," Amnesty International USA (London, 1997).

17. Farida Shaheed et al., eds., *Shaping Women's Lives: Laws, Practices and Strategies in Pakistan* (Lahore, Pakistan: Shirkat Gah, Women's Resource Center, 1998); and Cassandra Balchin, ed., "Women, Law and Society—An Action Manual for NGOs," (Lahore, Pakistan: Shirkat Gah/WLUML, 1996).

18. "Pakistan: Violence against Women in the Name of Honor," Amnesty International (1999).

19. "An Open Letter to General Musharraf Published in *Pakistan Today* Creates an International Uproar," *Pakistan Today,* 17 March 2000.

Women, Violence, and the Human Rights System
Sally Engle Merry

∽ ALTHOUGH the idea of human rights grows out of a two-hundred-year tradition rooted in the European Enlightenment, the expansion of the contemporary human rights system is a product of the second half of the twentieth century.* Since the Universal Declaration of Human Rights in 1948, there has been a dramatic expansion in doctrines of human rights and mechanisms for enforcing them. The United Nations and its affiliated agencies are the most important institutions in this process, but they are supported in very significant ways by an exploding network of international nongovernmental organizations, or NGOs. Women's rights are a relatively recent addition to the domain of human rights. Their importance began with the first meetings on women and development in the 1970s. The right to protection from violence is one of the most recently articulated. First discussed as a human rights violation in the late 1980s, this issue expanded enormously in the 1990s. It grew from a focus on rape and battering in intimate relationships to rape and gender violence enacted by states in warfare, torture, and imprisonment as well as during interethnic violence. Trafficking of sex workers, the AIDS pandemic, and particular social practices that have an impact on women such as female genital cutting have recently been defined as instances of violence against women.

Thus, the content of women's rights has changed dramatically since 1948, as have human rights more generally. These changes are the result of the activities of states and transnational organizations such as the

United Nations and innumerable NGOs (Turner, 1997; Keck and Sikkink, 1998; Boulding 1988). Their activities constitute an international civil society actively engaged in expanding and monitoring human rights. Through transnational processes of information gathering, conferences, and discussions under the auspices of the United Nations and regional bodies, these groups have created a new quasi-legal order (see Santos, 1995). Conventions, treaties, and implementation systems are created by international teams, then ratified by states, which assume responsibility for enforcing them under the supervision of a global body (see Riles, 1999). Even though the human rights system lacks the sanctioning power of state law, its expansion and elaboration creates a new discursive legal space within the global arena, one constructed by actors outside Europe and the United States as well as within it. One dramatic illustration of the changing understanding of rights within the international human rights system is the emergence of a conception of indigenous rights, attached to groups rather than individuals and defining international law as competent over matters formerly considered within the domestic responsibility of states. S. James Anaya (1996) notes that international law is shifting back to the naturalist framework of early classical theory in that it is concerned with an overarching normative concern for world peace, stability, and human rights and is incorporating a discourse concerned with individuals and groups.

As a quasi-legal system, the human rights regime engages in distinctive practices of constructing and supporting rights. The human rights system is constantly changing, developing new conceptions of rights and new declarations for announcing them. This essay examines the emergence of violence against women as a human rights issue within the human rights system and explores how the quasi-legal form of global social ordering, characteristic of the contemporary human rights system, functions with reference to the definition of violence against women as a human rights issue.

The Expansion of Human Rights

Rights are a cultural phenomenon, developing and changing over time in response to a variety of social, economic, political, and cultural influences. Since 1948 the concept of human rights has shifted from its original meaning of civil and political rights rooted in liberal theory to an expanded notion of collective rights, cultural rights, and social and economic rights. The present system was born in radical French revolutionary thought at the end of the eighteenth century, but by the end of the twentieth, the new human rights system had become the preeminent global language of social justice in the world. As human rights has gradually displaced socialism and communism it has itself incorporated some of the features of these ideologies, such as economic and social rights to work and health care. In response to the demands of indigenous peoples, among others, human rights now include rights to culture.

The original creation of the human rights system was a response to particular historical circumstances. Although there was some discussion of human rights in the early twentieth century, the modern human rights system developed after World War II. After the Holocaust many argued that the protection of the human rights of individuals could no longer be the sovereign prerogative of states. The UN and the new international legal regime of human rights were founded on the assumption that no state could be entrusted with absolute power over its own citizens. Individuals needed protection from abusive states. The international regime of human rights argued that by virtue of their humanity, all individuals are entitled to a basic modicum of human dignity; that certain human rights are universal, fundamental, and inalienable and thus cannot and should not be overridden by cultural and religious traditions; and that the accident of birth in a particular social group or culture has no bearing on individuals' intrinsic worth or right to be treated as human beings (Zechenter, 1997). Thus, the human rights system was inspired not only by French Enlightenment theory but also by the world reaction to Nazism. Similarly, the decolonization movement of the 1950s and 1960s shaped human rights discourse. As colonized peoples began to press for decolonization, self-determination emerged as an important human rights concept (see Merry, 2000).

In response to these historical and social processes, the UN human rights framework has continued to evolve and change since 1948. This is a pluralized, flexible, and responsive system that develops over time. It has grown from a focus on individual rights to collective or group rights. The original focus on protecting individuals from the abuses of state power has expanded to protecting emerging states from colonial exploitation to protecting emerging nations (peoples) from the effects of the international political economy. Since the 1980s indigenous peoples have claimed rights to protection from the violations of states. Thus, the modern human rights concept is less individualistic and more egalitarian than its liberal political precedents. Civil and political rights were the earliest rights, but they have been joined by human welfare guarantees to employment and fair working conditions, health, food, and social security, education, and participation in cultural life of the community. These so-called positive rights came from socialist and welfare state conceptions that emphasized economic, social, and cultural rights over political rights. The United States accepts civil and political rights more enthusiastically than economic, social, and cultural ones; African states emphasize social, economic, and cultural rights over civil rights; populous Asian states such as China and Indonesia argue that individual political rights are foreign to their Asian communal cultural traditions and subsistence needs (Messer, 1997).

Collective rights are among the most recent rights, although collective rights have precedents going back to the early twentieth century in minority rights, language rights, and rights to self-determination (see, e.g., Anaya, 1996; Asch, 1988; Coulter, 1994; Sierra, 1995; Tennant, 1994; Trask, 1993; Wilmsen, 1989). Indigenous peoples in particular have sought rights that are collective and whose beneficiaries are historically formed communities rather than individuals or states (Anaya, 1996). As Anaya notes, these rights not only conflict with the dominant individual-state dichotomy, which underlies the creation of international standards, but it also challenges state sovereignty. To some extent claims to cultural rights demand assertions of cultural authenticity that are resonant with earlier anthropological conceptions of culture. The authentic and culturally distinct self-representations that this discourse sometimes requires may even constitute constructed misrepresentations or misunderstandings of shared histories (Beckett, 1996; Friedman, 1996; Rogers, 1996). In other words, making claims to cultural rights often requires framing these claims in terms of an essentialized, homogeneous, "traditional" culture (see Jackson, 1995; Merry, 1997). This requirement contradicts the flexible and changing nature of the cultural life of indigenous communities and often requires them to present claims in tragically inappropriate terms (Povinelli, 1998).

Thus, despite its Western Enlightenment origins, the human rights system is not fixed but changing in response to new global circumstances. It is the product of negotiation and discussion rather than imposition. As the concept has expanded from its initial meaning within liberalism—the protection of the individual from the state—to a series of obligations by states to its members such as rights to food, housing, self-determination, and other collective rights, the content, diversity, and nature of rights has changed.

Violence Against Women as a Human Rights Violation

The case of gender violence dramatically demonstrates the creation of new rights. Although gender violence had been an issue since the mid-1970s, it emerged as a major focus for women's rights in the early 1990s. Violence against women is not generally perpetrated by states but by private citizens. Yet activists argued that a state's failure to protect women from violence is itself a human rights violation (Bunch, 1990; Thomas and Beaseley, 1993).

The conception of gender violence as a human rights violation expanded rapidly during the 1990s. In 1992 the Committee on the Elimination of Discrimination against Women (CEDAW) formulated a broad recommendation that defined gender-based violence as a form of discrimination, placing it squarely within the rubric of human rights and fundamental freedoms and making clear that states are obliged to eliminate violence perpetrated by public authorities and by private persons (Cook, 1994). The doctrine asserts state responsibility for failures to protect women from violence, the obligation to protect being an internationally recognized human right (Bunch, 1990; Thomas and Beaseley, 1993; Cook, 1994). Although individuals are not legally liable under international human rights law, states are responsible for their failures to meet international obligations, even for acts by private persons if they fail to make an effort to eliminate or mitigate the acts (Cook, 1994). Within national legal systems, assault and murder are universally considered crimes, but wife beating is shielded by its location in a legally and culturally constructed private sphere (Report of Secretary General, 1995). Historically, in the United States as well as many other parts of the world, it has been regarded as less serious than other kinds of assault. Thus, the emergence of violence against women as a distinct human rights violation depends on redefining the family so that it is no longer a shelter from legal scrutiny.

Although gender violence was apparently not an issue in the 1975 and 1980 global women's conferences, the Nairobi Forward-Looking Strategies developed in 1985 placed violence against women as a basic strategy for addressing the issue of peace (Stephenson, 1995; Report of Secretary General, 1995). The 1979 Convention on the Elimination of All Forms of Discrimination against Women did not mention violence against women. However, in 1989 the Committee on the Elimination of Discrimination against Women adopted a recommendation against violence and in 1992 formulated a broad recommendation that defined gender-based violence as a form of discrimination, placing it squarely within the rubric of human rights and fundamental freedoms and making clear that states are obliged to eliminate violence perpetrated by public authorities and by private persons. In 1990 the Economic and Social Council adopted a resolution recommended by the Commission on the Status of Women recognizing that violence against women in the family and society derives from their unequal status in society and recommending that governments take immediate measures to establish appropriate penalties for violence against women as well as developing policies to prevent and control violence against women in the family, workplace, and society (Report of Secretary General,

1995). This recommendation suggests developing correctional, educational, and social services including shelters and training programs for law enforcement officers, judiciary, health, and social service personnel. The national reports prepared for the review and reappraisal of the Nairobi recommendations preceding the 1995 Beijing conference revealed that most countries now recognize the problem of violence against women and have placed emphasis on legal reforms. It is noteworthy that while most countries have adopted programs to prevent domestic violence, the initiative came from transnational NGOs. Groups with bases in several countries that have worked together across national borders have been in the lead in many of these changes.

At the 1993 UN Conference on Human Rights in Vienna, this issue became even more important (see Schuler, 1992). The Commission on the Status of Women recommended the formulation of an international instrument on violence against women and in 1993 developed the Declaration on the Elimination of Violence against Women, working with meetings of groups of experts. In 1994 the General Assembly of the United Nations adopted the Declaration on the Elimination of Violence against Women (Van Bueren, 1995). In the same year the UN Commission on Human Rights condemned gender-based violence and appointed a special rapporteur on violence against women (Report of Secretary General, 1995).

The 1995 Platform for Action of the Fourth World Conference on Women in Beijing included a section on gender-based violence. It named as a violation of human rights any act of gender-based violence in the family, the community, or perpetrated by the state that results in physical, sexual, or psychological harm or suffering to women in private or public life, including acts of violence and sexual abuse during armed conflict, forced sterilization and abortion, and female infanticide. The text reads:

> Violence against women both violates and impairs or nullifies the enjoyment
> by women of their human rights and fundamental freedoms. The long-stand-
> ing failure to protect and promote those rights and freedoms in the case of
> violence against women is a matter of concern to all States and should be ad-
> dressed. (sec. D, p. 112)

Violence against women is defined broadly as "any act of gender-based violence that results in, or is likely to result in, physical, sexual or psychological harm or suffering to women, including threats of such acts, coercion or arbitrary deprivation of liberty, whether occurring in public or private life" (sec. D, p. 113). By declaring the right of women and girls to protection from violence as a universal human right, the conference reasserted this dramatic expansion of human rights.

This global development of human rights declarations and concerns builds on extensive national and local social movements beginning in the 1970s. After two decades of work to mobilize state law to redefine battering as a crime, activists have globalized their approaches through NGOs and the UN. Grassroots feminist movements in Europe, the United States, Australia, Argentina, Brazil, India, the Virgin Islands, as well as many other parts of the world have developed strategies to protect women from violence in the home based on a critique of male power within gender relationships and using approaches such as shelters, support groups for victims, and criminalization of battering (Silard, 1994; Oller, 1994; Thomas, 1994; Bush, 1992; Morrow, 1994). Internet postings indicate new programs in Quezon City, Philippines, Budapest, Hungary, and New Delhi, India. The need for intervention is being widely recognized in the nations of the south as well as the north (e.g., Ofei-Aboagye, 1994). Many of these programs take inspiration from human rights. For example, an Internet posting in the late 1990s of the Hungarian group, NaNE!, proposed to make concrete suggestions for strengthening current laws and developing "new laws and protections in line with the U.N. Declaration of Human Rights and the European Charter of Human Rights, both of which have been signed and ratified by Hungary."

Thus, global declarations about gender violence and human rights grow out of local movements and in turn inspire and inform other local movements and programs in different parts of the world. This process of reappropriation may introduce unfamiliar categories of self and personhood, including a redefinition of women's rights to safety, but it is the result of local agents mobilizing national and global law in the face of local resistance rather than a global imposition of a new moral order. (See Freeman, 1994, for a description of the way local groups attempt to use international human rights norms to change national legal systems with reference to women's human rights in several African nations). There has been, in the last decade, a global exchange of model program approaches as well as human rights documents. For example, the Domestic Abuse Intervention Project developed in Duluth, Minnesota, in the early 1980s became the prototype for a batterer's intervention program in Hilo, Hawaii (Merry, 1995). In the Hawaiian program, perpetrators were taught to use negotiation and collaboration in dealing with their partners instead of violence, isolation, intimidation, and the exercise of male privilege, a philosophy depicted iconically in the "power and control wheel." The DAIP approach has been used in New Zealand for about the same length of time as in

Hilo, but there part of the program has been modified for Maori people, who participate in separate men's groups. Non-Maori New Zealanders, largely of European ancestry, participate in a program more similar to the Minnesota prototype. Similar programs operate in Germany, Scotland, Canada, and the United States, even in such culturally distinct locations as the Pine Ridge Indian Reservation and Marine Corps bases, according to Ellen Pence, DAIP originator. It is also in use in Israel, and in 1992 it was adopted on St. Croix in the Virgin Islands (Morrow, 1994).

The example of the DAIP shows how programmatic approaches to gender violence are spreading globally along with declarations of rights in the human rights system. In the late 1990s this process was facilitated by Internet communications. For example, in 1999–2000 a virtual working group under the auspices of UNIFEM conducted an e-mail exchange about approaches to violence against women that included 2,300 participants in 120 countries.

The development of an international approach to gender violence is complicated by the importance of at the same time protecting local cultural practices. Gender violence is inextricably linked to culturally rooted systems of kinship and marriage. There is an inevitable collision between protecting women and preserving marriages. If the only way to provide security and safety for a woman is to allow her to separate from her husband, reducing violence against women will diminish the permanence of marriage and the power of husbands over wives, and change the meanings of masculinity and femininity. It pits protecting the woman against safeguarding the marriage. In the United States protecting women from violence has typically meant separating the woman from her battering husband. Despite extensive interest in treatment programs for batterers, for example, success has been limited, and the surest route to safety has been separation. This kind of intervention challenges the permanence and sanctity of the family.

Thus, conceptualizing violence against women as a human rights violation typically means demanding changes in local cultural practices concerning sexuality, marriage, and the family. Women's vulnerability to violence depends on entrenched sociocultural practices involving marriage, work, and religious and secular ideologies of masculinity and femininity (see Bunch, 1997; Cook, 1994; Kerr, 1993; Schuler, 1992). Conventions on the rights of women typically require states that ratify them to change cultural practices that subordinate women. The 1992 Declaration on the Elimination of Violence Against Women issued by the CEDAW committee says that "states should condemn violence against women, and should not invoke any custom, tradition, or religion or other consideration to avoid their obligation with respect to its elimination" (Cook, 1994, p. 167, citing CEDAW General Recommendation 19). Discussions of violence against women in the human rights frame typically call for reforms of cultural practices such as dowry deaths, son preference, female infanticide, honor killings, and female genital mutilation (Schuler, 1992; Bunch, 1997). The 1995 Platform for Action from the Beijing Fourth World Conference on Women states:

> Violence against women throughout the life cycle derives essentially from cultural patterns, in particular the harmful effects of certain traditional or customary practices and all acts of extremism linked to race, sex, language or religion that perpetuate the lower status accorded to women in the family, the workplace, the community and society. (D, sec. 119)

Many states have opposed this conception of human rights on cultural or religious grounds and have refused to ratify women's rights treaties or have done so only with substantial reservations. By 1999, 163 countries had ratified CEDAW and 23 had not, according to the National Committee on UN/CEDAW, but it has more substantive reservations against it than any other international treaty (Bunch, 1997). One-third of the ratifying states have substantive reservations to parts of CEDAW (*Progress of Nations,* 1997). Some states such as China claim that UN documents on women's rights such as CEDAW violate their own cultural practices and have ratified the treaty only with extensive reservations. Some Islamic states and the Vatican opposed the 1995 platform, arguing that marriage, motherhood, and the family were the backbone of society. In its statement on the platform at the 1995 Beijing conference, the Holy See stated: "To affirm the dignity and rights of all women requires respect for the roles of women whose quest for personal fulfillment and the construction of a stable society is inseparably linked to their commitment to God, family, neighbour and especially to their children." Thus, women's rights to protection from violence seem diametrically opposed to the protection of culture. But this new category of human rights violation merges a wide variety of behaviors such as rape in wartime, wife battering, and female genital mutilation (Keck and Sikkink, 1998). These activities vary significantly in their local cultural support. Some are clearly illegal, such as rape in wartime; others are tolerated within the private space of the family, such as wife battering; and others are local cultural practices supported within local communities. Of this last group, many are currently being contested and some have been outlawed, such as female genital cutting, now illegal in several African states. To see violence against women as an opposition between culture and rights fails to acknowledge the contested and variable cultural support this variety of behaviors receives in different social groups. It assumes that all of these actions are part of "culture" and that there are no debates within any society about the acceptability of each one.

Some approaches to gender violence rely less on law and a conception of rights but instead on religion or community. They put less emphasis on separation. For example, some evangelical Christian churches provide anger management training programs while condemning divorce. Battered women are encouraged to engage in prayer and batterers are encouraged to seek divine assistance in controlling not only their hitting but also their angry thoughts. Biblical injunctions about ending marriage discourage divorce. Another alternative roots intervention in community identity. The current restorative justice movement, for example, relies on the strength and cultural values of local communities to resolve conflict. It grows out of community conflict resolution approaches found in some indigenous communities. In this model, community members help the perpetrator of violence move through repentance toward reconciliation. Although this approach is not generally applied to gender violence, it may be in the future.

Such alternative approaches, particularly those based on religious or ethnic identity, appear in global discourses as well. For example, the debates at the Beijing conference concerning violence against women focused on the extent to which the proposed language contradicted basic cultural practices and values, primarily ideas about the sanctity and religious meanings of the family and the relationship between church and state. A study in Canada found it was not always clear that aboriginal women preferred sentencing circles to criminal forms of intervention in battering incidents (McGillivray and Comaskey, 1999).

Human Rights as Quasi-Law

The human rights system has many features that are lawlike, but it lacks an enforcement mechanism parallel to that of state law. Like state law systems, human rights operates through statutes produced through quasi-legislative processes of commission meetings and deliberations with the assistance of experts under the auspices of UN organizations. The precise texts of the declarations and conventions, achieved by means of a painstaking process of examining words and meanings in a variety of preliminary and working group meetings, are then presented to the General Assembly for approval (see Riles, 1999). Once approved, conventions must be submitted to the constituent nations of the UN for ratification and become binding internationally only when a sufficient number of nations has ratified the agreement. Declarations, on the other hand, are simply passed by the General Assembly (Kim, 1991). Thus, the human rights conventions become part of national legal systems and are, in theory, enforced by those nations while declarations may gradually become part of customary international law, as has taken place with the Universal Declaration. Because the UN the system is grounded in a network of sovereign nations, it has no binding power beyond the consent of these constituent nations.

However, there are significant non-national actors engaged in this system. The most important are a growing network of transnational NGOs who provide expertise in the drafting of documents and assist in the process of monitoring compliance with agreements (Stephenson, 1995). The major weapon of human rights compliance remains communication: exposing points of violation of human rights documents and using international public opinion to condemn violating states. Such a mechanism is clearly dependent on the international system of power and the interests of powerful nations in pressing for human rights of various kinds. Inevitably, it will be the rights promoted by the most powerful nations that will be most effectively pushed on noncompliant nations. As violence against women has become a more important issue in the United States and Europe, for example, it has more often been promoted as a concern within the human rights system.

This mechanism of enforcement makes clear, however, that if an issue loses importance within the NGO community and among activists in politically powerful nations, it is likely to drop off the agenda of international concern. Margaret Keck and Kathryn Sikkink (1998) propose a boomerang model to describe this form of human rights pressure: local groups facing neglect of a human rights violation in their country appeal to international NGOs, who in turn mobilize political support within a dominant country and induce it to put pressure on the weaker country. Thus, the enforcement of human rights depends greatly on the international balance of power and the agendas of the economically and politically powerful nations, which means in effect the nations of the north rather than the south.

Yet the human rights system is also supported by public opinion and an extensive network of local and transnational institutions that use communications systems such as the Internet to bring global attention to behavior they define as human rights violations. Although these networks of communication and the consequent mobilization of public opinion cannot be called law, they can serve as powerful motivations to local actors concerned about public opinion on the international stage. Some documents of the human rights system have acquired the status of international customary law, such as the Universal Declaration, so that their force does not require ratification. Clearly, the mobilization of transnational public opinion through generating reports, information exchange, and the media and the arts contributes in important ways to strengthening the quasi-legal system of human rights.

Conclusion

This analysis of human rights as a developing and changing system enforced by transnational civil society and public opinion reveals the importance of ongoing political movements in support of particular human rights. Such rights emerge out of political movements, such as the women's liberation movement of the 1970s and the indigenous people's movements of the 1970s and 1980s. As these groups define their issues in terms of human rights and put them on the agenda of the major human rights institutions of the UN, they reshape the human rights system. At the same time, the strength and effectiveness of any human rights issue depends on continuing mobilization by these groups and sustained political activism in maintaining their visibility. In many ways, human rights represents a discourse available for framing problems rather than a system of law for preventing them. As a discourse, it can be used by local actors around the world who seek to define their problems in these terms. On the other hand, as a quasi-law system, its power is deeply dependent on continued activism by local groups as well as by transnational NGOs, governments, and UN bodies.

NOTES

*For their support of the research described in this essay, I am grateful to the National Science Foundation, Cultural Anthropology and Law and Social Sciences Programs.

WORKS CITED

Anaya, S. James. *Indigenous Peoples in International Law.* New York, 1996.

Asch, Michael. *Home and Native Land: Aboriginal Rights and the Canadian Constitution.* Agincourt, Ontario, 1988.

Beckett, Jeremy. "Contested Images: Perspectives on the Indigenous Terrain in the Late Twentieth Century." *Identities: Global Studies in Culture and Power* 3 (1996): 1–15.

Boulding, Elise. *Building a Global Civic Culture.* Syracuse, N.Y., 1988.

Bunch, Charlotte. "Women's Rights as Human Rights: Toward a Re-Vision of Human Rights." *Human Rights Quarterly* 12 (1990): 489–498.

Bunch, Charlotte. "The Intolerable Status Quo: Violence against Women and Girls." *The Progress of Nations 1997.* New York: UNICEF Publication, 1997.

Bush, Diane Mitsch. "Women's Movements and State Policy Reform Aimed at

Domestic Violence against Women: A Comparison of the Consequences of Movement Mobilization in the U.S. and India," *Gender and Society* 6 (1992): 587–608.

Cook, Rebecca J. "Women's International Human Rights Law: The Way Forward." *Human Rights Quarterly* 15 (1993): 230–261.

Cook, Rebecca J. "State Responsibility for Violations of Women's Human Rights." *Harvard Human Rights Journal* 7 (1994): 125–175.

Coulter, Robert T. "Commentary on the UN Draft Declaration on the Rights of Indigenous Peoples." *Cultural Survival Quarterly* 18, no. 2 (1994): 37–41.

Davies, Miranda, ed. *Women and Violence: Realities and Responses Worldwide.* London, 1994.

Freeman, Marsha A. "Women, Law and Land at the Local Level: Claiming Women's Human Rights in Domestic Legal Systems." *Human Rights Quarterly* 16 (1994): 559–575.

Friedman, Jonathan. "The Politics of De-Authentification: Escaping from Identity, a Commentary on 'Beyond Authenticity' by Mark Rogers." *Identities: Global Studies in Culture and Power* 3 (1996): 127–137.

Jackson, Jean. "Culture, Genuine and Spurious: The Politics of Indianness in the Vaupes, Colombia." *American Ethnologist* 22 (1995): 3–28.

Keck, Margaret E., and Kathryn Sikkink. *Activists Beyond Borders: Advocacy Networks in International Politics.* Ithaca, N.Y., 1998.

Kerr, Joanna, ed. *Ours by Right: Women's Rights as Human Rights.* London, 1993.

Kim, Samuel S. "The United Nations, Lawmaking, and World Order." In *The United Nations and a Just World Order,* edited by Richard A. Falk, Samuel S. Kim, and Saul H. Mendlovitz. Boulder, Colo., 1991. Pp. 109–125.

McGillivray, Anne, and Brenda Comaskey. *Black Eyes All of the Time: Intimate Violence, Aboriginal Women, and the Justice System.* Toronto, 1999.

Merry, Sally Engle. "Gender Violence and Legally Engendered Selves." *Identities: Global Studies in Culture and Power* 2 (1995): 49–73.

Merry, Sally Engle. "Legal Pluralism and Transnational Culture: The Ka Ho'okolokolonui Kanaka Maoli Tribunal, Hawai'i 1993." In *Human Rights, Culture and Context: Anthropological Perspectives,* edited by Richard A. Wilson. London, 1997. Pp. 28–49.

Merry, Sally Engle. *Colonizing Hawai'i: The Cultural Power of Law.* Princeton, N.J., 2000.

Messer, Ellen. "Anthropology and Human Rights." *Annual Review of Anthropology* 22 (1993): 221–249.

Messer, Ellen. "Pluralist Approaches to Human Rights." *Journal of Anthropological Research* 53 (1997): 293–317.

Morrow, Betty Hearn. "A Grassroots Feminist Response to Intimate Violence in the Caribbean." *Women's Studies International Forum* 17 (1994): 579–592.

Ofei-Aboagye, Rosemary Ofeibea "Altering the Strands of the Fabric: A Preliminary Look at Domestic Violence in Ghana." *Signs: Journal of Women in Culture and Society* 19 (1994): 924–938.

Oller, Lucrecia. "Domestic Violence: Breaking the Cycle in Argentina." In *Women and Violence,* edited by Miranda Davies. London, 1994. Pp. 229–234.

Peters, Julie and Andrea Wolper, eds. *Women's Rights, Human Rights.* New York, 1995.

Povinelli, Elizabeth. "The Sense of Shame: Australian Multiculturalism and the Crisis of Indigenous Citizenship." *Critical Inquiry* 24 (1998): 575–611.

Report of the Secretary General. *From Nairobi to Beijing: Second Review and Appraisal of the Implementation of the Nairobi Forward-Looking Strategies for the Advancement of Women.* New York: United Nations, 1995.

Riles, Annelise. "Infinity within the Brackets." *American Ethnologist* 25 (1999): 1–21.

Rogers, Mark. "Beyond Authenticity: Conservation, Tourism, and the Politics of Representation in the Ecuadorian Amazon." *Identities: Global Studies in Culture and Power* 3 (1996): 73–127.

Santos, Boaventura De Sousa. *Toward a New Common Sense: Law, Science, and Politics in the Paradigmatic Transition.* New York, 1995.

Schuler, Margaret, ed. *Freedom from Violence: Women's Strategies from Around the World.* New York: UNIFEM, 1992.

Sierra, Maria Teresa. "Indian Rights and Customary Law in Mexico: A Study of the Nahuas in the Sierra de Puebla." *Law and Society Review* 29 (1995): 227–255.

Silard, Kathy. "Helping Women to Help Themselves: Counselling Against Domestic Violence in Australia." In *Women and Violence,* edited by Miranda Davies. London, 1994. Pp. 239–246.

Stephenson, Carolyn M. "Women's International Nongovernmental Organizations at the United Nations." In *Women, Politics, and the United Nations.* Westport, Conn., 1995. Pp. 135–155.

Tennant, Chris. "Indigenous Peoples, International Institutions, and the International Legal Literature from 1945–1993." *Human Rights Quarterly* 16 (1994): 1–57.

Thomas, Dorothy Q. "In Search of Solutions: Women's Police Stations in Brazil." In *Women and Violence,* edited by Miranda Davies. London, 1994. Pp. 32–43.

Thomas, Dorothy, and Michele Beaseley. "Domestic Violence as a Human Rights Issue." *Human Rights Quarterly* 15 (1993): 36–62.

Trask, Haunani-Kay. *From a Native Daughter: Colonialism and Sovereignty in Hawai'i.* Monroe, Me., 1993.

Turner, Terence. "Human Rights, Human Difference: Anthropology's Contribution to an Emancipatory Cultural Politics." *Journal of Anthropological Research* 53 (1997): 273–291.

"Report of the Special Rapporteur on Violence Against Women, Its Causes and Consequences, Ms. Radhika Coomaraswamy." UN Commission on Human Rights, 1996.

The Progress of Nations 1997. UNICEF Annual Publication. United Nations, 1997.

The Fourth World Conference on Women, 1995, Beijing, China: Official Documents. See "Beijing Declaration and Platform for Action: Platform 3"; "Address to the Fourth World Conference on Women, Secretary General"; "Statement by Jordan"; "Statement by Egypt"; "Statement by the Holy See." New York, United Nations, 1996.

Van Bueren, Geraldine. "The International Protection of Family Members' Rights as the Twenty-first Century Approaches." *Human Rights Quarterly* 17 (1995): 732–765.

Wilmsen, Edwin, ed. *We Are Here: Politics of Aboriginal Land Tenure.* Berkeley, Calif., 1989.

Wilson, Richard A., ed. *Human Rights, Culture and Context: Anthropological Perspectives.* London, 1996. See esp. the editor's introduction.

Zechenter, Elizabeth M. "In the Name of Culture: Cultural Relativism and the Abuse of the Individual." *Journal of Anthropological Research* 53 (1997): 319–347.

Mainstreaming a Concern for the Human Rights of Women

BEYOND THEORY

Felice D. Gaer

∞ IN Beijing in 1995, the simple statement that "women's rights are human rights" was incorporated in the declaration that ended the Fourth World Conference on Women, the largest meeting of women ever held and the largest conference ever convened by the United Nations. It summed up the ongoing effort by women's advocates to demonstrate to the international community not only that women have human rights but that these rights are not beyond the reach of a growing number of human rights mechanisms and programs set up by international and national institutions.

At the Beijing Conference delegates agreed to maintain the separate UN bodies devoted to women that have played a catalytic and expert role in developing standards; but they also sought to engage all other programs of the UN in examining gender-related aspects of their ongoing work. This solution, commonly called "gender mainstreaming," involves a process of assessing the implications for women and men of any planned action, including legislation, policies, or programs, in all areas and at all levels. This definition makes explicit the need to link gender with other issues, such as violence, health care, or political participation, and also makes a point of stating that gender is not only about women—it is about women and men and the way each is affected.

Gender mainstreaming seeks to empower women by removing obstacles that have been constructed by societies that operate to the disadvantage of women. By evaluating laws, policies, programs, customs, practices, and an array of inequities from a gender perspective, women and men can identify those areas in which women have been discriminated against and develop new policies to overcome that discrimination.

Beyond the laws, customs, and programs that can be seen as obstacles to the advancement of women, there are often practical barriers at work. In 1998 the UN secretariat surveyed thirty-three UN programs and identified the following obstacles encountered in taking action to advance women: a lack of gender-disaggregated data for analysis of both problems and achievements; a lack of indicators for monitoring progress; inadequate human and financial resources devoted to these issues; low levels of commitment, both politically in some countries and in the management of some UN agencies; and cultural and other constraints in the delivery of technical assistance.[1] On a practical level, these are formidable obstacles.

In August 1995 the United States delegation to Beijing circulated a paper (in the author's possession) entitled "Gender," which summed up the need to mainstream gender concerns this way: "At the base of the use of the word gender . . . is the concept that biology need not determine everything that men and women do. That opens the door to change, to changing the balance of power and responsibility between men and women—in the home, in the workplace, the marketplace. . . . That is what the UN Charter of 1945 is about when it calls for equal rights of men and women. There is simply no way to say that and not mean change."

From the earliest days of the United Nations, those seeking to advance women's human rights have explored the best way to proceed. They have struggled with the comparative advantages of separation and of integration. On the one hand, establishing a separate institutional arrangement specifically to oversee and develop standards and practices regarding women's rights offers the prospect of like-minded advocates concentrating and progressing in a focused setting. On the other hand, "mainstreaming" women's human rights into other human rights programs and operational field activities promises that women's human rights will not be marginalized in a few weak and neglected programs that are peripheral to core activities undertaken elsewhere.

The greatest struggle has been simply to make the human rights of women visible, whether it is with regard to the use of violence against women, or in issues of employment, education, health care, or other rights. As the UN's human rights staff explained in December 1999, "gender mainstreaming is thus the process of bringing an awareness of the status of women into the public arena. In the field of human rights, this primarily involves realizing that there is a gender dimension to every occurrence of a human rights violation." Mainstreaming also requires increasing women's actual participation in the human rights mechanisms and, to ensure that mainstreaming has an enduring effect on the way human rights work is carried out, resolving a core bureaucratic problem of coordination and cooperation among the many parts of the United Nations system.[2]

These three elements—building awareness, increasing participation, and expanding coordination—may sound routine, but they have proved perplexing to implement.

Some of the progress in integrating gender into the human rights programming and mechanisms of the UN is discussed below. The case of Afghanistan offers a serious look into the achievements, obstacles, and prospects for integration of a human-rights-based approach, and a gender-based rights approach in particular, into the operational country programming of United Nations agencies.

The Response of Human Rights Programs to Gender Concerns

Building awareness of the human rights of women begins with making them visible. Indeed, much of the credit for putting this issue onto the agenda of UN human rights bodies goes to the nongovernmental women's activists and organizations who mobilized their efforts in conjunction with the preparations for the World Conference on Human Rights, held in Vienna in 1993. Before this, women's human rights was truly an invisible subject for the UN human rights programs.[3]

In the years preceding the Vienna World Conference, women advocates theorized, conceptualized, and conducted meetings locally and internationally. These meetings produced plans for the advocacy that would follow. The issue of violence against women became a focal point for much of the effort put into the conference, with women everywhere agreeing that violence was a priority matter directly affecting them and cutting across geography, class, and race. Violence against women also most closely resembled concepts already examined and addressed by human rights bodies: the systematic use of coercive and forcible measures to ill-treat, harass, or otherwise impair the capacity of individuals to enjoy their human rights. Unlike most human rights initiatives at the UN, the individuals on whom the spotlight was now placed were women and girls. Advocates identified patterns of violence directed against women, highlighted antiviolence strategies being used at the national level, clarified the international legal framework applicable to violence against women, and proposed governmental and intergovernmental measures that would combat such violence.[4]

One of the key outcomes of their efforts was to call for creation, in the Commission on Human Rights, of a special rapporteur on violence against women. This post, promised earlier, was specifically addressed in the Vienna Declaration and Program of Action, which emerged from the World Conference and was in fact established in 1994. Systematic attention would henceforth be placed—at every session of the Commission on Human Rights since—on violence against women by the state (particularly in wartime), in the community, and in the family. The Special Rapporteur, Radhika Coomeraswamy of Sri Lanka, has produced a series of ground-breaking reports on each of these issues, providing an array not only of country-specific information, but of legal and social analysis demonstrating how these issues fall within the human rights agenda, and offering concrete proposals for actions to be taken to address them.

Yet Coomeraswamy's work has faced a particular danger: if she were the only focus of attention to and reporting on women's human rights issues, the subject would be marginalized within the human rights bodies. Building awareness would require others to monitor, report, and examine how women's human rights were affected.

Human Rights Treaty Bodies and Special Procedures

Slowly, other UN bodies began to incorporate awareness of women's human rights. The work of the human rights treaty monitoring bodies, the focus of recommendations at both the Vienna and Beijing World Conferences, is one such area. The 1995 Beijing Platform for Action stressed the importance of applying the six international human rights instruments in ways that would clearly consider "the systematic and systemic nature of discrimination against women that gender analysis has clearly indicated" and that would ensure "full integration and mainstreaming of the human rights of women" (paragraphs 222, 231b and 231f). The Division for the Advancement of Women has pointed out that the treaty bodies are well placed to contribute to gender integration by clarifying not only the practices encountered but also the obligations of states to uphold women's human rights through their assessment of each country's compliance with its treaty obligations. The Division concludes that "for the most part these bodies have tried to take account of the situation of women" and are themselves "in the process of developing an awareness of the gendered nature of some human rights." However, it cautions that "these treaty bodies have not yet clearly acknowledged that gender is an important dimension in defining the substantive nature of all rights" and it recommends a great deal more must be done.[5]

Some of the country-specific and other thematic special rapporteurs of the Commission on Human Rights have begun to address various gender-related violations of the human rights principles that fall within their mandate. Many did so initially by creating a separate section, usually at the end of their reports, on how women were affected.

In 1999 the newly reformed agenda of the Commission on Human

Rights included, for the first time, a separate agenda item on "Integration of Gender and the Human Rights of Women." This change reflects years of effort. And yet it also creates an ongoing challenge—to avoid marginalization of the issue. For this approach to be successful, women's rights cannot be addressed only under a single agenda item that relates to nothing else; instead, the subject must enter into the thinking, planning, monitoring, and implementation of all human rights matters under consideration at any given session. Gender integration of women's human rights means breaking the silence, ensuring the visibility of abuses against women, clarifying the norms at issue, and pressing for accountability of those who perpetrate those abuses, and then coordinating action so that the issues are thought about and acted upon in multiple contexts.

Prodigious efforts by women's human rights experts have helped to make clear to UN human rights specialists why certain abuses of human rights are specific to women and how they affect women, while also making clear that these are abuses of "traditional" human rights. Within the United Nations, agencies such as UNIFEM and the Division for the Advancement of Women have joined with the Office of the High Commissioner for Human Rights to organize workshops on gender-related aspects of human rights. Participants in those workshops pointed to the sources of information that experts could consult to examine these topics and addressed ways to ensure both the clarity and consistency of the human rights standards at play. Participants emphasized the political and cultural environment within which women pursued human rights; they outlined the institutional framework necessary to ensure respect for, and protection, promotion, and fulfillment of, women's human rights.

Thus it was something of a breakthrough when, in 1999, the Special Rapporteur on Extrajudicial, Summary, and Arbitrary Executions, Asma Jahangir of Pakistan, drew attention to "honor killings" by the male relatives of women alleged to have committed adultery or seeking divorce. The Special Rapporteur stated that such killings cannot be explained away by tradition or culture or dismissed as private matters; they are nothing less than murder. She went on to demonstrate that state-sanctioned impunity for so-called honor killings ignores the rule of law and due process and undermines individual human rights protections. As such, these killings are the legitimate concern of the human rights community.

New posts such as the Special Rapporteur on Education and the Independent Expert on Extreme Poverty also brought a gender perspective to studies in those areas. Older posts looked at issues in new ways. For example, the Special Rapporteur on Freedom of Expression now addressed the right of women to seek, receive, and impart information, and the link between freedom of opinion and expression and the elimination of discrimination and violence against women. The Special Rapporteur on Religious Intolerance proposed undertaking "a series of studies on discrimination" against women.

Country-specific special rapporteurs on Iran, Nigeria, Somalia, Myanmar, and Sudan in 1999 addressed the treatment of women. The Special Representative on Iran concluded that, despite well-meaning declarations, the government has so far achieved little improvement in the condition of Iranian women. The Special Rapporteur on Nigeria criticized the slow pace of eradicating harmful traditional practices, such as female genital mutilation and early marriages. The independent expert on the situation of human rights in Somalia, drawing special attention to minorities, pointed out that rape, reportedly uncommon in Somalia before the war in the 1990s, has become a weapon of war for the militia and bandits as well as in camps for displaced persons and returnees. The Special Rapporteur on Myanmar (Burma), noted the serious psychological problems of women who suffered violent abuses. Cultural inhibitions linked to the subject of sex and the serious social implications of rape and assaults on women compound the problem. As a result, he concluded, female-headed households were less able to become self-reliant. Although the new constitution of Sudan contains some provisions for the equal rights of women, the Special Rapporteur on that country cited continuing discriminatory legislation and practices. He also noted a large number of women widowed by the war and separated from their children, who had been abducted during raids or forcibly conscripted.

According to a study by the Office of the High Commissioner of Human Rights (OHCHR), the issue still mentioned most often in the human rights rapporteurs' reports is "gender-based violence."

> Women are used as targets in various types of conflicts and in various types of violence. Women are raped, sexually abused, beaten, tortured and killed. Rape is more and more being used as a tactic of war. . . . Women widowed by war . . . are especially vulnerable with regard to their physical safety; the difficulties of replacing lost identity documents; their mobility; their rights to inherit and to have access to land and property; obstacles to their remarriage; the suffering of consequences for the political views of their male relatives. Widows often lose the protection of their husbands and their social status and have to take responsibility for the entire family.[6]

This study reports that, in 1999, violence against women both inside and outside the family was covered by the various reports and that most of the special rapporteurs have referred to women's human rights as encompassing "equal access to education, literacy, access to health services, access to property, access to loans, the right to inherit, and participation in the decision-making processes, as well as the persistence of harmful traditional practices."

It is important to note that, although nearly two dozen posts existed for special rapporteurs and experts, Radhika Coomeraswamy was the first woman appointed to such a post. For gender mainstreaming to succeed in the Commission on Human Rights, increasing the participation of women in the special procedures and mechanisms of the commission itself came to be a pressing concern. In 1997 Mary Robinson of Ireland took office as the High Commissioner, and changes began to take place. Once women were appointed to some of the special procedures—Independent Expert on Somalia, Special Rapporteurs on Extrajudicial Executions and on Education—the attentiveness to gender mainstreaming in the reports on these subjects grew significantly. The presence of women in the secretariat staff and in nongovernmental organizations at the meetings of the Commission on Human Rights also helped achieve gender mainstreaming. Particularly important was the presence of women on key delegations who were interested in expanding the focus on women's human rights within the broader programs of the UN's human rights bodies.

Afghanistan: Building Awareness and Gender Sensitivity

The United Nations Commission on Human Rights has been monitoring human rights conditions in Afghanistan since 1984, when a special rapporteur was first appointed. The changes in the way in which the human rights of women are discussed with regard to that country provide a dramatic demonstration of how the UN has developed gender sensitivity and raised awareness of this issue; yet these discussions also highlight the obstacles still facing those who seek to promote "gender mainstreaming" in UN human rights programs.

The first special rapporteur on Afghanistan, Feliks Ermacora of Austria, focused largely on restrictions on political rights, imprisonment, and torture, as well as humanitarian abuses, affecting the civilian population of Afghanistan in the course of the Soviet invasion and the prolonged armed conflict that resulted from it. In December 1993, after the Vienna World Conference on Human Rights, which put so much attention on the human rights of women, this issue was raised in the annual General Assembly resolution on human rights in Afghanistan. After discussing attacks on civilians, disappearances, and political imprisonment, the resolution referred to reports of rape, abduction, and other abuses, stating that the General Assembly was "deeply concerned about the violation of the human rights of women by warring factions in Afghanistan, and about the lack of respect toward them and their honour, physical integrity and dignity, as reported by the Special Rapporteur." Operative paragraph 9 of the same resolution called upon the Afghan parties to ensure their "honour and dignity" in accord with international human rights law. In this case, the term "human rights of women" clearly reflected growing awareness of the way this issue had become prominent in Vienna, and in the case of Bosnia as well. But the reference to rape as a lack of respect, as an offense against women's "honour" and "dignity," reflects a lack of understanding of rape in wartime as a form of violence against women, as a human rights issue, and as a humanitarian violation.

In 1994 the General Assembly, referring (in resolution 49/207) to the demise of the former Afghan government and the rise of factional fighting in the country, dropped the preambular (but not the operative) references to "honour," and added a reference to violations of human rights. The General Assembly stated that it was "deeply concerned about the recurring violations of human rights specific to or primarily directed against women by some members of warring factions in Afghanistan, and about the lack of respect toward them and their physical integrity and dignity, as reported by the Special Rapporteur." The operative paragraph called for ensuring respect for women's human rights, so that their "honour and dignity may be ensured." However, a later paragraph in the same resolution seemed to push the language forward: after referring generically to many abuses, including disappearances and torture in prisons, and humanitarian aid, the General Assembly called upon the Special Rapporteur "to continue to gather information about specific instances of grave human rights violations and to broaden and intensify efforts in addressing human rights violations that are specific to or primarily directed against women, in order to assure the effective protection of their human rights."

Progress could be seen a year later, in December 1995, immediately following the Beijing World Conference on Women, when the language used to refer to Afghan women's human rights and the scope of issues covered changed substantially. Reflecting the concerns of the new Special Rapporteur, Choong-Hyun Paik of the Republic of Korea, the General Assembly (in resolution 50/189) expressed its particular concern "at reports of abuses and violations of the human rights of women, including acts of violence and denial of access to primary and basic education, training and employment, affecting their effective participation in political and cultural life throughout the country" and urged all parties "to respect all human rights, including the rights of women and children, and to take measures to ensure the effective participation of women in social, political and cultural life throughout the country."

Special Rapporteur Paik discussed better protection of women and girls in his early 1996 report, pointing to deteriorating situations for girls, with schools now closed to them at the instruction of the Taliban authorities in Herat. The abduction of young girls (by opposing forces) had ceased with Taliban control of particular regions; on the other hand women were not permitted to travel out of their homes unless accompanied by close male relatives, and they could no longer work. UNICEF had suspended all aid in Kandahar and Herat because of the discriminatory practices against girls.

Increasing attention to the severe policies of the Taliban authorities toward women was now growing. In early 1996 the Commission on Human Rights (in resolution 96/75) called upon "all authorities in Afghanistan to ensure equal treatment to women and girls" and urgently called for local authorities in Kandahar and Herat to reopen primary and secondary schools for girls and "to reintegrate women in their previous jobs." Since the Taliban established its control in Jalalabad in September 1994, women had no longer been allowed to work in health care.

After the Taliban took control of Kabul in 1996, similar repressive measures against women were decreed there. Numerous high level UN officials, including the Secretary General, spoke out against the restrictions on women's rights, including the Taliban's denial of UN aid to women. On October 11 the Taliban's request for the UN seat held by the government of former President Rabbani was denied. Eleven days later the UN Security Council adopted resolution 1076, in which it called upon all Afghan parties to stop fighting and begin talks on a lasting political settlement and establishing a fully representative transitional government. In an unusual reference to human rights, the Council also denounced the discrimination against girls and women and other violations of human rights and international humanitarian law. The issue of the human rights of women had become "mainstream."

In resolution 51/108, adopted in December 1996, the General Assembly now called on all the Afghan parties "fully to respect and act in accordance with all human rights and fundamental freedoms, regardless of gender, ethnicity or religion," and urged full respect for the rights of women and children in another paragraph, calling for "measures to ensure the effective participation of women in social, political and cultural life throughout the country." The Assembly also deeply deplored "the grave deterioration of the human rights of women noted by the Special Rapporteur in his report," urging "the Afghan authorities immediately to restore respect for all human rights of women, including the right of women to work and the right of girls to education without discrimination."

Writing for the spring 1997 session of the Commission on Human Rights, Special Rapporteur Paik drew attention to the full range of measures put in place by the Taliban, pointing out that they were, at times, "enforced harshly by Taliban forces and in particular by the representatives of the department of religious police." In December, he explained, "women were warned to observe the veil more strictly and 225 women were reportedly beaten behind the closed gates of the presidential palace . . . while their husbands and relatives waited outside." Paik detailed restrictions on medical treatment, employment, education, clothing, shopping, and other social contacts.[7] The Special Rapporteur offered two comments: one to the Taliban authorities calling for restoration of women's human rights, and the other to United Nations personnel, demanding that they "apply a single system-wide policy on the issue of gender equality in accordance with the Organization's stated principles" and the UN Charter. He also appended the actual decrees affecting women.

Both the Commission on Human Rights and the Commission on the Status of Women have adopted resolutions that discuss, in considerable detail, the need for changes in the discriminatory policies adopted toward women in Afghanistan. It has been quite unusual for the Commission on the Status of Women (CSW) to adopt a country-specific resolution. (The only other current country-specific resolution is a perennial one on Palestinian women.) But the CSW has reverted to this practice in the case of Afghanistan. A resolution on Afghanistan has been adopted by consensus every year since 1998. In 1999 Linda Tarr-Whelan, U.S. Ambassador to the Commission on the Status of Women, noted that "few practices of the Taliban have aroused more worldwide condemnation than their treatment of women and girls." Tarr-Whelan said that "it was crucial to highlight the denial of women's and girls' access to health care in Afghanistan" and that the resolution would condemn "continuing grave violations of the human rights of women and girls, especially their right to an adequate standard of living, including health care, and their rights to education and employment."[8]

The 1999 CSW resolution "condemns the continuing grave violations of the human rights of women and girls . . . in all areas of Afghanistan, particularly in areas under control of the Taliban"; condemns its denial of access to health care, denial of access to education, employment outside the home, freedom of movement, and freedom from violence; and urges the Taliban and other parties in Afghanistan "to recognize, protect, promote, and act in accordance with all human rights and fundamental freedoms, regardless of gender, ethnicity or religion" in accord with international human rights instruments and humanitarian law. It also calls for urgent measures to ensure the repeal of legislative measures that discriminate against women; participation of women in all aspects of Afghan life; respect for the right of women to work (the 1998 resolution had added "outside the home"); the equal right of women to education, freedom of movement, and equal access to health care; and respect for the right to security of the person. Acknowledging the importance of accountability for human rights violations, the resolution also speaks of the need to see that "those responsible for physical attacks on women are brought to justice."[9] Missing from these lists is any direct reference to the killings, rape, torture, or other physical maltreatment of women during the Afghan civil war.

As it had in 1998, the 1999 CSW resolution asks the United Nations as well as other donors to ensure that UN-assisted programs in Afghanistan are formulated and coordinated to promote and secure participation of women in those programs and that women and men benefit equally. The humanitarian aid it envisions—including the UN's own programs—should be conducted so that it is "based on the principle of non-discrimination, incorporates a gender perspective, and actively attempts to promote the participation of both women and men." Calling on member states to "mainstream a gender perspective into all aspects of their policies and actions related to Afghanistan," it welcomes the new posts of Gender Coordinator and Human Rights Coordinator in the UN's Office for Coordination of Humanitarian Assistance for Afghanistan and urges implementation of the 1997 Gender Mission recommendations.

The absence from any of the CSW resolutions of a request for an ongoing investigation of the situation, or even for reports from other bodies, illustrates the difference in approach to the human rights of women by the CSW, which generally fields broad issues but does not examine specific cases of violations, and the Commission on Human Rights (CHR), which vests special independent experts (i.e., the special rapporteurs) with the authority to investigate, intervene, gather facts, analyze the situation, and make recommendations in public reports. The calling to accountability of those who perpetrate violence against women in Afghanistan is arguably a sign that the CSW may be ready to change its approach. Elsewhere in the resolution, the CSW calls upon the CHR's Special Rapporteur on Afghanistan to stress in his report the importance of ensuring the human rights of women and girls.

The resolution of the Commission on Human Rights in 1999 addressed most of the issues touched on by the CSW but in somewhat more detail. Reflecting upon the conclusions of both the former special rapporteur, Choong-Hyun Paik of the Republic of Korea, and the new rapporteur, Kamal Hossain, a former foreign minister of Bangladesh, the human rights body condemned the widespread pattern of human rights violations, including violations of the human rights of women and girls, particularly in areas under Taliban control. In other paragraphs of resolution 1999/9 focusing on women and girls, it urged all parties to put an end to all violations of the human rights of women and girls, and, getting down to specifics, called for urgent measures to ensure the repeal of discriminatory legislative measures; effective participation of women in numerous spheres, including the economy; respect for the right of women to work (the CSW called for "the *equal* right of women to work"), including reintegration into their jobs; fulfillment of the right to education (the CSW spoke of "the *equal* right . . . to education"); the reopening of schools and admission of women at all levels; respect for a woman's right to security of the person and freedom of movement; and equal access to facilities that protect her right to the highest attainable level of physical and mental health. As for follow-up, the CHR reappointed its special rapporteur for another year, asking him to maintain his scrutiny of the human rights of women and children. It encouraged the Secretary General to investigate fully all reports of mass killings, rape, and "other cruel treatment" and make a concerted effort to ensure a gender perspective in the selection of staff for the UN Special Mission to Afghanistan.

Resolutions adopted by each of these bodies in 2000 continued along the same lines, with some refinements and improvements in language. Both resolutions seem to place greater emphasis on field-based integration of human rights and gender concerns. Significantly, however, both the CSW and the CHR request that special attention to the human rights of women be "fully incorporated" into the work of the Civil Affairs Unit to be set up, at the recommendation of UN Secretary General Kofi Annan, as a human rights monitoring body under the UN mission in Afghanistan. The CHR resolution also calls upon the High Commissioner for Human Rights to ensure a human rights presence in the Afghanistan mission. Other new elements of the resolutions in 2000 were an emphasis on the importance of training and selection of staff with understanding of the human rights of women, and efforts to enhance the role of women in Afghanistan in preventive diplomacy, peacemaking, and peacekeeping activities. Both resolutions emphasize that all humanitarian aid programs in Afghanistan be based on principles of nondiscrimination.

In 2000 both the Special Rapporteur on Afghanistan and the Special Rapporteur on Violence against Women traveled to the country and issued separate reports. Stating that "the character of the existing authorities who rule without the consent and participation of the Afghan people is the root cause of human rights violations," Kamal Hossain emphasizes the right of all Afghans to participate in the government and decision-making processes; this means being able to make decisions "through freely chosen representatives." In a section based on interviews with refugees and internally displaced persons, he also highlights a large number of other violations against women's human rights. Among the key issues raised are rape, abduction of girls, and so-called "forced marriages." He concludes that the rule through "edicts," which have affected women so harshly, must be remedied through a "framework change."[10]

Coomeraswamy writes with extraordinary precision and clarity about "official, widespread, and systematic discrimination" against women exacerbated by war. She not only discusses restrictions on access to various social services and education but directly addresses issues of physical abuse of women, such as sexual assault, beatings by the religious police (including, for example, on the breasts), and public lashings. Coomeraswamy makes clear that religion is unacceptable as an explanation for the kinds of repressive measures against women found in the country: she states that "Taliban edicts are not Islam, but the Taliban's version of Islam." She goes beyond this analysis of facts on the ground, however, to examine and comment upon the UN's approach to its on-the-ground activities, based on her conversations with UN officials who eschew "confrontation" and call for dialogue. She warns, however, of the danger of United Nations "complicity" in human rights violations.[11]

A Principled Approach to Aid

At a July 1998 press briefing, then-UN Emergency Relief Coordinator Sergio Vieira de Mello characterized Afghanistan as "probably the most difficult place to work on earth," citing the hostile security environment, extreme chronic poverty, recurrent natural disasters, an ongoing armed conflict, and a discriminatory human rights regime. Yet the United Nations does work there. Its efforts focus on promoting a peaceful settlement to the country's extended civil war, stemming the flow of narcotics from Afghanistan (the world's single largest producer), and providing humanitarian aid to the internally displaced and others. Repressive measures against women decreed by the Taliban, estimated in 1999 to control some 80 percent of the country, continue along with armed conflict.

The appropriate means of operating on the ground in and around Afghanistan have been the subject of considerable attention, particularly in the period since the Taliban took Kabul and questions were raised about their discriminatory and repressive gender-related policies. Worldwide condemnation followed the instituting of repressive measures against women, as did intensive UN scrutiny. Violations of the human rights of Afghan women are nothing new. But the Taliban's policies and repressive enforcement actions, according to Amnesty International, have introduced a new type of repression. Women who fail to conform to the policies are beaten by Taliban guards in detention centers or in public places such as shops, streets, and bus stops. Amnesty International views women "detained or physically restricted on account of their gender" to be prisoners of conscience.

After the Taliban took control of Kabul, the capital, and repressive measures against women became more visible, many leading UN officials criticized them publicly, and some UN programs were suspended. Others were reevaluated and redesigned. In June 1997 the UN's Executive Committee on Humanitarian Affairs (ECHA) recommended that all UN agencies adopt a principle-centered approach to the gender issue in Afghanistan. Under its terms, UN agencies would continue to engage in life-sustaining activities that benefited any Afghans in need, male and female, but would not contribute to the Afghan authorities' institution-building efforts while the discriminatory practices continued. These agencies were also asked to keep up a dialogue with Afghan authorities, with a view to bringing about their adherence to the principles of the Universal Declaration of Human Rights.

But while UN and implementing agencies were asked, at least at first, to take a consistent approach in these matters, and to seek to ensure that all staff, national and international, male and female, would be allowed to work effectively, ECHA in 1997 added two cautionary notes. The first was a possible loophole stating that UN agencies would use appropriate sensitivity to the different approaches required when dealing with these issues in urban and rural areas. The second was a caution that could strengthen or weaken UN actions, depending on who is in charge, stating that "heads of UN agencies, funds, and programmes will no longer make unilateral declarations on UN policies and practices related to human rights observance in Afghanistan." Angela King, UN Special Advisor on Gender Issues and Advancement of Women, was authorized to review indicators and monitoring measures in UN agencies in Afghanistan.

In a 26 June 1997 letter appended to the Afghanistan Gender Mission report, Secretary General Kofi Annan "fully" endorsed the principle-centered approach, noting that, "while women have never really enjoyed normal freedom, their condition in the cities under Taliban control has deteriorated," and that Taliban policies contravene two core human rights treaties signed by Afghanistan. He stated that "these restrictions have also adversely affected the ability of the United Nations to deliver programmes of relief and rehabilitation."

In November 1997 the UN dispatched a seven-member Interagency Gender Mission to Afghanistan comprised of UN agency representatives from the United Nations Children's Fund (UNICEF), the United Nations Population Fund (UNFPA), the World Health Organization (WHO), the World Food Programme (WFP), and the Economic and Social Commission for West Africa (ESCWA), and a Norwegian donor-NGO representative, led by Angela King. The Gender Mission team, believed to be the first of its kind, examined the condition of women in Afghanistan and the ways in which external assistance is conceived and delivered; it recommended measures the international community could take to address gender concerns in the delivery of aid and indicators to ensure appropriate ongoing monitoring of aid activities.

The Gender Mission addressed two critical areas: the nature of gender discrimination and proper actions in the field by UN agencies and programs. According to the Report of the Interagency Gender Mission to Afghanistan, 12–24 November 1997, the Gender Mission "resulted in the development of a coherent set of guidelines for field staff for implementing a principle-centered approach to humanitarian and development assistance." But the report also revealed that UN agencies and their implementing partners in Afghanistan have done little to promote gender equality. Indeed, "most programmes and projects ignore women at all at stages of their design and implementation. Even women-specific projects are not designed in consultation with women," and "UN staff are notably unprepared to confront the challenges of reversing gender discrimination." Despite the new UN concern over gender-related abuses, the situation continued to deteriorate. The UN's powerful Administrative Committee on Coordination (ACC) subsequently emphasized that gender issues needed to be fully integrated into the strategic framework process for countries in crisis.

Among the Interagency Gender Mission's conclusions was that "long years of deprivation, war and competing traditions" in Afghanistan have been compounded by the policies of the current authorities. Thus, "changing attitudes and behavior . . . will take a long time." In certain problem areas, such as health-care service delivery, which was devastated by Taliban dismissal of women as teachers, medical students, physicians, and service providers, the report concludes that "rehabilitating the health care infrastructure is as critical a need as providing emergency care." Other areas of need, such as education, freedom of movement, and economic well-being, are also discussed. A major focus of the report is the way that the UN system has responded to such events: it finds that UN agencies and their implementing partners in Afghanistan "remain uncertain about their role in promoting gender equality," that the principles that frame gender concerns in assistance are "not formulated clearly or consistently. As a result, they have been applied inconsistently."

In addition, the report states that "most programmes and projects ignore women at all at stages of their design and implementation. Even women-specific projects are not designed in consultation with women." In what is perhaps its most devastating conclusion, the report reveals the ignorance of field-based staff about the application of human rights guarantees to everyone: "UN staff are notably unprepared to confront the challenges of reversing gender discrimination. Many staff are unfamiliar with the founding principles and human rights instruments of the UN, and their responsibility in implementing them."

The United Nations tried to balance principle and pragmatism in the field by negotiating a memorandum of understanding (MOU) with the Taliban. The UN sought to permit international civil servants to pursue assistance programs that arguably meet international human rights guarantees for women, as the subject had evoked so much international concern. Dated 13 May 1998 and signed by officials of the Islamic Emirate of Afghanistan and the United Nations, the MOU addressed security, privileges, immunities, and obligations of UN staff; participation of international and national female staff in UN assistance programs; access to health and education for women and girls; and coordination and follow-up.

Unfortunately, the text of the MOU reveals a casual disregard for international human rights principles and a willingness to accept cultural and religious conditions set down by local authorities as the guidelines governing their implementation. Indeed, the United Nations staff clearly made very significant compromises in the course of reaching the agreement to permit it to operate. The MOU is riddled with contradictory language and restrictions that flout most of the nondiscrimination "principles" of international human rights treaties that Afghanistan had ratified. In fact, its internal contradictions are extraordinary, even for a UN document.

While assuring that UN communications will not "be subject to censorship," the MOU declares that "the United Nations shall refrain from using or distributing material that would transgress Islamic morality." In this way, the UN not only accepted the Taliban authorities' capacity to define that morality but agreed to self-censor not only anything it distributes but even its own use of materials in its own program design and implementation. The agreement declares that UN recruitment policies will be "without distinction" as to race, gender, religion, or nationality, but that they will also be "with due respect to Islamic values and traditions." Appointment of national staff, however, will be vetted with the government authorities and subject to their "confirmation"—which promises to contradict previous assurances of nondistinction in recruitment. Another part of the agreement offers assurances that UN staff "shall refrain from political activities or religious proselytism." This is followed by the joint affirmation that "proper respect shall be paid to Islamic principles and local customs."

Further compromises appear on the issues of access to education and health. Trying to strike a deal that can be explained to those who support "principles" as well as those who support the local restrictions, the UN and the Islamic republic give lip service to principle while finding a way out for the local authorities to impose their own limitations of those rights. The Taliban and the UN "jointly commit that men and women shall have the right to education and health care . . . based on international standards and in accordance with Islamic rules and Afghan culture." The document states that "the Authorities plan to promote" health education "in accordance with Islamic principles." Acknowledging the "economic difficulties in the specific cultural traditions that make" the goal of "participation of men and women in health education, and food security," the MOU declares that "women's access to and participation in health and education will need to be gradual." It is apparent that some aspects of the right to health and education may indeed require a gradual approach; for example, some medicines or facilities may be unavailable, thus rendering it impossible to offer them promptly. However, the access to such rights *on an equal basis* with men is a key issue essential to nondiscriminatory participation and "access" to these rights should be available to all immediately.

As the Human Rights Committee has concluded (in its general comment number 28) on equality of rights: "State parties are responsible for ensuring the equal enjoyment of rights without any discrimination. Articles 2 and 3 mandate State parties to take all steps necessary, including the prohibition of discrimination on the grounds of sex, to put an end to discriminatory actions both in the public and the private sector which impair the equal enjoyment of rights."[12] Affirming that women can have access only on a "gradual" basis is an unacceptable departure from the obligations of all states to ensure the rights of women. The statement that "the Ministry of Public Health . . . will continue to allow women to work . . . in accordance with its principles" allows the government to set the terms—including terms that may be discriminatory as to which professions, if any, women can participate in. Employment discrimination and a lack of access to employment has been shown to be a key factor in entrenching women's poverty and their low status in society.

In the period following the signing of the agreement, there were no signs of, in deMello's words, "tangible, measurable" progress in the matter of equal access to health and education. Taliban authorities had tightened the understanding they had reached with the UN about the movement of international UN employees and national ones. They declared that no Muslim female employee of the United Nations—from *any* country—could travel to or within Afghan territory under their control unless accompanied by a male relative. As the year progressed, threats to the security of

UN personnel and to foreign NGOs increased as well. Compromises were worked out, but harassment of UN officials continued, and eventually even Kabul's home-based schools for girls and women were closed.

The security situation became increasingly untenable for foreign personnel, particularly after the U.S. air strikes on alleged training camps associated with terrorist Osama bin Laden in retaliation for the bombings of U.S. embassies in Africa. In August 1998 Taliban forces captured the city of Mazar-i-Sharif. Massive abuses, and worse, followed, according to a Human Rights Watch report of 1 November 1998, including detentions "of thousands of men from various ethnic communities" and a massacre directed against members of the Hazara ethnic group—a "killing frenzy" believed to be in retaliation for the killing of some two thousand Taliban soldiers after their surrender fifteen months earlier.

In a July 1998 press briefing, de Mello, the emergency relief coordinator, publicly questioned the efficacy of cutting UN aid programs because of gender concerns: Is "it better in view of unacceptable violations of human rights, to withdraw and condemn, or [is] it better to remain engaged and to try to make a small difference on the ground however tenuous the chances of success might be?" He added: "At what point should humanitarian agencies draw the line and withdraw?" and, further, "What level of security risks to . . . staff was acceptable?"

The answer came soon enough. After the shooting of UN personnel serving in Kabul, with one dead, the world organization evacuated its staff from the country, as did most NGOs. They were gone by November. Yet, almost immediately, they began negotiating the terms of their return. Indeed, by March 1999 the United Nations was returning to Afghanistan. On 3 June 1999, in a "Briefing of the Security Council on Emergency Situations Outside the Federal Republic of Yugoslavia," de Mello explained that the return to Kabul and elsewhere has been "a difficult and painstaking process," but "I am confident that we are well on the way to posting staff in all six locations agreed to earlier."

In the spring of 1999, a report by the UN's Special Rapporteur on Afghanistan suggested that restrictions on women had eased slightly in Kabul. Kamal Hossain said after visiting the capital that he had "observed some relaxation of the restrictions imposed on the rights of women, as a few women doctors and nurses were seen at work in a hospital attending to female patients." A more flexible attitude was reportedly expressed by Taliban representatives with regard to the access of girls to education, and a recent edict granted exemption to needy widows from the restriction against the employment of women in urban areas.

Visiting the capital in May, Pamela Constable related a similar view in the 11 May 1999 *Washington Post:* "the burqa [a garment that covers a woman's body] is said to be only a partial covering in Kabul; some women doctors are permitted in a few hospitals; some religious schools were said to exist for girls; and the UN has signed agreements to build four colleges for women at some appropriate future point." She added, however, that she was constantly accompanied by two male officials, who were present when she was told about or shown such "improvements" in Kabul. When she asked questions of people she met, these officials often answered for them. Other restrictions limited her ability to investigate actual conditions. Constable concluded that the changes, however modest, were in response to outside pressure on the Taliban.

Still, both the Commission on Human Rights and the Commission on the Status of Women continue to view the situation as very dismal when it comes to respect for the human rights of women. At a press briefing in Geneva, Special Rapporteur Hossain sought to make clear that "the situation was very negative in all fields regarding women," that clear-cut indicators of improvement were lacking, and that "the emergence of a framework for building peace . . . aimed at establishing a broad-based multiethnic and fully representative government" was needed to improve the overall human rights situation in Afghanistan. And, as noted above, visits by Hossein and Coomeraswamy in September 1999 revealed extensive violations, including abductions and gender-specific abuses, as well as the ongoing problems with "access" to human rights by women.

In Stockholm, on 21–22 June 1999, a meeting of the Afghan Support Group (ASG), a group of states that contribute to programs in the country, was convened (as usual without UN involvement). According to the chairman's summary, participants "took stock of the progress in integrating gender considerations into assistance activities." The nature of that progress is not indicated, other than a brief reference to the group's support for "rights-based programming and in particular the recruitment by the UN Coordinator's Office of a human rights advisor and a gender advisor." Still, various UN officials continue to resist the idea of giving any serious attention to gender-related issues in their decisions and programming for humanitarian assistance in Afghanistan, as evidenced by their written reports. For example, a paper on "Gender Issues in Afghanistan" delivered on 12 June 1999 at the Stockholm ASG meeting by the office of the UN Coordinator in Islamabad put forth the following argument:

> Any underestimation of the influence of the cultural, socio-economic factors contributing to shaping the status quo of Afghan society and economy will lead either to the failure of these interventions to achieve their objectives or worse, to reduce the very narrow margin of access to social services and em-

ployment women have at present. . . . There is a great need for the donor community, . . . if they wish to create a climate conducive to gender equity in Afghanistan, to make a more intensive effort to look into Afghan society rather than to look at it.

The gender paper goes on to note that a senior gender advisor has joined the UN office in Islamabad and will be responsible for "the engagement, follow-up, and coordination, through the principled common programming approach, of gender mainstreaming in Afghanistan." A gender action plan, outlined in the document, calls for dialogue with the local community, with technical departments affecting women, and with political and religious leaders. It also calls for sensitization workshops and related training on the capacity of the UN system for gender mainstreaming, advising the UN system on gender-related policies and guidelines, and working closely on gender-related issues with the NGOs involved in Afghan-related matters. Notably, what it does not call for—or mention—are specific actions to implement nondiscrimination policies.

Another indication that gender-related concerns have been relegated to a low level in UN programming for Afghanistan and in the donor community as well can be gleaned from two UN documents issued in June 1999. One is a 25 June press release issued in Islamabad by the UN Spokesman for Afghanistan, Stephanie Bunker, who noted the three major concerns, expressed at the Stockholm meeting, of donors to Afghan programs: the lack of national reconciliation, the need for a political solution to the conflict, and concern over forced repatriation of refugees from Iran. Nowhere is discrimination against women mentioned in the press release.

Gender-related concerns also have taken a backseat in the Secretary General's quarterly report on the UN's Special Mission to Afghanistan, a report mandated by the General Assembly.[13] It addresses military, political, humanitarian, and human rights aspects of the Afghan situation without so much as mentioning gender-related issues. A brief reference to education mentions female education in passing. Yet, in contrast, reportedly the gender advisor attached to the United Nations in Afghanistan has visited Kandahar and Kabul without an accompanying "male relative" and not wearing a burqa, and has met with top Taliban officials.

The overall devastation in Afghanistan—physical, economic, social, and political—presents enormous problems at many levels for those seeking to provide aid and assistance of many kinds; thus gender may well be downplayed deliberately. The security situation is another major obstacle to the presence of the United Nations and other groups seeking to assist in this complex emergency. A lack of program resources merely compounds the problems involved in implementing policy and planning operational activities.

The Afghan Support Group (ASG) called for the UN Coordinator's Office to present a Human Rights Plan of Action for meeting in Ottawa in December 1999. It also noted that resources are vital to any attempt at implementing "principled programming" on gender and human rights. Most significant is the statement in the 21–22 June 1999 chairman's summary that "progress from a rights-based perspective would require a long-term engagement and a broad interpretation of priorities in terms of human rights in Afghanistan." Women have never been a priority in such assistance programs in this region in the past, and an emphasis on the long term rarely means a focus on the status of women.

Human Rights: Improvement or Complicity?

In late 1999 Secretary General Kofi Annan reported to the Fifty-Fourth General Assembly that the UN's "Strategic Framework for Afghanistan" had three pillars: peacemaking, humanitarian assistance, and human rights. Annan proposed, and the Security Council agreed, that the on-site UN Special Mission to Afghanistan (UNSMA) would take on primary responsibility for conducting UN peacemaking activities in Afghanistan and would gradually move to Kabul. He stated that it would establish a civil affairs unit with a new monitoring function, the main objective being to promote respect for minimum humanitarian standards and deter massive violations of human rights in the future.[14]

According to a UN strategy paper, the civil affairs unit will assess the human rights of most immediate concern as well as in-country means of safeguarding human rights, prepare analytic reports on the human rights situation, develop a dissemination program on enhancing understanding of human rights, and develop a strategy on the most appropriate means of improving human rights. When conditions are right, a second phase would assist civil society and interact with governance rules and other matters, implementing the concerns about human rights.

The approach to be taken by this new unit is not likely to satisfy most human rights monitors, who believe that public reports and shining a public spotlight on abuses can deter human rights violations. The strategy document prepared by the Afghan civil affairs unit posits three approaches to be taken in situations of conflict with extensive human rights violations—persuasion, denunciation, or substitution—and insists that persuasion entails some compromise in terms of making abuses public. A persuasion approach, the authors of the strategy paper claim, requires a "collaborative relationship with de facto authorities" that must be built upon "trust and mutual respect." Seeking to persuade the Taliban that respect for human rights is in their interest, the authors explain that they will need to act with "confidentiality and utmost discretion." The paper explains that it will be a constant challenge to succeed at this effort, conceding that "it may be necessary to make concerns about particular gross violations public" at some point, as "it would be difficult to remain silent in the face of gross and systematic violations of human rights." Regular reporting by the UN, it cautions, "should provide a balanced analysis of the human rights situation so that the authorities get credit for positive steps or achievements." In contrast, a "condemnatory approach will not be effective in convincing the authorities, especially the Taliban, to respect human rights." But the civil affairs unit must not "be seen to acquiesce or condone abuses by the authorities." Suggesting that the UN has learned little from its failed operations in Bosnia and elsewhere, the document concludes that "maintaining access to endangered civilians generally means that humanitarian agencies avoid a confrontational approach when confronted with human rights violations."[15]

Special Rapporteur Radhika Coomeraswamy obviously encountered this mindset in her visit to the region, as evidenced by her comments critical of it:

> The United Nations and its partners have adopted a dual approach in its work in Afghanistan as part of the Strategic Framework process. With regard to humanitarian assistance, a non-confrontational approach . . . is considered the best strategy. With regard to other issues, the policy makers appeared to be divided. One school of thought, favored . . . by the gender focal point is that the United Nations should enter into a dialogue with the Taliban authorities and work toward incremental change with minimum confrontation. Other policy makers were of the belief that the UN would compromise its principles if it were officially to tolerate the Taliban principles while implementing projects. From a human rights perspective, the Special Rapporteur is of the belief that certain Taliban policies fundamentally compromise the human rights of women and that rights-based programming is necessary for the UN system to respond effectively to human rights violations. Certain of her interlocutors expressed concern that confrontational statements by foreign organizations would worsen the situation by angering local authorities and producing stricter conditions. However, UN complicity in the violation of the rights of Afghan women is also a serious matter. The Special Rapporteur is of the belief that humanitarian assistance requires a different approach, that of constructive engagement in human rights issues. The hardships suffered by the Afghan people require this type of effort."[16]

Coomeraswamy offers some recommendations that go beyond the effort to be nonconfrontational, quiet, and balanced—the preferred approach of the civil affairs unit. The Taliban, she argues, "unless and until it is ready to meet its international obligations with regard to the rights of women," should not be given international recognition. The abuses require "firm and consistent international action based on humanitarian intervention." She calls for consideration of action to "compel the Taliban to respect a minimum core of women's human rights." In addition, she states that the flow of nonhumanitarian aid into Taliban-controlled areas "should cease unless the aid can be delivered without discriminating against women. International standards with regard to the rights of women cannot be compromised for policies of 'constructive engagement.'"

This picture is by no means comforting to the advocate of integrating a concern for the human rights of women in UN operational programming regarding Afghanistan or any other nation. There is evidence emerging from other sources of UN movement toward downplaying the human rights of women. A consultant to the UN indicated that UN personnel posted to the UN Special Mission in Afghanistan vigorously and repeatedly questioned the validity and effectiveness of the human rights concerns raised by member states and nongovernmental organizations regarding their work in the country. The field-based UN personnel argued that recent human rights reports of the special rapporteurs and other human rights groups were not "balanced" (reporting only on Taliban abuses) and were distinctly unhelpful in that they antagonized the Taliban authorities. These UN personnel stressed that raising the human rights issue directly was neither effective nor helpful to people suffering abuses. Many of these international aid officials argued that the process for the realization of women's human rights must be gradual and that rural women's lives had not been affected as much as those in the cities, particularly Kabul. A number claimed that those most vocal about Taliban abuses of women in Kabul were "elitist." Most UN agencies are focused on a gradual "rights-based" approach that seeks to change the Taliban's policies through "constructive engagement" and point to some recent "loosening up" of a few of the restrictions against women in Afghanistan as "significant progress."

The reality, according to the UN consultant, is that while it is true that restrictions have been lifted to some modest degree, they could easily be tightened at the drop of a hat. Moreover, the loss of rights for women in Afghanistan who previously enjoyed a wide range of rights is so dramatic that the current situation is only slightly less abhorrent. "At the current rate of progress," the consultant states, "women may regain the rights they had before the Taliban—in about 40 or 50 years."

Conclusion

Although there have been major efforts on behalf of the advancement of the human rights of women throughout the UN human rights system in the past decade, there is still a long way to go, particularly with regard to the integration of these concerns into the field-based UN programs. This is illustrated by the high-profile case of Afghanistan.

Standard-setting, reconceptualization, and new reporting on gender equality and the elimination of violence against women has progressed, but practical application of remedies and principled field-based policies are not yet the norm. There is, in particular, much greater awareness of the dimensions and prevalence of violence against women, but measures to address this issue effectively are still rare, and precise data remains scant.

The participation of women in the review and reporting of human rights conditions has grown in many important ways, but there is still a long way to go in this area as well. Cooperation and coordination of principled policies to address international guarantees of the human rights of women in the field remains underdeveloped in the programming of the United Nations.

While improvements may come in the UN's field-based programming, a tendency to take an easier path—favoring a nonconfrontational approach to humanitarian assistance—may overwhelm the need for direct and insistent action on the enforcement of international human rights guarantees to women. Still, the developments of the 1990s have spurred a fuller realization of the human rights of women. With concerted effort and creative enthusiasm, action can follow awareness, and the obstacles before us—human, resource-based, or political—can undoubtedly be overcome, one by one.

NOTES

1. See United Nations Document E/CN.6/1998/3.

2. See UN Document E/CN.4/2000/67, 21 December 1999.

3. For more on the development of this trend, see Felice Gaer, "And Never the Twain Shall Meet? The Struggle to Establish International Women's Rights as Human Rights," in *The International Human Rights of Women: Instruments of Change,* edited by C. Lockwood et al. (American Bar Association, 1998), pp. 1–89.

4. See, for example, "Combatting Violence Against Women," International League for Human Rights, 1993; and Charlotte Bunch and Niamh Reilly, *Demanding Accountability: The Global Campaign and Vienna Tribunal for Women's Human Rights* (New Brunswick, N.J.: Center for Women's Global Leadership, and New York: UNIFEM, 1994).

5. "Integrating a Gender Perspective into UN Human Rights Work," *Women 2000,* Division on the Advancement of Women, United Nations, December 1998, based on a report for a meeting of chairpersons of human rights treaty bodies. See also UN Doc. HRI/MC/1998/6.

6. UN doc E/CN.4/2000/67, 21 December 1999.

7. UN doc. E/CN.4/1997/59.

8. U.S. Mission to the UN, press release, 11 March 1999.

9. UN doc. E/CN.6/1997/L.7.

10. UN doc. E/CN.4/2000/23.

11. UN doc. E/CN.4/2000/68.

12. UN doc. CCPR/C/21/Rev. 1/Add.10.

13. UN doc. S/1999/698, 6/20/99.

14. See A/53/695-S/1998/1109, and A/54/536-S/1999/1145, para. 86.

15. "Overall Strategy/Approach, Annex IV," document in the author's possession.

16. UN Doc. E/CN.4/2000/68, add. 4, para. 80.

II: WOMEN AND HEALTH

Women's Health and
Human Rights
Julie H. Levison and
Sandra P. Levison

∞ WOMEN'S health is not only influenced by genetics, biology, and physiology but also by women's role in society. The field of women's health has developed in response to increasing knowledge of the non-reproductive differences between men and women, with physicians, scientists, nurses, women's advocates, social workers, and administrators collaborating in a multidisciplinary effort to understand and promote women's health and general well-being. The National Academy of Women's Health Medical Education published a comprehensive definition for women's health which reflects a multidisciplinary approach to considering women's health. "Women's health is devoted to facilitating the preservation of wellness and prevention of illness and includes screening, diagnosis and management of conditions which are unique to women, are more common in women, are more serious in women and have manifestations, risk factors or interventions which are different in women." Women's health also

recognizes the importance of the study of gender differences, recognizes multidisciplinary team approaches, includes the values and knowledge of women and their own experience of health and illness; recognizes the diversity of women's health needs over the life cycle and how these needs reflect differences in race, class, ethnicity, culture, sexual preference and levels of education and access to medical care; includes the empowerment of women, as for all patients, to be informed participants in their own health care.[1]

Inequalities in the social and economic status of men and women dis-proportionately deprive women and their children of good health. Com-pared to men, women worldwide tend to earn less money, are economically dependent, attain a lower educational level, and have fewer legal rights. This disparity leads to a power imbalance between genders, with women having an inferior status. The influence of these factors is seen in diseases and conditions such as HIV/AIDS; violence against women, including do-mestic abuse, sexual molestation, rape, sexual harassment, female genital mutilation (also known as female circumcision), honor killing, dowry-related murder, selective malnutrition of girls, forced prostitution, and tor-ture; infringement on reproductive rights; limitations on access to health care and drugs; and underrepresentation of women in clinical trials.

While women live longer than men and females outnumber males in most regions of the world, less than half of the world's population is com-posed of women. The different patterns of morbidity and mortality in men and women show that women have particular health risks. These risks be-gin in childhood, when parents and by extension society make decisions on the value of females and males. For example, in some areas where there is little social value in women, sex selection is practiced; abortion may be used to eliminate female fetuses, and female babies may be the victims of selective malnourishment or infanticide. In many areas, social and cul-tural factors deny girls and women the same nutrition, health care, and other support that males receive.[2]

These values on gender roles and status influence health later in life. In regions where women are malnourished (as are half the women in most of Asia and Africa), marry very young, start having children at a young age, and do not have access to health care or contraception, the prospects for the health of mother and child are diminished. Maternal deaths are associated with malnutrition, high-risk pregnancies, deliveries that occur without the benefit of trained personnel, and abortions, particularly those that are ille-gal or performed under unsterile conditions by untrained individuals.

From a health policy perspective, the challenge of providing health care is forming a consensus over what constitutes health. Human rights tenets indicate that the ability to attain the highest possible standard of health is not a privilege for the elite but a right that comes with being human.

A greater knowledge of the link between human rights and health ex-poses the social factors that foster illness and the spread of disease. It is becoming apparent that efforts to promote health care that do not include attention to human rights issues are incomplete and ultimately ineffec-tive. Therefore, the challenge of promoting public health, and in particu-lar women's health, is unquestionably linked to the challenge of upholding human rights.

Promoting women's health means valuing fundamental human rights such as the right to education, the right to employment and equal pay for equal work, and the right to participate in the political life of one's community. In 1945 the United Nations was founded on the principles of protecting and promoting human rights. The document that resulted as a universal standard for humanity was the Universal Declaration of Human Rights (UDHR) in 1948. The UDHR is not a legally binding agreement but has gained legitimacy on the national and international level when nations have incorporated the UDHR's precepts into their national constitutions and referred to portions of the document when upholding another nation to these standards for human rights. The International Covenant on Economic, Social, and Cultural Rights (ICESCR) and the International Covenant on Civil and Political Rights (ICCPR), written in 1966, elaborate the scope of the UDHR. They are legally binding in the capacity that states agree to comply and regularly be assessed of their compliance with the covenants. Together, the United Nations Charter, UDHR, ICESCR, and ICCPR form the International Bill of Human Rights. The acceptance of these documents makes individuals, governments, and local communities accountable for the protection of human dignity.

This essay attempts to describe deficiencies in women's health and their inextricable connection to women's dignity and human rights. Our goal is to explain how support for the rights of women is not just a matter of social justice but is recognized through national laws and international covenants. When individuals and societies are held accountable to these standards, communities thrive. Effective long-term health planning should include the realization of women's potential as active community participants.

Women and HIV/AIDS

HIV/AIDS is a global problem. Although 85 percent of HIV/AIDS cases are located in regions of Africa and Southeast Asia, modern transportation and technology foster the rapid spread of people and their products throughout the world. Thus the virus disperses without regard for geographic or civil boundaries. The United Nations estimates that there are close to 35 million women, men, and children living with HIV, and over 70 percent of the viral infections occur through sex between men and women.[3] HIV/AIDS is rampant in conditions where poverty, lack of education, and political instability are widespread and where the value of life, the rights of the individual, and the dignity of women are not sacrosanct.

Gender inequities and stereotypes that limit women's participation and influence in society contribute to the spread of HIV. Gender inequality is increasingly being understood as a significant factor in HIV transmission.

Indeed, the number of cases of HIV/AIDS in women is growing at a staggering rate. Over half of the 35 million cases of HIV/AIDS worldwide are reported in women. In the United States in 1994, AIDS was the fourth leading cause of death for women, and is the primary cause of death for women between the ages of 20 and 40 in some of the major cities in Western Europe, sub-Saharan Africa and the Americas.[4] In the United States women of color comprise the fastest-growing population with HIV infections.[5]

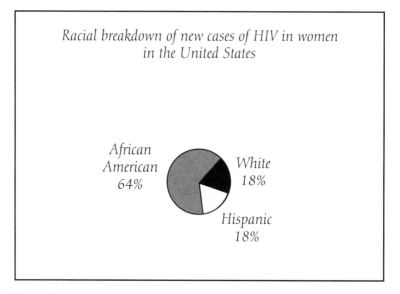

Racial breakdown of new cases of HIV in women in the United States

African American 64%
White 18%
Hispanic 18%

Source: Centers for Disease Control and Prevention, as reported in Lawrence Altman, "Focusing on Prevention in Fight Against AIDS," *New York Times,* 31 August 1999.

In both developed and developing nations, social, political, and economic systems that discriminate against individuals based on their gender, race, creed, sexual preference, or religion further weaken individual and societal defenses against HIV/AIDS and undermine public health policies that target the spread of the infection.

As the response to the HIV/AIDS crisis has developed since the beginning of the global response in the early 1980s, so too has the manner of controlling HIV/AIDS in women. In the beginning of the AIDS crisis in the 1980s, public health prevention strategies focused on individual risk and promoted change in individual behavior. This strategy was based on an assessment of HIV/AIDS using classical methods of epidemiology that identified the determinants of HIV/AIDS as results of individual behavioral choices. In the late 1980s, with the epidemic transformed into a global pandemic, the understanding of HIV/AIDS became much more complex as public health programs began to consider the social conditions that influence individual choices. While public health messages that have focused on individual risk and behavioral change have shown elements of real success in the populations of injecting drug users, sex workers, and gay men, the epidemic has persisted on a global scale. An analysis of the epidemiology indicates that the most vulnerable populations to HIV infection are women, urban minorities, and injecting drug users.

Since an overwhelming majority of new cases of HIV are transmitted through heterosexual sex, HIV/AIDS has disproportionately infected young individuals in the prime of life. As mothers, wives, caregivers, and laborers, women hold a complex place in society. Thus, the infection of women with HIV is far-reaching. Women play a critical role in the community and economy, and as an increasing number of women become infected with HIV, these traditional caregivers become invisible to society. Women with HIV/AIDS and their similarly afflicted relatives are left without the social support to sustain them through their illness because of the perpetual role of women as domestic caregivers.[6] As mothers die of AIDS, a generation of children is orphaned. When older relatives and grandparents become surrogate parents, they suffer the burden of not only grief and shame from the loss of a relative due to HIV/AIDS, but also the responsibility of caring for a child later in life, when they have their own geriatric medical challenges.[7] The increasing infection of HIV/AIDS in women and in younger populations has devastated traditional social and economic systems and norms.

Differences in HIV/AIDS Based on Sex

Men and women suffer from sexually transmitted diseases in almost equal proportion. Yet the consequences of infection in women are unique. Part of this is due to women's biological susceptibility to sexually transmitted infections. While a number of longitudinal studies in Africa that compare male-to-female and female-to-male HIV transmission have been inconclusive due to the size of the samples and the timing of the surveys, one study of HIV-1 infection in rural Uganda indicates that men are twice as likely as women to introduce HIV infection into a marriage, and within serodiscordant marriages (in which one partner is HIV-positive and one is HIV-negative), women are twice as likely to contract HIV from their husbands as husbands from their wives.[8] This data supports research from Europe, the United States, and East Africa, along with studies on other sexually transmitted diseases that suggest that women are more likely than their male partners to contract infection from heterosexual intercourse.

Women are particularly susceptible to HIV/AIDS based on their anatomy and biology. Consequently, diagnosing, facilitating prevention, and treatment present challenges to health-care providers. The biological characteristics of the female reproductive anatomy contribute to women's greater vulnerability to HIV infection. The mucosal surface that covers the female genital tract is a large surface area, which the HIV virus can penetrate during heterosexual contact.[9] The specific correlation between viral exposure and the location of cervical lesions or the interaction between HIV infection and the menstrual cycle, pregnancy, and hormonal contraception have only recently begun to be elucidated.

The consequences of infection from sexually transmitted diseases in women is often more severe than in men. Inflammation of the genital tissue due to infection with other sexually transmitted diseases increases a woman's susceptibility to contracting HIV. Ultimately these infections can lead to pelvic inflammatory disease; complications in pregnancy, delivery, and the development of the child; premature death of the fetus or infant; cervical cancer; and infertility.[10]

The diagnosis of HIV infection, along with other sexually transmitted diseases in women, can be delayed or misclassified because women often present with few symptoms or clinical manifestations different from those men present. For example, the first AIDS cases were identified in 1981, when young homosexual males presented with *Pneumocystis carinii* pneumonia in metropolitan centers in the United States. Initially the criteria for diagnosing HIV were based on observations from male cases, so that women with cervical dysplasia or cervical cancer were not diagnosed or treated for HIV infection because clinicians were unfamiliar with this manifestation of the disease. It was not until 1993 that the AIDS surveillance case definition was expanded to include cervical cancer in adolescent and adult females.[11] As a result of delays in diagnosis and treatment, historically women have not been able to benefit equally from medical regimens to extend life and improve well-being.

Gender Roles and HIV

Women's gender—their role in society as determined by their sex and shaped by sociocultural expectations—also influences how HIV infection has an impact on women's lives. The social, economic, and cultural analysis of the AIDS epidemic shows that the unequal status of men's and women's roles in societies contributes to the spread of HIV/AIDS. Thus preventing HIV infection presents multifaceted problems. Men and women are not monolithic categories but rather differentiated by cultural, ethnic, and economic variants in gender roles. But the contents of these gender definitions are interdependent. For example, traditionally women have been expected to act as caregivers. Their identity is tethered to the domestic realm, while men are often the family breadwinners, control the family income, and have the ability to participate in political life. With the responsibility of domestic work, raising children, and caring for the elderly, women tend to have less opportunities to seek education, receive remuneration for their labor, and ultimately empower themselves. Therefore women tend to be economically dependent on male partners and lack the personal freedom to travel, access information, and exert authority in the decision-making processes in the home and in their communities.

This imbalance in power between men and women threatens women's health and is lethal when HIV enters the gender ecology. Since life-saving HIV medical therapies cost more than $15,000 per year and are unattainable in poorer countries and communities, control of the AIDS epidemic, particularly its transmission to unborn children, depends on prevention. The epidemiologist Jonathan Mann suggested that programs that educate and motivate women about HIV prevention along with the availability of condoms are still unsuccessful in preventing HIV because of gender inequities. Educated women with access to condoms are still vulnerable to HIV if they cannot refuse unwanted or unprotected sex from a partner.[12] These women often fear verbal and physical abuse or the debilitating social and economic repercussions of divorce, which can include loss of property, children, and status within the community.

It is not enough for women to be monogamous in order to prevent the spread of HIV. Women's susceptibility to HIV is tied to the behavioral practices of their male partners, who can choose to have a greater number of sexual partners and extramarital relationships. In fact society condones promiscuity in males—"boys will be boys." Changes in gender stereotypes and expectations are necessary in strengthening AIDS policies. When rape, whether within or outside the bounds of marriage, is not considered a crime, when sex is a conquest rather than an act of intimacy, and when women are valued as vehicles of pleasure rather than as human beings, there is a higher probability for HIV transmission.[13] Human rights doctrines provide a language of accountability to develop effective, gender-sensitive HIV/AIDS policies.

The Future of HIV Policy: Human Rights

In the almost twenty years in which the AIDS epidemic has developed, it has become clear, based on the distribution of the disease, that both the public health model, which associates individual risks as determinants of HIV/AIDS, and the biomedical model, which targets the pathology of HIV/AIDS, have failed to explain the complex social networks in which the epidemic flourishes. The World Health Organization defines health as "a state of complete physical, mental, and social well-being and not merely the absence of disease or infirmity"; this definition supports the notion that biomedical threats and social injustices determine health. Addressing the determinants of HIV/AIDS means also confronting the determinants of human well-being and empowerment. In order to protect women against susceptibility to HIV it is necessary to provide them with the means for safer sex and for men to be responsible and choose to practice safer sex. For public health practitioners and policy makers, human rights provides a common language to identify the power imbalances in gender roles present in society that fuel the spread of HIV.

When we apply human rights standards to health we have an analytical tool to identify the social preconditions for health and the prevention of HIV transmission. As Jonathan Mann argued, successful HIV/AIDS prevention programs entail three difficult tasks: mobilizing political and governmental support so that those in power recognize the threat of HIV to women; addressing social mores that perpetuate gender roles and expectations that are harmful to women's health and dignity; and confronting disparities in wealth and resources that isolate women to poverty and dependency.

Specific rights that protect against HIV/AIDS discrimination are enumerated in several human rights documents: the Universal Declaration of Human Rights (UDHR); the International Covenant on Civil and Political Rights (ICCPR); the International Covenant on Economic, Social, and Cultural Rights (ICESCR); the Convention on the Elimination of All Forms of Discrimination Against Women (CEDAW); and the Convention on the Rights of the Child (CRC). These documents protect against violations of dignity that promote HIV vulnerability and the promotion of healthy living conditions. Under article 25 of the UDHR, article 12 of the ICESCR, article 12 of the CEDAW, and article 24 of the CRC there is support for conditions that promote health. Article 12 of the ICESCR calls for states to make special provisions for the prevention, treatment, and control of epidemic diseases. The Commission on Human Rights and the Sub-Commission on the Prevention of Discrimination and the Protection of Minorities Resolution, adopted in 1996, calls for the protection of an individual's health rights regardless of the individual's health status, including HIV/AIDS status.[14] Under the nondiscrimination of clauses in articles 2 and 3 of the ICESCR and the ICCPR, article 2 of CEDAW, and article 2 of CRC, the enumerated rights are to be applied regardless of an individual's sex or "other status," which could apply to HIV status. The governments and organizations, such as the World Health Organization (WHO) and the Joint United Nations Program on HIV/AIDS (UNAIDS), that have adopted the precepts set out in these documents therefore uphold the notion that an individual cannot be subject to HIV-related discrimination under the guise of protecting public health.

Since women's dependent role in various aspects of community life leads to their vulnerability toward HIV infection, human rights can be used to empower women within the community by elevating their status. The three main paths to reducing women's risk of HIV are access to education, improved economic status, and increased political power for women. Education, in its broadest sense, is fundamental to expanding an individual's worldview. For women and adolescents increased access to information on HIV/AIDS, reproductive health, and family planning leads to their self-empowerment. The UDHR (article 19) and ICCPR (article 19) protect the right to seek, receive, and impart information and the importance of education in fully developing the human personality within a free society (UDHR, article 26; ICESCR, article 13). With respect to HIV-related information, the ICESCR acknowledges the right of everyone "to enjoy the benefits of scientific progress and its applications" (article 15). It is important for adolescent girls and boys to know about HIV prevention strategies as part of their role as responsible members of a free society. The CRC protects children's rights to seek, receive, and impart information and to have access to education and scientific knowledge (article 28) with a respect for equality of the sexes (article 29). Yet, as much as education can promote well-being and a respect for dignity, by itself education is insufficient to transform women into active members of their communities.

These educational and health programs are most effective when they tailor their message and services to the community they are intended to reach. In the first example of educational messages, sexually active girls and boys have been shown to demonstrate different attitudes toward the use of condoms.[15] Therefore, condom availability programs and sexual health education should address feelings of embarrassment, confidentiality issues, and gender-related norms on control in sexual relationships that appear to inhibit girls from using condoms or accessing condom availability programs. An often-ignored population is women who have sex with women. Studies have shown that such women are at risk for HIV from unprotected sex with men, injection drug use, and from unscreened semen for artificial insemination. Therefore, education programs that counsel this population should be sensitive to the complicated interaction between sexual identity and sexual behavior.[16] With regard to health services, when health centers are gender-sensitive they support the social realities of women's lives: they are in accessible locations, operate during hours that accommodate women who work during the day, and provide child care.

Human rights, in supporting access to education and HIV-information as well as treatment for all individuals, supports the multifaceted determinants to HIV/AIDS infection.

The economic independence of women endows them with the ability to participate freely in society. Living in poverty burdens women's lives, and immediate survival foreshadows a concern with HIV/AIDS. The opportunity to seek employment, earn a wage income, build credit, own property, or manage their own finances is necessary for women to raise their social status and obtain the personal freedom to make choices that benefit their health and the livelihood of their children. Human rights guarantee everyone the right to work, to freely choose employment, to create labor unions, and to work under conditions free of discrimination and where equal work is remunerated with equal pay (UDHR, articles 23 and 24; ICESCR, articles 7 and 8). The CEDAW specifically addresses the rights of women to gain employment and property regardless of marital status as well as the right to work in an environment free of discrimination and harassment (CEDAW, articles 11, 13, and 14.). The rights of women and girls, including access to Social Security benefits, are protected during pregnancy and disability, including HIV/AIDS (UDHR, article 25; ICESCR, article 10.2; Commission on Human Rights and the Sub-Commission on the Prevention of Discrimination and the Protection of Minorities). By achieving financial independence in an environment that protects equality, women gain a sense of individual agency. Elevating their economic status broadens women's vision for their lives and redistributes the responsibility of the caregiving role, which traditionally rests on women and limits their ability to achieve complete health.

When women can actively engage in political and community life, they can participate in developing HIV-prevention programs and policies that are gender-sensitive. Historically women have been instrumental in building self-help organizations. In addition, as the primary domestic caregivers, women can carry these organizational skills into the community for the benefit of social action toward HIV prevention. Often women are restricted from political and public roles because of religious, cultural, and social mores that confine women to the private sphere. However, international human rights documents recognize the importance of every individual to freely participate in the development of society. The UDHR states that "everyone has duties to the community in which alone the free and full development of his personality is possible" (article 29.1). In contributing to the process of HIV/AIDS prevention on the local, national, and international level, women shape policies that affect their lives and help to develop the legal backing of their human rights.

The case of HIV/AIDS in women is an important model for the intersection of health and human rights. Through education and access to sexual health information, both men and women build the communication and negotiation skills to practice safer sex so that they both have equal influence in their sex lives. Ethnicity, race, and class are also major determinants of behavior. Power, control, and self-esteem are critical elements of sexual relationships, and indeed studies have indicated that women with high self-esteem and sense of control over their lives are less likely to participate in sexually risky behaviors.[17] Therefore, changes in gender expectations and gender-related sexual responsibilities are part of the long-term goals of education, economic independence of women, and their free participation in the development of their communities. A gender-sensitive analysis of the HIV/AIDS epidemic shows the necessity of elevating women's status in society by fostering changes in male behaviors.

Violence against and Abuse of Women

Poverty, violence, malnutrition, and overwork are detrimental to health. The threat of violence is a potential at any point in the life span of an individual. Since violence is based on an abuse of power, it often targets the weakest members of the family and society—children, women, and the elderly. Not only is violence a social problem but it is a major burden on health resources. Victims of violence require disproportionate use of health-care resources in comparison to those women not having been exposed to rape or assault.

Certain forms of violence are gender-based: wife or heterosexual partner or homosexual partner abuse, incest, forced prostitution, female genital mutilation/female circumcision (FGM/FC), female child abuse, and honor killings. In addition to physical and sexual violence, other forms of violence are psychological and emotional. While violence may take many forms, it arises when an individual or group uses its power or control over another. In addition, the abuser may use male privilege by treating the woman less than equally; withholding access to money; and using the children as a form of coercion by threatening to remove them or eliminating visitation. Children also may be injured deliberately or accidentally during the assaults on their mother.

Violence against women is common; in fact, it is almost a universal phenomenon.[18] The most common form of abuse occurs when men abuse women; abuse can also occur between men and less frequently between women. Violence and abuse also may occur in teenage and elderly relationships. Despite its staggering prevalence, violence is thought to be the single most underreported crime because of social and legal barriers that impede the accurate collection of data, including varying definitions used in surveys as to what constitutes violence; fear of retaliation; shame about being a victim; irrational feelings of guilt and mistaken sense of loyalty and ambivalent feelings about the abuser, who is often a relative or intimate partner. Violence against women that is perpetrated by a husband, relative, or intimate partner is most prevalent between the ages of twenty-four and thirty-two and is the most pervasive form of gender violence.[19]

Although violence and abuse are an integral part of the lives of many people, and the single greatest cause of injury to women, the subject of violence has not been systematically addressed as a major issue in women's health.[20] Many studies on the prevalence of spousal abuse in developing countries indicate rates ranging from 22 to 75 percent, depending on the sample that was surveyed and how the abuse is defined.[21] However, only a limited number of national surveys address the repercussions of violence on women's health on a global scale. Studies in Tanzania, Ecuador, Chile, New Guinea, Sri Lanka, and Peru report that 60 to 70 percent of women were beaten by their husbands or partners. In at least half of these instances the husband used a weapon. The United Nations Secretariat's Division for the Advancement of Women compiled a study in the mid-1980s on domestic violence in thirty-six countries worldwide and included some of the following associations between violence and health.[22]

- In Kuwait, one-third of women surveyed admitted to being assaulted. Eighty percent of women surveyed said they knew of friends or relatives who had also been victims of violence.
- Fifty percent of married women surveyed in the largest slum of Bangkok admitted to habitual abuse by their husbands. Of a group of malnourished children treated at a Bangkok social services center, 25 percent came from families where the mother was regularly beaten by her partner.
- In the United States, 30 percent of female homicides were committed by a husband or partner.

Prevalence figures for domestic violence diagnosed in U.S. health-care settings vary according to the service provided: 25 percent of the women who seek treatment at hospital emergency departments and 37 percent of women who seek treatment for a violent injury do so because of domestic violence. Of women seen in primary care offices, 25 percent have been abused at some time in their lives; one out of six pregnant women is abused during pregnancy.[23]

Rape

Rape and other sexual crimes are underreported probably because of the stigma associated with this crime. Most of the perpetrators are known to the victim. In the United States several studies report that the occurrence of rape is between one in five and one in seven women over their lifetime.[24] Cases of rape in the United States reach a peak incidence between the ages of eighteen and twenty-four.[25] Many adolescents believe that there are times when it is acceptable for a man to physically force a woman to engage in sex. Forced sex within marriage constitutes rape. In many cultures women do not recognize the abuse as such because they have been socialized to believe that the husband's marital rights include physical and emotional punishment. It is important that the society and the legal and medical systems sympathize with the victim of violence and rape and create the environment to permit detection and treatment. Where the perpetrator of the rape is a friend, relative, or family member whom the victim sees on a regular basis, there is a risk of revictimization. Health-care professionals, representatives of the law, or concerned friends can detect the rape, develop a safe plan, and help the victim to leave. Barriers that prevent health-care personnel from effectively detecting and treating rape include their own bias resulting from unresolved personal violence; embarrassment; ignorance and lack of training; poor community services; and fear of legal involvement. Complications of rape include the possibility of pregnancy and the contraction of a sexually transmitted disease, including HIV.

Factors Responsible for Violence against Women and Girls

Violence will persist in locations that condone the abuse and beating of women and children and classify this behavior as being consistent with normal gender and family roles. While violence presents a serious risk to women's health, family violence traditionally has not been perceived as violence; thus attempts at detection, regulation, punishment, or education have been nonexistent. The health-care system and law enforcement have been slow to respond to these problems. In fact, behaviors that would be criminalized between strangers, such as assault, have been ignored when they occur within the family.

Other cross-cultural factors that foster domestic violence include the association of masculinity with domination, toughness, and honor. Abuse within the family is perpetuated by the economic dependence of women on men; legal systems that give women an inferior status to men and do not have mechanisms to protect women; insensitivity of police and the courts to women's issues; the tendency to regard domestic violence as a private matter; the failure of the economic structure to empower women to be financially independent by limiting their access to education and jobs; preventing women from being able to access cash; discriminatory laws defining limits of property rights for women and inheritance; the acceptance of violence as legitimate; the ability of men to control the behavior of women and have proprietary rights over them; and a political organizational structure that marginalizes the needs of women so they cannot seek relief.[26]

Historically women in the United States have not been protected against gender-based violence, but some progress has been made in publicizing partner abuse and keeping guns out of the possession of men involved in previous occurrences of domestic violence. The renewal in 2000 by Congress of the 1994 Violence Against Women Act and increased advocacy of women's rights, in this regard, are necessary beginning steps.

Prevention of Violence

While domestic violence occurs throughout the world, in all races, religions, and economic classes, the changes in rate of occurrence may be influenced by race and socioeconomic status. For example, a May 2000 report from the U.S. Department of Justice's Bureau of Justice Statistics describes a widespread change in reported violence involving intimate partners. The results of the study underscore how the likelihood of violence depends on complex and interacting factors. One of the reasons suggested for the decline in violence against black women in the United States in the 1990s is that women began to take advantage of resources available to them since the enactment and implementation of stricter laws protecting women against violent partners. Another possible factor in the decline of partner abuse among African-Americans was the absence from the home of violent black men, who, compared to whites, receive disproportionately long prison terms.[27] On the other hand, although white women were more often the advocates for these reforms, as a group they did not benefit from a reduction in partner violence between 1997 and 1998, when the incidence of violence against white women increased for the first time since 1976.

Women are at greater risk for violence when they attempt to leave abusive relationships. In the United States increased rates of partner abuse among white women in comparison to black women might be explained by the more frequent use of protection orders by white women. As more support groups are created and legal advocacy services are directed to protect individuals against domestic violence, women may rely on options to protect themselves so that they do not have to resort to homicide to end a dangerous relationship. However, men still kill as a manifestation of uncontrolled anger. As black women have become more educated, they have come to possess greater financial resources to leave dangerous relationships. Domestic violence is about control; since many men reason that, "If I can't have her, nobody will," the risk to women rises as they attempt to leave.

Health-care providers are in a uniquely favorable position to diagnose and treat abuse as well as refer patients to available resources. The presence of health-care providers who are familiar with the community and professional and legal resources is of great assistance to the patient. It also helps diminish the social isolation that these woman experience. Health-care providers who discuss domestic violence as a health issue with all their patients provide a supportive environment by increasing awareness of safe options for the victim and her children. Globally, members of the community should recognize domestic violence as a crime and work to protect women and children who are victims and see that offending partners are punished.

Sex Selection

In non-Western countries like China, Korea, and India, male offspring are preferred. In these societies girls are considered burdens because they have a lower status and require a dowry for marriage. A life as an unmarried woman is not an option. Females usually do not get educational opportunities or work outside the home and therefore are untrained to support themselves and their families. Today sex selection prior to birth can be achieved with amniocentesis or chorionic villus sampling. Female fetuses are selectively aborted. Where such technology is not applied, female children will be discreetly killed shortly after birth. In countries where there is a strong preference for males, the rate of neonatal death in girls is more than six times that of boys; there also is a higher neonatal mortality for girls born to families with no sons. Sex selection continues after birth by means of preferential allocation of food and access to needed medication.[28] Population studies estimate that, as a result of these practices, at least 100 million women are "missing" from the world population, primarily from China, Korea, and India.[29] Aside from immediate malnutrition, the long-term effects of depriving girls of protein- and iron-rich foods include chronic anemia, exacerbated by menstruation, and complications of pregnancy.

Factors that influence food deprivation of girls include education status, class, occupation, region, migratory patterns, and presence of land reform[30]; selective malnutrition occurs among the poor in some areas and among the more prosperous in others. Where food deprivation occurs, boys are breastfed longer, receive supplementary milk, subsequently are given protein-rich food (when it is available) such as milk, meat, fish, and eggs, and are given more than one portion, even when girls have received little if anything.

Studies suggest that where there are more opportunities for education of girls and mothers, sex selection decreases and greater investment is made in girls. Even where there are home visits to educate families about maintaining their daughters, the presence of prenatal sex determination technologies may enable couples to prevent the birth of girls. As long as education is withheld and women are deprived of self-determination, old traditions harmful to girls and women will be maintained.

Female Genital Mutilation/Female Circumcision

FGM/FC is a ritual performed on approximately 5 million girls per year and involves between 80 and 120 million women in more than thirty countries, from Muslim, Christian, and indigenous African cultures, including individuals from varied ethnic groups and socioeconomic classes.[31] The practice is not an established Muslim tradition, nor is it seen in Saudi Arabia or the Gulf states. Despite international efforts to criminalize the custom, the number of procedures may be increasing. With immigration the practice is moving to the United States, Canada, and Great Britain, and physicians from all countries are now confronted with public health problems that result from serious immediate and chronic medical complications of this procedure. The estimated numbers of girls and women with FGM/FC in Great Britain is 20,000.[32] In the United States in 1996 more than 150,000 women and girls were at risk. In Egypt the Giza Reproductive Morbidity Study, performed in 1989–1990 in two rural Giza villages adjacent to Cairo, determined that the entire sample, including women originating from Cairo or other urban areas, had been circumcised. In this study the extent of FGM depended on the age of the woman, with older women having more extensive genital removal.[33]

Where practiced, FGM/FC reflects cultural standards of femininity, the "socialization" of girls, and a physical sign of a girl's marriageability; it is perpetuated by all members of society. FGM/FC is a public event symbolizing the onset or approach of menstruation. It is usually performed by midwives on girls between the ages of six and twelve. The many cultural justifications for FGM/FC are associated with morality and family honor and include preservation of virginity and protection against promiscuity. The roots of these beliefs are deep and include religious customs, distinctions of gender roles, and superstitions.[34] It also has been a symbol of social status in Egypt and the Sudan. Women who live in societies where marriage is the only guarantee for economic security believe that the ritual is not optional but a prerequisite for marriage since the men require wives whose genitals have been excised.

FGM/FC is performed by a variety of individuals from trained midwives to untrained practitioners. The use of soap and water and the availability of needles and knives vary. The extent of the cutting and stitching varies. A razor or glass shard is often used by lay practitioners as the cutting instrument. The procedure ranges from partial or complete removal of the clitoris to total infibulation, which involves removal of the clitoris, cutting of the labia minora, and cutting and stitching together of the labia majora to cover the urethra and entrance to the vagina. Only a small opening is left for the passage of urine and menstrual blood.

If a comparable procedure were to be performed in men, it would range from amputation of most of the penis to total removal of the penis along with some of the scrotum. Although it is important to understand the cultural perception that FGM/FC aims to protect women and is in their best interest, the procedure results in genital removal and scarring.[35]

Usually girls and women have little knowledge of the anatomy and function of their reproductive organs. They are taught that their genitals are the property of their husbands. Because of this and the fact that very few of these women were warned about the impending procedure before it occurred, the relationship between limiting women's sexual pleasure and the medical and psychological consequences of FGM/FC are very complex.

Common complications include immediate hemorrhage, severe pain, shock, and death. More chronic complications include painful intercourse and loss of sexual pleasure with intercourse, chronic anemia, growth retardation, infection, abscesses, ulcers, blood stream infection, tetanus, gangrene, obstruction of urine flow, chronic urinary tract infection, obstruction of menstrual blood flow, menstrual pain, chronic pelvic and back pain, chronic pelvic infection, cysts, scars, recurrent stitch abscesses, risks with child birth, interference with delivery, tears, vesicovaginal fistulas (abnormal communication between vagina and bladder), and urinary incontinence. The psychological effects of FGM/FC vary depending on the extent of the procedure and whether the practice is common and legal. Girls and women who live in countries where FGM/FC is practiced experience conflicts between the trauma and complications of the ritual and the need to adhere to the social necessities to be "good marriageable girls." While the extent of sexual impairment, including the ability to achieve orgasm, is unsubstantiated in the research, often most of the girls and women subjected to FGM/FC manifest subtle psychological symptoms that may be difficult to uncover because of strong forces of denial and pres-sures exerted by social norms in these communities.[36]

Women and girls who have undergone FGM/FC and immigrated to countries where the practice is neither performed nor condoned experience a different set of complications, which range from problems with develop-ing sexual identity to problems with childbirth when they are attended by health-care professionals with little or no experience in this area. Immi-gration and travel have brought this health issue into countries where it has heretofore been absent, necessitating the dissemination of information to health-care workers and members of the judicial system so that they can prevent, detect, and treat girls and women with FGM/FC.

Multilateral agencies such as the World Health Organization (WHO) and many governments have opposed the practice on the basis of human rights violations. In 1993 the Vienna Declaration of the World Conference on Human Rights ruled that FGM/FC is a violation of human rights. This policy has been adopted by other United Nations health and human rights organizations. In addition, statements condemning FGM/FC and calling for its abolition have been issued by the International Federation of Gynaecology and Obstetrics and the World Health Assembly (the highest authority within WHO). This latter resolution was sponsored by several African nations and Lebanon. Several countries have criminalized FGM/FC. In 1996 the U.S. Congress passed a law making FGM/FC a felony punishable by up to a five-year prison term. But criminalization of FGM/FC is insufficient in eradicating the ritual. Health-care profession-als can play an important role by validating a family's concerns about promiscuity while educating girls and young women so that they make ap-propriate choices about sexuality that are consistent with the family's val-ues without FGM/FC.

Social and Political Action to Curb Violence

As women have organized to oppose totalitarian regimes, the oppression in their own lives has become an issue. In the 1970s the UN Decade for Women brought attention to the importance of women in international development and provided international money and support for women-focused nongovernmental organizations (NGOs). Grassroots community-based actions against gender-based violence include neighborhood women watches, social sanctions, and public humiliation of the perpetrator. In In-dia government-sponsored affirmative action is directed at improving the lot of women. The government has mandated that a certain number of col-lege seats and government jobs be reserved for women. In 1992 the Pan-chayat Act gave women one-third of council seats as well as one-third of village chief positions. Women in India have formed Women's Rights Unions, and there has also been activity to outlaw child marriages.

Gender-based violence is now emerging as an international issue. Women's health advocates have done much to promote the issue, often despite the official indifference of world health leaders. The view that violence against women is a factor in the AIDS pandemic and should be considered in strategies for AIDS prevention has gained currency. The challenge moving forward is to be able to consolidate the grassroots activities and the international interest in gender-based violence so that national polices are changed.

Although representatives of many countries have signed international agreements promising to rewrite or repeal laws that discriminate against women, these agreements have been ignored. In Spain and Portugal violence against women was unofficially condoned until these countries joined the European Union. Organizations like Equality Now, in New York, are focusing on holding these governments accountable for these agreements. The support of enlightened men is critical to the resolution of the problem of violence against women.

Human rights codes uphold the individual's right to well-being. However, the ways in which societies provide for that right differ. Where women have poor health status, this is usually attributable to issues of access to health care and the state's health services. Another factor that compromises women's access to health care is the rift between the ideals of a given health system and the prevalence in some locations of superstitions. Women will not access health care if they have a belief system that does not include modern medicine or when they consider themselves unworthy of healing. For example, in India some village women believe that illness is caused by evil spirits lurking in trees. Furthermore, many of these Indian women believe that their worth is determined exclusively by giving birth to sons and by laboring in the fields.[37]

Even when women have access to health care, their diagnosis and treatment may be compromised because they have not been able to benefit from the scientific information derived from research. Data from men cannot be extrapolated to women if women have been excluded from clinical trials. Racial differences, such as in the metabolism of drugs and health outcomes, must also be taken into account in clinical trials. Research must be conducted on diverse populations in order to have wide applicability. Improved care for all women must thus address scientific, ethical, and political issues.

Governments vary in how they prioritize health. Nations modeled on the welfare state provide some type of universal health care because the state considers health a public good comparable to housing, employment, and education. Conversely, in some countries, like Afghanistan, controlled by religious extremists, women have poor if any health care since they cannot be attended by male physicians and are themselves barred from medical school and all types of education. In the United States health care is a case of both excess and deprivation. Women who belong to disadvantaged groups, and who generally lack health insurance, are at great risk of poor health. For example, they are much less likely to access preventive services, like mammography, than insured women.

The advancement of community and global health is bound with the status of women's health. Central to this issue is what governments and societies believe is possible in terms of health and what patients believe they deserve. Women as health-care managers for themselves and their families substantially influence the capacity of human development and ultimately social justice. The advancement of social justice is not based on the correction of past inequities but on present practices, which include addressing both subtle and blatant health discriminatory practices.

Reproductive Rights and Access to Pharmaceuticals

As the twenty-first century began, world population was estimated at six billion people. The United Nations estimate of world population in 2050 is 7.7 to 11.2 billion. Because of changes in culture and the availability of contraception, the birthrate in developing countries has been dropping. But unplanned and unwanted pregnancies continue to occur. It is estimated that, of the 200 million pregnancies each year, approximately 50 percent are unplanned and 25 percent unwanted. The unwanted children that result often become the victims of various forms of neglect, including abuse or abandonment. Couples who have the knowledge and resources to plan their pregnancies have greater control of their future and healthier women and children result. But contraception is not a substitute for good health-care services. The combination of the ability to choose contraception, access to better education and health care, as well as equal rights for women is essential.

The core rights issue in reproductive health is the ability of women to have agency and make decisions that shape the course of their lives, such as determination of when to start a family, its size, and the interval between children. These rights entail services related to family planning, maternal health, treatment of HIV/AIDS and sexually transmitted infections, infertility, and reproductive cancer. Reproductive rights include the right to a safe and legal abortion. Women should be able to make decisions about reproduction free of discrimination, coercion, and violence.

Globally there has been a wide spectrum of governmental policies aimed at family planning. In the People's Republic of China, public policy has strictly curtailed the number of children to one child per family, with punishments for those who disobey. In India public information campaigns about contraception have increased usage and decreased family size. The United States has seen a long-standing political, religious, and moral controversy over access to and the legality of abortion. For some time issues of contraception and abortion have consumed the energy of American women and advocates of freedom of choice. Worldwide, there are an estimated 26 million pregnancies legally terminated and an estimated 20 million illegal procedures with an associated mortality of 78,000 deaths. In the United States the mortality of surgical abortion is 0.6 per 100,000 women.[38] But because of harassment of physicians who perform abortions, in 1995, 86 percent of U.S. counties had no health-care provider to perform this procedure. There is interest in safe drugs for the termination of pregnancy, particularly in areas where qualified personnel are absent. Because the abortifacients do not require anesthesia, they may be used safely very early in the pregnancy. The availability of contraception varies around the world. Emerging nations with large populations and high poverty rates have seen decreasing financial support for contraceptive programs because of political and economic crises as well as shrinking U.S. aid.

Teen Pregnancy and Adolescent Access to Contraception

Adolescent pregnancies have traditionally been considered a private family matter. In many developing countries, arranged marriages for girls at a very young age have been socially desirable. Consequently these young girls are not permitted to complete their formal schooling and become teenage mothers, frequently having sequential pregnancies. With improvements in public health, availability of antibiotics, and improved survival of infants and children, in developing countries there is now an opportunity to advocate for delaying the age of marriage and permitting the education of girls.

Whereas sexual activity in teenage girls in developing nations occurs mainly in the context of their early marriages, in developed nations teenagers often engage in sex before they are married. The requirements for parental consent and the absence of confidentiality often deter teenagers from seeking needed contraceptive and reproductive services. Considerable interest has been focused on adolescent pregnancy because of public awareness of their negative social and economic repercussions. Adolescents have a greater likelihood of having a premature, low-birth-weight infant with all the resulting complications. They also are less prepared for the financial, emotional, and psychological consequences of caring for a child. Teen mothers frequently leave school, require public assistance, lack occupational skills, and have repeat adolescent pregnancies.

In the United States there has been a decline in teenage pregnancies, which reflects reductions in the numbers of sexually active adolescents and the increased use of contraceptives by sexually active teens. Although condom use has increased since 1980, adolescents use them inconsistently. Abortion rates are also declining (with half of all abortions in the U.S. occurring in women under twenty-five). The teen birthrate in the United States remains among the highest in the industrialized world, and the proportion of unmarried teenage pregnant mothers continues to rise.

In the United States and other Western nations, health-care professionals, politicians, and religious organizations discourage both youthful marriage and premarital teen sex. Yet the media is saturated with sexuality, and thus teens receive mixed messages. Efforts focused on motivating adolescents to delay early sexual experience must take account of the ambivalence about sex in adult society. In societies where there is no future for the poor, sex gives immediate gratification and a baby gives status to the new parents, even if this attention is short-lived. Efforts to prevent pregnancy must also be linked to prevention of sexually transmitted disease. Linking prevention of pregnancy with abstinence and condom education programs is vital in curbing the growth of STDs, not least of which is HIV. Ultimately, success in preventing teenage pregnancy depends on the adolescents themselves, who must have a clear sense that they have a good future, which early child-bearing would limit.

Adolescent pregnancy prevention requires more than education about reproduction and access to family planning. Youngsters need education about the risks of substance abuse and the relationship of this behavior to unplanned pregnancy as well as preventive strategies. Encouraging male responsibility in teenage pregnancies is one vital step; social norms that depict responsible male sexual behavior can be revived through the media and within communities. Another step is to incorporate family planning services in the physician-patient relationship, with accessible, affordable family planning and outreach services, with convenient hours, situated near schools. Efficient linkages between these services and schools is critical.

Often teenagers do not seek help from health-care professionals because they do not view these individuals as confidential sources of care. They fear that information will be disclosed to their parents or guardians who will disapprove of or abuse them. When adolescents are aware of their rights to confidentiality they are far more likely to use medical facilities for HIV testing and contraceptive services. Among many physicians in the United States, confidentiality in providing reproductive care to adolescents is a controversial issue. Physicians are concerned about parental rights and reactions. But minors do have rights to obtain confidential medical care; physicians, nurses, social workers, teachers, counselors, and advocates must become more familiar with the legislation that permits teenagers to receive confidential services. The U.S. Supreme Court has found that minors have a constitutional right to privacy, which gives them a certain amount of autonomy in deciding reproductive health issues. Federal laws guarantee minors access to confidential family planning services. The courts have consistently struck down laws that prevent minors access to contraception without parental consent.

Although it is important to encourage youngsters to communicate with their families, there is evidence that mandating parental consent for abortion delays treatment and increases risks.[39] The Supreme Court has ruled that requirements for parental consent for abortion are not constitutional unless they provide for rapid confidential judicial bypass procedures. The American College of Obstetricians and Gynecologists and the Society for Adolescent Medicine have supported physicians' recognition of the importance of patient confidentiality and the parental role as well as the need for communication between adolescents and their parents. However, the physician must act appropriately to protect a minor where the teen pregnancy occurs as a result of incest or abuse by a relative. In these circumstances, teenagers may not wish to disclose the pregnancy or their intention to seek an abortion. The provision of teen pregnancy prevention requires interdisciplinary care. In view of the diverse needs of adolescents, federal support should include a full spectrum of services beyond abstinence.

Promoting Women's Health

Since the founding of the UDHR in 1948, and with the greater awareness of women's status internationally achieved in the 1970s, there has been an increased collaboration of governments and nongovernmental groups to discuss the advancement of women's lives. (See appendix.) The 1995 United Nations World Conference on Women in Beijing was one such example. In the years since Beijing, continued inaction on the value of women threatens women's health. Women are still the majority of the world's poor; they labor in unsafe working conditions with few if any social services; and they are underrepresented in leadership positions where policies are decided. Even within their homes, many women are treated as chattel, subject to abuse, and unable to control intimate sexual activity. Educating women is insufficient to overcome women's rights abuses without social support and access to resources that empower women to fulfill their potential as individuals committed to their communities.

Health-care policy and practice concerning women's health must take account of several issues: the health of girls and women over the life span; improvement in the inclusion of women in research protocols and the analysis of findings to include sex and gender; safe and healthy work environments; detecting and eliminating traditions that have a negative impact on women's health; treating women with respect and providing for their education so that women can participate in their care. When international human rights doctrines are ineffective, whether because they are unenforceable without national or regional laws or only sporadically enforced, the role of the health-care professional takes on great importance. Health-care workers can document human rights violations, expose abuse, and advocate for the elimination of the abuse.

As respected community members, health-care workers have the unique opportunity to point out potential injury to women before it may be apparent to most, including the women involved. Physicians and health-care workers can be effective in increasing public awareness by joining or forming coalitions that work to recognize and eliminate human rights abuses and change laws; that influence the drafting of new legislation; and that induce changes in the judicial and police systems to advance human rights for women.

Assessments of the status of women show that even where there is legislative support to improve women's health and well-being, a better system of holding nations to standards of accountability is still required. Support of women's rights may still be met with cultural and political unwillingness. In some countries crimes against women go unpunished; women may not inherit property and lack the right to vote. Educating men to support the value of women and their rights promotes changes in male behavior, which in turn allows the advancement of women.

Human rights are not privileges but an inextricable part of being human. Indeed, because the attainment of health is dependent on the protection of all human rights, the status of women's health is a representation of the value of women's dignity in society. Therefore, the appreciation of women and their role in society is an affirmation of the value of human dignity. Recent advances in human rights have provided the legal underpinnings for the protection of women's health. However, the universal acceptance and application of these principals remain as the future challenge.

Appendix: A Chronology of Support for Women's Human Rights[40]

1946	UN Commission on the Status of Women: calls for global monitoring of activities related to women and promotion of the rights of women.
1952	UN Convention on the Political Rights of Women: mandates political equality for women throughout the world through granting the right to vote and hold office.
1957, 1962	Conventions guaranteeing equal rights to women in marriage and divorce.
1967	Declaration on the Elimination of Discrimination against Women.
1976–1986	Decade of the Woman. The World Conference on Women initiates the collection of statistics on women.
1979	Convention on the Elimination of All Forms of Discrimination Against Women.
1980	World Conference on Women, Copenhagen: further collection of statistics on the status of women.
1985	World Conference on Women, Nairobi: reviews the collected statistics about women's conditions and adopts "Forward-Looking Strategies for the Advancement of Women."
1989	Convention on the Rights of the Child.
1993	Second Conference on Human Rights: identified gender-based violence as an abuse of women's health rights.
1995	World Conference on Women, Beijing: established specific goals and timetables which could serve as benchmarks to evaluate the progress of governments on issues such as the elimination of laws that discriminate against women and increasing the number of women in public service.

NOTES

*The authors dedicate this essay to the memory of Jonathan Mann, M.D., M.P.H., educator, health care activist, and the first Director of the World Health Organization's Global Program on AIDS. He understood and promoted the linkage between women's human rights and women's health.

1. National Academy of Women's Health, Medical Education, *Women's Health in the Curriculum: A Resource Guide for Faculty*, Glenda Donoghue, ed. (Philadelphia, 1996), p. 10.

2. United Nations, *World's Women 1970–1990: Trends and Statistics.* Social Statistics and Indicators Series K no. 8 (New York, 1991).

3. World Health Organization, *The World Health Report 1999* (Geneva, 1999).

4. This WHO survey estimates HIV/AIDS prevalence based on reports from WHO member states. Therefore the reliability of the data is dependent on the reliability of the state in accurately reporting these cases.

5. D. Huddleston, "Women and AIDS/HIV," citing National Institute of Allergy and Infectious Diseases, in *Annual Review of Women's Health 2,* edited by B. J. McElmurry and R. Spreen Parker (New York, 1995), p. 226.

6. P. Farmer, *Inequities and Inequalities: The Modern Plagues* (Berkeley, Calif., 1999).

7. D. Joslin and R. Harrison, "The 'Hidden Patient': Older Relatives Raising Children Orphaned by AIDS," *Journal of the American Medical Women's Association* 53, no. 2 (1998): 65–71.

8. L. M. Carpenter et al., "Rates of HIV-1 Transmission Within Marriage in Rural Uganda in Relation to the HIV Sero-status of the Partners," *AIDS* 13 (1999): 1083–1089.

9. Carpenter et al. (1999), p. 1087.

10. C. Ingram Fogel, "Sexually Transmitted Diseases," in *Annual Review of Women's Health 2,* edited by B. J. McElmurry and R. Spreen Parker (New York, 1995), p. 206.

11. M. Chamberland, J. W. Ward, and J. W. Curran, "Epidemiology and Prevention of AIDS and HIV Infection," in *Principles and Practice of Infectious Diseases,* 4th ed., edited by Gerald L. Mandell, John E. Bennet, and Raphael Dolin (New York, 1995), p. 1174.

12. J. M. Mann, "Human Rights and AIDS: The Future of the Pandemic," in *Health and Human Rights: A Reader,* edited by Jonathan M. Mann et al. (New York, 1999), p. 216.

13. H. Jackson, "Societal Determinants of Women's Vulnerability to HIV Infection in Southern Africa," *Health and Human Rights* 2, no. 4 (1998): 9–14.

14. See D. Whelan, "Human Rights Approaches to an Expanded Response to Address Women's Vulnerablity to HIV/AIDS," *Health and Human Rights* 3, no. 1 (1998): 24; and Commission on Human Rights and the Sub-Commission on the Prevention and Discrimination and the Protection of Minorities Resolution 1996/43 and E/CN.4/Sub.2/1996/L/21.

15. S. Guttmacher et al., "Gender Differences: Differences in Attitudes and Use of Condom Availability Programs among Sexually Active Students in New York City Public High Schools," *JAMWA* 50, no. 3–4 (1995): 99–102.

16. M. B. Kennedy et al., "Assessing HIV Risk among Women Who Have Sex With Women: Scientific and Communication Issues," *JAMWA* 50, no. 3–4 (1995): 103–107.

17. See, for example, D. Paone et al., "Sex, Drugs, and Syringe Exchange in New York City: Women's Experiences," *Journal of the American Medical Women's Association* 50, no. 3–4 (1995): 109–114.

18. See, for example, D. Levinson, *Violence in Cross-Cultural Perspective* (Newbury Park, Calif., 1989); P. R. Sanday, "The Socio-Cultural Context of Rape: A Cross-Cultural Study," *Journal of Social Issues* 37, no. 4 (1981): 5.

19. L.L. Heise et al., "Violence Against Women: A Neglected Public Health Issue in Less Developed Countries," *Social Science Medicine* 39, no. 9 (1994).

20. United Nations, *World's Women 1970–1990: Trends and Statistics,* Social Statistics and Indicators Series K no. 8 (New York, 1991), p. 19.

21. L.L. Heise et al., "Violence Against Women" (1994).

22. *World's Women 1970–1990: Trends and Statistics* (1991).

23. S. A. Eisenstadt and L. Bancroft, "Domestic Violence," *New England Journal of Medicine* 341, no. 12 (1999): 886–892.

24. M. Koss, "Detecting the Scope of Rape: A Review of the Prevalence Research Methods," *Journal of Interpersonal Violence* 8, no. 198 (1993).

25. Anne Flitcraft, "Violence, Abuse and Assault over the Life Phases," in *Textbook of Women's Health,* edited by L. A. Wallis et al. (Philadelphia, 1998).

26. Levinson, *Violence in Cross-Cultural Perspective* (1989).

27. As reported by Fox Butterfield, "Study Shows Causal Divide in Domestic Violence Cases," *New York Times,* 18 May 2000.

28. Barbara Miller, "Social Class, Gender and Intrahousehold Food Allocations to Children in South Asia," *Social Science Medicine* 44, no. 11 (1997): 1685–1695.

29. Gita Sen and Rachel C. Snow, eds., *Power and Decison: The Social Control of Reproduction* (Boston, 1994).

30. Miller, "Social Class, Gender and Intrahousehold Food Allocations" (1997).

31. Controversy surrounds the appropriate term to describe the ritual. Use of the term "female circumcision" is believed by some to be euphemistic, as it masks the violence the ritual entails and the negative impact on women's health and sexuality; those who object to its use also decry the parallel suggested with male circumcision. Those who place the ritual in a cultural context oppose the term "female genital mutilation," which they believe slanders a tradition. See Layli Miller Bashir, "Female Genital Mutilation: Balancing Intolerance of the Practice with Tolerance of the Culture," *Journal of Women's Health* 6, no. 1 (1997): 11–14.

32. Tammi L. Bishop, "Female Genital Mutilation," *Journal of the National Medical Association* 89, no. 4 (1997): 233–236.

33. C. V. Dugger, "Tug of Taboos: African Genital Rite vs. American Law," *New York Times,* 28 December 1996. H. Khattab, "Women's Perception of Sexuality in Rural Giza." Reproductive Health Working Group Monographs in *Reproductive Health.* Cairo: the Population Council Regional Office for West Asia and North Africa, November 1, 1996.

34. Bashir, "Female Genital Mutilation" (1997).

35. Nahid Toubia, *A Technical Manual for Health Care Providers Caring for Women with Circumcision* (New York, 1999).

36. Nahid Toubia, "Female Circumcision as a Public Health Issue," *New England Journal of Medicine* 331, no. 11 (September 1996): 712–716.

37. Mary Anne Weaver, "Gandhi's Daughters: India's Poorest Women Embark on an Epic Social Experiment," *New Yorker,* 10 January 2000, 50–61. R. M. Martinez and M. Lillie-Blanton, "Why Race and Gender Remain Important in Health Services Research." *American Journal of Preventative Medicine*, 12, 5 (1996): 316–317.

38. Sophie Christine-Maitre, Philippe Bouchard, and Irving Spitz, "Medical Termination of Pregnancy," *New England Journal of Medicine* 342, no. 13 (March 2000): 946–964.

39. American Academy of Pediatrics. "The Adolescent's Right to Confidential Care When Considering Abortion," *Pediatrics* 97 (1996): 746–751.

40. Adapted from United Nations, *World's Women 1970–1990: Trends and Statistics* (New York, 1991), p. 7.

The Rights of the Girl Child
Julia Chill and Susan Kilbourne

Prelude: Rosario's Story

∽ ROSARIO was the ninth child of twelve in a poor family in Manila.[1] Her mother died when she was nine years old. For a while her older brothers and sisters cared for the younger children. After a few years they were unable to keep their small house, and the children were split up and left to fend for themselves. That is how Rosario ended up on the streets in Manila, scavenging for food. It was there that she met Peter, a twelve-year-old who had been on the streets for several years. In addition to begging, he also worked the streets for a local brothel. After a few days of scavenging together, Peter led Rosario to the brothel and told her that she could trade doing odd chores for food and shelter.

Also in Manila at that time was Heinrich Rimer (not his real name), an Austrian medical doctor who visited Manila frequently for rest and relaxation. Dr. Rimer was well known in Manila for his predilection for young girls. During this visit, like others, he contacted Peter at the brothel and asked him to bring a young female to his hotel.

Peter brought Rosario. Dr. Rimer paid Peter twelve dollars and asked him to stay. He gave Rosario a drink with a powerful muscle relaxant in it and then proceeded to rape her with Peter watching. Rosario said later that the doctor hurt her terribly. But even then he was not finished. He took out a vibrator from his suitcase and inserted it into Rosario's vagina, where it broke into several pieces. Dr. Rimer then removed the vibrator, paid Peter another ten dollars, and told him to take Rosario away.

Out on the street Rosario complained that she was hurting. Peter took her to a local doctor who gave her pain pills. They told no one what had happened to Rosario. The pills helped a bit and Rosario felt better for a few days. Then she began to complain of a fever and chills and general malaise. When they went back to the doctor, he gave her an antibiotic. She felt better again for a while, but about four weeks later, she developed severe pains in her abdomen and the fever returned. She wandered the streets like this for several more weeks before she collapsed. She was taken to the local hospital, where, three days before she died, she told a nun what had happened to her.

The nun ordered an autopsy and several pieces of the vibrator were found in Rosario's cervical area. The nun reported Rosario's death to the police, who went looking for Peter. When they found him, he told them the story of Dr. Rimer, who visited frequently and always asked for young girls. For the first time, the government was galvanized. Law enforcement agents contacted officials in Austria, and Dr. Rimer was identified. He was extradited to the Philippines and tried, but let off on a technicality. He returned to Austria and resumed his medical practice.

It is impossible to tell how may Rosarios there are in the world today. A recent estimate indicated that 75,000 child prostitutes now populate the Philippines.[2] But the very nature of sexual trafficking—the underground furtiveness—precludes an accurate count of the number of child victims. Similarly, it is impossible to say for sure how many children are serving as soldiers in the world's conflicts, but reliable estimates run into the hundreds of thousands, with girls a substantial proportion of that number.[3] It is also difficult to say how many girls are working as domestic servants, but in one city in Bangladesh alone, estimates place the number at 300,000.

Horrible things happen to children every day, in every corner of the world. Boys and girls alike face unimaginable abuses, exploitative labor, forced military recruitment, exposure to fatal disease, and denial of fundamental human rights—all exacerbated by the fact that the individuals who suffer are so small. For girls, the human rights violations are compounded by gender bias, physical limitations, and traditional societal roles. From the earliest stages of life, girls experience persistent inequality and discrimination that result in physical and psychological harm. Infanticide, differential access to nutrition and health care, child marriage, forced prostitution and trafficking, rape, and domestic abuse all harm the chances of their surviving into adulthood, much less as healthy women.

This essay focuses on human rights problems faced by children, especially those problems of special significance to girls. The international legal framework for analyzing these problems and searching for solutions is

the Convention on the Rights of the Child (CRC). As discussed briefly below, several other international instruments are relevant to many of these
issues; however, the CRC was drafted specifically to address children's
needs.

Background to the Convention on the Rights of the Child

The first international document establishing the concept of general children's rights was the Declaration of Geneva, adopted by the League of Nations in 1924. This declaration recognized that "mankind owes to the
child the best it has to give," and its five brief principles focused on the
provision of care for all children. In 1959 the United Nations General
Assembly adopted a more comprehensive Declaration on the Rights of the
Child. The 1959 declaration included not only principles that echoed the
care and protection model of the previous declaration but principles that
began to establish rights for the child.[4] The rights language is evident in
the preamble and principle one, which proclaims that "every child, without any exception whatsoever, shall be entitled to these rights, without distinction or discrimination on account of race, colour, sex, language,
religion, political or other opinion, national or social origin, property,
birth or other status, whether of himself or of his family." However, neither the Declaration of Geneva nor the 1959 Declaration on the Rights of
the Child were legally binding international law.

The first reference to children's rights in legally binding United Nations instruments occurred in the International Covenant on Civil and
Political Rights (ICCPR) and the International Covenant on Economic,
Social and Cultural Rights (ICESCR), two treaties that, with the Universal Declaration of Human Rights, are commonly referred to as the International Bill of Human Rights.

Most of the articles of the ICCPR and the ICESCR employ general language that refers to all human beings, including children. However, article
24 of the ICCPR specifically recognizes the child, stating that every child
has a right to a name, to a nationality, and "to such measures of protection
as are required by his status as a minor, on the part of his family, society,
and the State." ICCPR article 10 also notes that "juvenile offenders shall
be segregated from adults and be accorded treatment appropriate to their
age and legal status." The ICESCR also addresses the child in article 10,
requiring that

> special measures of protection and assistance should be taken on behalf of all
> children and young persons without any discrimination for reasons of
> parentage or other conditions. Children and young persons should be pro-

tected from economic and social exploitation. Their employment in work harmful to their morals or health or dangerous to life or likely to hamper their normal development should be punishable by law. States should also set age limits below which the paid employment of child laborers should be prohibited and punishable by law.

In 1979 the United Nations celebrated the twentieth anniversary of the Declaration of the Rights of the Child by proclaiming it the International Year of the Child. During that year the Polish government proposed the drafting of a legally binding convention focusing on the rights of the child. Although the initial plan envisioned a treaty based primarily on the 1959 Declaration, the rejection of the CRC's first draft led to a vastly expanded treaty.[5] Over the next ten years, representatives from governments and nongovernmental organizations (NGOs) participated in the drafting of the CRC. It was unanimously adopted by the U.N. General Assembly on 20 November 1989 and received more signatures during its first day open for signature than any other treaty. The CRC entered into force less than a year later—a record for an international human rights treaty. It is the only instrument that has been ratified by all but two member states in the United Nations, Somalia and the United States.[6]

The CRC integrates the rights included in previous declarations, the ICCPR, and the ICESCR. Its fifty-four articles include civil and political rights, as well as economic, social, and cultural rights. Article 1 of the CRC establishes that the definition of "child" is "every human being below the age of eighteen years unless, under the law applicable to the child, majority is attained earlier." Other articles cover a host of topics including civil rights, such as freedom of expression, freedom of religion, freedom of association, and access to information; and economic rights, such as the right to education, health care, social security, and an adequate standard of living. The CRC also contains protections against the many abuses faced by children: physical violence; sexual exploitation; sale, trafficking, and abduction; drug abuse; capital punishment; torture; deprivation of liberty; and exploitative labor. Moreover, the CRC includes guidelines for the regulation of adoption, child protective services, juvenile justice systems, refugee processes, and care for disabled children. Throughout its articles, the CRC exhibits strong respect for the role of the parents and family as the child's primary support structure.

The CRC also includes a monitoring body, the Committee on the Rights of the Child. This committee, composed of nationals from ten States Parties (those countries that ratify the CRC), is responsible for receiving reports from States Parties. Reports are required two years after becoming a State Party, and then every five years. The reports are intended to demonstrate how countries are implementing the CRC's provisions and highlight areas where improvement is needed. The committee reviews State Party reports, meets with State Party representatives, receives reports from NGOs within the country in question, and then issues comments and recommendations for improving the development and implementation of children's rights programs and policies. There is no enforcement mechanism in the CRC, and the CRC includes no provisions for sanctions or prosecutions of any kind. The only "enforcement" of the CRC comes from domestic and international political pressure exerted on States Parties by citizens, NGOs, and other countries.

The CRC is based on four basic principles, found in articles 2, 3, 6, and 12. First, article 2 protects the child's right to be free from discrimination. All children are entitled to the rights contained within the CRC "without discrimination of any kind, irrespective of the child's or his or her parent's or legal guardian's race, colour, sex, language, religion, political or other opinion, national, ethnic or social origin, property, disability, birth or other status." This principle is essential for ensuring the implementation of the CRC as a whole. The CRC further requires that States Parties must "take all appropriate measures to ensure that the child is protected against all forms of discrimination and punishment on the basis of the status, activities, expressed opinions, or beliefs of the child's parents, legal guardians, or family members."

Second, article 3 contains the general principle of the best interests of the child: "In all actions concerning children, whether undertaken by public or private social welfare institutions, courts of law, administrative authorities or legislative bodies, the best interests of the child shall be a primary consideration." The language of the article indicates that the best interests of the child (however that term is defined in a particular context) must be one of the primary factors considered (but not necessarily the only or the most important factor considered) when certain public bodies make decisions that affect an individual child, a group of children, or children as a group in society. The best interests principle is intended to apply broadly and generally to each of the CRC's provisions and to the implementation of the treaty as a whole.

Third, article 6 establishes the crucial right to life: "States Parties recognize that every child has the inherent right to life. States Parties shall ensure to the maximum extent possible the survival and development of the child." Article 6 states a deceptively simple principle—every child has the right to life—that is the heart and soul of the CRC. In short, States Parties must act to protect the most vulnerable of their citizens. Moreover, States Parties themselves must not take any actions that will rob children of their lives. This limitation is explicitly drawn in the CRC's absolute ban on capital punishment for children.

Fourth, article 12 requires States Parties to "assure to the child who is capable of forming his or her own views the right to express those views freely in all matters affecting the child, the views of the child being given due weight in accordance with the age and maturity of the child." Article 12 further provides that "the child shall in particular be provided the opportunity to be heard in any judicial and administrative proceedings affecting the child, either directly, or through a representative or an appropriate body, in a manner consistent with the procedural rules of national law." The principle of the child's right to be heard is crucial to the CRC's underlying goal of child empowerment. Although this article does not guarantee that the child's views will prevail in a judicial or administrative proceeding, his or her views will at least be heard and considered. For the first time, a major international legal instrument has enshrined the concept of the child as an active participant in his or her own life, rather than as a piece of chattel for disposal, or, more charitably, as an object in need of protection.

Of course, the many rights and protections elaborated in the CRC are complex and interrelated. For the purposes of this discussion about girl children, perhaps it is most appropriate to highlight the ideal of nondiscrimination. As mentioned above, article 2 emphasizes the importance of applying all the CRC's rights "without discrimination of any kind." But girls and women face discrimination, gender stereotyping, and sexual harassment every day and in many different ways, some subtle and some violent. A particularly egregious example of the discrimination that women and girls endure was forced into the world's consciousness in late 1996, when the Taliban regime took control of Afghanistan. According to the Physicians for Human Rights, the Taliban regime issued edicts

> forbidding women to work outside the home, attend school, or to leave their homes unless accompanied by a husband, father, brother, or son. In public, women must be covered from head to toe in a burqa, a body-length covering with only a mesh opening to see and breathe through. . . . Houses and buildings in public view must have their windows painted over if females are present in those places. . . . [A temporary hospital] facility was designated as the sole facility available to women. At that time the facility had 35 beds and no clean water, electricity, surgical equipment, X-ray machines, suction, or oxygen. . . . Education must be limited to girls up to the age of eight, and restricted to the Qur'an.[7]

What happened in Afghanistan shocked the world. But millions of girls face similarly damaging discrimination on a smaller scale—and the world turns a blind eye. The issues of health, labor, education, and sexual exploitation affect both boys and girls. But their particular impact on girls is compounded by gender bias and sexual discrimination. The Committee on the Rights of the Child, in its January 1995 report on its work preparing for the Fourth World Conference on Women, noted that "girls [are not] a special group entitled to special rights"; rather, they "are simply human beings who should be seen as individuals and not just as daughters, sisters, wives or mothers, and who should fully enjoy the fundamental rights inherent to their human dignity."

Health

The World Health Organization recognizes that "the enjoyment of the highest attainable standard of health is one of the fundamental rights of every human being without distinction of race, religion, political belief, economic or social conditions." *Health* is defined not only by the absence of disease and illness, but by physical, mental, and social well-being. It involves all aspects of life and is affected by more than access to health care: biological, psychological, and sociological influences play a critical role. Violations of human rights clearly affect the ability to enjoy the highest standard of health. Human rights standards regarding violence, discrimination, and harmful practices are important in addressing the poor status of girls' health in many countries, as are those rights that address education and child labor.

In some communities the preference for male children leads to prenatal sex determination and selective abortion as well as female infanticide. In India one doctor's advertisement for amniocentesis read: "Spend Rs [rupees] 500 now and save Rs 50,000 later," referring to the dowry savings for an aborted female.[8] The increasing availability of technology permitting determination of fetal sex also creates an atmosphere in which women may be pressured by family members to undergo testing and abortion for a fetus of the "wrong" sex.

When abortion is not available, infanticide may occur. A girl child may be directly killed after birth or she may be killed by deliberate neglect (the denial of proper nutrition, care, or health services). Studies of South Korea and China show that, among all births, the ratio of females to males is 892 to 1,000 and 884 to 1,000, respectively; for second-order births in China, the number is 833 to 1,000, and for third- and higher-order births in South Korea, 540 to 1,000.[9] In New Delhi a study by the National Commission for Women found that the ratio of females to males decreased from 970 to 1,000 in 1901 to 926 to 1,000 in 1991.[10] A study of twelve villages in Tamil Nadu revealed that more than half of the infant female deaths were the result of infanticide. In the six villages where infanticide occurred, the ratio of females to males was 940 to 1,000 as compared to 1,019 to 1,000 in the other villages.[11]

As a girl grows older, she is at risk of other harmful practices. Female genital mutilation (FGM) is the name given to the traditional practice of cutting and removing parts of the female genitalia. According to the the Center for Reproductive Law and Policy, approximately 130 million girls and women throughout the world have undergone FGM, and every year an additional 2 million face the procedure. Performed mainly on girls between the ages of four and twelve, it may occur in infancy, prior to marriage, or during the first pregnancy. It is practiced in approximately twenty-eight African nations and specific areas in the Middle East and Asia, as well as among some immigrant communities in Europe, Canada, and the United States.

In some communities, proponents of FGM justify the procedure as a religious necessity or a rite of passage into womanhood. Other communities believe that it protects virginity and prevents promiscuity or has purifying, aesthetic, or hygienic benefits. FGM is especially significant in communities where women's economic and social survival is dependent upon marriage and where the procedure is a prerequisite for wifehood.[12]

The CRC requires that States Parties protect children from "all forms of physical or mental violence, injury or abuse, neglect or negligent treatment" in article 19 and specifically addresses the issue of traditional practices in article 24, affirming that "States Parties shall take all effective and appropriate measures with a view to abolishing traditional practices prejudicial to the health of children." Members of the committee have exhibited specific concern about FGM in numerous observations to States Parties, suggesting that State Party authorities make a determined effort to eradicate the procedure. Recognizing that traditional practices cannot be eliminated solely by legislative actions, the committee has also recommended that States create comprehensive educational programs, engage all segments of society in their efforts, and support the work of NGOs working to end FGM.

The CRC guarantees every child's inherent right to life, and to the maximum extent possible, her survival and development. It also calls on States Parties to "recognize the right of the child to the enjoyment of the highest attainable standard of health" in article 24. Although the CRC does not address the question of when life actually begins, it requires that States Parties balance the conflicts arising in issues of abortion and family planning. However, the overarching principle of nondiscrimination must influence the decision making of all States Parties. The committee has unambiguously called on States Parties to challenge attitudes and practices allowing the continuation of infanticide and other customs and policies harmful to the girl child.

Education

One of the most basic human rights, and one of the most important to the quality of girls' lives, is the right to education. As a general matter, educated individuals are more productive members of society. Parents who are better educated are also more likely to understand their families' health and nutrition needs. However, an estimated 130 million school-age children in the developing world do not have access to basic education.[13] This is because the children are working full-time, their families cannot afford the costs of sending a child to school, or there is no school to attend. For countless other children, school conditions are hardly conducive to learning. Overcrowded classrooms and overworked teachers are common, and educational materials are scarce and of poor quality. Tensions often run high in such conditions, and teachers may resort to corporal punishment to maintain discipline. Frequently, the lessons taught in school are of little use in the lives of the children.

According to UNICEF, a number of unmistakable connections link education for girls and important benefits for women and society:

- The more educated a mother is, the more infant and child mortality is reduced.
- Children of more-educated mothers tend to be better nourished and suffer from less illness.
- Children (and particularly daughters) of more-educated mothers are more likely to be educated themselves and become literate.
- The more years of education women have, the later they tend to marry and the fewer children they tend to have.
- Educated women are less likely to die in childbirth.
- The more educated a woman is, the more likely she is to have opportunities and life choices and to avoid being oppressed and exploited by her family or social situation.
- Educated women are more likely to be receptive to, participate in, and influence development initiatives and send their own daughters to school.
- Educated women are more likely to play a role in political and economic decision-making at community, regional, and national levels.[14]

As cases in point for these statistics, UNICEF cites Pakistan, where one additional year of schooling for 1,000 girls would end up preventing an estimated 60 infant deaths; Brazil, where the fertility rate of 6.5 for illiterate women compares quite unfavorably to the fertility rate of 2.5 for women with a secondary education; and the Indian state of Kerala, where literacy is universal, the fertility rate is India's lowest, and the infant mortality rate is less than that of any developing country.[15]

The benefits of education for girls are unarguable, yet education seems to be beyond the reach of too many girls in the developing world. According to UNICEF, of the estimated 130 million school-age children who are not receiving an education, approximately 73 million are girls.[16] Girls are often kept at home to perform gender-based chores or discouraged from attending school because of gender stereotyping. Girls who do attend school frequently face substantial gender bias and sexual harassment in the classroom. Many girls drop out of school when they reach puberty because of the lack of separate toilet facilities to accommodate menstruation.

The CRC addresses both access to education and quality of education. Article 28 requires States Parties to "recognize the right of the child to education, and with a view to achieving this right progressively and on the basis of equal opportunity." Article 28 goes on to elaborate that, in particular, States Parties must:

a. Make primary education compulsory and available free to all;
b. Encourage the development of different forms of secondary education, including general and vocational education, make them available and accessible to every child, and take appropriate measures such as the introduction of free education and offering financial assistance in case of need;
c. Make higher education accessible to all on the basis of capacity by every appropriate means;
d. Make educational and vocational information and guidance available and accessible to all children;
e. Take measures to encourage regular attendance at schools and the reduction of drop-out rates.

Further, Article 28 requires States Parties to "take all appropriate measures to ensure that school discipline is administered in a manner consistent with the child's human dignity."

The content of the child's education is covered in article 29, which calls on States Parties to agree that the education of the child shall be directed to:

a. The development of the child's personality, talents and mental and physical abilities to their fullest potential;

b. The development of respect for human rights and fundamental freedoms, and for the principles enshrined in the Charter of the United
Nations;

c. The development of respect for the child's parents, his or her own cultural identity, language and values, for the national values of the
country in which the child is living, the country from which he or she
may originate, and for civilizations different from his or her own;

d. The preparation of the child for responsible life in a free society, in the
spirit of understanding, peace, tolerance, equality of sexes, and friendship among all peoples, ethnic, national and religious groups and persons of indigenous origin;

e. The development of respect for the natural environment.

Article 29 also provides for the continued liberty of "individuals and bodies to establish and direct educational institutions, subject always to the
observance of the principles set forth in . . . the present article and to the
requirements that the education given in such institutions shall conform
to such minimum standards as may be laid down by the State."

Applying articles 28 and 29 to the educational problems faced by girls
primarily in developing countries requires exceptional gender sensitivity.
UNICEF has offered a ten-point strategy for improving schools and promoting girls' attendance. UNICEF's key measures include:

- providing free or subsidized education, so that parents do not have to
choose between sending a son or a daughter to school;
- designing a "child-centered learning experience" to encourage individual learning;
- recruiting and training teachers to be more aware of and sensitive to
gender issues and children's rights, including recruiting more women
teachers;
- ensuring that school administrators are trained in and sensitive to gender issues;
- eliminating gender bias from educational materials;
- involving communities and families in schools;
- placing schools closer to families' homes;
- scheduling classes flexibly so children can assist with family duties;
- providing early childhood education programs, so children are prepared
for school;
- maintaining education data.[17]

These and other measures are proving effective. UNICEF offers the
example of the Islamic Republic of Iran, where girls' enrollment rate in

primary schools has risen from 80 percent to 96 percent since 1986, and where for the first time, in 1999, girls made up 52 percent of the students accepted into Iran's public universities. However, many barriers to girls' education still remain. Traditional cultural views on gender segregation have necessitated training more women teachers and increased spending to provide separate schooling for boys and girls up to the university level. Additionally, a recent survey revealed that 25 percent of the families in three Iranian provinces feel that education is unimportant for their daughters because of their future roles as wives and mothers. Thirty-four percent indicated that their daughters were prevented from attending school because of the cost of supplies and uniforms, even though schooling itself is free and compulsory.[18]

Child Labor

The simple fact of working does not violate a child's human rights. However, much of the labor performed by child workers in developing countries around the world is hazardous, exploitative, and detrimental to their development. Moreover, it is an undeniable violation of human rights. International Labor Organization (ILO) and U.S. Department of Labor statistics indicate that an estimated 250 million children, ranging in age from five to fourteen years, are involved in economic activity in developing countries; 120 million of these children work full time.[19] The figure of 250 million working children fails to include children who work full time in their own families' homes.

Many factors interact to create the pressures that force children to work. The single most significant factor is poverty. As UNICEF, in its *State of the World's Children 1997: Focus on Child Labour,* notes:

> Where society is characterized by poverty and inequity, the incidence of child labour is likely to increase, as does the risk that it is exploitative. For poor families, the small contribution of a child's income or assistance at home that allows the parents to work can make the difference between hunger and a bare sufficiency.

Another important factor is the availability of schools and compulsory education. When school attendance is not mandatory, or when the school is so far from home that attendance is too expensive, working becomes a more attractive option for the child and his or her family. Gender and class bias, violent conflicts, and traditions regarding adulthood also prevent school attendance or create pressure for a child's early entry into the workforce.

According to ILO and U.S. Department of Labor statistics, most working children, an estimated 61 percent, live in Asia; 32 percent are in Africa; and 7 percent are in Latin America. However, although Asia has the largest number of child workers, a much larger proportion, 41 percent, of Africa's children between five and fourteen years old are working. In Asia and Latin America respectively, approximately 21 and 17 percent of the child population is working. The ILO has noted that the less developed a country is, the greater the proportion of children who work. Determining the number of child laborers in developed countries is much more difficult.

Girls as well as boys participate in many different kinds of labor, much of it hazardous. In developing countries, 70 percent of child laborers work in agriculture, fishing, forestry, and hunting; the rest are employed in industries such as manufacturing, mining, sales, and personal service.[20] All of these employment sectors hold significant risks for children, many of whom begin working at very young ages. Child workers are exposed to dangerous and heavy machinery and tools, chemicals, toxins, and diseases. They work long hours under grueling conditions, usually to the detriment of their schooling, their physical health, and their emotional well-being.

The available data indicate that more boys than girls are working. However, girls' employment may simply be less visible as a result of the difficulty of accurately counting domestic workers. UNICEF estimates that "domestic work is the largest employment category of girls under age 16 in the world"; 90 percent of the world's domestic workers are girls.[21] UNICEF studies show that an estimated 250,000 child domestic workers, known as *restaveks,* 20 percent between seven and ten years old, reside in Haiti. In Jakarta, the capital of Indonesia, there are approximately 700,000 child domestic workers. According to the U.S. Department of Labor, the Philippines has some 300,000 child domestic workers.

Child domestic workers face very difficult conditions. Separated from their families, these girls spend most of their time in their employers' homes, cooking, cleaning, and caring for children. They are often not allowed to leave the house, and are frequently physically and verbally abused. In many cases, the wages owed to these girls are never paid.

The CRC and the International Labor Organization Convention 182 on the Worst Forms of Child Labor are important instruments in combating hazardous and exploitative child labor. Article 32 of the CRC requires States Parties to "recognize the right of the child to be protected from economic exploitation and from performing any work that is likely to be hazardous or to interfere with the child's education, or to be harmful to the child's health or physical, mental, spiritual, moral or social development." In particular, States Parties must "provide for a minimum age or minimum ages for admission to employment; provide for appropriate regulation of the hours and conditions of employment; [and] provide for appropriate penalties or other sanctions to ensure the effective enforcement" of these requirements. The ILO Convention, a landmark multilateral treaty adopted in 1999, requires each ratifying nation to "take immediate and effective measures to secure the prohibition and elimination of the worst forms of child labor," which includes "all forms of slavery or practices similar to slavery, such as the sale and trafficking of children, debt bondage and serfdom and forced or compulsory labour, . . . [and] work which, by its nature or the circumstances in which it is carried out, is likely to harm the health, safety or morals of children."

But simply outlawing hazardous and exploitative child labor is not enough. Little progress will be made unless the pressures that drive children into the labor force are reduced. Therefore, any program to eliminate unacceptable forms of child labor must also include plans to replace those hazardous jobs with alternatives, especially education and expanded employment opportunities for adults.

Sexual Exploitation

It is difficult to conceive of a more fundamental human right than the right to bodily integrity. Yet all over the world children's bodies are exploited and their spirits demeaned on a daily basis. Sexual exploitation of children takes different forms but primarily occurs in three areas: trafficking for sexual purposes, prostitution, and pornography.

Trafficking is the sale of children for sexual purposes, involving moving women and children between countries or within a country for that purpose. Trafficking, prostitution, and becoming subjects for pornographic depictions are forced on the child victims for the purposes of profit and pleasure for adults. Meanwhile, the children involved experience severe physical and psychological trauma, disease, risk of pregnancy, and drug addiction. The U.S. Department of Labor in 1998 found that, in one Bangkok shelter for former child prostitutes, half of the girls, whose ages ranged from fourteen to eighteen years, tested positive for HIV.

The number of children being exploited sexually is impossible to pinpoint, but by all estimates (those cited here are by UNICEF and the U.S. Labor Department) the numbers are staggering. An estimated two million children enter the sex industry through the force, deception, or simple betrayal of strangers or even family members. In the city of Dhaka, Bangladesh, alone, there are about 10,000 child prostitutes. Approximately 92 percent of the prostitutes in Nicaragua are between the ages of twelve and eighteen. On a major sexual trafficking route between Nepal and cities in India, thousands of girls, many as young as seven, are trafficked every year, increasing the estimated number of 200,000 Nepalese prostitutes in India.[22]

Another appalling aspect of the problem of sexual exploitation is the lure of sex tourism. According to many child advocacy organizations, several countries are identified as destinations for men who desire sex with children. Sex tourism is increasing in Central and South America, bringing those areas into competition with long-time sex tourism centers in Asia—notably Thailand, the Philippines, Vietnam, and Taiwan.[23] Ofelia Calcetas-Santos, the United Nations Special Rapporteur on the sale of children, child prostitution, and child pornography, noted that "it is contended that ex-servicemen may be operating as many as 30 sex tours that take men from the United States to Thailand and surrounding countries."[24]

The CRC contains several provisions that address the multiple issues involved in sexual exploitation. Article 34 requires States Parties to "protect the child from all forms of sexual exploitation and sexual abuse." In particular, States Parties are required to prevent:

a. The inducement or coercion of a child to engage in any unlawful sexual activity;
b. The exploitative use of children in prostitution or other unlawful sexual practices;
c. The exploitative use of children in pornographic performances and materials.

Article 35 requires States Parties to take measures "to prevent the abduction of, the sale of or traffic in children for any purpose or in any form." Article 36 requires States Parties to "protect the child against all other forms of exploitation prejudicial to any aspects of the child's welfare." Article 7 protects the child's right to be cared for by his or her parents—a right that is violated when girls are trafficked for the purpose of becoming domestic workers.

An Optional Protocol to the CRC on the Sale of Children, Child Prostitution, and Child Pornography was adopted by the U.N. General Assembly and opened for signature by member nations on 25 May 2000. The Optional Protocol is a separate treaty containing provisions that are focused on the issues involved in the commercial sexual exploitation of children; it will be legally binding on the countries that ratify it, just as the CRC is legally binding on its States Parties. The Optional Protocol will require each of its States Parties to ensure that its criminal or penal codes will cover "the offering, delivering, or accepting by whatever means a child for the purpose of . . . sexual exploitation" or prostitution, and "producing distributing, disseminating, importing, exporting, offering, selling, or possessing . . . child pornography." In addition, the Optional Protocol includes requirements intended to ensure that States Parties recognize the vulnerability of the child victims of sexual exploitation and provide for their special needs during legal proceedings. As noted above, the ILO Convention 182 is another important legal tool in the international fight against the commercial sexual exploitation of children. This landmark multilateral treaty requires ratifying countries to "take immediate and effective measures to secure the prohibition and elimination of the worst forms of child labor," which are defined as, among other things, "all forms of slavery or practices similar to slavery, such as sale and trafficking of children, . . . the use, procuring or offering of a child for prostitution, for the production of pornography or for pornographic performances."

These international instruments are effective only if they are employed by governments with the will to end the commercial use of children's bodies. As a result of the near universal ratification of the CRC and the publicity that has surrounded too many tragedies—such as the death of Rosario, whose story introduces this essay—many countries have moved to improve their laws. According to Laura Lederer of the Protection Project, following Rosario's death, Austria, Germany, and a few other Western European nations passed laws prohibiting child sex tourism and making it a crime to sexually abuse a child in a foreign country. Other countries, such as the Philippines and Sri Lanka, have increased their penalties for the commercial sexual exploitation of children.

Conclusion

Rosario's death also sparked the formation of an international NGO (ECPAT International: End Child Prostitution, Child Pornography and Trafficking of Children for Sexual Purposes) whose mission is to end child prostitution, child pornography, and trafficking of children for sexual purposes. NGOs working together with concerned governments can make a tremendous difference in the lives of abused, neglected, and exploited girls. Empowering girls and women to assert their internationally protected human rights through the mechanism of NGOs and governmental agencies is one of the best ways to create lasting change in the situations that threaten so many girls and women with so much harm. As Margaret Mead said, "never doubt that a small group of thoughtful, committed citizens can change the world. Indeed, it is the only thing that ever has."

The problems outlined in this essay are only representative of the adversities faced by girls. Many individuals, NGOs, and governments are working tirelessly to improve conditions for girls and boys, and for women and men. The Universal Declaration of Human Rights, a statement of principles unanimously adopted by the United Nations in 1948, asserts that the "recognition of the inherent dignity and of the equal and inalienable rights of all members of the human family is the foundation of freedom, justice and peace in the world." There is still so much to be done before our daughters—the Rosarios of the world—can freely, safely, and with honor occupy their rightful places in the human family.

NOTES

1. As told by Laura Lederer, director of the Protection Project, School of Advanced International Studies, Johns Hopkins University. This story is part of the Protection Project's Survivor Story Database, which houses the stories of many young women and girls like Rosario. Some of the names and certain details have been changed, but this story is true.

2. U.S. Department of Labor, *By the Sweat and Toil of Children,* vol. 5: *Efforts to Eliminate Child Labor,* Washington, D.C. (1998). See p. 32, citing International Labor Organization, *The Sex Sector: The Economic and Social Bases of Prostitution in Southeast Asia,* Geneva (1998).

3. Maggie Black, "War against Childhood," in *In the Firing Line: War and Children's Rights* (London: Amnesty International, 1999).

4. See Cynthia Price Cohen, "The Developing Jurisprudence of the Rights of the Child," *St. Thomas Law Review* 6, no. 1 (1993).

5. See Cohen, "The Developing Jurisprudence of the Rights of the Child" (1993).

6. For information about the United States' failure to ratify the CRC, see, e.g., Susan Kilbourne, "Opposition to U.S. Ratification of the CRC: Responses to Parental Rights Arguments," *Loyola Poverty Law Journal* 4 (1998).

7. Physicians for Human Rights, *The Taliban's War on Women: A Health and Human Rights Crisis in Afghanistan,* Boston (1998), pp. 2–3.

8. L. Lingam, "Sex Detection Tests and Female Foeticide: Discrimination Before Birth," in *Understanding Women's Health Issues: A Reader,* edited by L. Lingam, New Dehli (1998), pp. 209–218.

9. East West Center Program on Population, "Evidence Mounts for Sex-Selective Abortions in Asia," *Asia-Pacific Population and Policy Report,* no. 34 (May-June 1995).

10. *Annual Report 1992–1993: Assessment of the Progress of Development of Women* (New Delhi: National Commission for Women, 1993).

11. S. George, R. Abel, and B. D. Miller, "Female Infanticide in Rural South India," *Search Bulletin* 12, no. 3 (July-Sept. 1998).

12. Nahid Toubia, *Caring for Women with Circumcision,* New York (1999).

13. UNICEF, *State of the World's Children 1999: Education* (New York, 1999).

14. *State of the World's Children 1999: Education* (New York, 1999).

15. UNICEF, *State of the World's Children 1999,* citing Lawrence H. Summers, *Educating All the Children,* Policy Research Working Papers Series, (Washington, D.C.: World Bank, 1992), and *The Education of Girls and Women: Towards a Global Framework for Action* (Paris: UNESCO, 1995).

16. UNICEF, *State of the World's Children 1999,* citing *The Education of Girls and Women: Towards a Global Framework for Action* (Paris: UNESCO, 1995).

17. UNICEF, *State of the World's Children 1999.*

18. UNICEF, *State of the World's Children 2000* (New York, 2000).

19. Kebebew Ashagrie. *Statistics on Working Children and Hazardous Child Labor.* Geneva: International Labor Office (1997; revised April 1998). *By the Sweat and Toil of Children,* vol. 5: *Efforts to Eliminate Child Labor,* Washington, D.C.: U.S. Department of Labor, (1998).

20. U.S. Department of Labor, *By the Sweat and Toil of Children,* vol. 5: *Efforts to Eliminate Child Labor* (Washington, D.C., 1998), p. 17.

21. "Child Domestic Work," *Innocenti Digest 5* (Florence, Italy: UNICEF International Child Development Centre, May 1999), p. 3.

22. *Issue Summary: Sexual Exploitation of Children,* United States Fund for UNICEF, available at *http://www.unicefusa.org* (posted April 2000); U.S. Department of Labor, *By the Sweat and Toil of Children,* vol. 5: *Efforts to Eliminate Child Labor* (Washington, D.C., 1998), citing Child Workers in Nepal Concerned Center, *State of the Rights of the Child in Nepal 1998: Country Report Released by CWIN* (Kathmandu, January 1998).

23. Laura Barnitz, *Commercial Sexual Exploitation of Children: Youth Involved in Prostitution, Pornography and Sex Trafficking,* Washington, D.C.: Youth Advocate Program International (1998).

24. United Nations Economic and Social Council, *Report of the Special Rapporteur on the Sale of Children, Child prostitution and Child Pornography,* E/CN.4/1999/71, 55th Session, 29 January 1999, para. 8.

Psychocultural Factors in the Adaptation of Immigrant Youth

GENDERED RESPONSES

Carola Suárez-Orozco

CURRENTLY there are more than 130 million migrants worldwide. Of those, approximately 12 to 18 million are considered refugees who are escaping political, religious, ethnic, or gender persecution. In addition to those who are officially recognized as refugees, a much larger number of individuals are designated as asylum seekers who are not granted formal status. Although asylum seekers often share with refugees similar motivations for leaving their place of origin, they are not recognized for a number of nonobjective reasons, including inadequate interpretation at hearings, poor documentation, and political relations between the countries in question. As so many individuals' lives have been affected by displacement, it is crucial that we develop a deeper understanding of the realities they face as well as how they may be adapting.

Psychologists lag far behind economists, sociologists, and demographers in terms of basic research on the topic of immigrants and refugees. There is a smattering of clinical writings on the impact of these displacements on individuals and families. While these are important contributions to our understanding, such research is typically limited in terms of generalizability. Most of the research that does exist has emphasized the adult immigrant experience. Given the number of children involved, surprisingly little research has focused on the experiences of children. In the United States, for example, children of immigrants are the fastest-growing sector of the child population. Currently one in five children is the child of an immigrant. By 2040, the number of children of immigrants is projected to be one in three.

Just as the research on immigration has emphasized the experiences of adults, the lens has been focused largely on men. After years of neglect, in the late 1980s and 1990s the specific issues facing immigrant women began to gain attention. Although there are more immigrant women than men, we still know little about the gendered experiences of immigrants. Knowledge about immigrant girls, and more specifically immigrant adolescent girls, is sketchier still. This essay summarizes fundamental information that both researchers and service providers interested in the experiences of immigrants—and thus adolescent girls as a subgroup within that larger group—should keep in mind. To paraphrase the anthropologist Clyde Kluckhohn, immigrant girls are like all other immigrant children, like some other immigrant children, and like no other immigrant children. Therefore, I begin by outlining issues pertaining to the children of immigrants generally. (In discussing the children of immigrants, I refer to both the first generation—those born abroad—as well as the second generation—those born in the new land of both foreign parents.) I then turn to the more specific issues pertaining to immigrant adolescent girls.

The Stresses of Immigration

Multiple pathways structure immigrants' journeys into their new homes. Many enter a new land because their families are fleeing economic or political instability. Others come not for reasons of survival but rather to thrive by taking advantage of the economic and professional opportunities provided in new settings. The three major categories of motivation for migration are socioeconomic factors, factors relating to fear of persecution, and family reunification. In the real lives of migrants, the pathways are not always distinct; often a family's decision is motivated by a variety of factors.

Nevertheless, these categories are useful for understanding the experiences of immigrant families and their children. For immigrants leaving their homes for a better life or to be reunited with loved ones, optimism may help to attenuate the losses that inevitably accompany migration. For refugees who have been pushed out of their homes after massive trauma, the cumulative losses they sustain may be overwhelming. On balance, immigration results in substantial gains for many families. But it also exacts considerable costs.

By any measure, immigration is one of the most stressful events a family can undergo. Immigration removes individuals from many of their relationships and predictable contexts—extended families and friends, community ties, jobs, living situations, customs and (often) language.

Immigrants are stripped of many of their sustaining social relationships as well as of the social roles that provide them with culturally scripted notions of how they fit into the world. Without a sense of competence, control, and belonging, they may feel marginalized. These changes are highly disorienting and nearly inevitably lead to a keen sense of loss.

Many of the forms of stress discussed here are common to both immigrants and to refugees. However, refugees and asylum seekers suffer particular stresses that require separate discussion. The serious human rights violations suffered as a result of political or ethnic repression have long-standing repercussions. Many refugees and asylum seekers are subjected to long imprisonments, torture, the destruction of homes, and the disappearance of loved ones. Others may not endure these experiences directly but are subjected to the terror of the "uncanny" that may be occurring all around them. Many suffer the loss of beloved family members and friends. In addition to the predictable period of grieving that is inevitable given the loss of loved ones, refugees often also experience transient as well as long-term symptoms of Post-Traumatic Stress Disorder (Cole, Espin, and Rothblum 1992; Somach 1995). Symptoms frequently include recurrent memories of the traumatic event as well as nightmares. Sufferers generally alternate between a general psychic numbing of emotional responses and a persistent sense of heightened arousal. As a result they may experience a wide range of emotional responses including anxiety, irritability, and anger. Refugees and asylum seekers may also have difficulty concentrating and be experiencing insomnia (Horowitz 1986; Smajkic and Weane 1995). Children may become extremely withdrawn and depressed; they may act out, becoming behaviorally disruptive (Bylund 1992). There may be some gender differences, dependent on cultural factors, in the way symptoms are manifested.

In situations of political and ethnic repression, women and adolescent girls are frequently subjected to the gender-specific trauma of rape (Agger 1992; Camino and Kruhlfeld 1994, Friedman 1992). These systematic sexual assaults "make political use of sexuality in the service of repression" (Agger 1992). At the community level these assaults function to terrorize the targeted community and establish the power of invading forces. At the individual level the assaults break down the victim's defenses and weakens her sense of personal identity. The ramifications for the victim and those who love her are far-reaching.

Domestic violence also increases as a result of the destabilization of the family. Male family members all too often behave violently toward their wives and daughters in response to their womenfolk's perceived loss of virtue. This perceived contamination, coupled with the man's heightened vulnerability resulting from the stresses of traumatic events and exile, lead to increased rates of domestic violence (Agger 1992; Friedman 1992). As a consequence, for refugee women there may be no safe haven either outside or inside the home.

The human rights violations suffered by a refugee lead to disruptions in the relationship she has with herself as well as with others. The process of turning oneself off, becoming numb, to withstand trauma and its aftermath becomes less functional over time, creating a sense of unreality that interferes with everyday functioning (Agger 1992). Relations with others are disrupted as basic trust is profoundly violated (Robben and Suárez-Orozco, in press). "Extreme violence 'unmakes' the internalized culturally constituted webs of trust, based on social norms, world views, and moral conventions" (Robben and Suárez-Orozco, 2000). Furthermore, trauma frequently is transmitted "radioactively" from the inner world of the victim across generations, perpetuating conflicts (Gambel 2000).

Human rights violations in the context of political or social unrest are not the only sources of trauma for migrants. For undocumented immigrants, the actual border crossing often proves to be a traumatic event for adults and children alike. At the U.S.- Mexican border, for example, those crossing the border risk heat exhaustion and violence at the hands of border agents and paid crossing guides (Eschbach et al. 1997). Women are at particular risk of being physically abused, raped, robbed, or murdered during border crossings (Friedman 1992; Amnesty International 1998).

In addition to violence experienced prior to or during migration, all too many immigrant children witness a high level of violence in their new neighborhood and school settings. Many move into neighborhoods that are fraught with violence and dismal social situations. Simply walking to school can become a traumatic event. In one sample (conducted by the Harvard Immigration Project, of the Harvard Graduate School of Education, codirected by the author and Marcelo Suárez-Orozco), of four hundred recent immigrant children attending fifty schools in two American cities, many voiced concerns about school and neighborhood violence, including rape and murder in their school, the stabbing of a teacher in front of her class, a shooting in the school parking lot, a face slashing, a bomb explosion, an armed prison escapee chased by police on school premises during school hours, and gang and drug activity. Violent incidents in the new setting may perpetuate previous traumas or subject immigrants to new traumas.

In many cases, children are separated from their parents for long periods of time as a result of migration. Parents often leave children with relatives as they forge pathways in the new country. At other times the child comes with one parent, leaving the other parent behind in the homeland. In the Harvard Immigration Project sample, 80 percent had been separated from one or both parents for periods of several months to several years. During this time the child is likely to attach herself to a new care-taker, who may or may not affectionately attend to her needs. If the child succeeds in attaching to a new caretaker, the separation from this care-taker in order to be reunited with the parent may be quite painful (com-pounding the mourning and loss that follows immigration). The fallout from the period of separation can lead to significant tensions between par-ents and children (Falicov 1998).

A much less dramatic but nevertheless significant form of stress for all migrants has been termed "acculturation stress" (Berry 1998; Flaskerud and Uman 1996; Smart and Smart 1995). This is the process whereby in-dividuals learn and come to terms with the new cultural "rules of engage-ment." The individual's place of origin provides her with familiar and predictable contexts; these predictable contexts change in dramatic ways following immigration. As Eva Hoffmann, who immigrated from Poland to the United States, has written, immigration results in falling "out of the net of meaning into the weightlessness of chaos" (Hoffmann 1989, p. 151). Without a sense of competence, control, and belonging, migrants are often left with a keen sense of loss, disorientation, and marginality.

Many immigrants experience a sense of euphoria upon arrival (Sluzki 1979). Expectations are high and possibilities seem boundless as the im-migrant attempts to find work and a place to live. As the realities of the new situation are confronted, individuals normatively begin to experience a variety of psychological problems (Ainslie 1998; Arrendondo-Dowd 1981; Suárez-Orozco 2001). Most frequently, the cumulative losses of loved ones and familiar contexts lead to feelings along a spectrum of sad-ness to depression to "perpetual mourning" (Volkan 1993). The disso-nances in cultural expectations and of predictable contexts lead many to experience an anxious disorientation. Disappointed aspirations and dreams, when coupled with a hostile reception in the new environment, may lead to feelings of distrust, suspicion, anger, and even well-founded paranoia (Grinberg and Grinberg 1989).

The repercussions of the responses at the individual level can have deeply destabilizing effects on the family, which may be felt particularly by the children. The structure of the family is changed—former family lead-ers may be "demoted" and the nature of culturally scripted gender rela-tionships may shift (Hondagneu-Sotelo 1994). When immigrant women move into the formal workplace, their new role as family providers may at once lend them independence and create tensions within their relation-ships. Some immigrant families become entrenched in traditional gender roles in an effort to ward off acculturation.

Many immigrant families incorporate extended family members and are more interdependent and hierarchical than traditional Anglo-American families (Smart and Smart 1995). Some of these characteristics are in part culturally determined but others may be secondary to migration. Extended families will often live together to share both the financial and the childcare burdens. In the absence of other social support networks, they may rely on each other considerably more than most nonimmigrant families.

Immigrant parents often become fiercely protective of their children in the new environment. One of the things they fear is that the children may become too Americanized. They may set limits that are significantly more stringent than those they would have set in their home country. At the same time, immigrant parents are often quite dependent on their children, who develop language skills more quickly and consequently serve as interpreters and errand-runners for the family. As the roles of parent and child and their interdependency becomes more complex, significant tensions arise.

As many immigrant parents must work several jobs, their physical absence from the home compounds the psychological unavailability that often accompanies parental anxiety and depression (Athey and Ahearn 1991). Many immigrant children are left to their own devices long before it is developmentally appropriate. While in some cases this leads to hyperresponsible, internalized children, in other cases it leads to depressed kids who are drawn to the lure of alternative family structures such as gangs.

Children usually adapt more quickly to the new context than do adults. In the school setting, children are forced to contend more quickly and more intensely with the new culture. The parents' workplaces require less in the way of language skills and are likely to be populated by other members of the immigrant community (M. Suárez-Orozco 1998). Parents may feel uncomfortable with the pace of their children's adaptation; children may feel embarrassed by or fiercely protective of their parents' "old country" and "old-fashioned" ways.

In immigrant families the potential for miscommunication between members must not be underestimated. Most children long to be like their peers and thus show a preference for the language of the dominant culture (Portes and Hao 1998). Indeed, the children often learn the new language more quickly than do their parents. Their level of fluency in the home language is likely to atrophy over time (Wong-Fillmore 1991). Hence, the child is likely to have difficulty communicating subtleties of thought and emotion in that language, even as the parents have trouble doing so in the new language. In complex discussions, subtleties of meanings are likely to be missed. It is not uncommon to overhear discussions in which parents

and children switch back and forth between languages and completely
miss one another's intent.

The Sending Context and the Ethos of Reception

A number of factors may significantly influence the response to the transitions and stress of immigration. These mediating variables can be broken
down into two categories—sending factors and receiving factors.

Each individual brings with him characteristics, traits, and experiences
that are referred to as sending (or antecedent) factors. The circumstances
surrounding the migration can play a key role. If the immigrant is lured
out of her homeland by the promise of opportunity and adventure, she is
likely to be more positively disposed to the experience than if she is pushed
out by ethnic, religious, or political conflict, chronic hardship, or famine
in the homeland. The individual initiating the migration is likely to be
more enthusiastic about the experience than an initially reluctant spouse,
elderly parent, or child (Shuval 1980). Children and adolescents often do
not share their parents' motivation to migrate. They do not experience ea-
ger anticipation but rather take the migration as an imposition upon them
from which they have little to gain.

A variety of other sending factors, including socioeconomic background, can help to mediate the stresses of the migration process. Possessing the language of the new country clearly is an asset. Religiosity and
connection with a church may also play a positive role. The rural to urban
shift (a not uncommon pattern for many immigrants), on the other hand,
may complicate the transition. Rural children often lose the freedom to
play and roam the neighborhood in the new urban environment.

Personality and temperament also play a significant role in how the individual responds to the migration process (Garcia-Coll and Magnuson
1997). Individuals who are particularly rigid, or who have a high need for
predictability, are likely to suffer more than those who are flexible and
comfortable with change (Wheaton 1983). Traits such as shyness, pride,
sensitivity to outside opinions, and suspiciousness complicate the process
of adaptation.

Conditions in the new host milieu, such as the efficacy of the social
support network, the quality of interpersonal relationships, and the availability of social companionship, naturally influence adjustment to the new
environment. Whether the immigrant is able to share in the general quality of life also depends on her status as "documented" or "undocumented."
On an emotional level, feeling "hunted" by agents of the immigration authorities leads to anxiety and paranoia; on a practical level, legal status determines the kind of work available to the immigrant.

For children, the quality of their schools and neighborhood safety affect the process of transition. Many immigrant children find themselves in segregated, conflict-ridden schools in areas with high rates of poverty. "Affordable" urban housing is often located in areas that resemble war zones. Because of concerns about safety on the streets, parents may require children to stay within the confines of their cramped living spaces. Thus immigration is often felt as a loss of freedom.

All over the world, intolerance of newcomers is historically an all-too-common response. Complicating matters, today's immigrants are more diverse than ever in terms of ethnicity, skin color, and religion. Prejudice and discrimination against immigrants of color is particularly widespread and intense (Coll-Garcia and Magnuson 1997). Exclusion of newcomers can take a structural form (when individuals are excluded from the opportunity structure) as well as an attitudinal form (in the form of disparagement and public hostility). These structural barriers and the social ethos of intolerance and racism that many immigrants of color encounter intensify the stresses of immigration.

In the late twentieth century, widespread concern about the influx of new immigrants led to several dramatic anti-immigrant initiatives designed to prevent immigrants (largely undocumented but also documented) from receiving benefits or public services. In the United States, immigration controls (in the form of legislation such as California's Proposition 187) over the years have moved from the border, to the school house, to the hospital and welfare agencies. These practices generate a pattern of intense exclusion and segregation—in the workforce, the schools, and residential patterns—between large numbers of immigrants and the larger society. The patterns of institutionalized segregation are further intensified by increasing segmentation in the economy (Portes and Zhou 1993). Furthermore, while immigrant youth have made gains in terms of level of completed education, those gains are not being rewarded proportionally in terms of wages or earnings (Myers 1998).

Attitudinal social exclusion also plays a toxic role. How does a child incorporate the notion that she is an "alien," an "illegal," unwanted and not deserving of the most basic rights of education and health care? Fear of the cultural dilution of the country's institutions and values is an enduring preoccupation feeding the anti-immigrant ethos (Espenshade and Belanger 1987). Immigrants who do not speak the language of the new setting and who "look" different from the dominant majority make many nonimmigrants uncomfortable. At best they are viewed as unwelcome competitors, at worst as sinister. Negative attributes are projected onto them as they become the target of what the cultural psychologist George DeVos terms "psychological disparagement" (DeVos and M. Suárez-

Orozco 1990). They become the object of symbolic violence, which stereo-types them as innately inferior (lazy, prone to crime, and so forth) and thus less deserving of sharing in society's benefits.

Many immigrant and minority children are subjected to a social mir-roring that is predominantly hostile. Assumptions about them on the part of nonimmigrants include expectations of sloth, irresponsibility, low intel-ligence, and even danger. When the child sees herself reflected this way in a number of mirrors, including the media, the classroom, and the street, the outcome is devastating. Immigrant children are keenly aware of the prevailing ethos of hostility. The Harvard Immigration Project asked its sample of children to complete the sentence: "Most Americans think that [Chinese, Dominicans, Haitians, Mexicans—depending on the child's country of origin] are . . ." The modal response was the word "bad." Other responses were "stupid," " useless," "garbage," "gang members," "lazy."

Psychologically, what do children do with this reception? Are the atti-tudes of the host culture internalized, denied, or resisted? The most posi-tive possible outcome is to be goaded into defiance, a desire to prove that the labels and stereotypes are wrong: "I'll show you. I'll make it in spite of what you think of me." This response is relatively infrequent. Children more often respond with self-doubt and shame, setting low aspirations in a kind of self-fulfilling prophecy: "They're probably right. I'll never be able to do it." Yet another, not uncommon, response is a desire to punish the host culture by proving its expectations to be correct: "You think I'm bad. Let me show you how bad I can be."

A number of theoretical constructs have been developed over the years to explore the immigration experience in the United States, a society whose founding narrative is based on both steady streams and periodic waves of immigration. Models developed to examine immigration in the United States were historically largely based on immigrants of European origin. These immigrants' pattern of assimilation was depicted as a gener-ally upwardly mobile journey; the longer they were in the United States, the better they seemed to do socially and economically.

Patterns of Immigration and Adaptation

The current immigration—a wave that began after 1965—is one of remarkable diversity. The new immigrants come from highly diverse so-cioeconomic and skill backgrounds. Some are among the most educated portion of the population, thriving, for example, in the high-tech indus-tries; others have very little education and are therefore entering the serv-ice industry with little prospect for advancement. The new immigrants bring with them remarkable diversity in terms of culture and languages.

More than 100 languages are spoken in New York City public schools, more than 90 in Los Angeles schools. Over 70 percent of today's immigrants are people of color, coming form Latin America, the Caribbean, and Asia. These new immigrants are contributing significantly to our increasingly diverse society. In a society that historically has not easily handled race relations, this diversity factors into a somewhat different pathway of immigrant insertion in American society. Today, many of the children of immigrants are not following the traditional trajectory of upward mobility in the course of assimilation.

Today the pattern of adaptation is more complex. In broad strokes, several studies on the performance of immigrant children in schools have pointed to a trimodal pattern of school adaptation (a critical predictor of success in this society). Some immigrant children do extraordinarily well in school, surpassing native-born children in terms of a number of indicators—including grades, performance on standardized tests, and attitudes toward education. Other immigrants tend to overlap with native-born children. Still others tend to achieve well below their native-born peers (Kao and Tienda 1995; Rumbaut 1995; Suárez-Orozco and Suárez-Orozco 1995; Waters 1996).

Another disconcerting pattern has consistently emerged from an array of research on immigrant groups: length of residency in the United States is associated with declining health, school achievement, and aspirations. A large-scale study by the National Research Council considered a variety of measures of physical health and risk behaviors among children and adolescents from immigrant families, including general health, learning disabilities, obesity, emotional difficulties, and various risk-taking behaviors. The NRC researchers found that immigrant youth were healthier than their counterparts from nonimmigrant families. The researchers noted that these findings are "counterintuitive," as it would be expected that the racial or ethnic minority status, generally lower socioeconomic status, and high poverty rates of many immigrant children and families would place individuals at higher risk. They also found that the longer youth were in the United States, the poorer their overall psychological health and the more likely they were to engage in risky behaviors such as substance abuse, violence, and delinquency (Hernandez and Charney 1998). It should be noted that a Canadian study of a similar nature yielded nearly identical findings (Besier, Hou, Hyman, and Tousignant 1999).

In the area of education, a survey of more than fifteen thousand high school students in California and Florida found a negative association between length of residence in the United States and both grade-point average and aspirations (Rumbaut and Portes 1997). Another study conducted in high schools across the country also found a pattern of decline associated with "Americanization" (Steinberg, Brown, and Dornbusch 1996).

Of the 400 children interviewed for the Harvard Immigration Project, 98 percent agreed with the statement: "School is important to get ahead." In a more open-ended question asking the children to name their favorite thing about life in the United States, 44 percent spontaneously mentioned school. In the sentence-completion task, "In life the most important thing is . . . ," 47 percent responded "school." In the sentence-completion task, "School is . . . ," 72 percent gave positive responses such as "my life," "my other family," "the pathway to success." Their incoming attitudes are remarkably positive, but the verdict is still out regarding what will happen in time.

Immigrant Adolescent Girls

With these experiences of immigrant and refugee children and their families in mind, one can apply the key issues of adaptation specifically to immigrant and refugee adolescent girls.

The data on the mental health and risk-behavior practices of immigrant girls is sketchy. No comprehensive study has yet been done on immigrant girls, though some studies address issues of particular groups such as Latina girls or Filipina girls. Some ethnographic, clinical, and survey data suggest greater depression, low self-esteem, and tendency to commit suicide among female children of immigrants (Olsen 1997).

A number of studies report that substance abuse is substantially lower in Hispanic girls than it is in Hispanic boys. Other studies suggest that Hispanic boys and girls born abroad are less likely to abuse substances than their native-born counterparts (Khoury, Warheit, Zimmerman, Vega, and Gil 1999).

One team of researchers reviewed the literature and considered the relationship between acculturation and mental health among Latinos (Rogler, Cortes, and Malgady 1991). They considered three hypotheses: one postulated that less acculturated individuals would be at greater risk because of loss of relationships and economic and social stresses; another predicted that greater acculturation would lead to greater risks of depression because of the exposure to toxic mainstream attitudes and potential internalization leading to low self-esteem; and a third hypothesis predicted that risk is greatest at the high and low ends of the spectrum. Review of the literature yielded no consistent support for any of the hypotheses, nor were gender differences established. One conclusion, consistent with the National Research Study findings (of both males and females) mentioned earlier, was that the first generation was somewhat hardier while the second generation was at greater risk.

A number of studies have reported gender differences in responsibilities at home. Immigrant girls have far more responsibilities at home than do their brothers. Their roles include translating, advocating in financial, medical, and legal transactions, and acting as surrogate parents. Eldest children in particular are expected to assist with such tasks as babysitting, feeding younger siblings, getting siblings ready for school in the morning, and escorting them to school (Valenzuela 1999)

Other studies have noted significant family tensions around dating (Espin 1999). In some immigrant communities, becoming "Americanized" is synonymous with being sexually promiscuous. As a result, immigrant adolescent girls' activities outside the home are heavily monitored and controlled. While boys may be encouraged to venture forth into the new world, girls and women are more likely to be kept close to home. Because girls tend to place greater value on social and family ties, they may be more reluctant to struggle to separate from the family (Goodenow and Espin 1993). However, adolescent girls often experience the burden of being torn between the pursuit of romantic love and the role of dutiful daughter (Olsen 1997).

As a result of their parents' concerns about dating and their many domestic responsibilities, immigrant girls are often heavily restricted in their activities outside the home. These restrictions are often experienced by adolescent girls as "unfair" and "oppressive" and may be the focus of family conflict. Yet the restrictions may indeed have benefits (Smith 1999). First, girls may be less exposed to toxic circumstances such as violence or gang-related activities. Indeed, several researchers have found that girls are less likely to be involved in gangs, and when they are, their involvement is more symbolic and less intense. They are more likely to remain in school and more easily make the transition out of the gang phase, moving relatively smoothly into the labor market (Smith 1999).

Since the beginning of this century, among most ethnic groups, immigrant girls have tended to complete more years of school than have their male counterparts (Olneck and Lazerson 1974). Among Asian Americans, an analysis of census data found that for the children of immigrants, females reach higher levels of educational attainment than do boys (Brandon 1991). A study of Afro-Caribbeans in New York showed that girls are more likely to complete school (Waters 1996).

The educational anthropologist Margaret Gibson notes that "there is mounting evidence that among some groups, ethnic girls tend to remain in school longer and receive higher grades than boys, while in others, their performance lags behind that of their brothers" (Gibson 1997, p. 42). This overall pattern is true in the United States as well as in much of Europe. Religion and culture have a tremendous influence on the experiences of immigrant girls. Girls of Hindi Indian, Muslim Afghani, Catholic Mexican, or Buddhist Chinese backgrounds will face quite different issues. For example, arranged marriages for teen girls are normative in some cultures; for a girl raised in a postindustrial society steeped in media images of what life should be like, including the expectation that both girls and boys complete a prescribed amount of schooling, this pathway will be much more conflicted than if she were being raised in her country of origin (Olsen 1997). In cultures where parents discourage their daughters from remaining in school past marriageable age (which in some cultures is the mid teens), educational pursuits for girls will be truncated.

How can we account for girls' more successful educational trajectories among some immigrant groups? For immigrant girls who are more restricted by their parents than boys, "time at school then becomes a precious social experience" (Olsen 1997, p. 125). In contrast to mainstream American teenagers, who tend to talk about their time in school as a "prison experience," immigrant girls tend to experience their days in school as times of relative freedom (Olsen 1997). They may feel more positive about their schooling experiences and therefore be more engaged. By and large immigrant girls take their schooling seriously. But as anthropological evidence makes clear, among ethnic groups that have historically been depreciated and disparaged, academic engagement is threatened for boys and girls alike. However, for boys from these groups, their performance in school is, on the whole, more at risk. This is true, for example, for Afro-Caribbean youth in Britain, Canada, and the United States, for North African males in Belgium, and for Moroccans and Algerians in France.

A number of hypotheses explain why boys are more at risk. Parents may exert less control over their sons' behaviors than their daughters'. It has been persuasively demonstrated that family and community control play a significant role in the well-being of youth (Earls 1997). Furthermore, boys and girls encounter different teacher expectations. Adolescent minority boys are often seen by teachers and administrators as threatening. Another factor contributing to boys' poorer performance in school may be the strong peer pressure for boys to reject school (Fordham 1996; Gibson 1982; Smith 1999; Waters 1996). Behaviors that boys engage in to gain the respect of peers often put them in conflict with their teachers.

Girls are also more likely to have specific career goals and plans than do boys (Olsen 1997). Girls often develop certain skills that make them more easily employable. Because girls are more likely to have helped their mothers as translators and in negotiating social institutions, they develop such "soft" skills as translation, advocacy, and explaining. It is no accident that they are more likely to enter the work force as youth counselors, medical assistants, daycare workers, caseworkers, and other social-service-related positions (Smith 1999).

Finally, let us turn to the quintessential task of adolescents—that of defining oneself vis-à-vis the society at large. The children of immigrants must construct identities that will, if successful, enable them to thrive in the disparate social settings of home, schools, the world of peers, and the world of work. In *Childhood and Society* (1964), the psychologist Erik Erickson argued that for optimal development, there must be a certain amount of complementarity between the individual's sense of self and the varied social milieus he or she moves among. Immigrant children, however, must move across discontinuous social spaces. Immigrant children today may have their breakfast conversation in Farsi, listen to African American rap with their peers on the way to school, and learn in mainstream English about the New Deal from their social studies teacher. Therefore, the experience of the children of immigrants offers us a particularly powerful lens through which to view the workings of identity.

Immigrant adolescents face particular challenges in their identity formation (Aronowitz 1984; Phinney 1998). When there is a great deal of cultural dissonance, when the cultural guides are inadequate, and when the social mirror reflects back negative images, adolescents will find it difficult to develop a flexible and adaptive sense of self. Many are torn between the attachment to the parental culture of origin, the lure of the often more intriguing adolescent peer culture, and aspirations to join the American mainstream culture (which may or may not welcome them).

Studies suggest that immigrant girls seem to feel less pressure to make choices about their ethnic identity (Smith 1999; Waters 1996). Boys feel more strongly pressured by peers to take on a racial identity. Furthermore, identities and negative expectations are less likely to be imposed upon girls by the dominant society. Immigrant boys of color in particular are more likely to perceive that they are unwelcome by mainstream society. Perhaps as a result, girls tend to perceive more future opportunities than do immigrant boys of color.

There is some consensus that the boundaries between identities are "more fluid and permeable" for girls, who seem to find it easier to assume transcultural competencies and make successful bicultural adjustments (Waters 1996, p. 66). Such bicultural strategies are critical to the individual's well-being.

In forging new identities, the children of immigrants are drawn into three primary styles of identity formation that fall along a continuum. These identities and styles of adaptation are powerfully linked to social context and social mirroring; they are fluid and may shift in the course of development, being highly dependent upon the social environment the youth moves in.

At one extreme, adolescents may structure their identity by identifying with the dominant mainstream culture while rejecting the culture of their origin. Adolescents who forge an identity of ethnic flight may avoid speaking their parents' language and forge relations with mainstream youth. Though they may gain access to privileged positions within the mainstream society, they will still need to deal with issues of marginalization and exclusion. By mainstream standards, this strategy is often quite adaptive in terms of "making it." But the identity achieved often comes at a significant social and emotional cost: self-disparagement and estrangement from their culture of origin.

At the other extreme of the identity continuum are youths who develop an adversarial stance, constructing identities upon the rejection of the institutions of the dominant culture (which have already rejected them). Immigrant youths who find themselves structurally marginalized and culturally disparaged are likely to respond in ways similar to other marginalized youths (such as African Americans in the U.S., Koreans in Japan, and Algerians in France). Youths with adversarial identities often encounter problems in school, have high dropout rates, face unemployment in the formal economy, and are overrepresented in the penal system.

The most adaptive strategy is creatively to fuse aspects of both the parental and the new culture. Among youths who successfully mold a transcultural identity, the culturally constructed patterns of social control of immigrant parents retain legitimacy. At the same time, these youths develop the social competencies required to function effectively within the dominant society. Transcultural youths have the instrumental competencies necessary both to cope successfully in the new setting and to retain the affective, emotional sustenance of the community of origin.

Forging a transcultural identity is a challenge. It is all too easy to become encumbered by self-doubt and to internalize self-hate. Gelareh Asayesh, an Iranian immigrant, describes the tensions:

> The need to belong is a powerful thing. It pits those of us who are children of other worlds against ourselves and one another. . . . I try to catch the eyes of people passing by, hungry for the opportunity to show them that despite my appearance, I am not one of them. Let me speak a sentence full of colloquialisms. See, I am fluent . . . I have no accent! I'm like you. Don't consign me to the trash heap, where the unforgivably different belong. . . . This inner dialogue fills me with shame, yet I am helpless against it. I have become a party to my own disenfranchisement. The worst part of being

told in a thousand ways, subtle and not, that one is inferior is the way that message worms itself into the heart. It is not enough to battle the prejudice of others, one must also battle the infection within. (Asayesh 1999, pp. 210–211).

Withstanding the tremendous stresses of migration and the social pressures and tensions of the new homeland requires an often-elusive alchemy of effort, resilience, and optimism. The support of family and mentors is essential for maintaining that youthful drive. Immigrant youth bring with them tremendous hope and energy, and host societies would do well to harness that energy and repay that hope with opportunity and recognition of cultural pride. The achievement of transcultural competencies is the surest path toward the successful transition of immigrants.

WORKS CITED

Agger, Inger. *The Blue Room: Trauma and Testimony among Refugee Women: A Psychosocial Exploration.* London, 1992.

Ainslie, Ricardo. "Cultural Mourning, Immigration, and Engagement: Vignettes from the Mexican Experience." In *Crossings: Mexican Immigration in Interdisciplinary Perspectives,* edited by Marcelo M. Suárez-Orozco. Cambridge, Mass., 1998.

Amnesty International. "From San Diego to Brownsville: Human Rights Violation on the USA-Mexico Border." *New Release,* 20 May 1998.

Aronowitz, M. "The Social and Emotional Adjustment of Immigrant Children: A Review of the Literature." *International Review of Migration* 18 (1984): 237–257.

Arrendondo-Dowd, P. "Personal Loss and Grief as a Result of Immigration." *Personnel and Guidance Journal* 59 (1981): 376–378.

Asayesh, Gelareh. *Saffron Sky: A Life Between Iran and America.* Boston, 1999.

Athey, J. L., and F. L. Ahearn. *Refugee Children: Theory, Research, and Services.* Baltimore, 1991.

Besier, M., F. Hou, I. Hyman, M. Tousignant. "From New Immigrant Children: How Are They Coping?" Conference Workshop Paper for Investing in Children: A National Research Conference. Available: http://www.hrdc.gc.ca/strapol/arb/conferences.

Brandon, P. "Gender Differences in Young Asian Americans: Educational Attainment." *Sex Roles,* 25 (1991): 45–61.

Bylund, Maria. "Women in Exile and Their Children." In *Refugee Women and Their Mental Health: Shattered Societies, Shattered Lives,* edited by Ellen Cole, Olivia Espin, and Esther Rothblum. New York, 1992.

Camino, L.A., and R. M. Kruhlfeld. *Reconstructing Lives, Recapturing Meaning: Refugee Identity, Gender, and Culture Change.* Amsterdam, 1994.

Cole, Ellen, Olivia Espin, and Esther Rothblum. *Refugee Women and Their Mental Health: Shattered Societies, Shattered Lives.* New York, 1992.

De Vos, George, and Marcelo Suárez-Orozco. *Status Inequality: The Self in Culture.* Newbury Park, Calif., 1990.

Eschbach, Karl, Jacqueline Hagan, and Nestor Rodriguez. *Death at the Border.* Houston, Tex., Center for Immigration Research, 1997.

Espenshade, Thomas J., and Maryanne Belanger. "Immigration and Public Opinion." In *Crossings: Mexican Immigration in Interdisciplinary Perspectives,* edited by Marcelo M. Suárez-Orozco. Cambridge, Mass., 1997, pp. 365–403.

Espin, Olivia. "Psychological Impact of Migration Latinas: Implications for Psychotherapeutic Practice." *Psychology of Women Quarterly* 11 (1987): 489–503.

Espin, Olivia. *Women Crossing Boundaries: A Psychology of Immigration and Transformations of Sexuality.* New York, 1999.

Falicov, Celia Jaes. *Latino Families in Therapy: A Guide to Multicultural Practice.* New York, 1998.

Flaskerud, J. H. and R. Uman. "Acculturation and Its Effects on Self-Esteem Among Immigrant Latina Women." *Behavioral Medicine,* 22 (1996), pp. 123–133.

Fordham, Signithia. *Blacked Out: Dilemmas of Race, Identity, and Success at Capital High.* Chicago, 1996.

Friedman, Amy. "Rape and Domestic Violence: The Experience of Refugee Women." *Women and Therapy* 13 (1992): 65–78.

Gambel, Yolanda. "Reflections on the Prevalence of the Uncanny in Social Violence." In *Cultures under Siege: Collective Violence and Trauma in Interdisciplinary Perspectives,* edited by Antonius Robben and Marcelo Suárez-Orozco. Cambridge, U.K., 2000.

Garcia-Coll, Cynthia, and Katherine Magnuson. "The Pychological Experience of Immigration: A Developmental Perspective." In *Immigration and the Family: Research and Policy on U.S. Immigrants,* edited by Alan Booth, Ann Crouter, and Nancy Landale. Mahwah, N.J., 1998.

Gibson, Margaret. *Accommodation without Assimilation: Sikh Immigrants in an American High School.* Ithaca, N.Y., 1988.

Gibson, Margaret. "Complicating the Immigrant /Involuntary Minority Typology." *Anthropology and Education Quarterly* 28 (1997): 431–454.

Goodenow, C., and Olivia Espin. "Identity Choices in Immigrant Adolescent Females." *Adolescence* 28 (1993): 173–184.

Grinberg, Leon, and Rebecca Grinberg. *Psychoanalytic Perspectives on Migration and Exile.* New Haven, Conn., 1989.

Hernandez, Donald, and Evan Charney, eds. *From Generation to Generation: The Health and Well-being of Children in Immigrant Families.* Washington, D.C., 1998.

Hoffmann, Eva. *Lost in Translation: A Life in a New Language.* New York, 1989.

Hondagneu-Sotelo, Pierrete. *Gendered Transitions: Mexican Experiences of Immigration.* Berkeley, 1994.

Horowitz, Ruth. *Honor and the American Dream: Culture and Identity in a Chicano Community.* New Brunswick, N.J., 1986.

Kao, Grace, and Marta Tienda. "Optimism and Achievement: The Educational Performance of Immigrant Youth." *Social Science Quarterly* 76 (1995): 1–19.

Khoury, Elizabeth, George Warheit, Rick Zimmerman, William Vega, and Andres Gil. "Gender and Ethnic Differences in the Prevalence of Alcohol, Cigarette, and Illicit Drug Use Over Time in a Cohort of Young Hispanic Adolescents in South Florida." *Women and Health* 24 (1999): 21–40.

Myers, Dowell. Dimensions of Economic Adaptation by Mexican-Origin Men.

In *Crossings: Mexican Immigration in Interdisciplinary Perspectives,* edited by Marcelo M. Suárez-Orozco. Cambridge, Mass., 1998.

Olneck, M. R., and M. Lazerson. "The School Achievement of Immigrant Children: 1900–1930." *History of Education Quarterly* 14 (1974): 453–482.

Olsen, Laurie. *Made in America: Immigrant Children in Our Public Schools.* New York, 1997.

Phinney, Jean S. "Ethnic Identity in Adolescents and Adults: Review of Research." In *Readings in Ethnic Psychology,* edited by Pamela Balls Organista, Kevin M. Chun, and Gerardo Marín. New York, 1998.

Portes, Alejandro, and Lingxin Hao. "E Pluribus Unum: Bilingualism and Loss of Language in the Second Generation." *Sociology of Education* 71 (1998): 269–294.

Portes, Alejandro, and Min Zhou. "The New Second Generation: Segmented Assimilation and Its Variants." *The Annals of the American Academy* 530 (1993): 74–96.

Robben, Antonius, and Marcelo Suárez-Orozco. *Cultures under Siege: Collective Violence and Trauma in Interdisciplinary Perspectives.* Cambridge, U.K., 2000.

Rogler, L. H., D. E. Cortes, and R. G. Malgady. "Acculturation and Mental Health Status Among Hispanics." *American Psychologist* 46 (1991): 585–597.

Rumbaut, Rúben. "Life Events, Change, Migration and Depression." In *Phenomenology and Treatment of Depression,* edited by W. E. Fann et al. New York, 1977.

Rumbaut, Rúben. "The New Californians: Comparative Research Findings on the Educational Progress of Immigrant Children." In *California's Immigrant Children,* edited by Rúben Rúmbaut and W. Cornelius. La Jolla, Calif., 1995.

Shuval, J. "Migration and Stress." In *Handbook on Stress and Anxiety: Contemporary Knowledge, Theory, and Treatment,* I. L. Kutasshm, L. B. Schlesinger et al., eds. San Francisco, 1980.

Sluzki, Carlos. "Migration and Family Conflict." *Family Process* 18, no. 4 (1979): 379–390.

Smajkic, A. and S. Weane. "Special Issues of Newly Arrived Refugee Groups." In *Issues of War Trauma and Working with Refugees: A Compilation of Resources,* edited by Susan Somach. Washington, D.C., 1995.

Smart, J. F., and D. W. Smart. "Acculturation Stress of Hispanics: Loss and Challenge." *Journal of Counseling and Development* 75 (1995): 390–396.

Smith, Robert. "The Education and Work Mobility of Second Generation Mexican Americans in New York City: Preliminary Reflections on the Role of Gender, Ethnicity, and School Structure." Paper presented at the Eastern Sociological Society Meeting, Boston Mass., March 1999.

Somach, Susan. *Issues of War Trauma and Working with Refugees: A Compilation of Resources.* Washington, D.C., 1995.

Steinberg, Laurence, B. Bradford Brown, and Sanford Dornbusch. *Beyond the Classroom: Why School Reform Has Failed and What Parents Need to Do.* New York, 1996.

Suárez-Orozco, Carola. "Identities Under Siege: Immigration Stress and Social Mirroring Among the Children of Immigrants." In *Cultures under Siege: Collective Violence and Trauma in Interdisciplinary Perspectives,* edited by Antonius Robben and Marcelo Suárez-Orozco. Cambridge, U.K., 2000.

Suárez Orozco, Carola, and Marcelo Suárez Orozco. *Children of Immigration.* Cambridge, Mass., 2001.

Suárez-Orozco, Marcelo M. *Central American Refugees and U.S. High Schools: A Psychosocial Study of Motivation and Achievement.* Stanford, Calif., 1989.

Valenzuela, Abel. "Gender Roles and Settlement Activities among Children and Their Immigrant Families." *American Behavioral Scientist* 42, no. 4 (1999): 720–742.

Volkan, V. D. "Immigrants and Refugees: A Psychodynamic Perspective," *Mind and Human Interaction* 4, no. 2 (1993): 63–69.

Waters, M. "The Intersection of Gender, Race, and Ethnicity in Identity Development of Caribbean American Teens." In *Urban Girls: Resisting Stereotypes, Creating Identities,* edited by B. J. Ross Leadbeater and N. Way. New York, 1996.

Wheaton, B. "Stress, Personal Coping Resources, and Psychiatric Symptoms: An Investigation of Interactive Models." *Journal of Health and Social Behavior* 24, no. 9 (1983): 208–229.

Wong-Fillmore, Lily. "When Learning a Language Means Losing the First," *Early Childhood Research Quarterly* 6 (1991): 323–346.

III: WOMEN, ACTIVISM, AND SOCIAL CHANGE

Women's Rights as Human Rights

WOMEN AS AGENTS OF SOCIAL CHANGE

Temma Kaplan

∞ UNTIL the1990s, discussions of human rights focused on torture and genocide and other extreme forms of abuse. The term "human rights" usually referred to violations of people's bodily integrity by agents of the state. Indeed there have been far too many instances of such violations in Argentina, Chile, Guatemala, Northern Ireland, Bosnia, Rwanda, and South Africa, resulting in torture and murder. But women grassroots activists, including survivors of such atrocities, have increasingly extended the term "human rights" to indicate a location and a process of direct democracy by which people reveal secrets those in power wish to hide. They include under the rubric of "human rights" opposition to various forms of violence, including economic and social inequalities against which activists have increasingly been struggling.

In the1990s grassroots women's organizations pressured the official human rights organizations to discount the apparent separation between public and private life and to characterize as human rights abuses such violent acts as female genital mutilation, enslaving servants and child prostitutes, dowry death, domestic abuse, and the use of rape as a strategy of war. They have led marches and invasions of buildings worldwide to force the United Nations, and through it member governments, to stop abetting the abuse of women. Women's international social movements, basing their strategies on participatory democracy, on leading by pedagogy, and on integrating everyday life and politics to meet human needs, periodically express themselves through mobilizations, by which they have redefined "human rights" to mean universal social transformation.

Grassroots movements of women have generally mobilized around quality of life issues they associate with human rights. Concerned with the survival of their families, neighbors, and racial, ethnic, or class communities, when they decide to move, they oppose conscription of their sons; they protest against increases in the cost of living that prevent women from providing food, fuel, shelter, health care, and safety for their families and communities; they resist the siting of toxic-waste dumps near homes belonging to members of a repressed minority who may be poor and seemingly defenseless; they demand information about family members who have been kidnapped or arrested; they call for the end to violence at home, in public, and in hidden prisons and torture chambers; they claim their rights as human beings.

"Grassroots" is a term that defies any narrow definition since it is as common as grass and as difficult to uproot. Grassroots groups can frequently ally people from different classes, races, and ethnicities. Like "movement," used as both a noun and an adjective to describe the New Left in the 1960s, "grassroots" also suggests a process that may result in a variety of different organizations. Grassroots organizations can sometimes ally with churches, political parties, and trade unions, but they are never under their control. To the women claiming to be from the grassroots, the term means being free from any constraining political affiliations and being responsible to no authority except their own group. Grassroots women recognize the power of corporate and governmental opponents, but they also toy with powerful opponents, subjecting them to ridicule designed to shame them in public for what they prefer to do in private. These women assert their moral superiority: their right to be community activists, not according to official laws, but on their own terms.

During the last decade, grassroots women's groups all over the world have been intensifying their call for "women's human rights" in what amounts to a political theory in motion. Arguing that abuse of women and girl children are not only unfortunate occurrences but are actually violations of women's human rights, women from groups such as WILDAF (Women in Law and Development, Zimbabwe), ILANUD (Programa Mujer, Justicia, y Género, Costa Rica), INFORM (Information Monitor, Sri Lanka), WLUML (Women Living Under Muslim Law), ASCENT (Asian Centre for Women's Human Rights, the Philippines), and the Center for Women and Global Leadership at Douglass College, Rutgers University, among others, have reshaped the language of politics. Such advocacy groups have voiced demands for collective need, drawing on implicit theories of human rights, seeking to make community health and freedom from violence in the country and in the home a corollary of justice, with justice deriving its power from commonsense notions of human need rather than from codified law.[1]

The New Human Rights

What began as a strategy to make visible what powerful groups tried to keep secret has created the embryo of future democratic institutions. If calling for human rights were merely a defensive strategy to protect the line beyond which women could not afford to retreat, it would be interesting. But "human rights," linked to "democracy," as it so often is on the lips of grassroots women, is actually a claim for a new vision of politics. In part, the women proclaiming their human rights want the supports some social democracies provide. Women advocating human rights, democracy, and justice today are also attempting, at least in their visions for the future, to promote entirely new institutions.

In an age when multinational corporations, supported by the International Monetary Fund, the World Bank, and the World Trade Organization, wield more power than all but seven nation states, there is no existing political body able to defend and promote the political interests of the majority of the world's people. The United Nations provides a space where ethical ideas can be expressed and where certain social, economic, and political arrangements can be made. But no existing institutions mediate between individuals and the IMF in the Southern Hemisphere or between individuals and the WTO anywhere. Lobbying at United Nations conferences, such older groups as the Conference of NGOs (nongovernmental organizations) in Consultative Relation to the United Nations (CONGO) help constitute just one of the embryonic forms of the institutions grassroots women around the world are in the process of creating.[2] The relationship of "human rights" to the attempts to protect entire communities from the incursions of authoritarian governments or clandestine international organizations reached a peak in the last decade of the twentieth century. To meet national and international threats that violated not just bodily integrity but the possibilities for survival and hopes for the future of millions of women and men, grassroots organizations of women have moved out of their local and national territories to mobilize and lobby at an international level. They have elbowed themselves into international forums and have attacked those who would torture and destroy the body politic. Targeting various conferences of the United Nations, activist women of every description have put their bodies and their minds at the center of global power. Not merely resisting unjust authority, these women, sometimes in conjunction with men of their class and sometimes alone, have begun to create new political institutions dedicated to making human rights, broadly construed, a central element in the international political agenda. Grassroots women's groups have been moving back and forth between demands for material goods necessary for survival and demands for more ephemeral goals such as "justice."

By justice they mean equal distribution of resources and of access to influence over decision making. By human rights, they mean what socialism used to mean: a good life, free from violence, filled with creativity, with food, clothing, shelter, health care, and housing readily available. The grassroots organizations generally try to decentralize decision making and introduce what activists in the Civil Rights Movement and New Left groups of the 1960s in the United States and elsewhere called "participatory democracy." The slogan of the Third World Conference on Women, held in 1985 in Nairobi, Kenya, "to think globally but organize locally," might be called the motto of such human rights-oriented grassroots movements of women.

Slowly at first and now at an accelerating pace, women human rights activists are on the move. Over the past century, when a crisis ensued and the patterns of everyday life lost their form because of health threats, housing shortages, disruptions in the social order, or economic crises, often caused by shifts in global economic arrangements, such women sometimes argued that justice required that they intercede. By justice, they often meant more balanced behavior, an end to violence, and equal distribution of social necessities. Certain politically active feminists have joined with women of the working classes and subordinated ethnic and racial groups to make claims for justice, representing their demands as selfless and their provenance as universal. They have challenged rights of private property, unfettered markets, and structural adjustment policies, substituting claims for economic equality, social transformation, and democracy. Very much committed to improving conditions for themselves and their families, these women look toward new social and economic relations; they are visionaries who speak for a new ethical order, one based on principles of justice that transcend the rights of private property.

The particular brand of justice women evoke in these kinds of movements rests with fundamental human rights that no existing government or legal system now promotes. But these rights—to eat, use water, have shelter, remain well, and live in peace—are so much a part of what every human being in every culture knows is necessary to survival that only tyrants are willing to say that others should not strive for them. Women in grassroots movements increasingly have compared their own collective treatment at the hands of powerful companies and governments that endangered the health of their families to violations of justice and human rights. And these women have not been alone. In grassroots movements all over the world, militant women have shown in public displays how social and economic requirements fit into their conceptualization of human rights.

Speaking on 24 April 1998, at the memorial held at the General Assembly of the United Nations in New York for Bella Abzug (1920–1998), the feminist human rights and environmental activist, one high UN official praised Abzug for bringing civil society into the United Nations. To an audience of women from around the world—many wearing big hats in her honor—speaker after speaker recalled how she had helped translate theory into practice and practice back into theoretical arguments about the gendered nature of human rights. Abzug and her group WEDO (Women's Environment and Development Organization) provide an example of how women have made their presence felt to link individual feminist goals for equity to collective demands for social justice. Women's onslaught on the UN has been dedicated to showing how women of all races, classes, ethnicities, and nationalities can lobby the UN about many of the broad social and economic issues the UN addresses.

The call for human rights is not merely a shift in rhetoric; rather, it represents a groping toward an ill-defined but increasingly visible alternative social and political formation. Probing the meaning of human rights in the present context of grassroots movements points to the relationship between survival and the promotion of a new set of social relations and political institutions. The new organizations that grassroots women are creating provide a sense of entitlement based on what human beings need to survive. These organizations raise the question of whether we can go too far in subordinating political rights to the equally dire need for social and economic rights. If we can envision a new arena in which grassroots groups of women are struggling and creating new democratic institutions, we may have to move away from any notion of public and private, of the state and civil society. If these dualities no longer suffice to explain how political identities become established and what customs and practices enable ordinary women to form self-generating institutions, we need a new language to explain what grassroots women's groups mean by human rights.

Increasingly, since the 1970s, international women's federations and grassroots women activists have occupied public spaces to denounce violations of women's human rights. They have gathered at the United Nations and at the meeting of the World Trade Organization, held in late 1999 in Seattle, Washington. On 1 December 1999, the day after the police in Seattle had rioted, women scheduled to hold a teach-in about the effects of the WTO on women, decided to organize a peaceful demonstration downtown. Wearing gags to make visible the way they felt silenced, they marched in front of the police wearing riot gear. Once the police were given the signal that President Bill Clinton had safely reached his destination, the police, according to Ruth Caplan, dropped their batons, lifted their visors, and assured the women of their support.[3] By liberating space from which ordinary women previously had been barred, women's human rights advocates in Seattle and others around the globe have been publicizing the activities that those in power prefer to keep secret.

One Woman's Story

The story of Luz de las Nieves Ayress Moreno, a political revolutionary in Chile in the 1970s who suffered through three years of torture, exemplifies the struggles by women for human rights under extreme conditions under authoritarian regimes. Ayress is remarkable for her commitment to human rights as a matter of justice that links global concerns with local action. Now an exile living in New York, Nieves Ayress works as a nanny and helps organize a community center called Vamos a la Peña del Bronx in the South Bronx.

Nieves Ayress links her international concerns with local struggles for human rights. She has developed a feminist critique of some of the excessive resort to guerrilla tactics that endangered her life and contributed to the death of many with whom she was associated. As a student activist committed to winning social justice for the poor in Latin America in the late 1960s, Nieves Ayress left Chile to support revolutionary struggle in Bolivia. Tired of the sexual inequality among the guerrillas, she returned to the university in Chile to fight closer to home. She returned to working with the Socialist Party, but centered her activities in the poor area of La Legua, and she enrolled in the university. Because all students were suspect, she was arrested immediately after the military coup on 11 September 1973, which overthrew President Salvador Allende's government and brought General Augusto Pinochet to power. She was taken to the National Soccer Stadium, which became a holding pen and series of torture chambers, and suffered electric shocks all over her body. When speaking of her experiences, she hurries over that aspect of her life, noting that everyone suffered the military's use of electric cattle prods. But the second internment shaped her future life.

Living apart from her parents, she returned to the university as a twenty-three-year-old graduate student to study child development. At the same time, she became active in an underground movement to resist the military regime in the months following the coup. An Argentinean called Alberto or Comandante Esteban infiltrated her group. He claimed to be a leftist guerrilla and promised to provide arms and military training to resist Pinochet. Ayress, who recognized the futility of armed struggle and was suspicious that Esteban was an agent working with the military, urged her group to avoid any contact with Esteban. Those who ignored her and followed Esteban's lead were found dead in December 1973 with marks of extensive torture.

Ayress remained underground, but one day in January 1974, she thought it was safe to visit her father at his small technical machinery factory. When she arrived, she found Comandante Esteban and some soldiers waiting for her. She, her father, and her fifteen-year-old brother were taken first to Londres 38, a notorious torture center, run by Chilean army intelligence in downtown Santiago. Then began nearly three years of torture sessions at three different concentration camps.

In a communique dated 18–21 February 1975 to the Third Session of the International Commission on Crimes of the Military Junta in Chile, Fanny Eleman, the Secretary General of the International Democratic Federation of Women, told the story of Nieves Ayress. The federation was formed in Paris at the end of World War II and consisted of women from the Resistance and survivors of the Nazi extermination camps. Devoted to fighting against fascism, they circulated Ayress's story to as many human rights and women's organizations as they could reach. Ayress's mother, Virginia Moreno, had succeeded in finding her daughter and meeting with her a month after Ayress's capture. Moreno, who had written a dozen letters a day to get her family's story out, was able to reach certain people in Washington and Paris with her daughter's story. Ayress told how the torturers were men from Brazil, Bolivia, Uruguay, Paraguay, and Argentina as well as from Chile, who were forming an international league, known as Operation Condor, designed to repress resistance to their various military dictatorships. Experimenting on Ayress to see what prisoners could survive, the torturers introduced hungry rats into her vagina, and even tried to have her own father and fifteen-year-old brother rape her. As a measure of her importance as an experimental animal, General Manuel Contreras, Commander of DINA, the Chilean secret police, which reported directly to Pinochet, became one of her torturers.[4]

Ayress had managed to survive in jail until December 1976, when she and eighteen others who were also considered threats to national security were released from jail and exiled from Chile.[5] She traveled to Germany, Italy, Cuba, and Mexico, wherever there were Chilean relief organizations and exiles fighting to overthrow Pinochet. In Cuba she met her future husband Victor Toro, a Chilean revolutionary who had also been brutally tortured. Ayress and Toro left Cuba for Mexico, where their daughter was born, and then settled in the South Bronx, one of the poorest urban areas in the United States. In 1987 they founded Vamos a la Peña del Bronx, a community center that distributes food, helps people with AIDS, and—for Ayress, one of the most important services of all—serves as a center for women who have suffered physical or psychological battering as a result of domestic violence.[6]

The way Nieves Ayress narrates her life story is to emphasize the continuities, especially her continued work as a grassroots political activist. What enabled her to survive so many years of torture was her ability to create a collective life. When she was held in solitary confinement, she spoke to the dishes and to the bars on her cell. She recreated collective life with fellow prisoners. Ayress's story was one of those gathered by Joan Garces, director of the Salvador Allende Foundation in Madrid. Garces provided a significant portion of the evidence that Judge Balthazar Garzon of Spain used in his 1998 request that Pinochet be arrested on 16 October 1998 in London, where he had gone for a back operation. Acting under Spanish law and according to the 1984 UN Convention against Torture and Other Cruel, Inhuman or Degrading Treatment or Punishment, Garzon asked that Pinochet be extradited for the torture and murder of Chileans of Spanish descent and other victims of torture in Chile. Ayress and other survivors went into action, publicizing what they and the people of Chile had endured. Although Pinochet never reached Spain or France or Sweden, where charges against him also were lodged, he was held under house arrest in the United Kingdom until March 2000. He then returned to Chile, where nearly 150 indictments for murder and torture have been brought against him.

More than twenty years before Pinochet's arrest, a mass movement against him began in 1978. On 8 March 1978, International Women's Day, a consortium of students, workers, artists, intellectuals, and journalists gathered under the auspices of a group calling themselves the National Union of Homemakers. They called a meeting at one of the largest theaters in downtown Santiago and demanded the end of violence. In April the copper miners' union called an impromptu meeting and faced brutal repression. May Day provided another opportunity for thousands to congregate at a monument in a downtown square to demand civil and political rights in the biggest demonstration since the 1973 coup.[7]

Throughout the 1980s groups of shanty-town dwellers and women of all classes formed organizations and demonstrated against Pinochet. These social movements helped destabilize the Pinochet regime and forced him to hold a plebiscite in 1988, which led to the formation of a new representative democracy in Chile in 1990. As early as 1985, while Pinochet imposed martial law to repress the social movements mobilizing against him, representatives of the women's movement in Chile attended the

Third International Women's Conference in Nairobi, Kenya. Even under the Pinochet dictatorship, grassroots women activists were able to join their sisters in Nairobi, to call upon women to "think globally and organize locally."

The Importance of the Beijing Conference

The Decade of Women began in 1975 with a meeting in Mexico City that brought women's grassroots movements into public view. Following that were UN conferences on women in Copenhagen in 1980, in Nairobi in 1985, and in Beijing in 1995. In addition, women, first led in this effort by Bella Abzug's Women's Congress for a Healthy Planet at the 1991 UN Earth Summit in Rio de Janeiro, have liberated space at all UN meetings (and at the would-be-secret meeting of the World Trade Organization in Seattle). Grassroots women's groups, lobbying official delegations representing states, have been participating in UN conferences by organizing simultaneous tribunals and forums. At the UN Conference on Human Rights held in Vienna, grassroots women dramatically invaded the hall where delegates were meeting and presented a petition signed by 300,000 women, organized through the Center for Women and Global Leadership. With this demonstration, grassroots women forced the delegates to recognize that violence against women in all its forms—including the use of rape as a form of torture, holding women and girl children in sexual slavery, or killing women because their dowries were insufficient—is a violation of women's human rights. Facing down the delegates, grassroots women from around the world made visible with their own bodies the invisible violence against women taking place all over the world.

The Beijing Conference of 1995 brought the world's women together beyond nationalism to formulate an international agenda. At the First World Conference of Women, in Mexico City in 1975, feminists such as Betty Friedan and women's grassroots activists such as the Bolivian mining-community leader Domitila Barrios de Chungara publicly argued about what women needed and whether middle-class women from the industrialized countries had anything in common with those from poor nations.[8] In Beijing the effort to define women's rights as human rights bridged the gap.

At the other Women's Conferences in Mexico, Copenhagen, and Nairobi, Arab women and Israeli women locked horns as did other antagonists. Nationalist issues had frequently predominated over international goals; but since Beijing, the worlds converged, and the motto of "Women's Rights as Human Rights" has defined the relationship between feminists and members of grassroots movements of women—a pact that increasingly appears in joint public demonstrations. By creating a third space that is neither public nor private, grassroots activists have opened up an arena in which human dignity, not national law or custom, prevails.

The Beijing Conference marked a turning point. Women from Zimbabwe, Zambia, and South Africa, who marched as a group, brought the experiences of grassroots legal and medical movements together. Having discovered that 42 percent of women in Sub-Saharan Africa report that they are beaten regularly and that nearly 100 million African girl children are victims of genital mutilation, southern African women activists publicized these practices not as individual and cultural problems but as violations of human rights for which the United Nations and participating states should be held responsible. Women from southern Africa led the struggle to view mistreatment of women in universal terms that make such treatment unacceptable whatever the religious, cultural, and traditional justifications. Effectively, these women and the majority of other participants challenged the notions that cultural context determines women's needs for bodily integrity. Women grassroots leaders from all over the world attempted collectively to supplant cultural differences with universal ethical human standards applicable to all women.

Women involved in environmental justice movements around the globe took up issues about sustainable development and about how so-called globalization really meant globalization of markets, not of human needs for water, a clean environment, or access to public resources. In fact, activists from many continents discussed how trees necessary to maintain the water table were being leased to corporations, which deforested the land. They discussed how it might be possible to target certain companies that pollute several continents; grassroots women activists contemplated suing those companies in some countries, boycotting them in others, striking against them in other places where the rights of labor were relatively protected. With so many activists gathered together, women discussed the ways even progressive companies such as an American conglomerate, which provided canvas shopping bags to all participants of the Beijing Women's Conference, in fact employed women in sweat shops. The participants from the forum issued a public statement, chastising the company and shaming it in public. The company later agreed to raise wages and provide toilets for its workers. Although the conversations and programs of activists may be ephemeral—finding their ultimate expression in movements far away and years later—the document produced by official government representatives, the Beijing Platform for Action, represents some of the goals and strategies developed among the activists at the forum.

The Beijing Platform for Action, passed by 132 of the 185 governments participating in Beijing, placed increased emphasis on a broad spectrum of economic and social as well as political demands as part of human rights. The Platform for Action called for an end to gender discrimination in education by the year 2005; it demanded that women hold at least 30 percent of all decision-making positions in government; but it did not set targets for reducing the "feminization of poverty," or for controlling the World Trade Organization, the International Monetary Fund, or the World Bank. Despite the difficulties of holding governments accountable to their pledges, the ethical issues raised in Beijing go to the heart of what politics will be in the twenty-first century. Although feminist theorists such as Denise Riley and Iris Marion Young have considered the problem of whether we can speak of "women" at all—given that differences of class, race, ethnicity, ability and disability, and sexual preference confer identities that are steadily gaining currency—grassroots leaders attempt to blur differences in favor of universal human rights.[9]

While feminist lawyers have written the language of rights for women in national as well as UN documents, grassroots women activists have been less constrained by the language of existing legal systems. Women in grassroots movements want individual rights, but they also demand greater protection for the communities for which they speak. In other words, they want to transform international priorities to fulfill human need despite what customary laws or legal systems may dictate, and despite the agreements that so-called neoliberal or late capitalist governments have made.

Perhaps most important, the majority of countries in Beijing endorsed the priority of international human rights for women over national and customary law. A new language of human rights has been developing at the United Nations conferences in Vienna, Cairo, and Beijing. This idea about human rights attempts to transcend national boundaries to talk about universal human rights, with the emphasis on "human" rather than on "rights." They propose to go beyond national law, culture, religions, practices, and customs. At the preparatory conference for Beijing +5, held in New York in late February and early March 2000, the representatives of the 132 signatories to the Beijing Document began discussing what standards they will use to evaluate the progress they have made toward fulfilling their commitments. CONGO, WEDO, and the Center for Women and Global Leadership have helped brief groups from all over the world who came to New York to lobby official governments to represent the interests of ordinary women. Activists have established a model for combining direct and representative democracy that goes to the heart of what democracy might mean in the twenty-first century. By providing mechanisms to have women at the base advise government representatives, the Center for Women and Global Leadership establishes a new form of representation that can keep women's human rights at the forefront. Women increasingly advise the delegates directly through their mobilizations. In such institutions, democracy blends with activism in pursuit of human rights.

Members of grassroots women's movements also gathered to make their presence felt at every meeting. Certain women have argued for years that gender must be considered not only in areas where equity for women seems obvious but also in areas, such as government budgets, tax codes, penal codes, and trade agreements, that might at first seem gender neutral. At the preparatory conference for Beijing +5, women lobbied governments to make sure they recognized that gender transcended social relations and that gender must be incorporated in economic and political concerns.

Activism and Accountability

The effort grassroots women's groups have devoted to articulating women's human rights not only creates a new universal claim, it also demands that the government go beyond the boundaries between what used to be considered public and private life. If enacted as national law, the force of the state could come into play against the vagaries of religious and customary practices and the brutality of individual family members. Authorities become responsible for protecting women against violence, rather than permitting women and their defenders to demand protection. Some fear that state intervention might infantilize women just when they need to empower themselves. And, as feminist activists have always worried, such growth in state power, which blurs the separation of civil society from the state, could put governments squarely back into the bedroom. Will this ultimately help or hurt women and gays? What must we do to gain the benefits of state support while keeping the state at bay?

It might be argued that, in any case, international politicians only pay lip service to ethical goals while they carry out business as usual. Yet consider the Convention Against All Forms of Discrimination Against Women (CEDAW), written in 1979, passed by the UN in 1985, and endorsed by 135 countries, but not by the United States. The CEDAW amounts to an international equal rights amendment and has had an enormous impact on the countries that have passed it. They must now survey their own accomplishments and failures and explain how they plan to improve their records.

Instead of depending on hereditary or elected officials chosen to represent states at United Nations conferences, women working for reproductive rights, against sexual slavery, and for accountability about women's access to scarce resources such as land and water can advise the diplomats directly. No longer satisfied with working through the somewhat blocked arteries of representative government, women's international grassroots movements have been arguing with their bodies to add an element of direct democracy to the international struggle for human rights. In embryonic institutions, direct democracy blends with activism in pursuit of human rights. When such women lobby diplomats directly through their mobilizations, they effectively create a fourth estate: one that is neither judicial, legislative, nor executive. In such practices, democracy blends with activism in pursuit of human rights.

Conclusion

Since the 1990s activists have embarked on a mission to create a new global community, and the notion of women's rights as human rights is intrinsic to it. Women's human rights now hold out the promise of a good life, free from torture, intimidation, scarcity, and pollution, with access to good education, health care, choices about childbearing, and meaningful work. The Beijing Platform for Action and Beijing +5 may not have solved the problems of pollution, poverty, homelessness, or violence against women, but commitments to international platforms set moral standards, providing women's grassroots movements with leverage they can apply to their own governments, and enabling grassroots activists to organize across borders to compel governments to comply.

Women's constant appearance in public spaces such as the international meetings of the United Nations is part of a strategy to weave women into every conversation. The slogan for that process is "human rights." That form of human rights has never been codified in national or international law, but the increasing frequency with which grassroots women's groups have demonstrated for it indicates that human rights—as a social and ethical goal as well as a democratic process—may hold more revolutionary potential than any of us had previously imagined.

NOTES

1. Julieta Kirkwood, a Chilean feminist, first called for "democracy in the country and in the home" in August 1983, during a demonstration against Augusto Pinochet. In the 1980s grassroots women activists began linking the struggle for democracy to the fight against domestic and state violence.

2. The proliferation of grassroots organizations and NGOs (such as Planned Parenthood) and caucuses dealing with specific issues such as women's health is so great that many members of organizations that have participated in various UN conferences have coordinated their activities through an older coordinating body called CONGO. By mid-2000, CONGO had developed an NGO Coordinating Committee to consult with official delegates as they wrote the report. See the following web sites for more detailed material on the work of CONGO and its con-

stituent groups: WomanWatch: http://www.un.org/womenwatch. UNIFEM: http://www.unifem.undp.org.

3. Reported in a speech by Ruth Caplan, of the Alliance for Democracy, delivered at the Annual Central Pennsylvania Consortium Women's Studies Conference, Gettysburg College, Gettysburg, Pennsylvania, 25 March 2000.

4. Fanny Eleman, Secretary General of the International Federation of Women, Report to the Third Session of the International Commission for Research on Crimes Committed by the Military Junta of Chile, 18–21 February. Subsequently listed as the International Federation of Women. Four typed pages, photocopied and in the possession of the author. Carlos Villalón, "Una Historia de Amor al Estilo del Bronx," *La Información* (New York) 15–30 November 1998, pp. 9–14. Personal interviews with Nieves Ayress in New York City, 14 January 1998 and 16 December 2000.

5. Interview with Nieves Ayress by Jorge Ramos, "Así me torturó Pinochet," *El Diario* (New York), 14 January 1999, p. 43.

6. Personal interview with Nieves Ayress in New York City, 17 July 2000.

7. *Chilean Resistance Courier No. 9: Bulletin of the Movement of the Revolutionary Left (MIR) Outside Chile* (Oakland, Calif.) 18 (May–June 1978): 16, 52.

8. Domitila Barrios de Chungara, *Let Me Speak! Testimony of Domitila, A Woman of the Bolivian Mines* (New York, 1978).

9. Denise Riley, *Woman, "Am I that Name?" Feminism and the Category of "Women" in History* (Minneapolis, 1988); Iris Marion Young, "Gender as Seriality: Thinking about Women as a Social Collective," in *Rethinking the Political: Gender, Resistance, and the State,* edited by Barbara Laslett, Johanna Brenner, and Yesim Arat (Chicago, 1995), pp. 99–124.

The Forgotten Minority

Jean Trounstine

☜ EACH fall, on the first day of my Voices Behind Bars class at the community college, I ask my students to describe those who live in prison. What are they like, I ask, these people we call "inmates"? We list all the common notions: "poor," "uneducated," "from dysfunctional families," "addicts." I press them for stereotypes: "big guys with tattoos," "gang members," "psychopathic killers," "mean and violent people." We spend the next hour discussing their assumptions, dissecting perceptions created in part by the media and in part by fear. Then, after the chalkboard is filled with words, some they've crossed out and others they've added, I throw them the clincher. Why hasn't anyone mentioned women? At first they look at me with blank faces and soon they say, oh women, there just aren't that many in prison, and anyway, a student or two will admit, they aren't cool like dangerous guys. Women in prison aren't sexy, as "B" movies make them seem, or scary, like the real-life Charles Manson or the actor Sean Penn in *Dead Man Walking*. Besides that, women are just not at the heart of the matter.

By the end of the semester, my students have come to see that criminal justice systems in most countries think the same way. Women aren't at the crux of the prison problem. The number of women behind bars in 1999 in the United States was approximately 138,000, more than triple the number in 1985.[1] Women compose only approximately 7 percent of America's burgeoning jail and prison population.[2] Female prisoners are often overlooked; they are treated both inequitably—not offered services, educational programs, or facilities comparable to men's—and unjustly, as though they have the same needs as men.[3] Also of great concern is the information on sexual abuse that organizations like Amnesty International and Global Rights Watch have released. Perhaps this is why, I tell my students on that first day of class, you don't realize the subtle and not so subtle injustices that occur behind bars. You don't know enough of the truth about the people who live in prison.

Inside a Women's Prison

"Turn around and face the wall. Hands out to your sides. Spread your legs. That's it. All right, take off your shoes. Show me the bottoms of your feet. Good. Head forward. Hair. Behind the ears. Good. Stick out your tongue. Okay, open your mouth wide." I knew why she had to do it but I wanted to strike out against the officer invading my private spaces. She had violated the rules I lived by. I had been forced to submit to her will.

This was my first search in 1986 when I entered Framingham Women's Prison in Massachusetts, the state's most secure facility for females, where I would teach college classes and direct plays for ten years. It was not unlike the first moment of many women who enter a prison, although they are more likely to be strip-searched than merely patted down. It is what I consider the beginning of my political education, the moment at which I first began to realize the humiliation and shame felt by women who do time all over the world. It is emblematic of a system that operates on a military model, believes that criminal women are fallen women, and perpetuates the notion of the keeper and the kept.

Of course there are people in prison who need to be there and who make searches necessary. But because of the abrupt manner of my pat-search, the shock of it, I began to put myself in the shoes of the women who spend day after day behind bars. I said to myself, if this small experience can provoke such enormous feelings for me, what must it feel like for those who have been sexually abused and are guarded by men, those who cannot speak the language where they are incarcerated, those who out of desperation trade cigarettes for sex, or those whose children live too far away to visit? The search made me seek to answer questions: Who are these women and what does it feel like to live behind bars?

Bertie, twenty-one, was far away from her family in Jamaica, and by 1986 she had done two years at Framingham. Her style: flamboyant hats even though she had nowhere to go; an actor's sense of timing; a habit of telling someone off with her whole body; and a Caribbean way of tripping over words with a lilt. At first, Bertie never talked about her crime, the murder of her four-month-old baby girl, and was scorned as all bad mothers are in prison. Bertie found shelter in Dolly, an older woman she called "Ma," who accepted her and kept others at bay. Dolly reminded me of a racetrack bookie. She used to bring her knitting to class. A grandmother and pushing fifty, she was the second woman in the history of Framingham to earn an associate's degree. She was a hairdresser and trained as a Eucharistic minister, and Dolly later was awarded a humanitarian award by the officers at Framingham. She often said that she went to prison because of loving the wrong man, Frank, who killed their neighbor in a fight. Although she maintained that Frank acted alone, Dolly was convicted on the theory of "joint venture," aiding and abetting her partner in the murder. Having served fifteen years of a life sentence, she was refused a commutation, although at the time the governor was told that Dolly had congestive heart failure and would not live long if she did not get proper medical treatment outside prison. After fifteen years, she applied for parole and was one of the 2 percent in Massachusetts who are successful the first time around.

Kit, a forty-something junkie from the projects who called herself "white trash," wore her hair up in a tight ponytail with strands of hair straggling out, making her look bedraggled and old. She had purplish rings under her eyes and no teeth. A single mother, she lost her young daughter, whom she called "Joan the Bone," to Social Services. Kit's mother, an alcoholic, could not take care of Joan, and without a husband or sister, Kit had no place for her daughter to live. Kit was in and out of prison a few times before going to pre-release. When I knew her she wrote essays, poetry, and humorous sketches as well as stage-managed and performed in plays.

Gloria, a middle-aged black woman, killed her husband in self-defense. She was housed in a red room at Framingham. She said it haunted her, "the color of the blood she'd shed." She kept photos of her husband and children on the walls and prayed for them every day. Soon after I started teaching at Framingham, I saw Gloria on the news, talking about her crime. Her young son was also on camera, standing outside the prison by the barbed wire fence, a microphone in hand, a newscaster at his side. "Mama, I wish I could have done it for you," he said, sadly. I remember thinking, he's only seven and his mother is serving time for murder.

Luz said she didn't start the fire although arson was considered her crime. She was from a large Puerto Rican family but her children seldom visited, never wrote, and as she said, "*Dios mio,* who has the money to call collect." Luz talked about dreams she had "in the free world," about wanting to be a vet, taking her children to visit the graves of her ancestors, and having enough money so her mother never had to clean another house for the rest of her life.

It is easier to forget these women when we do not add names and faces to statistics. Then we can be content with what we see on the news, nodding our heads at the fact that, in this country, according to the Sentencing Project, ten times more black and Hispanic women are likely to go to prison or jail at least one time during their lifetime than white women.[4] Or we can, like my students, look askance when I say that of all the industrialized nations in the world, only Russia, a society in flux, has a higher incarceration rate.

We do not like to think about the humanity of the people we incarcerate, preferring instead to concentrate on their crimes, the more dramatic the better. But most women behind bars are not incarcerated for crimes as dramatic as the ones I mentioned above. The women who gravitated toward my college classes were the long-termers; they were more motivated to find ways to deal with their sentences. Most women behind bars are not there for years. They are women caught in a cycle of crime and poverty. The majority are in prison for economic crimes such as shoplifting, check forgery, crimes against property, and illegal credit-card use, according to a report issued in May 1994 by the Women's Economic Agenda Project, a California-based organization. The crimes that women commit often involve drugs.[5] In fact, says Meda Chesney-Lind, a noted researcher on women in prison, "while the intent of 'get tough' policies was to rid society of so-called drug king-pins, more than one-third of the women serving time for drug offenses in state prisons are there on charges of possession."[6]

Women Inmates: Particular Problems and Needs

Although many have violence in their backgrounds, by and large women in prison are not there for violent crimes. In my experience, many have been prostitutes and have drug or alcohol problems. They have chronic health problems, poor self-images, and, raised in families where neglect is the rule, have often been drawn to destructive relationships. Most are mothers who have not finished high school, with young children at home. They report significant histories of abuse, both physical and sexual, and many get pregnant and marry early to escape from home life.[7]

According to Margaret Shaw, a research associate at Concordia University in Montreal, "The history of women's imprisonment has been remarkably similar in most countries." From the moment a woman enters prison, she is met by the same system of power that has exerted control over her since childhood. She is treated either as a "childlike creature" who needs to be taught "maternal and domestic duties," or as someone too far gone to be reformed.[8]

What does it mean for a woman to experience submitting to the will of the keepers of the keys? Jean Harris, the school headmistress who became known for the murder of her lover, said that a typical day for her at the Bedford Hills correctional facility in New York State involved having doors unlocked and locked for her on the average of ninety times.[9] Being locked up includes being at the mercy of others and surrendering aspects of personal power we take for granted.

Dolly wrote a piece in one of my writing classes in which she described how hard it was for her to sleep knowing that, due to understaffing, officers were forced to patrol several units at a time each night. She said inmates who slept four to a room might be left unchecked for an hour without any guard available. What if a fight broke out, or a fire, or someone got sick, she worried. She wouldn't be able to leave her cell, and she feared such helplessness.

A prisoner's life is controlled by the guards who manage the prison, and while on the surface that seems logical and at times even useful, with women prisoners it is troubling. First of all, in this country most correctional officers are male. According to Human Rights Watch, men working in female correctional institutions outnumber their female counterparts by two and in some cases three to one—the major factor contributing to sexual abuse by officers. In fact, Human Rights Watch says, the practice of men "holding contact positions over women" often leads to violations of the United Nations Standard Rules for the Treatment of Prisoners.[10]

In a strange way, the principles of equal opportunity and civil rights are responsible for men guarding women. It is difficult to find grounds for denying men the job of prison guard. Nina Siegel is the author of a chilling article about the experiences of a woman in a California prison. According to Siegel, men's employment makes up 94 percent of all employment in prisons in this country. This situation, she argues, can lead to women being raped. In the case of the woman who was the subject of her article, the situation led to her being savagely beaten and sodomized for hours by guards; she was later threatened when a complaint was made to officials. This is not the exception, says Siegel. "For vast numbers of women behind bars, prison is a hell of sexual terror."[11]

Although numerous reports worldwide speak of such criminal behavior by officers toward inmates, rape and other kinds of sexual assault are not the only abuses that occur. In 1998 Amnesty International reported that many women in prisons and jails were victimized by male staff, in the form of "sexually offensive language; male staff touching inmates' breasts and genitals when conducting searches; male staff watching inmates while they are naked."[12] Because of poor supervision and training of male officers, these behaviors in many cases go unpunished. Despite their outrage, prisoners historically have been too frightened for their welfare and the welfare of their children to speak out.

One evening in 1995 at Framingham, the cast poured into a play rehearsal I was holding to tell me that over 100 pretrial detainees were awakened in the middle of the night by male and female officers in masks, screaming abusive language at the inmates. At first, I didn't know what to believe. They were so upset, all of them, talking at once, telling me how awful it was, how unjust, that it was like a nightmare. The officers made sixteen of the women strip, submit to a search, and give urine samples; my students swore that this had to be illegal. At the time, I was like so many who discount the stories of prisoners; I thought they had to be exaggerating. But in 1997, as reported by Amnesty International USA, the inmates won a lawsuit against the Department of Corrections, settling for $80,000 and the promise that future drug raids could not be carried out in such a fashion or with men present for searches. Their courage in the face of abusive treatment taught me that, as difficult as it is for women in the free world to speak up and counter the stereotype that a woman's word is worthless, it is even more difficult for women behind bars to break the silence and seek justice.

Some male jailers bring discriminatory attitudes about male dominance to their jobs. In some countries, the mistreatment of women in custody "appears to target their sexuality in a deliberate attempt to degrade them, and by extension their male family members." Egyptian security forces have been known to order female relatives of Islamic militants to strip naked and place them together with male detainees in a closed room in an effort to humiliate them and their families. Women in Pakistani jails who try to report rapes risk being accused of "sexual intercourse without being validly married."[13] They are marked for life.

While most of the sexual abuse of female inmates is about power and occurs with male guards, Nina Siegel has noted that prison ministers, doctors and male nurses, low-level administrators, and wardens have been the targets of allegations. In October 1999 the ABC program *Nightline,* hosted by Ted Koppel, did a series detailing the case of Anthony DiDomenico, a doctor from a California women's prison. The doctor had administered unneeded pelvic exams to women inmates, remarking that women appreciated these exams, "the only male contact" some of them got. Only after the information was broadcast, was DiDomenico transferred to another facility.

A male teacher in the college program at Framingham was conveniently transferred to a men's prison when women accused him of being "too familiar" in classes. A top official I knew made it his business to flirt with inmates, call them "girls" behind their backs, and overlook certain guards' actions. Sexual abuse by female officers is less frequent, but it does occur. Once a woman guard inappropriately touched my breasts when she pat-searched me; when I complained to the head of education, it was laughed off.

We most often hear of men raping other men in prison, but such acts happen occasionally with women inmates. Poor supervision and training can lead to neglect. Shirley, a young woman who played a lead in one of my plays, was about to make her entrance at the dress rehearsal. She stood up from the circle of chairs lining the stage apron, grabbed her kerchief, then clutched her apron, and fell, convulsing onto the wooden floor at the stage periphery. She began a sort of soundless groan, pulling her knees into her chest, and finally, curled up like a small child, lay motionless.

Her fellow cast member, Jen, was on her feet at once, at her friend's side, and the other women got water, a sweater, anything to help. Bertie, the Jamaican student who by now had been in three plays, knew the ropes and instructed me to find the recreation officer, who could call a nurse. Meanwhile a guard arrived and tried to talk to Shirley. Jen, shaking, looked up at him. "She hasn't been eating again. I know she's pretty sick."

The guard asked Shirley if she wanted to go to the health unit, but she shook her head no, over and over, tears streaming down her face. Finally, after what seemed like hours, a nurse appeared. She took Shirley's pulse and repeated the same questions. Jen was the only one who could get Shirley to speak. They decided to go back to her unit, Jen admonishing her fearfully, "You have to eat Shirley. You can't starve yourself to death." None of us realized then that that was exactly what Shirley, tormented by secrets and suffering from anorexia, was trying to do.

It relieved and surprised me that Shirley made it back the next day; in fact, Shirley's performance was the hit of the show. But I was shocked when, later, Bertie confided that Shirley had been raped a year earlier by a woman in the Awaiting Trial Unit where she'd been before sentencing. "I didn't want to mention it while we were in rehearsal. The woman who raped her was in the play too. They say she stuck a broom up her."

In some way, I felt responsible. Why, I wondered, had anyone let the two women be in an activity together, and why hadn't they let me know? Didn't anyone connect her anorexia with sexual abuse? At the time I didn't realize how much goes on in prison without communication and without repercussions. Framingham had kept her from committing crimes but had not protected her from being a victim of rape. I asked an officer about it, but he shrugged it off. "All that's hearsay. Until there's a conviction, there's nothing we can do. Anyway, around here, rape is something these women are all too familiar with. Who knows if Shirley was lying to get attention?"

Increasingly, women are speaking out, although for years the fear of repercussion silenced them. But still, as Siegel notes, Justice Department figures show that only ten prison employees in the entire federal prison system were disciplined in 1997 for sexual misconduct. Some believe that, in a system created by men, men's concerns are paramount. Chesney-Lind calls it "vengeful equity"—the result of a male imprisonment model, one that treats female offenders as though they were men.

Prison Policies

In 1917, when fourteen states in America had prisons for women, the idea was to reform those who had gone astray and teach women to be good housewives, helpmates, and mothers.[14] As old-fashioned as that sounds, some of the early reforms did recognize that women and men prisoners had different needs, even though they also encouraged women's dependency and subservience. But by 1935 reformatories had merged with custodial prisons—those built to house and keep criminals under lock and key—and by 1990, when the prison population was exploding, custodial prisons, a booming business, were being built at a fast pace with little thought for what might be best for women. Officials rationalized that because the number of women incarcerated was still so low compared to the number of men, it was not economical to meet women's needs.

When my community-college students took a tour of Framingham, they saw a sprawling campuslike environment. They said the reality was different from the image they had formed, based on TV, of four men crammed into a cell that stank of urine and feces. But I told them that Framingham's environment, held over from early reformatories, is deceptive. Four women still might be confined to one room the size of a large closet, and although buildings are spread out, inmates do not have access to the grounds without supervision.

Whereas there are twenty-two custodial facilities for men in Massachusetts, there is only one secure facility for women. That means that children who live miles away have trouble seeing their mothers and that visits of other family members are often infrequent. There are few programs for women offering education, exercise, or skill-training. Men might learn carpentry or plumbing, yet it took years before the women at Framingham could get a program called Women in the Building Trades. At first, officials would not allow tools in the prison, saying they were too dangerous for the women.

As a result of a 1990 study, Canada has done somewhat better, instituting five smaller regional facilities instead of one prison for women, putting in place women-centered programs, opening an Aboriginal healing lodge, revamping classification (the system that determines where a woman is housed), and retraining the staff to heed women's needs.[15] Canadian women in any part of the country now can get sentenced to a facility nearer to where they live. But in most countries, the distance between a prisoner's home and the prison is of little concern.

The equal rights of male and female inmates does not necessarily mean that males and females should receive exactly the same treatment; but it does mean they should have access to services that respond to their particular situations and characteristics. Amnesty International points out that, to be effective, some programs must be tailored to the needs of women. According to a 1997 AI study, the majority of women's prisons in this country lag behind in developing programs specific to female offenders in the areas of substance abuse, domestic violence, health education and victims of crime.

I watched Framingham's gym go to seed over a period of two years. The roof leaked; the floor boards buckled; there was no sign of renovation plans. That meant that women were deprived of an exercise facility for that time. Although there was a small weight room in operation, there was nowhere for volleyball, basketball, or aerobics. Women often told me how men in the state had better access to fresh vegetables and healthy food, religious services, and college classes. They felt that they deserved equal services in these areas.

One of the newest attempts to equalize men and women behind bars is through the chain gang, which uses shackled workers to toil on highways or in fields. As a result of a "tough on crime" policy, chain gangs have returned in several states, including for women. The most notorious instance is in Arizona, whose sheriff pronounced himself an "equal opportunity incarcerator," defended keeping women in "dank, cramped disciplinary cells," three or four to a room, and asked inmates "to sign up 'voluntarily' to fifteen-women chain gangs."[16]

Many prison activists feel that chain gangs are a kind of restraint and constitute cruel and unusual punishment, evoking images of slavery. The United Nations forbids restraints in prison except as a precaution against escape during a transfer, on medical grounds with specific instruction from the medical officer, and if other methods fail, to prevent a prisoner from injuring herself. But restraints are being used in many other cases. Amnesty International reports that sick women are sometimes chained to their hospital beds and that others are shackled even when giving birth and holding their newborns. The use of shackles on women seems difficult to justify in most situations. Relatively few women behind bars try to escape, least of all while giving birth. Most likely the use of shackles reflects another part of the system's strange distortion of equity: if we chain men, the argument goes, then we must chain women.

The use (and misuse) of restraints is an example of humiliation for its own sake, which perversely thrives in women's prisons. Kit, the feisty woman I worked with, had her false teeth taken away, the Department of Corrections claiming they might be a weapon. Restraints also are part of a larger issue of health care abuses for women behind bars. In one of my early composition classes, Dolly wrote a letter to the superintendent complaining about her humiliating experience going to get a mammogram. First she was strip-searched before she left Framingham. Then, she was waist-chained to four other women in a prison van and had shackles put on her ankles while riding to the prison hospital forty-five minutes away. Once at the hospital, she was kept in a room with a one-way glass mirror for most of the day. She ate from a plate slipped under her door, had to be escorted to the bathroom past a roomful of male prisoners who hooted and howled at her, and after eight hours, never got to see the doctor. She swore that she would never go for a mammogram again. The superintendent did not respond to her letter.

Health care has improved since I taught at Framingham but only because it could not get worse. One woman's complaints about falling were ignored by officers until she had to be rushed to the hospital and was discovered to have brain cancer. While I worked at the prison, several women committed suicide by hanging themselves in their cells, exposing some of the neglect, understaffing, and misdiagnosis that occurs behind bars. Getting to see a doctor has always been difficult since they are few and far between, and a woman can be on a waiting list for dental care for months. Dolly was dependent on medicine and care by a doctor for her heart condition, neither of which were available to her at Framingham. Most women in prison who are seriously ill risk not getting the treatment they need, and in some cases this means death.

Medical Care

Poor medical care for women has resulted in "late-term miscarriages; untreated cancer; other life-threatening diseases and increased disability as a consequence of poor or nonexistent care."[17] In countries such as India and Kazakhstan, as reported in "Prison Conditions and the Treatment of Prisoners," by Human Rights Watch, prisoners suffer from overcrowding, malnutrition, unhygienic conditions, and lack of medical care, even for AIDS; prisoners in Uganda, Zambia, and Sierra Leone suffer from lack of food, dehydration, malnutrition, dysentery, and pneumonia left untreated. In Kenya's Lang'ata Women's Prison, each cell holds three or more people who share the same small, tattered mattress and old blankets. Prisoners are not allowed to wear shoes or slippers and are constantly sick with foot ailments and chronic colds. The most common cause of death in Moroccan prisons is disease from overcrowding, malnutrition, and lack of hygiene and medical care.

In the United States, the 1990s saw the rise of tuberculosis cases in prisons due to the same conditions that cause the disease elsewhere, poor air circulation, overcrowding, and unsanitary conditions. Staff at Framingham were warned to get vaccinated, and even though prison health care is now being privatized in many locales, a result of the prison health issues of the 1990s, tuberculosis remains a problem.

The upswing of tuberculosis cases in this country is in part associated with AIDS, and over the years many prisons have seen the rise of HIV cases. The Human Rights Watch Prison Project report, "HIV/AIDS in Prisons," states that French prisoners are estimated to be HIV-positive at the rate of ten times that of other adults; in Brazil and Argentina, among other countries, there is an even higher level of HIV infection. In California, from 1981 to 1997 the number of HIV-infected women rose more than 88 percent, with 2,000 the total number in 1997. Male prisoners in that state received specialized HIV-related medical services. Women did not.[18]

At Framingham in the early 1990s, uninfected women prisoners often isolated themselves from those with HIV because of fear. The lack of education about the disease and disrespect from officers toward women with HIV was also a problem. In one of my plays, a woman was to portray a character with HIV. The actress quit a month or two into rehearsals, saying that she didn't want anyone in the prison to think she had the virus. Another woman treated in the prison hospital told me how awful it was to see female inmates with AIDS there, abandoned by their families, in pain, dying alone. The stigma was only reinforced, I felt, when officers started wearing rubber gloves. At first I thought it was only for the purposes of the pat or strip search. But soon I began to see officers wearing rubber gloves simply to escort women down the hallways.

One could argue that prisoners deserve to be disregarded. Most have broken the law. What indeed are the human rights of prisoners, in spite of their criminal background? They have their freedom taken away, they are separated from family and loved ones, and they toil at mostly meaningless jobs. Should they also receive inferior medical care?

The Importance of Work and Alternatives to Prison

Work behind bars ought to lend women a sense of self-worth and help them develop job skills. But watching many at their "chores," like cleaning the halls, I wondered what jobs they would be prepared for when they got out. Making microfiche and sewing flags, what Framingham called "industries," hardly seemed preparation for the outside world. Women are often given jobs in prison that reinforce traditional female roles. Not only do they clean, do laundry, and work in the kitchen, they work in the beauty shop, learn manicuring, and do secretarial jobs serving the prison administration.

In her book, *Women in Prison: Inside the Concrete Womb,* Kathryn Watterson points out that, under the Slave Emancipation Act of 1965, slavery and involuntary servitude were abolished for everyone except convicted criminals. In 1995, although some states paid nothing, the average weekly wage for prisoners was $2.00. Prisoners do have expenses, and most do not have bank accounts or families that can support them. At Framingham they buy toiletries, personal hygiene articles like tampons or deodorant, and this money comes out of their "account." At some institutions nationwide, women make cloth from which they sew their own uniforms, make soap, and, like male prisoners, do farming, run printing presses, and work in canneries. This work is said to constitute job training, but much money is made off prisoners as a cheap source of labor. Most jobs are more for the prison's benefit than for the women's future employment. Contemporary prisons are not uncommonly money-making operations run by for-profit companies, and they make more money by paying prisoners poorly, offering menial jobs, and spending as little as possible on services to rehabilitate.

In 1995 Congress approved a bill that took away all Pell grants supporting college classes for prisoners. Women suffered particularly from this loss, as education provides a way out and a way to deal with the separation from children. Although education has been shown to prevent repetition of criminal activities by former inmates, the mood nationwide is still to lock up criminals and throw away the key.

Gloria, the battered woman who killed her husband, often talked about how her son had no one to bring him to see her. At some prisons, according to Watterson, women may not touch their children during visits. In most states, pregnant inmates must give up their babies a few days after birth. Many argue that this is, in a sense, punishment of the innocent, since the child also suffers the loss. A few states, like New York and Nebraska, have prisons that allow infants to stay with nursing mothers for up to eighteen months. In most cases, incarcerated women give up their babies and have difficulty maintaining contact with their children. Given that over half of the children in the juvenile justice system nationwide have an inmate parent,[19] and most women in prison are convicted of nonviolent crimes, alternatives to prison should be considered for many so as to avoid punishing the children as well as the mothers.

The supermax, a state-of-the-art maximum security unit, advertises its aim to protect society from violent prisoners. But given that most females behind bars do not exhibit violent tendencies, isolation units within those facilities are inappropriate for female prisoners. Abuses of women in supermax facilities have been reported as recently as 1999 in California. Meanwhile alternatives to prison that would be effective in preventing recidivism do exist. These include community service work, restitution, job training assistance, alcohol and substance abuse treatment, probation, deferred sentencing, suspended sentences, conditional or supervised release, dispute resolution, fines, house arrest, residential care, and counseling. Not only are alternatives to prison more humane and effective, they are less costly. Incarceration estimates range from $30,000 to $59,000 per year. Alternatives begin at $2,000 per year for supervised community service up to $20,000 in residential substance abuse programs.[20]

Conclusion

Towards the end of my Voices Behind Bars class the students visit a pre-release facility where men and women are doing time. We spend two hours with men and women who have been sentenced to hard time for years and are finally at a lower-security institution. The students come away visibly moved, understanding that prisoners are human beings. The men invariably tell stories of survival behind bars. The women invariably tell stories of abuse and injustice. One student was so disturbed by hearing some of their stories that she wrote to congressmen and congresswomen around the country questioning our prison policies. For many, this experience is an eye-opener into a world that few want to enter.

When the women I worked with presented plays at Framingham, what many requested was to perform for their families. They needed to share their successes, as they have so few opportunities to show themselves, their families, or the world at large what they can do. The International Covenant on Civil and Political Rights says that "reform and social readaptation of prisoners" is "an essential aim" of imprisonment. Yet there is little indication that we are preparing prisoners to find ways back into society. To understand the forgotten minority, you must go inside what Kathryn Watterson calls "the concrete womb," where inequity, abuse, and long-term loneliness make clear that, if we are to think of ourselves as a civilized society, we must reconsider what we do with those women we lock away.

NOTES

1. Gail Walker, "A Caravan for Prison Justice," *Peace and Freedom: Women in Prison* 59, no. 5 (1999).

2. William Allen and Kim Bell, "Push to Cut Costs Poses Risks—And Not Just to Inmates," *St. Louis Post-Dispatch,* 27 September 1998.

3. Kristen Flurkey, "Abused Behind Bars: U.S. Women Inmates Suffer Human Rights Violations," *Peace and Freedom: Women in Prison* 59, no. 5 (Nov.–Dec. 1999).

4. Walker, "Caravan" (1999).

5. Amnesty International USA, "Not Part of My Sentence: Violations of the Human Rights of Women in Custody," 1999.

6. Meda Chesney-Lind, "The Forgotten Offender," *Corrections Today* 60, no. 7 (December 1998): 68.

7. Lori B. Girshik, "No Safe Haven: WILPF Member Writes Book on Women in Prison," *Peace and Freedom: Women in Prison* 59, no. 5 (1999).

8. Margaret Shaw, "Women in Prison: A Literature Review," *Forum of Corrections Research: Women in Prison* 6 (January 1994): 12.

9. Jean Harris, *Stranger in Two Worlds* (New York, 1986).

10. "All Too Familiar: Sexual Abuse of Women in U.S. Prisons," Human Rights Watch Publications, December 1996, p. 2.

11. Nina Siegel, "Locked Up in America: Slaves to the System," *Salon,* online magazine, www.salon.com, posted 1 September 1998.

12. Amnesty International USA, 1999, V-1.

13. "All Too Familiar," Human Rights Watch (1996).

14. Kathryn Watterson, *Women in Prison: Inside the Concrete Womb* (Boston, 1996).

15. Kelly Hannah Moffat, "Unintended Consequences of Prison Reform," *Forum of Corrections Research: Women in Prison* 6 (January 1994).

16. Chesney-Lind, "Forgotten Offender" (1998), p. 68.

17. Flurkey, "Abused Behind Bars" (1999), p. 13, quoting AI report.

18. Flurkey, "Abused Behind Bars" (1999).

19. Joyce R. Best, "WILPF Branch Helps Children Visit Moms in Prison," *Peace and Freedom: Women in Prison* 59, no. 5 (1999).

20. Kristen Flurkey, "Working for Alternatives to Incarceration," *Peace and Freedom: Women in Prison* 59, no. 5 (1999).

Degrees of Separation

Jane Stapleton

∞ THE theory of six degrees of separation holds that one human being is connected to another whom he or she does not know through six individuals who, at first glance, also seem to be complete strangers. The playwright John Guare, in his play *Six Degrees of Separation,* which was also made into a 1993 film, uses the theory to emphasize the potential for close connections between people who least expect it, people who on the surface have little or nothing in common. This possibility of being connected to women who live far away from me has always intrigued me. I look for them as I travel outside the United States, hoping to meet on a bus headed for the highlands of Guatemala or in a crowded Moroccan medina. That I may not talk with all of these women does not stop me from looking for ways in which we are connected. Our experiences as women draw us together. This essay is built on the assumption that one of the things that connects all women is the reality of gender-based violence.

The Realities of Rape

My life changed dramatically in the spring of 1987, when I, along with the college community in which I lived, learned that three men had raped an undergraduate woman after a fraternity party.[1] I did not know the woman, but I was particularly disturbed and intrigued by the case, not only because of what happened to her, but also because of the way people responded to the new term "acquaintance rape." I was enrolled in my first year of a graduate program in sociology at the Family Research Laboratory of the University of New Hampshire, Durham, the world's foremost research center on family violence and the subject that was the focus of my studies. Yet I had never come across the term "acquaintance rape," and I did not know anyone who had experienced this phenomenon.

The case received considerable coverage in the local and national media. The majority noted that while the incidence of acquaintance rape might be common on college campuses, it was different from "real" rape. "Real" victims were thought to be women who were held hostage at knifepoint by strangers who jumped out of the bushes on dimly lit paths. Then, as now, stranger assaults comprised the minority of rape cases in the United States.[2] From the beginning, media attention focused exclusively on the fact that Sara, the victim, was extremely intoxicated and was thus to blame for what happened to her. She was presented as a person who voluntarily drank until she was inebriated and who, because of this condition, wandered into the wrong dormitory room where three men had sex with her without her consent. Despite her initial inability to recall what had happened, the details were corroborated by one student who happened to walk into the room during the assault and five other students to whom the perpetrators described in detail what they had done. The specifics of the case, the media's representation of it, and the administrative and criminal proceedings that followed provided me with a new lens through which to view men's violence against women. Until the time that the case went public, I was familiar with national studies that quantified domestic violence victimization in the United States. Feminist writers offered theoretical explanations and qualitative data on women's experiences of violence. Members of the battered women's movement helped professionals find ways to make a difference in the lives of women who were being victimized. However, each understanding was incomplete and separate from one another. As a woman who had never been sexually or physically assaulted, I had the luxury of not needing to pull all of these pieces together. Sara's experience changed all of this for me. Although I did not know her, her reality surrounded me daily. Sara could have been any of the undergraduate women that I knew. She could have been me. I became keenly aware of the sense that little "separation" existed between us.

The media and many members of the university community articulated clear distinctions between stranger and acquaintance rape. But in my view, the legitimacy of victimization from one type of assault extended to the other. This is not to say that all incidences of violence are the same: such a position would diminish the complexity of women's experiences. But sexual violence, regardless of the perpetrator's relationship to his victim, is, simply and clearly, illegal and morally wrong. Originally, men who raped women whom they were married to and in some cases separated from would be charged with a lesser crime because of their relationship to the victim. (Delaware, Hawaii, and Maine had similar exemptions for men who had consensual sexual relations with women to whom they were not married.) But in the late 1980s most states had removed marital and voluntary social companion exemptions from rape or sexual assault statutes. This meant that the perpetrator's relationship to the victim was no longer relevant to the criminal prosecution of sexual assault cases.

Common notions lagged behind legal statutes. Giving less recognition to violence that occurred between people who knew each other made these types of assaults seem more acceptable. In such a climate, women often blamed themselves, and the seriousness of the crime was diminished by others. It came as no surprise, then, that Sara blamed herself and that other women blamed her too. At a time when she needed the support of other women, many participated in labeling her as guilty. It seemed at the time that this blaming of the victim derived from many women's sense that the same thing could have happened to them.

At the time, women employed different strategies to deal with the reality of rape. For my part, I became part of a grassroots student movement on campus that called attention to the fact that the three men's actions were wrong and against the law. We called into question the university's mishandling of the case and drew attention to the less-than-adequate support services and violence awareness programs on campus. I went on to study the emergence of "acquaintance rape" as a social problem and helped to start one of the first rape crisis centers on a college campus in the United States.

Not all women, however, walked beside me in my work. Many sought both consciously and unconsciously to protect themselves from the reality of rape. To do this, it was necessary for them to shift the knowledge of their own vulnerability. They created a false sense of safety by reasoning that, if they didn't do the things that Sara did, then they would never experience what she went through. For some women this worked, for some it did not. In the end, very few of us were really safe.

A World Context of Violence against Women

During a presentation at the Ninth Annual Women's Studies Conference, held at Southern Connecticut State University in 1999, on global issues for women, an Afghani woman, Ossai Miazad, described the current human rights violations against women under the Taliban regime. A diverse audience of three hundred people watched intently as a short video flashed images of women cloaked in pale blue coverings, known as burqas, shuffled silently through Afghani streets. The women peered through small mesh openings that covered their eyes, looking out at the world as if behind bars both externally and internally.

When the Taliban seized power in much of Afghanistan in 1996, they took all civil rights away from women and girls. Under an extreme interpretation of Islam, women are forbidden to work outside their homes and girls and women are denied access to any education. This regression is dramatic considering that prior to Taliban rule women represented 50 percent of students, 60 percent of teachers at Kabul University, 70 percent of schoolteachers, 50 percent of civilian government workers, and 40 percent of doctors in Kabul.[3] Women cannot leave their homes without being accompanied by a male relative, and women who do venture out alone risk being publicly stoned. Burqas must be worn in public at all times and women's shoes cannot make noise when they walk.

The audience was silent, as if overwhelmed, when the presentation was finished. It was no secret, what was happening in Afghanistan. The world was indeed watching as women's most basic human rights were being denied every day, every minute. Miazad then held up an article by Robin Givhan from the fashion section of the 18 September 1999 *Washington Post*. In the article, entitled "Dripping with Meaning," Givhan describes the British designer Alexander McQueen's latest fashions, which were "inspired by international news of female subjugation, the Taliban, and gender persecution." The writer lauds the designer for his brilliant work and commends him for mixing current-day issues with fashions for women. In the finale of McQueen's show, two "elevated women appear to be electrocuted or hanged as their bodies convulse in mock death throes." Was the mock abuse of women meant to show solidarity with oppressed women, or was it just a cynical exploitation of their sufferings for the purposes of entertaining an audience of fashion seekers?

One could not but be deeply moved by the plight of Afghani women. I found myself concentrating on the hundreds of women I had spoken to over the years who had experienced men's violence, and on the nature of women's human rights and gender-based violence in a global context. Of course, the status of women in the West, and specifically in the United States, is vastly different from that of Afghani women. Women in the United States can vote and hold political positions. They have freedom of movement. They are 46 percent of the work force, 56 percent of college students nationally, 26 percent of physicians, 30 percent of lawyers and judges; the fastest-growing small businesses in the country are those headed by women. The fact of American women's rights and freedoms is indisputable.

Yet when the safety of women in the United States is considered, a shocking picture emerges. According to the U.S. Justice Department Bureau of Justice Statistics, nearly one in three women experiences at least one physical assault by a partner during adulthood. The FBI's Uniform Crime Reports for 1991 show that physical violence by men is the leading cause of injury to women between the ages fifteen and forty-four. This represents more injuries than from car accidents, muggings, and rapes combined. Women are not the only ones hurt by men's violence. Each year, according to the Centers for Disease Control and Prevention, at least 6 percent of all pregnant women—about 240,000 pregnant women annually—are battered by their male partners. Additionally, the American Psychological Association's 1996 study, "Violence and the Family," estimates that 3.3 million children are exposed to violence against their mothers or female caretakers by family members.

As a citizen of the United States, I have found that it is easier, if not safer, to focus on what happens in someone else's country instead of my own. My ethnocentric lens into the world gives me a sense of being better, safer, and invincible. However, I have come to believe that it is not until I come to terms with the realities of my own life, in my own country, that I can truly provide Afghani women, or women anywhere in the world, the kind of support I seek to offer.

A Case in Point

I met Andrea (her name and characteristics and the details of her assault have been changed) when she was a junior in college. She was a biology, pre-med major and I was the coordinator of the Sexual Harassment and Rape Prevention Program, SHARPP, at the University of New Hampshire. SHARPP provides support services to sexual assault survivors and awareness education to the university community. She appeared in my office with her lab partner, Marianne, late one Thursday afternoon in October. Homecoming weekend festivities had just begun and the atmosphere on campus was as crisp and colorful as the leaves that fell from the maples that lined Main Street in this New England town. Visits from women just like them, young and in pursuit of their educations, with the rest of their lives ahead of them, were common. Underneath their pleasant exteriors, however, they had secrets about relationships or "bad experiences" that would haunt just about anyone who heard them.

Reluctantly, Andrea began our meeting by telling me that Marianne had persuaded her to come to my office. If it weren't for Marianne, she said, she never would have come. According to Andrea, the situation wasn't that bad, at least not yet. She was, however, a little nervous about this coming weekend. Marianne chimed in by noting that despite Andrea's attempts to minimize the situation, she thought that someone at the university should know what was going on with Andrea, just in case something bad happened over homecoming.

The story of Andrea's relationship with her boyfriend, Tim, unfolded over the next three hours. They had been together since they were seniors in high school. They lived in the same hometown, went to the same school, and shared many of the same friends, both at home and at college. Even their families had been long-time acquaintances. Apparently, Tim had always been the "assertive" one in the relationship, making most of the decisions on what to do and where to go. Andrea said that she liked it that way, and Tim had made it clear to her that this was how he wanted their relationship to be.

Things had been a little tense between Tim and Andrea since the beginning of the semester. Andrea was living off campus for the first time in a studio apartment on the edge of the university's grounds. Tim, who lived in an on-campus residence hall, spent much of his free time at Andrea's. He had the key to both her room and the front door of the building. He often went there between classes and to spend the night.

Andrea began by telling me about a "jealous rage" that Tim had shortly after the semester started. She was walking back to her apartment one afternoon with a guy in her psychology class. Her classmate lived in the fraternity house two doors down from her, and by coincidence they were walking in the same direction and started a conversation. When Andrea came into her room, Tim was waiting for her. He was very upset. He told her that he had been looking out the window and saw her talking to the "frat boy." Tim was talking in a very loud voice and pointed his finger in her face, asking her how long she had known this guy. He accused her of having a crush on him, even of having sex with him.

Confused, Andrea told Tim that she had just met Bruce on the way home from class and denied having a relationship with him or any interest in such a relationship. Tim calmed down some, but warned Andrea that she was never to walk home with Bruce again. He told her that he knew what "frat boys" were like and he didn't trust Andrea around them. Andrea assured him that she was faithful to him and that she wouldn't walk home with Bruce again.

After this incident, Tim began meeting Andrea outside each of her classes; he even left one of his classes early to be sure to get to Andrea's class before it ended. At first Andrea thought that this was romantic and liked the idea of being escorted. But she began to feel a little uncomfortable when Tim started showing up, during the day and at night, at the local bar and restaurant where she worked. He sat at the bar and drank beer while she served food in the restaurant. When Andrea's shift was over, they immediately went back to her place. Soon, Andrea was spending all of her time with Tim. It was rare for her to be alone.

One night while Tim waited for Andrea to finish her shift, Bruce came into the restaurant with several of his fraternity brothers. They sat in Andrea's section, so she waited on them. She was pleasant to them, but she made sure that she didn't engage in a direct conversation with Bruce. When Andrea finished her shift, she and Tim walked back to her apartment. They talked very little on the way home and Andrea could tell that Tim was angry. Once inside her studio, in her words, Tim "flew off the handle" and started yelling at her and again accused her of sleeping with Bruce. She denied it, but he insisted that she was unfaithful. He slammed the door and left. Andrea said she was very upset because she didn't want to lose Tim, but didn't know how to make him believe that she had been faithful. She had dated other boys, but Tim was her only real relationship to date.

Tim came back to Andrea's room the next morning. Andrea tried to talk with him about their fight, but Tim said he didn't want to. He did, however, warn her that if he ever found out that she was with another guy, she "would be sorry." Andrea told me that she felt uneasy that Tim didn't want to talk about what happened, but she also was a little relieved because she didn't want to provoke another incident like the one the night before.

Tim ate a bowl of cereal while Andrea took a shower. While she dried her hair, Tim jammed her desk chair under the bathroom doorknob so that the door was locked from the outside. Andrea politely asked Tim to let her out, as she needed to finish getting ready for her 11:00 class. He refused and told her that he wanted to make sure she wouldn't try to make contact with Bruce. Since she had class with Bruce on this day, Tim said that locking her in the bathroom was the only way he could be assured that she would not see or talk with him. Andrea pleaded with Tim to let her out, but he refused. He said he'd be back for her after his classes and he left for the day.

Andrea spent the entire day locked in her own bathroom. She banged on the door for a while, but got tired of pounding and knew that no one could get her out, even if they heard her. Besides, how would she explain the fact that her boyfriend locked her in the bathroom? Andrea felt angry with herself for letting this happen. She thought that this entire situation could have been avoided if she had asked a coworker to wait on Bruce and his friends the night before.

Andrea fell asleep on the bathroom floor and woke to Tim coming into her apartment. He opened the bathroom door and let her out. Overwhelmed with emotion, Andrea began to cry and Tim warned her again that if she talked to Bruce one more time, he would end their relationship. Andrea promised, but asked Tim to apologize for locking her in the bathroom. Tim refused and said that she deserved what she got. Andrea didn't respond. They ate the pizza that Tim brought for dinner and didn't talk very much before they both went to sleep. Andrea awoke around 3:00 a.m. with Tim on top of her, about to have intercourse. She stayed still and he continued. They both fell asleep shortly afterward.

Marianne found out what happened a week later, when Andrea came into lab with a swollen lip and a bruise on her right cheek. She asked Andrea if she was okay. Andrea's voice was shaky and she broke down in tears. The two talked after class and Andrea reluctantly told her that Tim had hit her two nights before. She said that he was drunk and had struck her several times because she hadn't waited for him after she ended her shift at the restaurant. She had a test to study for and Tim wanted her to stay with him at the bar. She declined and instead went to the library to study.

When Andrea returned home near midnight, Tim was waiting for her. He immediately started a fight, insisting that he was sure that she had been with Bruce and not studying for a test. She denied his accusations. He struck her several times and told her that she would pay for her actions. He left, and she had not seen him for a day and a half. Andrea knew he would eventually come back to her apartment and she was scared of what he might do. Marianne was supportive and encouraged her to call SHARPP. At first, Andrea refused to seek help. After Marianne said that she would go with her, Andrea agreed to talk with someone. It was at this point that they came to my office.

By the time we finished our conversation, Andrea said she was glad she had come. I had presented her with a range of options. She said she would carefully consider them and promised to be in touch with me the following Monday. However, she was adamant that she didn't want to get the police involved. Although she wasn't quite sure how she was going to handle things when she saw Tim, she did say that she would clearly tell him that she did not want him to hit her again. She said she was not ready to end the relationship. She loved him, knew that he cared for her, and thought that maybe they could still work things out. I gave her the 24-hour crisis line number and told her not to hesitate to call if she in any way felt unsafe or just needed someone to talk to.

Andrea did call the crisis line. It was 2:30 a.m. Monday morning, almost four days after our initial meeting. One of our advocates responded to the call and met her at the university's health center. On her way home from the library late Sunday night, she had passed through an empty parking lot. Tim and his friend Mark were waiting for her at the edge of the lot. They exchanged a few words and when Andrea went to leave, Tim pulled her behind a dumpster. While Mark held her, Tim tore her pants down. Tim said he was getting her back for being unfaithful and said that since she liked to sleep around, he thought Mark should, in his words, "get in on the action too." Andrea resisted and pleaded with them to stop, but one after the other they raped her. They finally stopped when a car drove through the lot. Tim and Mark exited through the woods. Andrea walked home and called the crisis line three hours later.

Andrea had extensive internal injuries and had sustained cuts and bruises on her legs and face. She didn't want to report the assault to the police because she said she was ashamed of what happened and thought that she was at least partly to blame. She said that she never should have walked alone through the empty lot so late at night. The attending physician and the advocate stayed with Andrea at the health center until daylight. She then returned to her apartment, packed a bag, called her mother, and drove to her parents' house.

We talked briefly on the phone the following day. She had decided to take the semester off and to quit her job. At her parents' urging she had definitely decided to leave the police out of it. She also didn't want to file administrative charges against Tim through the university's internal procedures. Rather, she agreed with her parents that the best way to resolve the issue was informally with Tim and his family. She told me that she preferred that I not contact her again and that she would be in touch with me when she was ready to talk to me. That was the last time I talked with Andrea. To my knowledge, she never returned to the university.

By the time homecoming 1994 was over, I knew of five women who had been sexually assaulted during the course of that one weekend. The actual number of assaults was probably closer to thirty, based on National Victim Center estimates of the incidence of rape. The five assaults that I was aware of involved people who knew each other to varying degrees. Prior to the assault, Andrea told me that she loved the man who would later rape her. Three of the five cases involved drug or alcohol use on the part of either the perpetrator or the victim. One woman suspected that she had been drugged at a party, but when the lab tests failed to substantiate this, the county attorney decided that the case wasn't strong enough to go in front of a grand jury. Hers was the only one of these cases that was reported to the police. None of these cases were reported in the student newspaper, although they were included in a story that presented SHARPP's statistics at the end of the academic year.

The majority of the university community never knew the intimate details of the assaults that happened on campus. In my role as advocate, I was told the dirty little family secrets and unspeakable truths of violence between intimates. These women had been carrying heavy burdens for days, months, and sometimes years. At times it was overwhelming to keep their secrets and burdens inside my head and heart. Having spent sleepless nights and lost my appetite because of what I'd been told, I tried to imagine what the women who had lived through the violence were feeling and how they were coping.

I myself was targeted for the work that I did. This reality flowed from my workplace to my home and at times wedged itself right between me and the people I was closest to. My tires were slashed, I got prank phone calls and harassing letters and dirty looks. When my house was broken into, I saw just how vulnerable to violence I was.

Friends and family often asked me how and why I worked at the rape crisis center. Most of them never understood the passion that I had for the work and the women who shared their lives with me. There was no denying that there was much pain involved in my work. But there was also an immense sense of satisfaction to be gained in knowing that I made a difference not only in the lives of women to whom I provided support, but also in the awareness of those with whom I had contact.

Making Connections

I was teaching an introduction to women's studies course the semester that Tim and Mark raped Andrea. During the section on violence against women, I emphasized that a national study had recently found that one in four college women experienced a sexual assault during her college career.[4] In most cases she was assaulted by someone she knew, often in her own home. One in twelve of the men surveyed indicated that they had engaged in behavior that met the legal definition of rape or attempted rape. An alarming percentage of men said that they would force a woman to have sex if they could be assured that they would not be held accountable for their actions.

Initially, these facts fell on deaf ears. While my students did not blame women who were victims of acquaintance rape outright, they did say they felt that these realities had nothing to do with them. They were more concerned with the "stranger type" assaults. When I asked them to explain why, the bottom line was that it was too uncomfortable for them to think about the possibility that someone they knew would hurt them.

Not only did these statistics question the kind of people with whom they associated, indeed whom they loved, they also called into question their own judgment. One student passionately explained that her parents had always told her to be aware of strangers. People whom she knew, family and friends, were the ones she could always trust. The information that

I presented challenged every notion of her sense of safety and made her vulnerabilities clear. Her comments reminded me of how exposed and vulnerable we as women really are.

After a long conversation, many of the students did say that they knew people who had been raped after parties or physically assaulted by men they dated. Several of the students confidentially told me that they had experienced violence themselves. Even though they knew women who had been victimized or had been victimized themselves, it took a newspaper headline reporting that a woman was raped by a stranger to make them pay attention. One student, who later disclosed to me that she was sexually assaulted by her uncle when she was a child, announced to the class, "I think you're all in denial."

We spent a good part of the month examining why men's violence against women was so prevalent in the United States, particularly among college students. U.S. Department of Justice statistics indicate that traditional-age college students and older high school students (sixteen to twenty-four years old) are at the highest risk for being both victims and offenders of sexual and domestic violence. They are the dating population, often experimenting with alcohol. For many of them this is their first time away from their parents for an extended period of time. They have a new sense of freedom, and with that a sense that "nothing bad will happen to me."

This is only a small part of the story. The characteristics of this age population provide only a portion of the background for men's violence against women. As much as college administrators would like to believe the contrary, banning alcohol on campus will not alone decrease the amount of violence against women. Instead, the root causes of violence must be dismantled. This is a much more difficult task and clearly one that extends far beyond the borders of the campus.

Understanding the foundation of violence against women starts with accurately naming the problem. For years, those of us in the movement talked about "violence against women" when in reality what we were describing was men's violence against women. The former term continues to be used today and is reflected in the name of the most comprehensive federal act in the United States to address the problem, the Violence Against Women Act of 1994. Crime statistics indicate that the more specific term is in fact accurate, as men are responsible for 95 percent of all violent acts against women in the United States. Why isn't the term used more often, and why are so many men and women uncomfortable with it? The reason is this: mainstream culture in the United States has created an environment that encourages, and in some cases requires, men's violence against women.

Despite U.S. laws against both sexual assault and domestic violence, both crimes go unreported and often unpunished. Men's entitlement over women, beginning with boys' entitlement over girls, is seen daily in today's media and is reflected in real relationships, whether in friendships, dating, or marriage. Double standards continue to exist for men and women. As a result, women continue to be portrayed as provoking sexual assault and deserving physical violence at the hands of their partners or spouses. Many violence prevention programs continue to focus on what women can do to stop violence directed at them; very little is directed at holding men accountable for their actions. Ultimately, men use violence as a means of keeping women in their place. The greater women's independence, the more does men's use of violence increase.

Some have charged that what I describe above creates a "victim mentality" among women.[5] Yet I maintain that ignoring the reality of violence does not make it go away. Not all women are victimized in their lifetimes, and likewise, not all men victimize women. However, ignorance will not stop those men who do rape and batter women from assaulting. Denial will not end abusive relationships. History has shown that silence creates a fertile ground for violence, particularly among intimates. Critics of the view that power relations between men and women must be changed risk distracting us from the realities of men's violence against women in the United States.

By the time November came, my students had a more solid understanding of the roots of men's violence against women. Another opportunity to highlight the connections among women came when a student group did a fifteen-minute oral presentation on dowry murder in India. The students had come a long way toward recognizing the scope of men's violence against women. The students who researched the topic had strong opinions, calling dowry murder "barbaric." But one woman's remark, "I'm so glad that I live in America and don't have to face such a thing as dowry murder,"—and the sight of several students nodding their heads in agreement—reminded me of how far they had yet to go in understanding the nature of violence and the connections between its various forms.

An essay by Uma Narayan sheds light on the dynamic of my classroom that day.[6] In an examination of the incidence of dowry murder in India, Narayan notes that the same cultural explanations that are employed to understand fatal forms of violence against women of the so-called Third World are missing from the analysis of fatal forms of violence against mainstream Western women. The assumption is that Third World women suffer "death by culture"—that is, they are are seen as "victims of their culture"—whereas mainstream Western women are presented as untouched by fatal forms of violence, as living in a culture that does not condemn them to second-class status.

Through a complicated search for incidence rates of fatal forms of violence directed at women in the United States, Narayan uncovers the dynamic involved in the "death by culture" explanation. She maintains that it is challenging, if not impossible, to find current information and comprehensive media coverage on the number of women who are killed by their male partners or husbands. Narayan found that the number of women in the United States who are victims of "domestic violence murder" and the number of Indian women who are victims of "dowry murder" is roughly proportional. This challenges the notion that the United States is a safer country for women and speaks to the fact that fatal forms of violence against women happen in both countries.

In many other classes I taught, students anxiously researched and critically analyzed issues such as dowry murder, genital mutilation, mass rapes of Bosnian women, and honor killings. Students, like the sources where they get their information, present these issues as outside the general context of men's violence against women, not only within the country under scrutiny, but also in relation to the United States. Narayan suggests that this is part of an overall process whereby Western feminists set the agenda for understanding issues that affect Third World women. Instead of seeing the connections between Western and Third World women, the latter are seen as "other." Western women's experiences are presented as the standard. However, their realities of violence are rarely, if ever, presented in a comprehensive way. The end result is that connections are denied, and it becomes much more difficult to reach across our differences to discover our similarities.

Women's Human Rights

The universality of violence against women has recently been the focus not only of the United Nations but also many nongovernmental organizations globally. The first major international acknowledgment of this issue came in 1979, when the United Nations General Assembly adopted the Convention on the Elimination of Discrimination Against Women, CEDAW, sometimes called the "International Bill of Rights" for women and girls (but not ratified by the U.S.). Although gender-based violence against women was not specifically addressed in the original document, it was clearly woven into the fabric of the convention. During the 1980s violence against women received little attention in official UN meetings. However, at a conference in Nairobi in July 1985 and at an expert group meeting on violence in the family sponsored by the Division for the Advancement of Women in 1986, discussion of the issue had a substantial impact on the attention it would later receive in the 1990s.

From 1991 to 1995, the United Nations significantly increased the attention paid to the issue of gender-based violence against women. The Economic and Social Council adopted a resolution in 1991 that urged member states to adopt, strengthen, and enforce legislation prohibiting violence against women. In 1992 gender-based violence was added to CEDAW. In 1993 the General Assembly adopted a draft of the Declaration to End Violence Against Women. In 1994 the Commission on Human Rights appointed a special rapporteur on violence against women, including its causes and its consequences. The Fourth UN Conference on Women, held in Beijing, included violence against women as a priority area in its 1995 Platform for Action.

This acknowledgment of the problem and importance placed on ending violence against women has had a ripple effect in breaking the silence that surrounds its incidence all over the world. For the first time, gender-based violence against women is being recognized not only as a public health concern but also a violation of human rights. An overview of population-based studies on violence against women around the world indicates that between 10 percent and 50 percent of women worldwide report being physically hit by an intimate male partner at some point in their lives.[7] Between 40 and 75 percent of these women suffer injuries, ranging from minor cuts and bruises to death, as a result of this abuse. It is estimated that as many as one in four women throughout the world are physically and sexually abused while they are pregnant. Unfortunately, many countries currently do not have national studies to document the pervasiveness of gender-based violence against women. There is no doubt, however, that violence against women crosses religious, national, cultural, and regional boundaries.

As we look to end men's violence against women, it is essential that we carefully consider the comparative realities of women globally. Although the world's women are inherently diverse, we share a common reality that cannot be denied. Indeed, the degrees of separation between women are very small when our experiences of violence are considered. In acknowledging this connection, we recognize that an incident of violence against one woman is violence directed at all women.

NOTES

1. For a detailed account of this case, see Paul Keegan, "Dangerous Parties," *New England Monthly* (February 1988).

2. National Institute of Justice, Centers for Disease Control and Prevention,

"Prevalence, Incidence, and Consequences of Violence Against Women: Findings From the National Violence Against Women Survey," November 1998.

3. Zora Rasekh, Heidi M. Bauer, M. Michele Manos, and Vincent Iacopino, "Women's Health and Human Rights in Afghanistan," *Journal of the American Medical Association* 280, no. 5 (August 1998).

4. Mary P. Koss, C. A. Gidyez, and N. Wisniewski, "The Scope of Rape: Incidence and Prevalence of Sexual Aggression and Victimization in a National Sample of Higher Education Students," *Journal of Consulting and Clinical Psychology* 55 (1987): 162–170.

5. See, for example, Katie Roiphe, *The Morning After: Sex, Fear, and Feminism* (Boston, 1994).

6. Uma Narayan, "Cross-Cultural Connections, Border-Crossings, and 'Death by Culture,'" in *Dislocating Cultures: Identities, Traditions, and Third World Feminism* (New York, 1997), pp. 83–117.

7. Center for Health and Gender Equity, "Populations Reports: Ending Violence Against Women," 23, no. 4 (December 1999).

Gender Apartheid, Cultural Relativism, and Women's Human Rights in Muslim Societies

Mahnaz Afkhami

∞ IN modern times women have moved from the margins to the center of history, playing increasingly important roles in families, communities, and states across the world. As women became increasingly aware and assertive, their demands for equality, participation, and access elicited reactions that range from curtailing their right to the privacy of their bodies and minds to policies that deny them experiences that are essential to their ability to compete in society. The infringement of women's rights is usually exercised in the name of tradition, religion, social cohesion, morality, or some complex of transcendent values. Always, it is justified in the name of culture.

Nowhere is this better demonstrated than in Muslim societies, where over half a billion women live in vastly different lands, climates, cultures, societies, economies, and polities. Few of these women live in a purely traditional environment. For most of them modernity represents, above all, conflict among contradictory values and forces that compete for their allegiance and call them to contradictory ways of looking at themselves and at the world that surrounds them. The most taxing of these contradictions is the one between the everyday requirements of living in the contemporary world and the demands advanced by the fundamentalist worldview, which singles out women's status and her relations to society as the supreme test of the authenticity of the Islamic order.

Fundamentalist movements as varied as Jama'at- i Islami in Pakistan, Ikhwan al-Muslimin in Egypt, FIS in Algeria, and the ruling elite in the

Islamic Republic of Iran rely for their legitimacy on various renditions of tradition that they assume invests social structures and mores with an ethic of gender relations appropriate to Islam. This ethic is symbolized by the institutions of *andarun* and purdah, which historically have translated to gender apartheid in the Islamic world. The ethic and the symbols, however, are becoming increasingly porous as Muslim societies, including a significant number of Muslim women, outgrow and transgress traditional boundaries.

It is important to note that the status of women in society—social, political, legal, economical—has been fundamentally the same across history for a majority of the world's population. Except for surface differences in manner and style, the basic arrangements for division of labor and power between men and women have been the same across the world. A woman's rights concerning major decisions about her children's future, place of residence, marriage, inheritance, employment, and the like have been severely curtailed in most of the world during most of human history.[1] Until the beginning of the twentieth century, when New Zealand became the first country to give women the right to vote, there was no place on earth where women shared in the political process. Nor did they have the same chance to train for a job, get a job, or, once having gotten it, receive equal pay. Indeed, in some of these areas, especially in the area of ownership of land, Muslim women fared better than women in the West.[2] Significantly, the first fundamentalist movement started in the United States at the beginning of the twentieth century. Protestant fundamentalism came into existence very much in response to the modern age and especially the new visibility and mobility of women. Everywhere, change in women's status has meant a change in the culture of patriarchy. In other words, cultural change is both a byproduct and requisite of change in women's status.

The contemporary threat to women and their rights in the Muslim world springs mainly from a resurgence of radical fundamentalist thought and politics in the last quarter of the twentieth century. The fundamentalist resurgence forces Muslim women to fight for their rights, openly when they can, subtly when they must. The struggle is multifaceted, at once political, economic, ethical, psychological, and intellectual. It resonates with the mix of values, mores, facts, ambitions, prejudices, ambivalences, uncertainties, and fears that are the stuff of human culture. Above all, it is a casting off of a tradition of subjection. Islamism reduces this complex, historical struggle to a metaphysical question. It does so by casting society in an idealized platonic "form" and by equating culture with the dogmatics of religion. This representation is functionally supported by an important strain in contemporary international discourse that takes off from the Islamic fundamentalists' assignment of private and public space to women rather than from freedom and equality as the core assumptions appropriate to modern times. Akin to a presumption of guilt in a court of law, this discourse reverses a universally accepted rule. To the extent that Islam, defined and interpreted by traditionalist Muslim men, is allowed to determine the context and contour of the debate on women's rights, women will be on the losing side of the debate because the conclusion is already contained in the premise and reflected in the process. This is the heart of the moral tragedy of Muslim societies in our time.

There are many reasons for the recent resurgence of Islamic fundamentalism, ranging from failure of sociopolitical and economic structures at home to neocolonial pressures. Devising appropriate strategies for improving women's rights and status requires an understanding of the reasons in each case of Islamist resurgence. However, no justification of the causes of economic failure, religious revival, or nationalist fervor may be validly used to justify the subjugation of women. My purpose in this essay is to show that neither Islam nor the culture of Muslim peoples is per se an obstacle to women's achieving rights. Rather, Muslim women face patriarchal structures that certain men in power or seeking political power misrepresent as religion and culture. The function of this misrepresentation is to keep women where they best serve the patriarchal priorities. Where the civil society has already somewhat developed, for example in Iran, the fundamentalist clerics seek to force women back to conditions women have surpassed and therefore find unacceptable.

The resulting tension between the attempt at establishing various degrees of gender apartheid in Muslim societies and women's determination to secure and preserve their human rights has led in recent years to widespread and continuous violence. In Afghanistan the Taliban has in fact forced women into total segregation, denying them any right or venue to participate in the affairs of society.[3] In Algeria a veritable war of attrition is raging where women are primary victims.[4] In Iran the Islamic Consultative Assembly, the Majlis, passed a bill last year that makes it illegal for newspapers and magazines to publish pictures of women, even when veiled, on their front pages, and another segregating hospitals and prohibiting male physicians to attend to female patients. All this is justified in the name of religion and culture.

The Islamist revival has succeeded in turning its representation of Islam into a dominant discourse not only in most Muslim societies but also in the West. The Islamist discourse seeks to establish a particular rendition of Muslim religion as the true image of Muslim societies as they "actually" exist. This presumed image is then presented as the actual "culture" of the Muslim people. All "rights" then, including Muslim women's, naturally flow from this culture. The Islamists present a cohesive, logical, and harmonious concept of women's place in society containing set answers to women's economic, social, ethical, and psychological needs. Gender apartheid is clearly defined in all laws and regulations pertaining to the role of women within the private and public spheres. Inheritance, dowry, guardianship, personal and professional boundaries, and other rules that limit women's spaces and movements are all worked out so that women's dependent and separate sphere is justified, protected, and perpetuated. Within this construct, women do not have rights as defined in the international documents of rights; rather, they have privileges that issue from the Qur'an, the shari'a (the body of Islamic sacred or "canon" law), and the hadith (reports of the sayings and actions of the prophet Muhammad), and supported by folklore and myth.

This vision is supported by the Western "Orientalist" understanding of Islam that tends to identify a concept of "Islamic ideal type" with the practice of living in the real Muslim world.[5] The Orientalist construct plays into the hands of the Islamists insofar as the latter pretend that Islam is both ontologically and epistemologically different from other religions. The Islamists argue that Muslim societies are fundamentally different from Jewish, Christian, or other societies. Muslim societies, unlike the others, remain religiously authentic despite the West's political hegemony and cultural onslaught. The non-Islamic traits in Muslim societies are aberrations resulting from colonial intrusion, and need to be eradicated. The present leaders of the Islamic Republic of Iran make a point of regularly emphasizing the perils of the West's cultural invasion of all Muslim countries.

Statements by Muslim religious leaders about women's rights, however, are rarely clear because of the ambiguity of meaning when words are used in different contexts. Terms such as *freedom, equality, equity, justice, authenticity, humanity, legitimacy, law, law-abiding* and the like are complex, changing meaning depending on who utters them and where and why. It is therefore essential to a fair understanding of them always to contextualize them. For example, to grasp the implications of Ayatollah Khomeini's *Islamic Government*[6] one must not only read it in its entirety but also place it within his worldview. Only then does one begin to understand from where the authority for arranging the affairs of society issues, who is competent to interpret this authority, and why it is one's obligation to obey the rule of the *faqih,* or the competent jurist.

Furthermore, that understanding is reflected in the Constitution of the Islamic Republic, which on the one hand sets forth the structures and rules that are to implement it, and on the other hand uses phrases about civic rights that seem to be taken verbatim from any modern social democratic document. The so-called "moderate" Muslim leaders usually speak with even less clarity, or, because listeners tend to understand utterances in terms of their own frames of reference, are not easily understood. When Iran's President Khatami speaks of *qanunmandi,* "the rule of law," most observers assume that it denotes the commonly understood concepts in secular law, when in fact he means, as he himself has insisted, the law as contained in and derived from the Islamic Republic's Constitution. The confusion, resulting partly from contextual difference, partly from deliberate subterfuge, and partly from the receiver's wishful thinking, however, is not always a handicap, because it creates room for dialogue.

The Relativist Discourse

The Islamist position on women's rights is advanced on two levels, one internal and the other external to the Muslim community. Internally, the argument invokes Islam and the inviolability of the text. The formulation is intellectually rigid, but politically well organized and ideologically interconnected across the Muslim world through chains of "traditions," clerical *fatwas* (decrees), and periodic government resolutions and legislation. Muslim women in significant numbers and from all social strata are currently objecting to this interpretation of Islam. The dimensions of the struggle are being defined as Muslim women strive for rights across the globe: what these rights are, how they relate to Islam epistemologically, how they resonate with social and political power in specific Muslim societies, and how strategies that seek to promote them will or should be developed. High on the list are the ways and means of interpreting religious texts: how should women approach the issue, what sort of expertise is needed, how can the issue be bridged to grassroots leaders, how may the intelligence received from the grassroots be brought to the interpretive process?

Scholars and activists are also looking into ways of educating the Muslim political elite: how to identify responsive decision makers, how to communicate reinterpreted text, how to develop criteria for judging the limits of political engagement, how to help executives, legislators, and judges sympathetic to women's human rights to implement change in the condition of women. They are also searching for appropriate patterns of mobilizing grassroots support, including ways to identify women leaders at different levels, communicating methods of pressuring political decision makers, and, most important, protecting women activists against moral and physical violence. The list, obviously not exhaustive, nevertheless signifies the dynamics of the relationship between women's human rights, politics, and the Islamic texts.

Externally, the Islamist position meshes with the idea of cultural rela-

tivity, which has been in vogue in the West for some time; in Western acad-
eme, relativist arguments are waged for reasons that usually transcend the
problem of right in its elemental form. The argument from relativity is
based on two sets of assumptions. The first has to do with our understanding of culture. "Culture" is defined as "the act of developing the intellectual and moral faculties esp. by education, . . . acquaintance with and
taste in fine arts, humanities, and broad aspects of science . . .; the customary beliefs, social forms, and material traits of a racial, religious, or social group . . ." (Merriam-Webster's Collegiate Dictionary, tenth edition,
1998). There are two distinct strings of meaning in these definitions. The
first suggests the best in the arts, manners, literature, music, philosophy,
science and all the other refined attributes that a civilization has achieved.
This meaning of culture is common to all societies. People everywhere and
always have been sensitive to the word itself for what it conveys about
their level of achievement in these areas.

The emotional attachment to this meaning of culture often creates mis-
understanding when the second meaning is intended. The second set of
meanings, namely, the concepts, habits, skills, arts, instruments, and so
on of a particular people, constitutes the more modern meaning attached
to the term and is originally an invention of the Western social scientists
who studied primitive societies in modern times. These societies exhibited
social habits that had remained substantially unchanged over time. They
resembled "ideal types," or, rather, they were construed as ideal types
which nevertheless actually existed. The idea of culture derived from these
societies was then extended to the study of "traditional societies," that is,
the non-Western peoples. A curious result of this process is that the Orientalists' reports of traditional Islamic societies serve to support contemporary fundamentalist claims to legitimacy, insofar as they suggest an
ideal-type Muslim society actually existing before it was corrupted by the
West.

This interpretation of culture is inapplicable to contemporary Muslim
societies. The more than a billion Muslims in the world live under different laws and practice vastly different customs. Even though they all identify themselves as Muslims, they do not all understand or practice Islam
in the same way. What is perhaps common to all is variety and contradiction resulting from uneven development. One must make a deliberate effort not to see the profound differences that exist—that have always
existed—between the majority of Muslims who live in South Asia and
Southeast Asia and others who live in the Middle East, Central Asia, or
Africa. Furthermore, all of these societies have undergone significant
social, economic, and cultural change in the twentieth century. More
important, each of these societies has experienced change unevenly.

Consequently, in any Muslim society different social types hold different mixes of indigenous and imported values. Often, these mixes create new forms, which are neither Western nor traditional. One might say they are modern in the sense of contemporary. The modern Muslim society is a mix of values, mores, and emotional responses. This is why any system of government that wishes to force uniformity on this dynamic variety will necessarily have to use considerable violence. Because fundamentalist Islam's worldview is defined mostly by its treatment of women, wherever Islamism has assumed power or otherwise become politically active women have born the brunt of the violence.

The foundations of the relativity argument are different in the West and in Islamist or other authoritarian circles. From this difference emerges the second error in the relativity argument. Its Western adherents base it on a claim to freedom of choice, particularly freedom to choose elements of cultures different from those of the white, Christian, European-American male. The claim assumes that the individual has the right to choose, but governments or social forces are stifling this right. The moral force of the argument derives from a universalist conception of individual freedom and human rights.

The Islamist position is quite the opposite. It says essentially that there exists no right outside the cultural norms defined by a designated group of "experts" to which individuals may appeal. This position denies that there is such a thing as universal rights. Rather, it insists that all rights are derivatives of Islam as interpreted by a select group of men. Most Muslim women object to this rendition of Islam or their rights. The Islamists use the confusion resulting from the similarity in terminology to advance their position by introducing the idea of cultural imperialism—a politically and emotionally potent subject that is nevertheless irrelevant to the argument. By suggesting that the West has invented the idea of universality of rights in order to impose its way of life on others, the Islamists attempt to disparage the validity of the argument for rights in the eyes of their peoples, including women. In this, they have been assisted by other "authoritarian" leaders, ranging from the Chinese to those in the Vatican. (For example, the Vatican joined Islamists to protest the 1994 Conference on Population and Development in Cairo and its Programme of Action.)

The central point in women's human rights is simple. Muslim fundamentalists always posit the question of women's rights within an Islamist frame of reference. That frame of reference determines the boundaries of the existence of every Muslim woman. The question I as a Muslim woman ask is: Why should I not have the right to determine how to organize my life? What gives another person the right to interfere in my personal life?

Why is it that a Muslim cleric arrogates the right to forcibly place me in a preordained framework? Does he derive his authority from God? Does he derive it from the text? Does he derive it from tradition? I reject all these claims. I argue that as a Muslim woman I know in principle as well as any man what God ordains or what the text says. I argue that tradition is no longer a valid source because societies change, cultures change, I change, and I am both willing and able to discuss these points with him. Before we begin this discussion, I grant him every right to be who he wants to be; to do what he wants to do; to preach what he wants to preach. I only demand that he does not force me to do what he wants me to do against my wishes, in the same way that I do not force him to do what I wish.

This frame of reference has nothing to do with the East, West, South, or North. It has nothing to do with color, creed, race, sex, or religion. There was a time when in the name of Christianity women were burned at the stake as witches because their behavior did not conform to the prevailing norms. Those who committed the murder justified their action by reference to Christian principles. Slavery was once the norm everywhere. Women were kept out of social and political decision making across the world. But times have changed. Christians have changed. Jews have changed. Muslims have changed. To the extent that this change has made me aware of my person as having a specific identity that I recognize independently of my race, creed, nationality, or religion, I resent and reject being forced to do things that I do not wish to do by reference to any of these properties. Indeed, any act of forcing me to do something against my will is an act of violence. The frame of reference, therefore, has to do with acceptance of the reality of change. It has to do with the fact that there no longer exists a monolithic Islam, if there ever was one. Therefore, to justify acts of violence by an appeal to Islam is disingenuous.

Clearly, this is not simply a question of law—religious or secular. Secular law may be as repressive as religious law. Rather, it has to do with the historical development of a kind of individual consciousness that defines the meaning of right. History moves from law to right—that is, from norms that have been given before the fact to norms that are established by participation and by dialogue among free individuals. Rights, therefore, cannot be severed from freedom.

Considered in this light, right is not only a property of the relationship between government and individual. It is, above all, a matter of individual space within the social system. It is the ability of a woman to speak, to move, to work, and to choose freely. Millions of Muslim women in Muslim societies demand but are denied this leeway by their governments or by the more powerful members of their male-dominated societies. Islamists complain that, whereas the claims of democratization by the Nasserists, the Ba'thists, and the Marxists are believed, the Islamists continue to be distrusted and their intentions doubted. I am not at all sure that Muslim women trust these groups. Nevertheless, there is a fundamental difference between the Islamists and these other movements: the authoritarian nature of state-society relations notwithstanding, all of the above-mentioned systems validated, at least on paper, women's claims to equal treatment under the law. Furthermore, none of these systems argued from principle that gender apartheid, women's unequal and complementary place in society, is preordained by immutable law. How many Islamist leaders are willing to make a statement such as this unequivocally? How many Islamist leaders are willing to state unequivocally that women's rights are theirs by virtue of the fact that they are human beings?

Right is also related to obligation, morally and instrumentally. This is the most central point to the concept of right, namely, that to demand it for yourself you must defend it for others. This also is an important aspect of the frame of reference. The statement is sometimes made that rights are stressed now whereas historically the accent has been on obligation; this statement needs clarification. To the extent that obligation represents legitimacy one is never less obligated because one has rights. Rights, in fact, create obligation, because they are always intertwined with legitimacy. Simply put, we cannot have rights without obligation because we cannot have rights that are not reciprocal. But we can be forced to perform tasks under threats that are disguised as obligation. This is precisely what many women in contemporary Muslim societies are forced to suffer and valiantly object to.

Muslim women who strive for recognition of their rights are not oblivious to history. They realize that cultures do not change uniformly, and therefore there are others in Muslim societies, men and women, who interpret reality differently than they do. This fact of cultural multiplicity, important as it is politically, nevertheless does not alter the moral foundation of their position—the frame of reference that rejects force and violence in religion and that respects the identity, privacy, freedom, and integrity of the human individual. This position recognizes that religious experience is a personal experience, and that all enforcement of religion is essentially not religion but political acts of violence perpetrated by one group of people against another. The basic principle, therefore, that "I" as a human being have the right to choose is, by definition, a universal principle—it is morally true whether I live in New York, Beijing, Katmandu, or Tehran. The fact that in practice I may not be able to exercise it everywhere is a matter for political and social analysis and action.

This point leads us to the relativity of means, which is a matter essentially of politics and implementation. There are many different ways to promote human rights across the world. The efficiency of approach usually is geared to the prevailing cultural and political conditions. Clearly, all of us must seek dialogue, not only because we need to communicate if we are to effect change, but perhaps also for a more fundamental reason. Right is not a property of any particular culture. It is a product of the evolution of human consciousness and the demands that the process produces. If so, then right has more to do with the possibility of individual choice than the choice itself. Thus, each culture may produce its system of rights, provided that the frame of reference, the universality of the possibility of choice and freedom, is maintained.

Conclusion

The international community now recognizes that women's rights are human rights and human rights are women's rights. These positions are recorded in several international documents, including, among others, the Universal Declaration of Human Rights (1948), the International Covenant on Economic, Social and Cultural Rights (1966), the International Covenant on Civil and Political Rights (1966), the Convention on the Elimination of All Forms of Discrimination Against Women (1981), the UN Declaration of the Elimination of Violence Against Women (1993), and the Vienna Declaration and Programme of Action adopted by the World Conference on Human Rights (1994). The main points of these documents were encapsulated in the Mission Statement to the Platform for Action of the Fourth World Conference on Women (Beijing, 1995), of which the first article is partly as follows:

> The Platform for Action is an agenda for women's empowerment. This means that the principle of shared power and responsibility should be established between women and men at home, in the workplace and in the wider national and international communities. Equality between women and men is a matter of human rights and a condition for social justice and is also a necessary and fundamental prerequisite for equality, development and peace. A transformed partnership based on equality between women and men is a condition for people centered sustainable development. A sustained and long-term commitment is essential, so that women and men can work together for themselves, for their children and for society to meet the challenges of the twenty first century.[7]

This worldview has been reinforced in recent times by the changes that have occurred throughout the world—changes that constitute the reality of our time. The argument and symbolism now advanced by Islamist patriarchs under the guise of religion is very similar to the argument and symbolism advanced nearly a century ago by the fundamentalists in the West. The English and American suffragettes faced the same opposition, vilification, ridicule, and attacks on their morality as contemporary Muslim feminists. The crass infringement of women's rights we see in the Muslim world has more to do with power, patriarchy, and misuse of religion as political weapon than with religion properly understood as individual faith. The Islamists draw on the discourse of relativity, now in vogue in the West, to deny or infringe women's rights by introducing or perpetuating a system of gender segregation. This we must oppose.

In a speech to the General Assembly on the occasion of the fiftieth anniversary of the Universal Declaration of Human Rights, UN Secretary General Kofi Annan stressed the fundamental bond that ties human rights to human nature. He said human rights did not belong to any government, nor were they limited to any continent. Rather, they belong to everyone. He called for prompt action to prevent the violations of human rights, saying that it was not enough to tell the victims of human rights abuses that we have done our best. Prevention, he said, must in fact be the priority. He called for the world to look again to the Universal Declaration of Human Rights for "a common standard of humanity for all of humanity."[8] In this, I believe, he should receive our support.

NOTES

*An earlier version of this essay appeared in *Religious Fundamentalisms and the Human Rights of Women,* edited by Courtney W. Howland (New York, 1999).

1. See, e.g., Yvonne Yazbeck Haddad and Ellison Banks Friendly, eds., *Women, Religion, and Social Change* (Albany, N.Y., 1985).

2. For example, until the mid-nineteenth century, at common law in the United States, once a woman married, her personal property became her husband's property and her real property became subject to his control for the duration of the marriage. See Cornelius J. Moynihan, *Introduction to the Law of Real Property* (St. Paul, Minn., 1962). In contrast, the Qur'anic legal system of centuries before gave a woman the right to own and manage property herself, and to keep possession of it after marriage. See John L. Esposito, *Women in Muslim Family Law* (Syracuse, N.Y., 1982).

3. See Physicians for Human Rights, *The Taliban's War on Women: A Health and Human Rights Crisis in Afghanistan* (Boston, 1998).

4. See Karima Bennoune, "S.O.S. Algeria: Women's Human Rights Under Siege," in *Faith and Freedom: Women's Human Rights in the Muslim World,* edited by Mahnaz Afkhami (London and New York, 1995).

5. The early European travelers to the Islamic Middle East called it the Orient, and thus they are generally referred to as the Orientalists. For a critique of Orientalist texts, see Edward Said, *Orientalism* (New York, 1978), who argues that

Western scholarship on the Orient is based on racist assumptions and "ineradicable distinctions between the West and the Orient." See Ann Elizabeth Mayer, *Islam and Human Rights: Tradition and Politics* (Boulder, Colo., and Oxford, 3d ed., 1999).

6. Ayatollah Ruhollah Khomeini, *Islamic Government.* Translated by Joint Publications Research Service (New York, 1979).

7. U.N. Doc. A/CONF.177/20 (preliminary version), 35 I.L.M. 401, 409 (1996).

8. See *Hamshahri*, Iranian Daily (Persian version) on http://www.neda.net/ hamshahri/770713/siasi.htm

Grassroots Organizations and Women's Human Rights

MEETING THE CHALLENGE OF THE LOCAL-GLOBAL LINK

Mary Geske and Susan C. Bourque

∽ ON 9 December 1999 Kofi Annan, Secretary General of the United Nations, announced an Optional Protocol to the convention on the Elimination of All Forms of Discrimination Against Women (CEDAW). The floor of the UN Assembly was sparsely populated. Only a few delegates—mostly women—attended the Secretary General's speech. But the gallery was filled with women attending the annual meeting of the National Council for Research on Women, a nongovernmental organization (NGO), with headquarters in New York, committed to promoting research on women. The protocol, the setting, the attendees, and the spatial arrangements for Annan's speech all reflect important dynamics in the current discussion of women's rights as human rights and the link between grassroots movements and global efforts to broaden and protect women's rights. The National Council held its meeting at the UN to signal the international scope of research on women and the importance of international networks for fostering improvements in women's status.

This essay, which explores the dynamics of local and global action, puts forth three arguments. First, the interaction between national and international approaches to women's rights has been crucial to our current understanding of women's rights as human rights. Second, the local-global link, at least for Latin America, is a central component in the maintenance of democratic regimes and the further liberalization of those regimes. Grassroots movements and NGOs have played critical roles in what has been called "the Third Wave of Democracy" in Latin America.

Third, addressing the emerging tensions between grassroots organizations and NGOs is vital to continued improvement in women's rights and human rights and the flourishing of liberal democratic regimes, that is, those that respect the rule of law and political and civil rights. Late-twentieth-century developments in women's human rights would not have been possible without grassroots movements and NGOs, which indeed may represent the emergence of a "global civil society."[1]

It is certainly the case that international trends in women's human rights have inspired changes in state policies. But as a number of cases in Latin America demonstrate, this is not necessarily a permanent "fix"; backsliding is a recurrent theme and palpable concern.

Global Trends and Women's Human Rights

Kofi Annan, in his address to the General Assembly on the opening of the fifty-second session on 22 September 1997, stated that "violence against women has become the most pervasive human rights violation, respecting no distinction of geography, culture or wealth." This observation was both a follow-up to the convention on the Elimination of All Forms of Discrimination against Women (CEDAW), adopted by the UN General Assembly in 1979, and presaged the 1999 Optional Protocol to the convention, which among other things would make it possible for women to file complaints directly to the UN after exhausting state remedies addressing discrimination. Specifically, Annan's remarks confirm the idea of women's human rights as a distinct issue and signal a recognition of and willingness to enforce global women's human rights. Alongside this hopeful development, however, are some disturbing global trends.

Human Rights Watch enumerates these trends in their *World Report 1999*. Specifically, the group cites the ongoing abuses of women's rights by states throughout the world, including Afghanistan, Guatemala, Iran, Morocco, Pakistan, and Rwanda, among others. The report further notes state-tolerated discrimination by private actors in Bosnia, Burma, Mexico, and Thailand, among others. While Human Rights Watch does note that progress has been made in, for example, India and Uganda, the cases of state-sponsored and state-tolerated discrimination against women stand in stark contrast to multilateral declarations and conventions. In an effort to reconcile these divergent national and international trends, Human Rights Watch notes that "as a direct result of the breadth and effectiveness of the women's human rights movement, countries throughout the world as well as intergovernmental organizations and international financial institutions appeared to understand that women's human rights could no longer be ignored"; yet at the same time, "member states showed their reluctance to deliver on the promise of human rights for women." Indeed, it is not uncommon to observe states making commitments to international declarations and conventions on women's human rights while at the same time sponsoring or tolerating the violation of women's human rights within their borders.

The Human Rights Watch report highlights another failure: although at a global level the influence of NGOs in various forums and intergovernmental organizations is notable, grassroots organizations and NGOs often find that national government representatives fail to act on issues those representatives have committed to in international arenas. What is more, locally, grassroots organizations may find a widening gap between their interests and those of NGOs. Thus another set of concerns arises: As NGOs have learned to function effectively internationally, have they lost their ties to grassroots organizations? By focusing on the national and international level, do they lose their appreciation of the issues and concerns of working-class women? Where this pattern occurs, what effect has it had on the struggle for women's human rights? The growth and influence of NGOs has led many observers to ask if they have eclipsed grassroots movements, weakening the links between the two and as a consequence weakening the critical ties between the global and local levels.

International Forums and Women's Human Rights

The United Nations has been a key player in expanding women's rights and broadening the definition of what constitutes those rights. As Annan pointed out in his remarks, at the time of the UN's founding in 1945 only thirty states granted women the right to vote. Early efforts to commit the UN to women's rights include the establishment of a commission on the Status of Women in 1949, the UN sponsorship of the Decade for Women and four UN Meetings on Women beginning in 1975 in Mexico City and ending in 1995 in Beijing, which were followed by the Beijing Plus 5 meetings in June of 2000. The establishment of CEDAW 1979 and the 1993 World Conference on Human Rights in Vienna were important in codifying and reemphasizing the centrality of women's human rights.[2] Indeed, international conferences and law are central to understanding the evolution of global efforts on women's human rights.

CEDAW and the Optional Protocol are our major points of focus for two reasons. First, the convention is a legally binding international treaty that formally recognizes and explicitly addresses the rights of women. According to Ilana Landsberg-Lewis, the convention

> is the principal legal instrument addressing women's rights and equality. Its
> uniqueness lies in its mandate for the achievement of substantive equality for

women, which requires not only formal legal equality but also equality of results in real terms. By recognizing that discrimination is socially constructed the convention sets the pace for a dynamic, proactive approach to women's advancement. It is no longer possible to say that there is no discrimination against women if laws and policies do not overtly discriminate against women. Under the regime of the convention, neutrality has no legitimacy. Positive actions are required of the State to promote and protect the rights of women.[3]

Similarly, the Optional Protocol is a treaty with the stated purpose to "ensure the full and equal enjoyment of women of all human rights and fundamental freedoms and to take effective action to prevent violations of these rights and freedoms."

Second, both the convention and Optional Protocol involve extensive interactions with NGOs or extensive global-local interaction. Focusing on the convention and Optional Protocol therefore allows us to examine the various actors responsible for the schism, delineated earlier, between internationally stated commitments and national failures to act. A focus on CEDAW and the Optional Protocol allows us to see the importance of international conferences like Beijing or other international forums like the UN Decade for Women. In the case of the latter, many suggest the UN Decade for Women was crucial in laying the groundwork for the convention. Many credit Beijing with contributing to the work of the administrative committee for the convention.[4]

Convention on the Elimination of All Forms of Discrimination Against Women

International attention to women's human rights first appeared in the form of the United Nations Commission on the Status of Women. Established in 1946, the Commission played a crucial role in identifying the various areas of inequality and discrimination affecting women. Culminating in its adoption in 1979, the convention on the Elimination of All Forms of Discrimination Against Women has been the most thorough and far-reaching treaty addressing women's human rights. An overall commitment to equality forms the basis for the convention. Three specific areas are addressed in detail. First, CEDAW enumerates the legal status of women with a focus on a number of particular rights, including political participation, representation, education, employment, and civil and business matters, among others. Second, it explicitly addresses reproductive rights. Issues of reproductive choice, maternity rights, and childcare all are referred to throughout the treaty. Finally, it focuses on culture and women's human rights. The emphasis is on the potential ways in which culture and tradition might limit women's human rights. A range of specific issues are stressed, including the role that stereotypes, customs, ideas, and norms play in the legal, economic, and political structures within states. The convention also provides for the establishment of the committee on the Elimination of Discrimination Against Women to monitor the treaty's implementation. Composed of twenty-three experts elected by ratifying states, the committee consults with states in their efforts to achieve the goals of the treaty. States are required to submit reports to the committee at least every four years.

The Optional Protocol allows women to take their case directly to the committee, assuming all state options for resolving the complaint have been exhausted. The committee then is authorized to investigate the complaint and issue a communication of its decision to the state. This may include an investigation within the accused state's territory with, of course, the state's consent. Ultimately, the committee issues a decision including relevant recommendations to the state. At various stages throughout this process, the state is given six months within which to respond to the committee's findings or decisions. Ultimately, the Optional Protocol provides an "opt-out" clause allowing states to deny the validity and jurisdiction of the committee. The Protocol seeks two additional requirements from states. First is the protection of any complainant. Second, the Protocol requires State Parties to "widely publicize the convention and its Protocol and provide access to the views and recommendations of the committee."

Like any international law, the convention and Optional Protocol are premised on the idea of state sovereignty and thus are beholden to and dependent on state interests and behaviors. A state might commit to the norms embodied in the convention and Optional Protocol for a variety of reasons yet fail to put the tenets of the treaties into practice, again for a variety of reasons. Indeed, some of the states cited as abusers of women's human rights in the Human Rights Watch report are parties to the convention and have signed the Optional Protocol.

Understanding this schism relies in part on understanding the relationship between local NGOs and grassroots organizations on one hand and international forums and states on the other. Are changes in state behavior more likely in cases where local NGOs and grassroots organizations are successfully brought into international forums? To what extent are women's human rights, identified locally, advanced by NGOs and through global conventions?

Local NGOs and Grassroots Organizations

Scholars are quick to point out the disjuncture between state commitments in international treaties and substantive state promotion or tolerance of discrimination against women. Charlotte Bunch writes:

The lack of understanding of women's rights as human rights is reflected in the fact that few governments are committed, in domestic or foreign policy, to women's equality as a basic human right. No government determines its policies toward other countries on the basis of their treatment of women, even where aid and trade decisions are said to be based on a country's human rights record.[5]

This is the gap that women's organizations have worked to bridge through a variety of international forums. Indeed, many, including Bunch, view the 1993 Vienna Conference on Human Rights as a turning point in the struggle for women's human rights. Elisabeth Friedman suggests three turning points that helped to advance women's human rights globally. First, women's human rights activists successfully pressured the major human rights organizations to focus some of their attention on women's human rights. For example, Amnesty International "started to work on women's human rights in the late '80s, when staff and membership realized that women were systematically underrepresented in their research." Second, and despite the convention, "the exclusion of women from international human rights norms and laws, as well as the possibility of using those norms and laws to advance women's rights, became clearer."[6] Third, women's groups became actively involved in the preparatory meetings for Vienna. Central to all three was the role of women's groups that tirelessly organized around and campaigned for women's human rights.

Both Friedman and Bunch note the important role of activists prior to the Vienna Conference. Despite its exclusion from the UN resolution announcing the 1993 conference, "gender-based violence and women's human rights emerged as one of the most talked-about subjects, and women were recognized as a well-organized human rights constituency."[7] The Vienna Declaration, along with the Optional Protocol, reflects the successful mobilization, organization, and influence of women's human rights activists internationally.

Optimism with respect to women's human rights is dependent on an ongoing global-local dialogue. In this spirit, the United Nations Development Fund for Women (UNIFEM) has successfully worked with the convention. Specifically, UNIFEM in cosponsorship with International Women's Rights Action Watch (IWRAW) Asia Pacific has held a number of Global to Local training sessions designed to increase the presence and influence of women's NGOs in countries reporting to the committee. Noeleen Heyzer, the executive director of UNIFEM, notes that the sessions are aimed at "strengthening women's rights advocates' understanding of the convention and of the committee's working methods, as well as exploring CEDAW's potential application to their advocacy work at the national level."[8]

The most recent UNIFEM/IWRAW Asia Pacific-sponsored training session took place from 18 January to 5 February 2000. Nearly forty women participated in the session, which focused on intensive training on the convention itself and on the CEDAW committee. According to Landsberg-Lewis, women from reporting countries come to learn about the reporting and monitoring process of the committee, specifically, how the committee interacts in a "constructive dialogue" with their government to enhance the implementation of the convention and, subsequently, the accountability of the country. This session includes specific training on writing effective reports and making issues or problems in their countries clear to committee members. Landsberg-Lewis contends that the growing role of NGOs in the reporting process has helped to make the committee sessions with governments dynamic and has assisted the committee in asking more informed, deeper, and more specific questions emanating from women from reporting countries.

It is important to note the growth and influence of NGO involvement in CEDAW sessions generally, especially since the Beijing Conference in 1995. The influence of a number of NGOs outside of those in the UNIFEM/IWRAW training demonstrates that women are interested in the reporting process, take the process quite seriously, and, in bringing their own information (i.e., shadow reports) into the process make the process itself more meaningful. Landsberg-Lewis credits the training session with increasing both governmental and committee responsibility to local women. Indeed, she cites examples of states making commitments or representations to the committee yet failing to live up to these commitments and representations upon leaving the UN. In several of these cases, local women's groups present in the training session achieved state commitments and representations through local publicity efforts and communication with state officials. Committee responsibility toward local women's groups has manifested itself not only in their meeting with these groups and accepting and reading their reports, but also in actually seeking women out to help clarify or substantiate information in the government reports.

Although the general dilemmas of international law plague CEDAW, the convention has nevertheless achieved or worked toward a number of important goals. First and perhaps most significant, it made women's rights human rights. Friedman quotes Roberta Clarke, coordinator for the Women and the Law Project of the Caribbean Association for Feminist Research and Action (CAFRA), whom she interviewed in 1993:

CEDAW was fairly important in bringing women into the "rights talk" arena. . . . Once your government has signed, it's a social contract that they're making with the women in the country. It gives you that tool, that leverage to say OK, this is the normative context within which women's status has to be dealt with—and it's a human rights document, so automatically you are in the basket of human rights.[10]

Second, CEDAW legitimizes women's claims for human rights. The deliberate incorporation of women's groups through the training sessions furthers this goal. Third, the convention demonstrates an international commitment to women's human rights, thus suggesting universalistic claims for women's human rights in contrast to those who claim "that equality between women and men should be made relative to culture and tradition."[10] Fourth, the convention has brought together a variety of actors with the shared goal of fostering understanding and respect for women's human rights. Most important are international organizations including UNIFEM, international activist networks such as the IRWAW, local NGOs, and states. International forums also have been important to CEDAW. Indeed, IRWAW was a product of the 1985 World Conference on Women in Nairobi. The Fourth World Conference on Women held in Beijing in 1995 was crucial in bringing together groups of women from around the world and providing a forum for raising and discussing new issues with respect to women's human rights.

In sum, the CEDAW is a prime example of the successful link between women's grassroots organizations, NGOs, and the United Nations. As noted above, the implementation of the convention and the condition of women's human rights depend on the maintenance of that link. The crucial key to the convention's success is its impact on human rights at the local level. Thus, continuing ties to local grassroots organizations must be a central concern. At the international level, UNIFEM has taken important steps to secure the link. In the section that follows, drawing on the experience of Latin America, we describe in greater detail how these ties emerged and the challenges posed in the current political climate.

Grassroots Women's Movements and Human Rights in Latin America: Broadening a Concept

The story of women's mobilization in Latin America has two interrelated components: first, Latin American women have insisted on an expanded notion of human rights and have used their demands for human rights to redefine the political and social roles available to women. In the process, they have been key players in the democratic transition that occurred in Latin America in the 1980s. The question, however, remains if this will continue to be the case during the process of democratic consolidation and democratic "decay" now under way. In assessing this potential, the crucial factors are the relations between women's organizations and national governments and among women's organizations (grassroots groups, NGOs, and feminists). An important component in that relationship is the international environment and most particularly the role of the United Nations. All the countries discussed here have signed and ratified CEDAW.

As the twenty-first century begins, it is commonplace to speak of the link between employment, education, reproductive rights, and health as key components of women's rights. This was not the case in the 1970s. Grassroots women's movements insisted on a more extensive definition of human rights. Perhaps the first case was the Housewives Committee of the Bolivian tin miners. Emerging in the 1970s to protest government efforts to dislodge the miners from their homes, the Housewives Committee enlarged the definition of human rights to include the right to food and shelter. This was repeated in the 1980s with the hunger march of Bolivian miners. In what would become a generalized pattern throughout Latin America, the extension of women's roles from the domestic sphere into the public sphere had a profound and far-reaching impact both on women and the political system. Discussing the Bolivian case, Marcia Stephenson concluded:

> While the miners' housewives originally mobilized around a set of needs directly linked to their roles in the home, the women's choice of the name Housewives Committees emphasized a political relation between the house and the larger community of resistance . . . throwing into question the boundary that otherwise separated the two spaces.[11]

The pattern noted in the Bolivian case came to be repeated in a variety of contexts throughout Latin America in the late 1970s and throughout the 1980s and 1990s. Women organized to protect basic human rights to food and shelter, as well as for the protection of their loved ones from the repressive acts of the state (arrest, kidnapping, torture, and disappearances). Protests that took traditional maternal roles as a point of departure served to broaden their roles to include explicit political demands and ultimately women's conception of human rights.

For Argentina, Chile, and Brazil, the 1960s and early 1970s were periods of intense political mobilization followed by brutal military repression. The authoritarian military governments that predominated until the 1980s violated human rights in each nation and gave rise to different patterns of grassroots mobilization among women. In all three countries, women organized to protest the torture and disappearance of husbands, children, and grandchildren. Because military regimes had repressed and restricted political institutions (in particular legislatures and political parties), new space was available for social movements. Women's organizations and human rights organizations filled the void.

Initially, the unusual nature of women's involvement in political mobilization gave them some protection and the ability to mobilize when men could not. This provided opportunities for action in uncharted space. Nevertheless, gender did not protect women for long and they soon suffered the torture and murder they had organized to protest. Accounts from women who were arrested and detained stress that their tormentors were particularly annoyed by the women's violation of their assigned roles. They had strayed beyond the appropriate nonpolitical sphere and were to be brutally reminded of that to deter further misbehavior.[12]

Women in the Southern Cone nations frequently justified their political involvement by reference to their maternal roles and the need to protect homes and families. They had been driven to public protest not out of a desire for an expanded political voice but rather to protest government violation of their loved ones—the appropriate role of a mother.

Contrary to expectations, a heightened notion of women as rights-bearing individuals developed during the transition to democracy, and the appropriate sphere for women's political action expanded. Many observers of grassroots movements had feared that political action built on women's traditional roles as mothers, grandmothers, and those responsible for the maintenance and well-being of the family would ultimately lock women into those roles and severely restrict their political action. María del Carmen Feijó, observing the Argentine Mothers of the Plaza de Mayo, was concerned that their success relied too heavily on the stereotyped view of women as self-abnegating, long-suffering, and "above" politics. Maruja Barrig raised the same concerns about women's communal kitchens in Peru. Over time such concerns have lessened as observers have seen women's organizations persist and provide women with critical organizing skills, expanding their capacity to petition the state and instilling a sense of self-worth and efficacy with long-term implications for the state.[13] Let us turn to several concrete examples of these patterns.

The defeat of the Argentine military in the war over the Falkland Islands, known in Argentina as las islas Malvinas, occasioned serious discrediting of the military and its right to rule. This in turn sparked thoughtful conversations on how to remake a stronger and more democratic Argentina. Women's organizations, which emerged during the period of repression, struggled over their proper role vis-à-vis the state in the new democratic framework. They also considered how social institutions could be restructured to provide better support for democratic values.

For some women, particularly the Mothers of the Plaza de Mayo, collaboration with the state was not possible. They insisted on a stance that separated the human rights organization from the emerging competitive party system. In contrast, for many feminists the challenge was to find a new entry point to the state, secure legislation for gender equity, and promote democratic values within the state. This tension, which is repeated in various forms throughout Latin America, underscores one of the signal issues for women's grassroots organizations: determining how they will resolve their ongoing stance toward the state and political parties.

In addition to the human rights organizations in Argentina, two other grassroots groups were significant: the Housewives committees, which emerged in full force in 1982 to protest the rising cost of living, and the various strands of the feminist movement. The feminist groups were well connected to the international women's movement and began to establish links with other feminists globally through their participation in the UN Decade for Women. Following the transition to democracy, feminists began to lobby for Argentine compliance with CEDAW. They also achieved success with the cancellation of restrictions on the use of contraceptives, and in 1991 Argentina established a quota system to guarantee women 30 percent of the upper-level positions on party tickets. The appointment of several noted feminists to high administrative positions within the government allowed members of the Argentine feminist movement to play significant roles in shaping the political agenda in Argentina, as well as the Argentine agenda for international meetings. Nevertheless, there were also setbacks, most notably the appointment of conservative women's groups—opposed to reproductive rights—to represent Argentina at the Fourth UN Conference in Beijing.[14]

In Brazil feminists and grassroots groups struggled together during the period of the greatest military repression. They were an important part of the groups that filled the political void when the military outlawed political parties and labor unions. Nevertheless, after the transition to democracy, many of the grassroots organizations were reluctant to engage with the state or join political parties. As Alvarez notes, women in the feminist movement struggled with the same issue: "During the 1970s, the formal political arena was not perceived as relevant to the feminist transformation process. . . . Rather, feminists felt their priority was to build a base in civil society to oppose the authoritarian social, political and economic order."[15] But feminists began to rethink this posture when legal opposition became possible. This exacerbated a long-standing tension within the feminist movement between those with political commitments to leftist parties (double militancy) and those who wanted the women's movement to remain autonomous.

In contrast to the tensions in the feminist movement, Alvarez found that the partisan tensions were less acute within neighborhood-based grassroots women's organizations. Political parties had little success recruiting working-class women, who remained skeptical, viewing partisan politics as a male domain. It was middle-class women who returned to claim political space within the new opposition political parties. Due to the differences in strategies, "ties to the neighborhood based women's groups gradually weakened. As a result, one critical source of Brazilian feminism's political leverage and legitimacy—its gender-based alliance with mothers' clubs and other working class women's organizations—was partially eroded."[16]

Nevertheless, feminist activity continued on two tracks—within the newly constituted political parties and in autonomous women's organizations. And the combination worked to the advantage of both groups. The women's movement and grassroots groups remained independent of the newly reconstituted parties and yet at the same time provided feminists who had chosen to rejoin political parties with a "legitimating constituency." As a result of their sense of an organized, mobilized grassroots base of support, Alvarez reports that the parties began to incorporate "core aspects of the feminist agenda" into their platforms, and the women working within parties found they had considerable clout. Parties competed for the votes of grassroots women's organizations and candidates addressed "issues such as day care, family planning, women's health and other women's issues in their campaign material."

The long transition period in Brazil brought groundbreaking innovations in gender and human rights, beginning with the establishment of State Councils on Women's Condition in 1983. The councils were an important source of innovation in family planning and women's health, and the São Paulo Council's Commission on Violence Against Women created the first police precinct staffed entirely by specially trained female officers to process cases of rape, sexual abuse, and domestic violence. The female police precincts were viewed as an important step in guaranteeing women's human rights, and they were attempted in a number of other Latin American nations.

In 1985, when the first civilian government was elected, the National Council for Women's Rights was installed in the Ministry of Justice. The majority of the new council members were women with long-standing links to feminist groups. But even with these innovations, serious problems remained. The women's police precincts (which were established throughout Brazil) were only partially successful. They still had to operate within an unreformed judicial system. Frustration with low rates of prosecution and conviction led to renewed efforts among women to organize against domestic violence and to insist on new definitions of rape in the civil code.

By the 1990s the brief flirtation of feminists with the state had run into serious limits—but feminism in Brazil's civil society was still a vital force. Moreover, grassroots feminism continued to flourish with new attention to race and class issues. Brazil's 1988 constitution showed the effects of feminists. But victory was short-lived and limited as the traditional male-dominated politics and institutions reasserted themselves. This becomes a familiar pattern, found in Chile and Argentina as well as in many other nations: those who win the war on the barricades lose the spoils in the process of institution building that follows.

In Chile women were actively involved in human rights struggles during the regime (1973–1989) of the military dictator Augusto Pinochet. Common cause was made between grassroots groups confronting dire economic conditions and human rights violations with those struggling for women's rights. Established politicians welcomed the women's groups during their efforts to end the military regime in the late 1980s. As women created organizations for human rights, economic survival, and political participation, "women raised their own gender issues," and women's mobilization helped democratize the Chilean political system and enlarged Chilean understandings of "the political."[17]

Nevertheless, the coalition governments that followed Pinochet were reluctant to pursue a feminist agenda. Instead they created a government agency, Servicio Nacional a la Mujer, (SERNAM) in January of 1991. SERNAM produced an Equal Opportunity Plan that promoted a comprehensive agenda from 1994 to 1999. It included a campaign against domestic violence. Despite women's involvement during the transition, political parties have been slow to include women in their ranks and the conservative trend in Chilean politics remains. Moreover, the disjuncture between feminists in government agencies and grassroots organizations has grown deeper. María Elena Valenzuela concludes: "Since the return to democracy the women's movement has been largely absent from politics. Even though there are an important number of grassroots women's organizations, they do not provide active or consistent support for those working on a women's agenda in the government."[18]

The pattern for Peru was somewhat different. The revolutionary government of the armed forces (1968–1978) was a stark contrast to those of the Southern Cone. Human rights abuses did not characterize the regime. Political parties continued to operate and the communist party expanded. The military government promoted a distinct pattern of inclusion and a program of social reform, and during the early years of the regime women were a part of its reform program. Concern for single mothers found its way into the government's Plan Inca and the 1978 constitution included an equal rights provision.

During this period, a spectrum of feminist organizations emerged and sought links with grassroots women living in the *pueblos jovenes* (young towns) surrounding Lima.[19] NGOs flourished and began to work with popular women's organizations. Peruvian feminists recognized from the outset that they would need to bridge class and ethnic divides to build ties to grassroots women's organizations. These self-help organizations, which included mother's clubs, nutrition programs for mothers and young children and communal kitchens, grew with the worsening economic crisis in the late 1970s and early 1980s. The grassroots groups were often wary of the feminist label, and feminists for their part feared that the popular organizations reinforced women's traditional domestic roles rather than raising gender consciousness. The grassroots organizations were focused on meeting the practical needs of women—most particularly feeding and sustaining their families as the economy went into a free fall.

With the return of democratic government in 1980, women's grassroots organizations increased dramatically in response to the severe economic crisis that accompanied the neoliberal economic reforms of successive governments. The communal kitchens became so widespread a necessity that they expanded to the level of a federation. Political parties and feminist groups competed to forge links with them. The communal kitchens were an important point of infiltration for *Sendero Luminoso*—the Shining Path revolutionary movement—and many grassroots organizations fell prey to internecine warfare waged by Shining Path.

Peru's worst human rights abuses occurred during the struggle with Shining Path from 1983 to 1992. Human rights violations were rampant. The civilian population, both rural and urban, was caught between the two violent forces of the army and the Shining Path. Paradoxically, it was in this struggle that several observers have concluded that women built roles as "visible protagonists of society." Mothers Clubs and Federations, relatives of the disappeared and migrant associations, communal kitchens and child nutrition committees, all gave women experience in working with one another and seeing new roles for themselves in their families and their communities.

> Women played lead roles in grassroots civic organizations that addressed the major practical rights issues—economic survival, war induced displacement, human rights violations, political stances toward Sendero and the State— that shaped a war torn and impoverished society. They became the organized claimants who channeled resources and political pressure beyond those mobilized by the masculinized political parties and grassroots organizations.[20]

In the rural areas, Andean peasant women played critical roles in wartorn regions. Coral Cordero described the developing consciousness of these women: "not only did they bury their dead, they found themselves searching for the living, helping those imprisoned and keeping households intact." The experience "profoundly affected and sensitized the women." Over time, confronting the task of defending human rights and organizing family survival, women formed stable organizations of Mother Clubs that grew to "14,000 Clubs and 80,000 affiliated women in the Ayacucho region by 1995." In this process, they established effective ties to NGOs for food, health and education. Cordero also concludes that for the first time they came to see themselves as "rights bearing individuals."[21]

Assessing the Patterns

In all four nations the grassroots women's organizations and feminist groups that organized in the 1970s and 1980s to protect human rights found that the links between them were strained by several tensions under the new democratic governments. First was the question of double militancy—the relation with political parties and the state. As political democracy returned, the question for many feminists was whether they would be more effective by remaining autonomous organizations or by reestablishing ties to the new state institutions and political parties.

The second question was how to maintain the link between grassroots organizations and feminist groups. One of the most important vehicles for the creation of those ties had been NGO work with grassroots groups. Feminists had created NGOs and worked within NGOs created by others. Many of the NGOs received their inspiration from the UN Decade for Women, and their financial backing came from international sources. Thus, as we look to the future, assessing these ties and the links between the global and local networks will be an important task.

Just as the patterns of military rule were distinct, so too the patterns of democratic transition and consolidation have varied. But for all nations the democratic transitions provided an ideal moment to rethink the constitution, the civil code, and the basis of citizenship. Women who had become organized to oppose the military and those who had begun to forge links to other women's groups through the emerging international networks of NGOs were well positioned to pressure and petition national governments for constitutional changes in women's status. The democratic opening brought new levels of guaranteed political participation in Argentina, women's councils and police stations in Brazil, SERNAM in Chile, and a constitutional equal rights provision in Peru. Also, during the period of democratic transition and consolidation, a bevy of new NGOs emerged—many of them with explicitly feminist goals.

Drawing on evidence from Argentina, Brazil, Chile, and Peru, Jane Jaquette and Sharon Wolchik stress "the need for permanently organized groups that are capable of mobilizing political resources to maintain existing gains and push new agendas."[22] Similar data from all four countries demonstrates that bureaucratic groups and women's ministries cannot operate without support from well-organized groups outside the government. But, as democratic consolidation has progressed, concerns about the ties between NGOs and women's grassroots organizations have been raised.

Alvarez notes the divergence between feminists who have learned how to operate in the global community of international governmental meetings and the world of grassroots organizations. She depicts the sharp contrast between the NGO Forum at Hairou and the official UN Conference on Women meeting in Beijing, seventy kilometers away. Despite the goal of the forum to influence the official Fourth World Conference on Women, most at the Latin American regional tent "appeared little concerned with and most minimally informed about the workings at the UN Conference itself."[23] Thus, one must be concerned that a lack of connection between groups linked to the grassroots movements and those with influence at the international policy level will result in a "women's agenda" that ignores the concerns of grassroots groups. In particular, Alvarez asks, will the concerns of racial and sexual minorities be obscured and will the issues of economic class be addressed adequately in a milieu that is dominated by educated and sophisticated women skilled in the intricacies of international diplomacy? As one analyst of the indigenous movement has written: "Those with the skills to lead internationally may be the least representative."[24] This reality poses a particular problem for the continuing representation of the concerns of women in grassroots movements and organizations.

Larry Diamond identifies a further set of concerns. International support for NGOs has been critical to their work with grassroots organizations and their efforts to promote democracy. It is difficult to imagine a flourishing civil society throughout the world without such support. Nevertheless, reliance on international donors raises questions of dependency. And, paradoxically, once the transition to democracy has occurred, there has been a tendency for international donors to "move on" to more desperate situations, leaving grassroots groups adrift during the consolidation period. The flight of NGO support may account for the shrinking of the political space available to grassroots groups once the transition to democracy has taken place. In the long run, this "retreat of civil society" may prove to be a severe hindrance to democratic consolidation.[25]

Conclusion: Constructing a Global-Local-Global Link

These concerns bring us back to the commencement of a new Optional Protocol to the CEDAW. They also recall the problems surrounding international efforts to address women's human rights given state interests on one side and the relationship between the global and local levels on the other. From the outset, the UN meetings had an impact on women's human rights in Latin America. The groups that organized around women's human rights in the Americas found important sources of support through the networks that became a part of each UN conference on women. For many governments the UN conferences marked their first efforts to compile data on the status and condition of women. At the same time, governments found themselves pressured by grassroots and feminist organizations for attention to priority items.

Today, the United Nations is again a key to the preservation and expansion of women's rights. CEDAW, for example, offers a potential conduit for NGOs and grassroots organizations both to air their particular concerns and hold their governments responsible for implementing policies in accord with the convention. What is more, the efforts of UNIFEM and IRWAW-Asia Pacific have successfully infused CEDAW with an effective mechanism linking local organizations to an international deliberative body. Given the challenges posed to grassroots movements, as the transition to democracy becomes the consolidation of democracy the global-local link is critical. Indeed, as the recent training sessions for CEDAW have suggested, local movements may be gaining momentum in their efforts to hold governments accountable to preserving women's human rights. At the same time, we might be witnessing a circling back to the global level, as international forums and bodies like the CEDAW committee also are learning from local organizations and adjusting their strategies and goals accordingly.

NOTES

1. Ann Marie Clark, Elisabeth J. Friedman, and Kathryn Hochstetler, "The Sovereign Limits of Global Civil Society: A Comparison of NGO Participation in UN World Conferences on the Environment, Human Rights, and Women," *World Politics* 51, no. 1 (October 1998): 1–35.

2. Technically, the committee on the Elimination of Discrimination Against Women is known by the acronym CEDAW. In turn, the convention on the Elimination of Discrimination against Women is referred to as the convention, the Women's Convention, and CEDAW. For the sake of clarity and consistency, we use "CEDAW" and "Convention" when referring to the convention and are explicit in our references to the committee.

3. Ilana Landsberg-Lewis, ed., *Bringing Equality Home: Implementing the Con-*

vention on the Elimination of All Forms of Discrimination Against Women (New York: UNIFEM, 1998), p. 1.

4. See Marjorie Agosín, ed., *Surviving Beyond Fear,* esp. the introduction (New York, 1993); and Elisabeth Friedman, "Women's Human Rights: The Emergence of a Movement," in *Women's Rights Human Rights: International Feminist Perspectives,* edited by Julie Peters and Andrea Wolper (New York, 1995).

5. Charlotte Bunch, "Transforming Human Rights from a Feminist Perspective," in *Women's Rights Human Rights,* ed. Peters and Wolper (1995), p. 12.

6. Friedman, "Women's Human Rights," in *Women's Rights Human Rights,* ed. Peters and Wolper (1995), p. 25, p. 27.

7. Charlotte Bunch and Niamh Reilly, *Demanding Accountability* (New Brunswick, N.J., and New York, 1994), p. 12.

8. Foreword to *Bringing Equality Home,* ed. Landsberg-Lewis (1998).

9. Friedman, "Women's Human Rights," in *Women's Rights Human Rights,* ed. Peters and Wolper (1995), p. 23.

10. Landsberg-Lewis notes the persistence of this cultural-relativism position and the importance of CEDAW in challenging its central tenets. *Bringing Equality Home,* ed. Landsberg-Lewis (1998), p. 1.

11. The actions of the Housewives and hunger strike eventually led to the downfall of the Banzer Suarez regime. The tactic of the hunger march was employed against another government in 1986 in response to neoliberal state demands. See Marcia Stephenson, *Gender and Modernity in Andean Bolivia* (Austin, Tex., 1999), pp. 192–195.

12. See the accounts of Domitila Barrios de Chungara, *Let Me Speak: Testimony of Domitila, A Woman of the Bolivian Mines,* with Moema Viezzer, trans. (New York and London, 1978), and *Si me permiten hablar,* with Moema Viezzer (Mexico City, 1987); and the analysis of Ximena Bunster-Burotto in "Surviving Beyond Fear: Women and Torture in Latin America," in *Women and Change in Latin America,* edited by June Nash and Helen Safa (South Hadley, Mass., 1986), pp. 297–325.

13. See María del Carmen Feijoó, "Women and Democracy in Argentina," with Marcela María Alejandra Nari, in *The Women's Movement in Latin America: Participation and Democracy,* edited by Jane S. Jaquette (Boulder, Colo., 2d ed., 1994), pp. 109–129; and Maruja Barrig, "The Difficult Equilibrium Between Bread and Roses: Women's Organizations and Democracy in Peru," in *The Women's Movement in Latin America,* ed. Jaquette, pp. 151–175. In her next article Barrig changed her mind about the political potential of such organizations: "Female Leadership, Violence, and Citizenship in Peru," in *Women and Democracy: Latin America and Central and Eastern Europe,* edited by Jane S. Jaquette and Sharon L. Wolchik (Baltimore and London, 1998), pp. 104–124. See also the discussion by Isabel Coral Cordero, "Women in War: Impact and Responses," in *Shining and Other Paths: War and Society in Peru, 1980–1995,* edited by Steve J. Stern (Durham, N.C., and London, 1998), pp. 345–374.

14. See the essays by María del Carmen Feijoó, "Women and Democracy in Argentina," in *The Women's Movement in Latin America,* ed. Jaquette (1994), pp. 109–129; and "Democratic Participation and Women in Argentina," in *Women and Democracy,* eds. Jaquette and Wolchik (1998), pp. 29–46.

15. This section draws heavily on Sonia E. Alvarez, "The (Trans)formation of Feminism(s) and Gender Politics in Democratizing Brazil," in *The Women's Movement in Latin America,* ed. Jaquette (1994), pp. 13–63 (with the quotation here

from p. 33); and Teresa P. R. Caldeira, "Justice and Individual Rights: Challenges for Women's Movements and Democratization in Brazil," in *Women and Democracy,* eds. Jaquette and Wolchik (1998), pp. 75–103.

16. Alvarez, "(Trans)formation," in *The Women's Movement in Latin America,* ed. Jaquette (1994), p. 36.

17. María Elena Valenzuela, "Women and the Democratization Process in Chile," in *Women and Democracy,* ed. Jaquette and Wolchik (1998), pp. 47–74.

18. Valenzuela, "Women and the Democratization Process in Chile," in *Women and Democracy,* ed. Jaquette and Wolchik (1998), p. 59.

19. See Maruja Barrig's discussion on this point in "Bread and Roses," in *The Women's Movement in Latin America,* ed. Jaquette (1994). See also Susan C. Bourque, "Urban Activists: Paths to Political Consciousness in Peru," in *Women Living Change,* edited by Susan C. Bourque and Donna Robinson Divine (Philadelphia, 1985), pp. 25–56. The military allowed the parties of the left to expand because it wished to undermine the traditional support base of APRA, the historical nemesis of the military.

20. Steve J. Stern, Introduction to Part 4, in *Shining and Other Paths,* ed. Stern (1998), p. 342.

21. See the discussion in Isabel Coral Cordero, "Women in War," in *Shining and Other Paths,* ed. Stern (1998), pp. 345–374.

22. Jane S. Jaquette and Sharon L. Wolchik, eds., *Women and Democracy: Latin America and Central and Eastern Europe* (1998), p. 10.

23. Sonia E. Alvarez, "Latin American Feminisms 'Go Global': Trends of the 1990s and Challenges for the New Millennium," in *Cultures of Politics, Politics of Cultures,* edited by Sonia E. Alvarez, Evelina Dagnino, and Arturo Escobar (Boulder, Colo., 1998), p. 293.

24. Alison Brysk, as quoted in Larry Diamond, ed., *Developing Democracy: Toward Consolidation* (Baltimore, 1999), p. 253.

25. Larry Diamond, ed., *Developing Democracy: Toward Consolidation* (Baltimore, 1999), pp. 252–255.

IV: WOMEN AND THE CULTURES OF DISPLACEMENT

"What Was She Doing There?"
WOMEN AS "LEGITIMATE TARGETS"
Barbara Harlow

Let me ask you something: what was she doing, vagabonding all over Guguletu, of all places; taking her foot where she had no business? Where did she think she was going? Was she blind not to see there were no white people in this place?

Yes, the more I think about this the more convinced I am that your daughter must have been the type of person who has absolutely no sense of danger when she believes in what she is doing.

What was she doing here, your daughter? What made her come to this, of all places. Not an army of mad elephants would drag me here, if I were her.

—Sindiwe Magona, *Mother to Mother*

∞ "WHAT was she doing there?" The question is part of the opening appeal in Sindiwe Magona's 1998 novel, *Mother to Mother*. The first-person narrator of the novel is Mandisa, who tells the story of her son, one of the young men from a Cape Town township who murdered the American Fulbright scholar Amy Biehl in August 1993. Although convicted of the crime, he eventually received amnesty from South Africa's Truth and Reconciliation Commission on the grounds that the action was "politically motivated." Addressed to Biehl's mother, the story is, however, as much that of Mandisa herself as it is that of her son or even of Amy Biehl. What

was she doing there?: the question applies not only to Biehl, but to Mandisa, who was brought to the township in the apartheid years of group areas acts, forced removals, influx control, and pass laws. In her Magona
creates a character whose experiences are typical of life for blacks under
the apartheid regime.

Ruth First was a South African investigative journalist, historian, and
an anti-apartheid activist. She had long militated against those strictures
of the apartheid regime portrayed in Magona's novel. First was assassi-
nated in Mozambique by a letter bomb sent to her from South Africa in
August 1982. Her assassins also applied to the TRC for amnesty. They argued inter alia that Ruth First was a "legitimate target," and that their
deed too was "politically motivated." They were granted amnesty in June
2000.

Biehl and First, hailing from two different continents, representing two
differing ideological histories, and coming out of two distinct generations,
had nonetheless each been committed to resisting discriminatory practices
and to defending human rights generally, and women's rights especially.
They insisted that human rights must necessarily include economic, social, civil, and political rights as well. Their separate lives converge in
their goals and in the violence of their deaths.

What makes a woman a "legitimate target"? What did Ruth First and
Amy Biehl do to be so considered?

Truth and Reconciliation

According to Human Rights Watch Report 2000, addressing abuses and
advances in human rights and their monitoring around the globe in 1999,
"for women coping with conflict and its aftermath, 1999 was a cross-
roads." The section on women's human rights states:

> Events in 1999 provided clear evidence that, with the rise of civil conflicts
> in which civilians are often the primary targets, women's rights are ever
> more at risk. Despite significant gains in securing international condemna-
> tion of the horrors typically visited on women in conflict zones, assaults on
> women were used as a weapon of war in every conflict waged in 1999. . . .
> Where fighting raged, women were raped; where conflicts subsided, women
> looked fruitlessly for protection, help, and justice; and where conflicts ended,
> women's hopes for improved rights met with disinterest and denial.

The section presents concerns geographically, from Algeria to Zimbabwe,
and also in terms of women's arenas of participation, war zones, displaced
persons camps, in the family and in the workplace. It shows that women

have been abused by the state and their male guardians, within civil and customary law. They have suffered political disenfranchisement and familial disinheritance, denial of asylum and refusal of reproductive health care. Clearly, the report indicates that much progress is still to be made if women are ever to have their rights recognized in light of the international conventions meant to ensure human rights.

In its "Africa Overview," the report decries a world that remains "indifferent to a continent in pain," recognizes the conflicts in West Africa, slavery in the Sudan, and Central Africa's role in the continental conflagration. Yet it observes that South Africa remains "on course," mentioning in particular the country's second democratic elections and citing the continued work of the country's Truth and Reconciliation Commission as exemplary in redressing the past as part of the process of addressing the future.

South Africa's Truth and Reconciliation Commission was established as part of the solution negotiated between the National Party government and the African National Congress and its allies. The two parties sought to put an end to apartheid's rule in the country and the decades-long struggle waged against it. According to the Promotion of National Unity and Reconciliation Act, passed by South Africa's first democratic government, elected in 1994, the TRC was charged with "investigating and documenting gross human rights violations committed within and or outside South Africa in the period 1960–94." In addition to the committee, which heard testimony on those violations and published its "Final Report" in October 1998, the Commission also included an Amnesty Committee and a Reparations and Rehabilitation Committee.

While denying the possibility of a blanket amnesty (such as had been proclaimed or legislated in Chile, El Salvador, and Argentina), South Africa's negotiated compromise nonetheless gave perpetrators the option of applying for amnesty; their application would be heard and adjudicated by the Amnesty Committee. To qualify for amnesty, applicants were required, first, to demonstrate that their action had been "politically motivated," and, second, to make "full disclosure" of the facts and circumstances relating to that action. The deadline for filing such application was in the event extended from 15 December 1996 to 10 May 1997, and although the TRC's final report on human rights violations was presented to then president Nelson Mandela in the fall of 1998, the Amnesty Committee's sessions continued into 2001. The Reparations and Rehabilitation Committee had barely begun its work, anticipating that if retribution was to be slow, restitution would face still more deferring pressures as succeeding governments sought to rectify the wrongs of the past and apply themselves to the present challenges.

The TRC's nearly two years of hearings into human rights violations were convened regionally, in significant part, in order to accommodate the testifiers and their communities. For testifiers to recount their experiences before not only a local but national and international audience would have been extremely painful. The Committee also held a series of special hearings into the roles of business and labor, the faith community, the legal community, the health sector, the media, the prison system, and compulsory military service; they also examined the role of children and youth and the ways in which women were affected by human rights violations. According to the report, the rationale for these special hearings was the imperative to "paint the backdrop against which such human rights violations occurred."

With particular reference to the question of women's suffering under apartheid, the Commission raised the question of the "ways in which [it] might be missing some of the truth through a lack of sensitivity to gender issues." The Centre for Applied Legal Studies, for example, had told the Commission that "over half of those who spoke [at the other hearings] were women, but that the roles and capacities in which women and men spoke differed. They saw that, while the overwhelming majority of women spoke as relatives and dependents of those (mainly males) who had directly suffered human rights violations, most of the men spoke as direct victims." The special hearings on women then elicited testimony on sexual abuse, psychological abuse, prison experience, and the ways in which "women's relationships were often used against them to weaken them and extract information." Presentations to the Commission described the authorities' taunting of women, charging that they had joined the resistance only because they were still unmarried or were prostitutes. Over and over the question implied was, What were they doing there? Mention is also made of Ruth First's prison memoir, *117 Days* (1965), in which she confesses her suicide attempt while held in detention.

Country of My Skull, published in April 1998, some six months prior to the Final Report, is Antjie Krog's account of her coverage for SABC radio of the TRC's hearings. In the chapter entitled "Bereaved and Dumb, the High Southern Air Succumbs," Krog focuses on women's contributions to the hearings. Describing the Eastern Cape sessions, she presents the narratives of women relatives and friends of Matthew Goniwe, one of the Cradock Four, killed in 1985. She cites one of the commentators covering the hearings:

> We're talking about two different social spaces: one in which violence was
> justified in the past. And the other, in the present, where abuses of human
> rights are condemned as immoral and wrong. By choosing the city hall in the

centre of town and not a community centre in the township, the Truth Commission wants to portray a symbolic break with the institutional frameworks of the past. This city hall is no longer the official domain of whites and perpetrators: it now belongs to all of us. (pp. 38–39)

That all-too-public space has become gendered, racialized, and historicized. Women have come forward, whether as "primary" or "secondary" victims, to present their stories of gross human rights violations under the system of apartheid. What were they doing there?

Amy Biehl

On U.S. Fulbright scholar Amy Biehl's next-to-last day in South Africa, in August 1993, she drove some of her friends home to their township of Guguletu—a trip from which she did not return. Guguletu, like other Cape Town townships, was the site of considerable violence during the turbulent years of conflicted negotiation that followed the release of Nelson Mandela and the unbanning of opposition organizations. Preceding the democratic elections of 1994, as part of her Fulbright scholarship Biehl had been assisting community organizations to prepare for the transition to a "post-apartheid South Africa." But in Guguletu at the time she was identified as an intruder. She was brutally murdered by a group of youths returning from a rally at nearby Joe Slovo High School.

Her murderers argued in their submission to the TRC's Amnesty Committee that they had acted out of political motivation, having been inspired by speakers at the rally. The Committee's decision granting the young men amnesty acknowledged that motivation: "Applicants . . . left the meeting with many others in a militant mood. They marched through the township . . . shouting ONE SETTLER ONE BULLET, determined to put into effect what they had been urged to do. This is how they got involved in the activities . . . which led to the killing of Amy Biehl." Biehl was twenty-six when she died.

In her Fulbright Scholarship application, Amy Biehl, a Stanford University graduate who had spent a year in Namibia and subsequently worked in Washington, D.C., described her proposed project in South Africa. She proposed spending an academic year at the University of the Western Cape (UWC) in Cape Town, to coincide with full-scale negotiations between the ANC and its partners and the National Party. "The focus of my research will be on gender rights in a new constitution," she wrote, including these questions: "How are proposals for gender rights in a bill of rights affected in the negotiations? How are women affected by various electoral mechanisms (i.e., does proportional representation benefit women)? How is gender affected by a strong central government (ANC) versus a decentralized regional government (NP [National Party])?"

The commitment to women's rights was, as Biehl hoped, finally written into South Africa's new constitution, although the promise made by such a historic commitment is yet to be fulfilled. The past still hangs heavy over efforts at implementation. It is that overburdened past, the history of women's struggle for a place on the agenda of human rights, that provides the grounds for Sindiwe Magona's novel, a fiction—in essence a kind of documentary—based on painful facts. "*Mother to Mother* is a book I did not plan," Magona said in an interview. "It's a book I didn't write at the moment of the act that provoked it. I was shocked. I was saddened. But . . . these things happen. You know, people get killed. My sadness, I must confess, was kind of distant and impersonal." Six months after Biehl's murder, Magona discovered that one of the four young men on trial for the crime was the son of a childhood friend.

> I wanted to explain [to the Biehls] that, sometimes with the best intention in the world, there are situations where parents cannot be effective parents. . . . The government of South Africa was waging war against African families. If the father was working it was never for enough wages. So the mother had also to be working; the children were being brought up by who? And today we wonder that all these young people are lost. We were not there. The parents were not there to raise their children. I wanted to explain this to the Biehls. Not that it excuses the people who killed their child.

And indeed, in the novel, Mandisa, the mother of Mxolisi (the name in all irony means "peacemaker"), makes a stark confession of guilt on her son's behalf that is at the same time a confession of her own powerlessness over him: "My son killed your daughter. People look at me as though I did it. As though I could make this child do anything" (p. 1).

Forced removals had brought Mandisa as a child to Guguletu—a name that means "our pride." The residents called it instead Gugulabo ("their pride"). Bulldozers and police vehicles of the apartheid state ruthlessly cleared the land of its native inhabitants, herding them to prescribed areas. Apartheid's dispossession of South Africa's black population began with the Natives Land Act of 1913—not repealed until 1991—which denied to black ("native") South Africans the right to own or hold land. As Sol Plaatje, one of the founders of the African National Congress in 1912, observes in *Native Life in South Africa* (1982; 1916), its sole objective was to "prevent the natives from ever rising above the position of servants to the whites" (pp. 70–71). The Natives Land Act provided the grounds for subsequent legislation, such as the Group Areas Act of 1950, which required the mass relocation of African, coloured, and Indian communities, in order to consolidate and expand the segregated demographics of the apartheid state. The Bantu Authorities Act of 1951 mandated the creation of "bantustans," separate living reserves for black South Africans, which divided blacks and prevented them from forming their own political organizations.

This explains what Mandisa "was doing there" in Guguletu. And it helps to answer questions about Mandisa's son and his collaborators. Magona, in her preface to the novel, asks, "What was the world of this young woman's killers, the world of those, young as she was young, whose environment failed to nurture them in the higher ideals of humanity and who, instead, became lost creatures of malice and destruction?" Was there really—in the words the apartheid government once used in its systematic response to questions about the increasing incidence of deaths in detention—"no one to blame"? Or was there a history that could still be called up?

The narrative of *Mother to Mother* takes place on the day of and the day after Amy Biehl's death. Behind these two days lies a long historical trajectory, the story of apartheid's assault on the black people of South Africa, from forced removals to police repression, deaths in detention, and assassinations at home and across the country's borders. There is much blame to be apportioned here, as well as amnesties to be granted and denied, and perhaps further, fuller disclosures yet, in the personal accounts of political processes.

Ruth First

Eleven years before Biehl's murder, in 1982, Ruth First was in Maputo, Mozambique, as a researcher at Eduardo Mondlane University, working on a collective project that involved migrant labor in southern Africa. Since 1979 she had been the Director of the Centre for African Studies at the university. First was the wife of Joe Slovo, the leader of the South African Communist Party and head of the ANC's armed wing of Umkhonto weSizwe. Slovo went on to become Minister of Housing in the new dispensation. After more than a decade of investigative journalism in the 1950s in South Africa, 117 days in prison there in 1963, and another decade and a half of anti-apartheid activism in exile in London, she had returned to southern Africa to assist in developing the region. That life's work was violently ended by a letter bomb sent to her by agents of the apartheid regime. She was fifty-seven at the time of her death.

First's assassins argued that she was a "legitimate target," a threat to the security of the South African regime. On 14 September 1998 one of the amnesty applicants, Craig Williamson, popularly referred to in South Africa as "superspy," when questioned by George Bizos, attorney for the Slovo family, said First had "played a political role as well as a practical role and this as far as the security forces and myself individually are concerned made her also an important target of the security forces." On 24 September 1998 Jerry Raven, another amnesty applicant, was questioned. Raven, an explosives expert, had at Williamson's behest manufactured the bomb that killed Ruth First. Bizos's assistant, Daniel Berger, asked: "When [Williamson] congratulated you, and you knew you had participated in the murder of a woman, did you feel any regret, yes or no?" Raven answered: "Do you say a woman or do you say Ruth First because in fact it was Ruth First. If Ruth First was in the eyes that be, a legitimate target, there would have been no regret."

First's assassination did not put an end to her work. *Black Gold: The Mozambican Miner, Proletarian and Peasant* was published posthumously in 1983. The volume was the seventh of First's books, preceded by *South West Africa* (1963), *117 Days* (1965), *The Barrel of a Gun: Political Power in Africa* (1970, published in the United States as *Power in Africa: Political Power in Africa and the Coup d'Etat*), *The South African Connection: Western Investment in Apartheid* (1972, with Jonathan Steele and Christabel Gurney), *Libya: The Elusive Revolution* (1974), and *Olive Schreiner* (1980, with Ann Scott). In addition, she had coedited, with Ronald Segal, the proceedings of a 1966 conference, *South West Africa: Travesty of Trust* (1967).

Among her unfinished work, however, were four additional projects that had been drafted in the 1970s, during her nearly decade and a half of exile in England. One of these outlines describes a proposed reader, titled *Vulnerability of African Independence, or the Dynamics of Stagnation,* which would have collected essays from contributing authors on such subjects as "the economic structure of independence, the resulting class/social structure, the political behaviour of these classes, the resulting economic constraints and self-reproducing nature of the economy." An alternative title to the volume was to have been *Africa: The Predicament of Independence.* A second project was conceptualized as a sequel to *The Barrel of a Gun* (or *Power in Africa*) and was to be called *Power Over Africa,* which would consider the international political pressures on and economic coercions of African independence, traced in a historical narrative from precolonial Africa, through the coming of European colonialism, slavery, imperial expansion, and concluding with decolonization. Not just the "relations of power inside Africa," that is, but the "power exercised from outside" would be the study's focus.

Still another research project left incomplete was *Popular Disturbance in*

Africa: Sources and Sequences. A second title proposed for this study—*Messiah, Mob and Guerrilla*—suggests its methodological and ideological emphases on contending strategies of mobilizing and organizing popular resistance in postindependence African countries. Finally, First left notes toward a project that are headed "profile of a corporation," and which are described as "reach[ing] out in a literary way to capture the personality of the Corporation." The contrasting case studies that First proposes are the Suez Canal Company and the Anglo American Corporation. Each of these unfinished projects relates in important ways to Ruth First's accomplished work and its persistently critical analysis of the struggle for and over African independence, the political and historic imperatives facing newly made nations, and the directions and directives available to the people and peoples whose future was then—and remains still—at stake.

Ruth First was born in 1925 in South Africa. Her father, Julius, was a prominent figure in the emergence and consolidation of the antiracial, socialist, and communist struggle in that country. Her mother, Tilly, would provide more than domestic support for her husband, her daughter, and her grandchildren as well. Ruth First attended the University of the Witwatersrand in the 1940s where she was active in student and national political activities. In 1949 she married Joe Slovo, whose own commitment to the struggle for social and economic justice in South Africa marked his political and military life until his death from cancer in early 1995. Throughout the 1950s First applied her probing intellectual skills as an investigative journalist and outspoken editorialist in publications (such as the *Guardian, New Age,* and *Fighting Talk*) that were repeatedly banned and repeatedly reconstituted. A resolute contributor to the mass-mobilized Defiance Campaign, launched in 1952, she was vehemently committed to the anti-pass movement, publishing many articles on that subject. According to Elizabeth S. Schmidt, although the "African National Congress (ANC) had been organising opposition to [pass] legislation since its founding in 1912," in the 1950s in particular it was "African women [who] played a leading role in the resistance to pass legislation because of the particular way in which influx control measures, implemented through the pass system, affected their position in society as well as African family life." First herself described that participation in a 1957 article in *New Age:* "Like those crackling veld fires that sweep over the dry Transvaal grass before the summer rains, the protest of African women against passes is spreading furiously from one area to another" (quoted in Pinnock, p. 67).

In Sharpeville in 1960, South African police opened fire on a peaceful anti-pass demonstration, killing more than sixty protestors, many of them women and children who were shot in the back as they attempted to flee the attack. Shortly thereafter, on 16 December 1961, Umkhonto weSizwe, the armed wing of the ANC, was formed and the armed struggle against apartheid launched. New legislation, such as the 90-Day Detention Law, was in turn drafted, and not just passes but prison sentences came to curtail the movements of those who trespassed against the guidelines of apartheid. In 1963 she was detained under the 90-Day Law, and held for 117 days. A forgotten copy of *Fighting Talk* in her home was one of the pieces of incriminating evidence of her contributions to the resistance struggle. Following her release, she and her three daughters joined Slovo in exile in England, where First continued to be active as writer, publicist, and campaigner in the international anti-apartheid struggle. She wrote scripts for BBC radio programs, taught at the University of Durham, and contributed to debates both large and local. In 1979 she returned to southern African, taking up her post at the Eduardo Mondlane University in Maputo, Mozambique.

In a special issue of *Fighting Talk,* published in June 1961 and devoted to significant dates from South African history, from the white miners strike in 1922 to the African miners strike of 1946, from Gandhi's passive resistance movement to the Defiance Campaign, Ruth First wrote:

> Looking back on the tale revealed in the chapters in this issue, who can doubt that here South African history was in the making?
>
> There are few heroes of gigantic stature in these episodes, few titans whose tremendous deeds are popularly associated with history. There are few dramatic moments in which the face of a country is suddenly transformed, few of those stark days when the whole fate of a nation is decided.
>
> Instead there is the record of a multitude of indecisive and inconclusive struggles, of strikes won and lost, of campaigns completed and uncompleted; there are a multitude of nameless, faceless ordinary people, some few remembered but many forgotten. Can this be history? Have we who live today left our mark on the future? (quoted in Pinnock, p. 77)

Nearly four decades later many individuals from that "multitude of nameless, faceless ordinary people" told their stories to the Truth and Reconciliation Commission, making for another kind of history. But Ruth First was no longer alive to tell her story. Like the killers of Amy Biehl, it was her assassins who provided one such narrative in their application for amnesty presented to the Commission and reviewed at its hearings in September and November of 1998 and reconvened in February–March of 1999. The assassins' version was radically challenged by the representatives of the struggle for which First had lived, worked, and died.

The Amnesty Hearings

South Africa's Promotion of National Unity and Reconciliation Act No. 34 of 1995 provided the framework for the establishment of the Truth and Reconciliation Commission inquiry into "gross human rights abuses" committed under apartheid, from 1960 to 1994. Two criteria were the sine qua non of the amnesty application procedures legislated by the act: that "the act, omission or offence to which the application relates is an act associated with a political objective committed in the course of the conflicts of the past" and that "the applicant has made a full disclosure of all relevant facts." The decisions handed down by the Amnesty Committee in two of the more high-profile cases that it heard suggest the significance of proving "political motivation" to its final determinations.

In the case of Steve Biko, for example, the Black Consciousness leader who died in detention in 1975, one of the officers who interrogated the prisoner, Gideon Niewoudt, was denied amnesty on the grounds that he was ignorant of the political reasons for his lethal brutality. According to the Committee, "Mr. Biko's death did not occur as a result of achieving or contributing towards countering political opposition." Niewoudt was judged to have been ignorant of Biko's support for a particular political party or cause. "Therefore the acts admitted by the applicant cannot be regarded as having been necessary to achieve or contributed to achieving the destruction of any opposition" (30 March 1999).

Just over a week after the Biko decision, the Committee hearing the amnesty applications from the killers of Chris Hani, a prominent leader of the ANC and the SACP who was gunned down outside his home in April 1993, also refused to grant them amnesty. The Committee argued that the killers, members of the right-wing Conservative Party (CP), had acted without instructions from the CP itself, and thus failed to meet the requirements for demonstrating "political motivation" (7 April 1999). In an editorial on that decision on 9 April 1999, however, the prominent South African newspaper *Weekly Mail and Guardian,* asked: "Was not Hani—the former military leader of a revolutionary party contending for political power by force of arms—a more 'legitimate' target than the young and idealistic Amy Biehl?"

The question of whether Biehl and First were "legitimate targets" at all in the calculations of their killers played a significant part in the unraveling of the stories told at the amnesty hearings. Four young men, Mongesi Manqina, Vusumzi Ntamo, Nzikhona Nofemela, and Ntombeki Peni, had been convicted of the murder of Amy Biehl and sentenced to prison terms. Applying for amnesty, Peni was asked by the chairperson of the hearings (which took place over three days in Cape Town in July 1997): "In your mind what did you achieve by killing Amy Biehl?" Peni replied, "Even though I am sorry that I contributed in the death of Amy Biehl, but I realised that the unrest at the time and the international recognition helped South Africa to be where it is." Later, Nofomela replied to another series of questions from the chairperson:

> Chairperson: And the fact that you were in "high spirits" was responsible for your conduct that day, is that it?
>
> Mr. Nofemela: Yes it's like that, even what we're told it's to ungovern the country.
>
> Chairperson: Had you not been in similar "high spirits" on previous occasions? . . .
>
> Mr. Nofemela: Are you saying before that day?
>
> Chairperson: Yes.
>
> Mr. Nofemela: We were used to that.
>
> Chairperson: Did you kill many people on those occasions?
>
> Mr. Nofemela: No we never did such a thing.
>
> Chairperson: Well why on this day?
>
> Mr. Nofemela: It's because she came to Guguletu during a very wrong moment.

At the time of Amy Biehl's murder, Nofemela was a student and PASO (Pan African Students Organization) organizer at Joe Slovo High School. Asked by one of the attorneys at the hearings, "Had Mr. Slovo been in the township that afternoon would you also have stabbed and stoned and killed him?" he replied, "No I would not have." "Why not?" he was asked. "Everybody knew him" was his reply.

A year later, in July 1998, nearly five years after the murder, Manqina, Ntamo, Nofemela, and Peni were granted amnesty for the slaying of Amy Biehl. "As members of PASO," the committee reported,

> which was a known political organisation of students, they were active supporters of the PAC (Pan African Congress) and subscribed to its political philosophy and its policies. By stoning company delivery vehicles and thereby making it difficult for deliveries into the townships, they were taking part in a political disturbance and contributing towards making their area ungovernable. To that extent, their activities were aimed at supporting the liberation struggle against the State. But Amy Biehl was a private citizen, and the question is why was she killed during this disturbance. Part of the answer may be that her attackers were so aroused and incited, that they lost control of themselves and got caught up in a frenzy of violence. One of the

applicants said during his evidence that they all submitted to the slogan of ONE SETTLER, ONE BULLET. To them that meant that every white person was an enemy of the Black people. At that moment to them, Amy Biehl, was a representative of the white community. They believed that by killing civilian whites, APLA was sending a serious political message to the government of the day. By intensifying such activity the political pressure on the government would increase to such an extent that it would demoralise them and compel them to hand over political power to the majority of the people of South Africa.

When the conduct of the applicants is viewed in that light, it must be accepted that their crime was related to a political objective.

The Amnesty Committee went on, however, to cite the contribution of Amy's parents in the presentation of its decision. Mr. and Mrs. Biehl had attended the hearings and were in South Africa to promote the Amy Biehl Foundation, which they had founded to honor their daughter by continuing her work in southern Africa. According to John Biehl, in his remarks cited by the TRC's Amnesty Committee:

You face a challenging and extraordinarily difficult decision. How do you value a committed life? What value do you place on Amy and her legacy in South Africa? How do you exercise responsibility to the community in granting forgiveness in the granting of amnesty? How are we preparing prisoners, such as these young men before us, to re-enter the community as a benefit to the community, acknowledging that the vast majority of South Africa's prisoners are under 30 years of age? Acknowledging as we do that there's massive unemployment in the marginalised community; acknowledging that the recidivism rate is roughly 95%. So how do we, as friends, link arms and do something? There are clear needs for prisoner rehabilitation in our country as well as here. There are clear needs for literacy training and education, and there are clear needs for the development of targeted job skill training. We, as the Amy Biehl Foundation are willing to do our part as catalysts for social progress. All anyone need do is ask. Are you, the community of South Africa, prepared to do your part?

Full Disclosure

Did those individuals who applied for amnesty for their role in the death of Ruth First know who she was? What did they think made her a "legitimate target"? There were nine applicants in the hearings, which were held in September and again in November of 1998, and concluded in February-March 1999. In addition to the First assassination, two other incidents were in question, each of them involving "cross-border" operations and implicating a significant part of the structure and policy of the South African Security Forces. These incidents were the bombing of the London headquarters of the ANC in 1982, and the murder by letter bomb in Angola in 1984 of Jeanette Schoon and her six-year-old daughter Katryn. Marius Schoon, husband and father of the victims, attended the hearings along with the three Slovo daughers. George Bizos, of the Legal Resources Centre, who had previously represented the families of Steve Biko, Neil Aggett, and others at inquests into deaths in detention under the apartheid regime, served as the lead attorney for the ANC and the Schoon and Slovo families. Amnesty was granted to all applicants on 15 October 1999 for the London bombing. The decision on the killings of Jeanette and Katryn Schoon and of Ruth First was still pending, nearly a year after the conclusion of the hearings in early March 1999. But the questions raised around the women's deaths remained urgent still. They were answered with amnesty in June 2000.

"Identification of targets" was a major topic of discussion in these amnesty hearings. What were the criteria for such identification? What were the consequences? The South African Security Forces had designated a unit to be assigned with this task of "identifying targets." Also invoked throughout the hearings was a more generalized standard of the "need to know"—an alleged limit on the intelligence and information available at any given time to the contributors to the assassination. There was thus also a limit on their culpability, their ability to identify higher-ranking officials. The invocation of the reputed "need to know" standard provided the alibis for a repetitive challenge to the amnesty requirement of "full disclosure." Did they know? What did they know? But even if they had known, what difference would what they knew have made?

Full disclosure was, and remains, important to the work of discovering and rendering as part of a public record the "truth." Truth is the elemental mandate of the Truth and Reconciliation Commission. But the second requirement of "political motivation" plays no less a significant role in the legacy inherited by the TRC and left to its successors in the international forums established to redress past violations of human rights and establish standards for the future. The question of whether Ruth First was a "legitimate target" for assassination by the combined South African Security and Defense Forces matters not only because her killers should be brought to justice, but because the example she set by her life and her life's work demands that her death be seen in the light of truth.

Bridget O'Laughlin, an anthropologist at the Institute of Social Studies in The Hague, had worked with Ruth First in Mozambique. She was in the university office when the lethal letter bomb detonated. In February

1999, at the TRC's amnesty hearings, she described First's work in Mozambique at the time of her death. The attorney who questioned O'Laughlin sought to establish that First was a "legitimate target." After all, what was she doing there? O'Laughlin countered that First was totally committed to the work she considered so important. "Maybe that's hard to accept," she told the attorney, "but she did." O'Laughlin dismissed the possibility that First had, in the questioner's ominously suggestive words, "private avenues along which she was working"—that is, avenues that might have made her a legitimate target.

According to Jerry Raven, who manufactured the letter bomb that killed Ruth First, the end, as he presented it on the twelfth day of the TRC's September 1998 amnesty hearings, was as follows: "Well, I believed in the powers that be, that a legitimate target had been identified. This target was a high ranking official of either ANC/SACP alliance and that whoever would open the packet, would at the worst be seriously injured but most likely, be killed." Raven went on to distinguish between a "potential activist" and a "potential terrorist": The activist was a "noncombatant who is not personally involved at grassroots level in . . . acts of terrorism." The terrorist is "also a member of said organisation, who does the acts of terrorism, planting bombs, etc. etc." Craig Williamson, who had passed the lethal orders to Raven to produce the bomb, responded to questions put to him by advocate Bizos by admitting that Ruth First was not as high-profile a target as her husband. But she was, he said, "a very high-ranking member of the South African Communist Party/ANC Alliance and one who was engaged in two levels of activity in Mozambique which related to the ANC/Communist Party struggle against South Africa. One is as a high level functionary of the Communist Party and the other as a member of the ANC structures—so she played a political role as well as a practical role and this . . . made her also an important target of the security forces."

In the November 1998 hearings, Mac Maharaj was called as a witness on behalf of the victims. Maharaj, who was at the time that he testified minister of transport, previously been a secretary of the ANC underground in Lusaka following his release from prison in 1976. He testified that "Ruth First was not involved with the internal struggle of South Africa, that is from the internal structures, military or political. . . . She was a member of the ANC like every other member. . . . She did work with the students who were in exile in Mozambique and . . . was doing major research work assisting the development process in Mozambique." Although "involved in the anti-apartheid struggle," she did so in a way that did not make her a legitimate target. The difference between the kind of work she did and that done by others was "a major distinction in my mind because the ANC maintained two separate structures, external and internal." In further questioning, Maharaj was asked whether he agreed with Gillian Slovo, Ruth First's daughter, "that her mother's death was a loss for the ANC?" Maharaj replied, concluding the day's hearing as well as the November session, "Yes Sir and a grievous loss to South Africa today."

Conclusion

What were they doing there? Amy Biehl and Ruth First were academics, activists, researchers committed to a narrative of development, a narrative that would be a story involving women in its writing, the story of a development that would place women's rights as human rights at the head of its agenda. They worked toward these ends and died midway through the process. Their stories continue to be reconstructed and examined. A poem commemorating Ruth First written by Jeremy Cronin, a former political prisoner who became Deputy General Secretary of the SACP and an ANC MP, and who attended portions of the hearings, contains these lines: "The struggle to be a person / Remains an endangered address."

WORKS CITED

Krog, Antiie. *Country of My Skull.* Johannesburg: Random House, 1998.

Magona, Sindiwe. *Mother to Mother.* Cape Town: David Philip, 1998.

Magona, Sindiwe. Interview. *Modern Fiction Studies* (spring 2000).

Pinnock, D. *Voices of Liberation: Ruth First,* vol. 2. Pretoria: HSRC Publishers, 1997.

Plaatje, Sol T. *Native Life in South Africa* [1916]. Randburg: Ravan Press, 1982.

Schmidt, Elizabeth S. "Now You Have Touched the Women: African Women's Resistance to the Pass Laws in South Africa 1950–1960." *Notes and Documents* 6, no. 83 (March 1983).

Truth and Reconciliation Commission of South Africa. *Final Report.* 5 vols. Cape Town: Juta, 1998.

How Long Does Exile Last?

Agate Nesaule

∞ I like to get my hair cut at the Salon Flamur. I like the name, which sounds glamorous and slightly erotic to me. I imagine it is French, a language I have never learned in spite of the five years in my childhood that I spent wandering homeless over Europe because of World War II. Flamur himself is young and energetic, and although he wears a white poet's shirt with flowing sleeves, he looks American. Scissors, clippers, and driers dangle like guns from his black leather holster, pointing down to his intricately stitched Western boots. His wavy upswept hair, discreet sideburns, and pale skin remind me of Elvis Presley, in his dreamier, more formal portraits anyway.

Flamur's employees, all women, are part of an American daydream as well—young slender girls dressed in cropped velvet tops revealing perfectly tanned bare midriffs in the summer and in unbuttoned velvet shirts and skintight pants in winter. They move efficiently yet gracefully between the chrome and glass shelves overflowing with expensive lotions and the rows of slightly threatening hair-dryers.

In reality Flamur is from Bosnia, and the Salon Flamur is a tiny place, no more than fifteen feet wide, wedged between an antiques dealer and a bakery in a nondescript mall in Wisconsin. Behind the polished plate glass in front, the windowless interior is long and narrow. Only the glittering mirrors, blazing lights softened by mauve surfaces, and careful scheduling keep one from feeling claustrophobic.

But one afternoon in late summer I can hardly get in because the place is full of women, with every seat taken on the short white leather sofa and two straight-backed chairs. They fall silent as soon as they see me, then jump up, like abashed school girls, and with repeated gestures urge me to sit. They watch me, as if a great deal depended on my good will, until I do.

In spite of my graying hair, I am not used to such uniform politeness from teenage girls and middle-aged women, not in America anyway, and there is nothing unusual about these women with their pale skins, dark hair, and slender bodies. Only details of their determinedly American clothes suggest other places and other times: Europe after World War II, Wisconsin and the Hmong people resettled here after Vietnam, the Baltic countries after the collapse of the Soviet Union. A summer dress with a snugly fitting dark top has an attached skirt of ugly checked black and brown flannel, a gathered gray polyester skirt cinched by a rubber belt is lengthened by a six-inch-wide insert of a faded flowered print near the bottom hem, the long sleeves of a thin white cotton blouse are covered with embroidery. The shoes are startling in their ugliness—black suede spike heels, split running shoes, scuffed sandals, cracked pumps—their polish unable to hide their flimsiness. These surface details speak to me of war and exile and poverty, as eloquently as words.

I am afraid to look into the women's eyes, and when I finally do, it is as bad as I have expected. They all have exile eyes: eyes that have lost everything and seen the unspeakable but are determined nevertheless to keep looking, eyes that remain wary and disillusioned even during shy smiles and suppressed giggles. I have seen those eyes before: in photographs of Latvian women and men who survived Siberia and on TV as two Rwandan girls were being interviewed by a journalist. The Hmong woman passing me on a Greyhound bus, the Chilean woman doctor who used to clean my house, my mother—they all had eyes like that.

Flamur beckons one of the women to his station, and they all troop along, surrounding and protecting. He studies her hair and her face, asks questions, makes suggestions. He waits patiently for the women to consult among themselves and agree before he snips so much as a hair. Under his skilled fingers the crudely chopped-off tresses take on a lovely sleek shape, and each individual strand glows.

I have never seen Flamur so gentle as he is when he speaks with the women in their language and his. And I see now that he too has those eyes: he knows or can imagine exactly what has happened to these women. So now he waits for their consent, even invitation, before he cuts. Flamur smiles at the young woman in the chair, and she smiles back at him. Because she likes her new haircut, she makes a playful little bow and even twirls around before the next woman sits down, but her eyes do not change.

I got my hair cut when I was younger, at the age of twelve, the year I came to America. I was alone in the dingy living room serving as a beauty shop in our slum neighborhood because my mother wanted me to keep my braids as much as I wanted to be rid of them. I believed that would make me less different from the American girls at school, that I would begin to belong. The woman holding the scissors above my head hesitated. "I don't want any trouble," she said. "All of you people from over there are pretty strange, I don't want your brothers to come beat me up." I pleaded with her that I had no brothers or other male relatives who cared that much about me, that Latvians did not have such strong beliefs about women's hair, that I would never tell she had been the one who cut. When she finally agreed, I closed my eyes as she worked and I prayed for transformation—from an exile into an American.

I do not envy these Bosnian women for getting far more elegant styles than my frizzy permanent and for being together rather than alone because I know some of the things that lie ahead. They will have to get the clothes right, of course, but after that they will have to learn English and how things work here, find jobs, try to get their educations accredited and failing that start all over, live among the poor and desperate until they can afford something else, make new friends, find lovers or husbands among the few people from their own country or face the suspicion of American families, learn not to mind when they are criticized for speaking English with an accent and their own language among themselves. Their names will be mispronounced or arbitrarily changed, their foreignness mistaken for ignorance and laziness, their longing for home confused with ingratitude to America. They will be asked perfunctory questions to which people cannot stand hearing honest answers. They will have to show a positive attitude while mourning their lost lovers, killed family members, destroyed homes, and devastated country. And in the unlikely event that they ever return, it is inevitable they will no longer belong there, just as they do not really belong here. I hope they do not suffer from nightmares. I hope they do not get silenced.

But America is also a wonderful country, which offers opportunities to exiles that would be unheard of in other places. I know, because through luck, persistence, and the generosity of others, I have an excellent education, professional status, and a comfortable middle-class existence. I am generally at ease in my adopted country.

Yet sometimes, almost fifty years after coming here, I still succumb to the longing to speak my own language, which can be so intense that, like other exiles, I will do things that make little objective sense—travel great distances, spend time with people with whom I have nothing in common, swallow the disappointment of most such encounters. Even go to church.

Actually, I lost my faith at age seven when Russian soldiers continued looting, beating, and raping women and girls in the basement as I obsessively repeated "Our Father, Which Art in Heaven." Nothing changed, no one was listening. And although in the last few years I have felt less cut off from the spiritual world, I go to Latvian church services mostly because of language.

The congregation is tiny, twenty-seven people; the majority are women in their seventies and eighties. The minister, although born in this country and serving a large American congregation, travels two hundred miles six times a year to conduct services in his pure, unaccented, sophisticated Latvian. I like him because he has such an open heart even after serving in Vietnam and because he knows how to speak so directly about love and forgiveness without ever haranguing his listeners.

I also like the small church the Latvian congregation rents for these late Sunday afternoon services. The white frame building with its modest steeple sits in an expanse of grass, far back in a triple lot. Framed by maples, oaks, and pines, it does not seem to be part of any city. Standing in front, looking neither left nor right, I can trick myself into believing I am about to enter a country church in Latvia, one that is all imagination, not memory.

Darkness is falling already on this dreary, wet afternoon in November, and it will be black when I leave because after the service there is always a social hour. The older women bring homemade apple cakes and traditional open-faced, beautifully decorated sandwiches, and we sit together for an hour or two at tables set with flowers and white tablecloths, sipping wine or strong coffee. Eighty-six-year-old Mr. M., who was a teacher in Latvia, a prisoner of war in France, and a factory worker and also teacher in Latvian Saturday schools in the United States, usually presents a secular program. But nature and the divine are so closely linked in Latvian culture that sometimes the poetry recitations, discussions, and songs seem like a continuation of the service.

Today Mr. M., who as a young man loved the theater, is reading and acting out parts of a sketch by a nineteenth-century Latvian dramatist. It recommends conduct for lovers, complete with advice that women should drop their handkerchiefs in front of men in the city and ask for help carrying milk pails in the country. The whole thing would be unspeakably trite in English, but its sexism and cliches are muted by time and place and language, so that it is actually funny.

Steps sound on the dark stairway behind Mr. M. Someone comes down, hesitates, stops.

And then the door bursts open, and a man crashes into the basement. Dressed in a shabby overcoat loose enough to hide a gun, unshaven and red-eyed, he looks at us contemptuously, then turns his back on us and goes upstairs. We listen hopefully for the outer door to close, signaling his departure, but it does not.

Whispers sweep over the old women: what is he doing up there? Is he stealing the undefended chalices? Defacing the altar? How are we going to pay for the damage to the Lutheran Church of the Deaf, which rents us this space and trusts us to take good care of it? And why is there no phone down here to call 911?

We hear steps again, and the man reappears. This time he strides into the bathroom behind Mr. M. and bolts the door. More terrified whispering, greater intakes of breath. The man is an African American, which increases his difference from these old Latvian Americans, who have arrived too late in their lives and avoided situations too well to learn much about the history and culture of various ethnic groups in the United States.

More steps sound on the stairs and a woman with bleached blonde hair and hard features inspects us, then turns and leaves. But, of course, the old women whisper, that is his floozy, his accomplice, she is the one who will keep us from escaping when the man comes out with guns blazing. What else can he be doing in the bathroom but assembling a rifle, loading a revolver, lighting an explosive?

Mr. M., true to the tradition of the theater that the show must go on, reads. I would laugh at the ridiculousness of the situation and the fear of the women, if I did not know that all of them have faced real guns and cowered from real bombs before they came as adults to the United States after World War II. And somewhere at the very back of my mind an image from when I was seven is trying to get my attention: my mother and sister and I sit on a muddy mattress in a basement and watch the door for more Russian soldiers who will come again and prod us with their guns.

The man opens the bathroom door, and face averted, sidles up the stairs. Someone must find out what is going on. Pastor K. stands up and goes to the other stairway in the kitchen. Except for Mr. M., who is now acting out women's lines with gestures and in a high-pitched voice, there is a brief hopeful silence.

But Pastor K. does not come back. Oh God, what are they doing to him up there? Have they overpowered him, taken him hostage, tied his wrists, put a gun to his throat? No place is safe, not even a church. Wasn't there a shooting during choir practice in a church just recently, yes, of course there was. America is getting to be as dangerous as Europe, the present as bad as the past. No place is safe anywhere, not a school, not a church. The worst has happened to Pastor K., and we are next. The women are no longer whispering, but speaking their terror aloud. Only Mr. M., unaware of what has gone on behind him to cause all this commotion, soldiers on.

And then, surprisingly, I feel myself stand up. I can go and see. If Pastor K. needs help, I can help. Surprisingly, I do not think about this abstractly: I do not reason that he has a wife and four daughters while I am older and more alone than he is, I do not remember my theoretical indecision about whether I, had I been an adult, would have hidden Jewish women from the Nazis or Latvian girls about to be deported to Siberia from the Soviets. It feels neither self-sacrificing nor heroic, just totally simple and natural to get up and go. Fifty years later, at this moment, I have finally transcended the fears of exile.

As it turns out, Pastor K. does need help, but very little. The man and the woman are insisting they want to wait in the empty church for a sign-language class that may or may not take place. But as is often the case, mere numbers change the situation. As soon as there are two of us to invite the couple to have some coffee and cake and wait downstairs with us, they decide to leave. Pastor K. and I see them out and lock the church door. The irony of this action is not lost on us.

Mr. M. is still reading. "Oh, you were so brave to go, Agatina," a woman whispers to me, using the diminutive of my name, which always touches me. "Where did you get such courage?" Part of me wants to make careful distinctions between courage and trust and to begin listing abstractly everything that has helped me—therapy, dreams, love, friendship, creativity, the stories of others—but deep down I know that I have experienced a small miracle. And because it is a miracle, I do not know when or if ever such a miracle will come for other women in exile.

Letters of the Law

WOMEN, HUMAN RIGHTS, AND
EPISTOLARY LITERATURE

*Joseph Slaughter and
Jennifer Wenzel*

∞ When U.S. Representative Lynn Woolsey tried to draw the attention of U.S. Senator Jesse Helms to an international treaty on the rights of women, she was met, ironically enough, with his dismissing her for not being ladylike. Woolsey had been trying for months to arrange a meeting with Helms about Senate ratification of the United Nations 1979 Convention on the Elimination of All Forms of Discrimination Against Women (CEDAW). Although former President Jimmy Carter signed the convention in 1980, the Senate has failed to ratify the treaty for more than two decades. As Chairman of the Senate Foreign Relations Committee since 1994, Helms has blocked ratification by not holding hearings on the treaty.*

Woolsey contacted Helms's office on 26 October 1999 and told his staff to expect her the next day. Twenty women, including Woolsey and other representatives, arrived at his office armed with poster-sized copies of a letter signed by over 100 representatives. Told by Helms's staff that the senator was "indisposed," his whereabouts unknown, the group planned to leave the letter in Helms's office. They were then tipped off that he was in fact at a hearing on China policy down the hall. The group entered the committee room, carrying the letter on three placard panels, and stood quietly at the back of the room. According to Woolsey, Helms then "brought the gavel down and said, 'I would like you to sit down and act like ladies.'" From the back of the room, Woolsey offered Helms the letter and asked if they could meet to discuss CEDAW. Helms replied, "You know, you're out of order, and I would not be discourteous to you where you work." He then urged Woolsey to "please be a lady . . . you are not going to be heard," and ordered Capitol police, "Escort them out! Escort them out!" Woolsey's place was in the House, as Helms inadvertently punned, but not his Senate committee room—although, as Woolsey noted in her account of the incident, "it's a public hearing, you know."

This undeliverable letter signed by women and addressed to men is a recent manifestation of a generic scene of "miscommunication." The scene of the dismissed missive reinforces a prejudicial distinction between the public and the private, between what men do and what women may talk about. Helms's and Woolsey's confrontation depends on a gendered division between public and private space that implies that to "be a lady" is "not to be heard," whether in Woolsey's previous attempts to communicate with Helms or in the forum of a public hearing. Donna Sullivan, in her analysis of the role of the public-private dichotomy in understanding and effecting women's rights as human rights, notes that the "demarcation of public and private life . . . is an inherently political process" and that the distinction "has long been permeable when the state seeks to exercise control over disempowered communities" (1995, p. 128). Helms seeks to silence Woolsey on both sides of the divide simultaneously, urging her to adopt the decorum that preserves a lady's privacy (and silence) even in public, at the same time that he has her forcibly removed from (his) public sphere.

Rights and the Public-Private Divide

The public-private distinction is modeled in human rights documents themselves, delimiting relationships among the individual, family, community, nation, and the international sphere. The gendered inflection of the public-private dichotomy is particularly clear in the International Covenant on Civil and Political Rights (ICCPR) and the International Covenant on Economic, Social, and Cultural Rights (ICESCR), which characterize the family as "the natural and fundamental group unit of society." In the Universal Declaration of Human Rights (UDHR), the public community is conceived as that "in which alone the free and full development of his [individual] personality is possible." The family unit is characterized as a feminine sphere, where motherhood and childhood warrant "special protection"; women's rights are filtered through that protection of the family. The CEDAW, in contrast, links the family with society, "recalling that discrimination against women . . . hampers the growth of prosperity of society and the family and makes more difficult the full development of the potentialities of women in the service of their countries and humanity." Article 5 more explicitly invokes the state's service "to ensure that family education includes proper understanding of maternity as a social function." While the UDHR, ICCPR, and ICESCR assume and fortify a gendered public-private split, the CEDAW acknowledges the historically gendered nature of that split and repositions women, both in and beyond their maternal relationships to family and society, in ways that deconstruct the division, locating women in a mediatory role between the public and the private.

Women are conceived in these documents as conduits for the entry of the public, in the form of culture, into the private, in the rearing of children. Arati Rao argues: "Historically, women have been regarded as the repositories, guardians, and transmitters of culture. Women represent the reproduction of the community . . . the primary caregivers in the family and therefore the earliest inculcators of culture in the child" (1995, p. 169). Rao attributes some of the discrimination suffered by women under the law to the "primary identification of the woman with the family and home, in a problematic separation of 'public' and 'private' spheres of existence, [which] contributes to her secondary status in the very realm where her future is debated and even decided: the public" (p. 169). But this codified mediatory role can be radically redefined when one of the vectors that transects the public and the private is the transmission of information. Freedom of information, understood as the right "to seek, receive and impart information and ideas of all kinds, regardless of frontiers," has the capacity to redescribe speech and association in ways that threaten the public-private split (ICCPR).

Susan Staves enumerates scenes of "miscommunication" in British and American history where the state refused to receive the petitions of women. The 1689 English Bill of Rights included the right to petition; Staves sees this inclusion as a unique contribution to the fledgling rhetoric and institution of human rights. The English Bill of Rights was an early elaboration of the Enlightenment's doctrine of human rights, whose conceptions of the individual, community, and nation remain the basis of human rights law today; its incorporation of a right to petition—"That it is the right of the subjects to petition the King, and all commitments and prosecutions for such petitioning are legal"—might seem a small step. Yet as Staves points out, the elaboration of that right was "quintessential . . . for those excluded from government, a crucial right for the disenfranchised" (1989, p. 165). The petition (not unlike the novel, whose development corresponds in great measure to the codification of human rights) provides a mechanism for making the private public and, as Staves notes, "rather touchingly invokes an enlightenment optimism that true grievances once expressed will be rationally and justly dealt with by government" (p. 166).

The right to petition not only provides a formal mechanism for airing grievances; the right also conceives of the individual as capable of identifying social and political activities and institutions that present obstacles to development and desire. It links private interest with the public good; encourages solidarity over isolation; and encourages complaint and correspondence (speech and writing) over rebellion and armed resistance. These features might explain why many have identified the right as having particular impact on women and disenfranchised members of society. In fact, although explicitly imagined as an individual right, petition has taken on an affiliative, international character, revised from its formulation in the Optional Protocol to the ICCPR, where complaint is the singular right of individuals "claiming to be victims of violations," to its most recent elaboration in the Optional Protocol to CEDAW, where petition can be undertaken by individuals and groups, and, more radically, on behalf of individuals and groups.

From the 1689 English Bill of Rights to the 1999 Optional Protocol to CEDAW, the right to petition has been elaborated in terms of freedom of thought and expression, a right to seek and disseminate information. Not only does the right to petition (particularly as it is elaborated in the international context of the United Nations) disrupt the categorical division of public and private, complementing the broader, evolving awareness of the mediatory position of women in society and the family. In its preamble, the CEDAW posits a mutually causal relationship between "international peace and security" (including disarmament and the elimination of racism and colonialism) and "the maximum participation of women on equal terms with men in all fields": international peace requires gender equality, and gender equality requires international peace. By connecting this most "public" realm of the "welfare of the world and the cause of peace" with women's rights, the CEDAW confirms the interrelationship of public and private concerns.

The Link between Rights and Literature

No less than the petitions provided for in these human rights instruments, literary letters have depended upon, and yet can disrupt, the notion that women's relationships to the world are essentially private. In his 1957 study, *The Rise of the Novel,* Ian Watt argues that changes in the domestic and economic situation of urban English women facilitated the novel's attention to the individual as hero or heroine through a gendered division of the public and private that relegated women's interaction with the world to the activity of letter writing. Watt explains that the position of the Georgian wife afforded a "new pattern of personal relationships made possible by familiar letter-writing, a pattern which, of course, involves a private and personal relationship rather than a social one, and which could be carried on without leaving the safety of the home" (pp. 187–188). Watt's identification of the rise of the novel (in particular its epistolary strains and precursors) with eighteenth-century epistemological and sociological shifts in the Anglo-European conception of the individual (and the attendant divisions of public-private, masculine-feminine, national, international, and domestic) and with an audience's interest in that individual, has become a critical standby in the literary-historical account of the novel and realist fiction.

Ruth Perry, in her 1979 study, *Women, Letters, and the Novel,* reexamines the identification of the novel as a feminine genre, as opposed to the masculine literary epics. "It is this emphasis," Perry writes in her introduction, "on individual consciousness, on the mental notions which accompany action, that is the connection between novels and women. For novels developed at a time when literate women—the sort that figured in such books—were dispossessed of all meaningful activity save marrying and breeding" (p. x). Perry claims that her study of epistolary fiction provides an analysis relevant to all literature because these stories "foreshadow the purposes of novels as we know them, providing a coherent world to experience and permitting readers to live vicariously in the borrowed emotional lives of the characters" (p. xii). The epistolary novel has a double didacticism in its generic formulation; it makes the private life of the individual available for public scrutiny and instruction and it provides a generic exemplum of letters to be copied.

As such, the "epistolary novel" is a misnomer, since an epistle is generally written with the intention of making public some didactic observance, but the classic epistolary novels purport to be collections of private letters made public through the intervention of an author or a narrative surrogate. This literary conceit is predicated on the distinction between public life (the world of society and politics) and private sentiment (the world of letters and the "inner workings of the mind"). That the genre itself depends upon the pretense of making public that which has been sealed suggests the risks entailed in maintaining a categorical division between the public and the private, as well as the peril, for a subject, of crossing those boundaries, the risk of finding one's experience outside of generic limits.

The literary trope of letters and letter writing might seem an odd point of entry into a discussion of women's rights, human rights, and literature, but it is our conviction that the three stories we read here—Helena Araujo's "The Open Letter," Tsitsi Dangarembga's "The Letter," and Janette Turner Hospital's "Dear Amnesty"—do something more than feature the letter as literary conceit, although certainly they modulate *belles lettres* and Ruth Perry's "borrowed emotional lives" with the urgency and borrowed time of human rights letter-writing campaigns. It is also important to note that each of the authors is identified with multiple countries and nationalities: Araujo with Colombia and Switzerland; Dangarembga with Zimbabwe, South Africa, and Sweden; and Hospital with Australia, Canada, and the United States. By thematizing the public and private constitution of the main characters—women who read and write letters— these stories recode the formal concerns and generic conventions of the epistolary novel in the service of radical resistance. The stories expose the limits of an antagonistic division between the private (correspondence and personal sentiment) and the public (petition and political activism); as literary letters, they constitute writing and reading subjects broadly in a field of local, national, and international rights and responsibilities. They reimagine processes of association and communication, filiation and affiliation, private and public correspondence, in ways that radically remap the globe in terms of commonality, solidarity, and interaction.

Literary Petitions and the Public Order

"The Open Letter" ("*Carta Abierta*") by the Colombian author Helena Araujo, concerns a Colombian social worker, Elvira, who lives in Switzerland and is coordinating the efforts of a "Solidarity Committee" preparing the presentation of a human rights petition to the visiting Colombian president and ambassador. Twenty-four hours of meetings, little sleep, and translating the president's speech into French take their toll, prompting Elvira to abandon the committee and her Swiss family, returning alone to Colombia. The meeting between Elvira's committee and the Colombian president offers little hope that the gravity of circumstances in Colombia can be fruitfully addressed in a Geneva hotel room, because the Colombian delegation ignores what should be "the most decisive moment of the audience," the presentation of the petition. Elvira, "straightening herself out with an awkward gesture, opening her eyes wide and looking around as if she's just emerged from the dark," leaves the meeting to emerge, textually, only in the note marked "urgent" that she dashes off to her husband from the Geneva airport.

The occasion for Araujo's intercontinental story was Decree 1923 of 6 September 1978, popularly known as the National Security Statute, that reinstituted the State of Siege under which the Colombian government had been operating almost continuously since its declaration in 1948. The statute, decreed by President Turbay Ayala within a month of assuming power, reassigned to the military judicial jurisdiction for cases of disturbance of the public order and targeted workers who participated in what the government designated "illegal strikes," mandating strict sentences for these crimes as well as for persons who possessed or disseminated "subversive propaganda." Implicitly recognizing the disruptive potential of communication and information to the maintenance of discrete spheres of public and private, the decree prohibited "information, statements, communiqués or commentaries relating to the public order, . . . or news items that incite to crime or make apology for it" from being transmitted via the public media "for as long as the public order is disturbed." The statute implemented emergency measures made possible by an explicit 1976 declaration that "the public order is disturbed." According to human rights reports from the early 1980s (including the Inter-American Commission on Human Rights report of 1981), implementation of the statute led to the detention, and in many cases torture, of more than sixty thousand individuals.

The declared disturbance of the public order provides the political context for "The Open Letter," although the story is explicitly staged in Geneva, the august home of the International Labor Organization, the United Nations High Commission on Human Rights, and Elvira's Solidarity Committee. The story thematizes the conflict between public discourse and private experience by contrasting the decorous delivery of the petition with Elvira's experience of that delivery. The Solidarity Committee works to address violations of Colombia's obligations on the right to organize, yet the only oblique reference to Colombian violations is summarized from the undisclosed contents of the open letter as "housebreakings, arrests, and torture." The story focuses on the noncorrespondence of the realities of human rights violations and the rhetoric and genre of petition, described in the Colombian Constitution as the right "to present respectful petitions to the authorities, on matters of general or private interest, and to obtain prompt action thereon."

The petition is, as the story has it, undeliverable, remaining folded on the table throughout the committee's meeting with Colombian officials. The only readers of the "open letter" are labor representatives from the Swiss signatories who reread the letter, recounting the signatures. The Colombian delegation acts "as if they know about the letter beforehand without having read it," the president remarking, with his elongated and plodding speech, that the Committee "had come to inform him of unknoooooown faaaaaacts." Elvira's frustration over the undeliverability of the letter presents itself in her lack of patience with the international labor organizations, their impossible acronyms, and their repeated reference to various ILO conventions: "She was starting to feel dizzy trying to remember what Martine told her the day before about the OIT [ILO], a violation of Conventions 85 and 86, no, 87 and 89."

Elvira's frustration conveys the inefficacy of the public invocation of numerically referenced conventions; compounding this failure of words and numbers to signify is the political undeliverability of the Solidarity Committee's letter of petition, for the Colombian president refuses to fulfill his role as audience. A rhetorical divorce occurs between the international effort to speak on behalf of those suffering—the repetitions of the diplomatically obvious—and the personal experience of that suffering accessed only metaphorically in the story. Elvira's own political activities consume both her days and her nights, "wearing down" her "resistance"; in some sense, her obligations to an international order displace her obligations to a national and domestic one, to the women workers who represent a portion of Colombian labor on whose behalf she signs her name. Her Swiss husband, familiarly known as El Flaco, shoulders some of the stress of solidarity by typing the petition and tutoring the couple's daughter, Chelita, in Colombian politics. But the stresses on Elvira result in her own "housebreaking": "I'm going to Colombia. Take good care of Chelita. I don't know whether or not I'm coming back."

What is Elvira resisting? Though titled "The Open Letter," and thus invoking a genre that asks the reader to substitute as audience for an addressee who has proven incapable or unwilling to respond to private complaint, the story creates other expectations on the part of the reader by drawing upon a different genre: torture survivor testimony. The opening lines evoke the trauma of torture: "Ugh!! Elvira could feel the air getting thicker, the lamps getting brighter, and the atmosphere closing in with each passing moment." The story delivers on the expectation created in these lines by invoking Elvira's editorial and custodial function, as she recalls the contents of a "file with the testimony of the prisoner whose head had been covered with a quilt before she was clubbed and then hung by her wrists." The story analogizes Elvira's responsibility for the collection of testimony and its redaction in the form of a petition with the sequestered victims' tortured relationships to speech and silence, to proclamation and secrecy. What Elvira cannot say, the topic upon which she cannot speak in her present circumstance, is violation itself: "They torture people! They can't deny it! Elvira wanted to scream it out to [the president]." The charge can be leveled in the public language of the petition, with its references to Colombia's international obligations. But what cannot be delivered—because a petition constitutes the generic "they torture" from a preponderance of individual testimony—is the private experience of violation.

Elvira's physical circumstance radically contradicts the emotive expectation of the first paragraphs; her sense of being out of place, of being in public rather than private, of speaking another's words rather than her own, of being one of the untortured rather than the tortured, confirms the disturbance of the public order: "And yet, there she was sitting in that armchair, hair freshly done, wearing a very tight tailored suit, calling him Mr. President and offering to translate into French what His Excellency was about to say." The normalcy of public interaction in a Geneva hotel room substitutes for the disorder in Colombia, standing in for, but also eliding, the fact that this scene of petition cannot take place in Colombia. Elvira's activities on behalf of the imprisoned, tortured, targeted, and silenced of Colombia within the "silken, embroidered walls of that suite of the Inter-Continental Hotel" textually parallel the displacement of the "voluminous puppet, a straw figure" president who does not "express himself of his own initiative, but rather [is] controlled by some other force, as if he were a ventriloquist's dummy," a parallelism that has her playing an equally alienated public role, translating his "already being repeated" phrases. Elvira's willingness to participate in this rarefied public order is wearing down; the absurdity of that order is reflected in the perversion of a postcolonial economic world in which a chocolate chalet, "no doubt a gift from Nestle's," sits on a table at the Colombian president's right hand. In her "improvised Spanish," Elvira's colleague Martine accepts the President's obligatory invitation to "the esteemed citizens of Switzerland here today to visit his country": "I accept invitation travel to Colombia. Want to see Modelo, Picota and Sacromonte prisons." Martine's transgressive response provides an exemplary disruption that further impels Elvira's disappearance from Switzerland.

In Elvira's case, Colombian politics are inherently a personal matter. Born into a Medellín family whose personal fortunes are bound to the public order, Elvira's life is not neatly delimited between private and public, between activities familial and political. In the years since she left Colombia, her brother has become manager of Coltejer (Colombia's chief textile operation), and his old classmate has received the Swiss ambassadorship. Her position as protagonist of the story complicates the public and the private, the international and the domestic, condensing the disorder of both nation and family. She imagines Ambassador Eugenio Vélez reporting to her brother: "even in Switzerland she was mixed up with 'those people'"—involvement with whom her brother had charged "was disrespectful to the memory of their dead parents."

The distance of Switzerland from Colombia, like that of the petition from the testimony, maintains, in Elvira's experience, a dangerous split between the public and the private. A decree that declares the public order disturbed identifies a bleeding across the lines of a public and private distinction that is unacceptable to authority; Elvira's rejection of the statist dichotomy necessitates her return to Colombia and disrupts the public order in an attempt to reconcile the public with the private. The chain of substitutions created by Elvira's remove from Colombia and her activities with the solidarity committee displaces, but cannot replace, the personal experience of violation. The integrity of her Swiss family remains threatened by the activity of her Colombian one. It is Martine's transgression of the public discourse, her improvised acceptance of an invitation that was not intended to invite, that reveals to Elvira the obstacles raised by a strict division between public and private. Although the open letter had seemingly little effect on the Colombian officials, the explicit addressees, its generic and rhetorical capacity, instead, moves Elvira. She assumes the role of audience for the document that she has helped to author and deliver, and as such, the open letter, which attempts to break down the barrier between public and private, reveals the superficiality of that split in Elvira's own life. Her acceptance of the letter precipitates her rejection of the seemliness of international petitioning and public discourse, developing an awareness of her own implication (through the family, nation, and the international) of her relationship to Colombian human rights violations.

Araujo's story locates the imaginative power of literature and letter writing in acts and metaphorical associations of substitution; such acts are "housebreakings" because they refuse to recognize the artificial boundaries between the public and the private that facilitate the Colombian president's refusal to receive the petition and acknowledge his government's continued violation of human rights. These "housebreakings" establish a correspondence between the public and the private, between Elvira as author and addressee, between Swiss and Colombian filiations, between language and action, and between open letters and urgent missives, that make possible Elvira's decisive act of subversion, her divorce from the "purely" public. As literature, the story suggests that these recognitions of correspondence are more than acts of literary imagination.

Postmark of a Day That Never Happened

Tsitsi Dangarembga's "The Letter," included in *Whispering Land: An Anthology of Stories by African Women* (1985), is a black South African woman's account of receiving a long-awaited letter: "This morning, I received a letter from my husband, the first in twelve years. Can you imagine such a thing?" the narrator asks at the story's opening. The story tells of the events of the day the woman receives the letter, the husband's reasons for fleeing their home twelve years earlier, and the "custom" of waiting that has become her daily routine ever since, a routine interrupted by the arrival of the letter.

Three years after her husband left, the woman had moved from the home they once shared in Sebokeng township, outside of Johannesburg, to go "back to my village in the homeland." The story unfolds colloquially, describing the routine of her life in that village. She visits the post office "every day of the week, except Sunday when the post office is closed . . . to see whether my husband has written." Juxtaposed with the rural normalcy of her routine is an account of the circumstances that led up to the husband's flight, a competing view of peri-urban "normalcy" and its humiliations—profound economic inequality, constraints on mobility, state violence directed against innocent and "random" targets—in South Africa under Prime Minister P.W. Botha. She concludes, "My husband and I observed these things together in Sebokeng . . . [and] we became political people. But in my country political black people, which is to say black people, are threatened with genocide." The state identified her husband as a "major security risk," a risk that necessitated "deploying squadrons of men, fleets of police cars and rounds of ammunition to capture a single black man in one little street of a decaying ghetto!" Despite the mobilization against her husband, he escaped by moving from house to house, "not liv[ing] as man and wife . . . until arrangements were finalized for his flight across one of our borders, which one I am not sure."

Dangarembga's choice of Sebokeng township in the Botha era (1978–1989) as the setting where the couple become politicized, and from which they flee, is significant in light of the public-private, international-domestic tensions in literary and human rights letter-writing. On 23 October 1984, seven thousand South African Defense Force (SADF) soldiers assisted police in conducting house-to-house raids in Sebokeng, to contain unrest in the townships that had been spreading since September. Addressing the UN Security Council on the same day (a week after he won the Nobel Peace Prize), Bishop Desmond Tutu commented on this unprecedented mobilization of the SADF against internal targets: "When you use the army in this fashion, who is the enemy? . . . The South African government is turning us into aliens in the land of our birth." Tutu's remarks highlight the perversion of public-private dynamics in late apartheid South Africa; the state waged an undeclared civil war within its borders, while the purported independence of the homelands worked to eliminate the possibility of citizenship for black South Africans.

Within this context, the homeland post office in the story is the locus where public and private concerns meet. The woman goes to the post office daily as "a ritual I performed in order to maintain my bond with the past." Keeping this private ritual without any expectation that the post office will deliver on its public function, the woman also suggests the widespread prevalence of such individual "customs," of which the postmaster is the nexus: "He understands my preoccupation with the mail because I am not unique—there are many families here in the village who have a father, a son, an uncle or a nephew who has not been heard of for many years, who has been imprisoned, or who has been reported missing or dead." This gendered culture of missing letters is constituted by a "self-sufficient . . . colony of women" waiting for but rarely receiving any reliable information.

When the woman finally receives her letter, she is torn between wanting to conserve the intimacy of her joy and wanting to wave the "letter like a victory flag." But her conflicted desires are informed as much by a sense of danger as by a desire for privacy. Her mother advises the woman to destroy the letter the moment she finishes reading it, and while she knows that "of course [her mother] was right," she replies instead, " 'It is a personal letter. . . . There can be no danger.' " Two marks on the exterior of the letter suggest the temptation to believe in, and the ultimate impossibility of, a safe, private letter: at the post office, the woman recognizes immediately the "familiar style" of her husband's handwriting, but she only notices once she arrives home the "South African stamp" and postmark that enable and trace its transmission to her.

Certainly the appearance of a letter "after all these years" is "strange"; her husband asks "why I had not replied to his other letters." But what concerns her more immediately is its consequence for her family. The letter's salutation, "My dear wife," assuages her fears about her husband's commitment to her, but his request that she "go to him in Botswana" with their daughter introduces a complication: she also has a five-year-old daughter conceived "during a few hours of my solitude." Just as the arrival of the letter transforms the hitherto private significance of the woman's post-office ritual, its message complicates her relationship to her daughters. Her life in the years of her husband's exile threatens to obstruct the reconstitution of her family outside the borders of South Africa.

But the woman's return letter, which informs her husband about the daughter, remains unsent and undeliverable, made public because it is among the "subversive . . . letters" found when her house is searched: "an armed vehicle and [six] camouflaged soldiers to arrest one small woman in a remote homeland village!" This fragment echoes the description of the police pursuit of her husband, underscoring the structural similarities and infrastructural ties between policing/defense activities in the homelands and South African townships. The soldiers take her to the police station, which is, we discover, where the woman sits as she narrates the events of the day.

Indeed, we discover that "The Letter" is a *letter*, a communication that escapes the confines of a homeland police station in a chain of transmission as opaque as that which brought both a long-awaited letter and an army jeep on the same day. The soldiers press her for a confession, but the narrator reveals not what she tells the men but rather the narrative situation itself: "I will not tell you how [the soldiers] threatened to shoot my children to make me confess to my terrorist activities, nor will I tell you how they beat my mother when she pleaded for me." In this "not telling," the narrator gives a second-person narratee—"you"—a private-public role as well.

The woman imagines two possibilities—being "charged with an act of treason plotted in Pretoria," or being detained until the officers "[concede] that my desire to be with my husband is not grounds for indictment"—that emphasize the public-private split upon which she is precariously balanced. But by invoking the second-person narratee, the woman establishes another context for correspondence and the exchange of information: "Whatever happens I know that they will make sure that we cannot reach Themba, but this is not my concern since I have told you my story, not to arouse your pity, but only so that you may know that these things are happening to us in our country." In this final moment the second-person narratee is implicated in an economy of knowledge: the woman is compensated for her knowledge ("I know") of a future without her husband by her acknowledgment of the narratee's knowledge ("I have told . . . so that you may know") of her situation, a specific instance of the generic "things . . . happening to us in our country." If the chain of transmission that brings the "personal" letter to her has been broken or coopted, so too can be the silence which surrounds women in detention.

The six references to this second-person narratee in the final paragraph amplify retrospectively the scattered references to "you" that seem stylistically, rather than structurally, colloquial until the end. But the formal structure of address is implicit from the beginning: "This morning I received a letter from my husband, the first in twelve years. Can you imagine such a thing?" The story's narration is an attempt to help the reader "imagine such a thing," as is evident in the scene where the woman receives the letter. Replacing direct narration, a series of imperatives encourages the implicit "you" to construct a scene that corresponds to the narrator's experience:

> So imagine my surprise when I saw the postmaster waiting for me . . . Feel how my heart stopped when he gave me the letter . . . Consider how my hand shook and the sweat trickled from my armpits in a dark patch down the sides of my dress as I took the letter from him . . . Do not think me rude when I tell you that I did not respond to his greeting. . . . To tell you the truth I did not see him or the post office or even the letter. All I saw was the writing, the familiar style with the "t"s crossed so heavily, occupying my field of vision, dominating all else.

The narrator attempts to construct a sympathetic, vicarious sight on the part of the narratee. Perception is then linked to the political: "*You see,* it was painful for me . . . *to see* my mother" neglect her children while caring for white children, "*watching* my father abused. . . . I *felt* my [brothers' frustration] *when I saw* them mutilate each other. . . . My husband and I *observed* these things together in Sebokeng . . . [and] we became political people" (emphasis added).

The narrator's initial question, "Can you imagine such a thing?," appears to be "merely" rhetorical, not expecting an answer, but the question becomes rhetorical in the Aristotelian sense, aiming to enlighten and persuade an audience. In the narrator's idiom of witnessing, whether "you can imagine such a thing" becomes urgent, as she exchanges her "concern" about her uncertain future for the narratee's knowledge of "what is happening to us in our country." The vicarious sight and sympathetic perception demanded by the narrator transform imagined experience into knowledge; by specifically disavowing an emotional response to this imaginative appeal as her goal ("not to arouse your pity, but that you may know"), the narrator revises the split between poetics and rhetoric—between epistolary fiction and petition.

The woman's stated aim reshapes the goals of rhetoric in another way as well: to *know* "what is happening" in late apartheid South Africa is indeed a subversive *act,* given the successive states of emergency from 1985, the year "The Letter" was published. Two audiences posed particular concern to the state in the censorship measures tightened after 1985: white South Africans and foreign audiences (see Marcus). Amnesty International reported in August 1985 that detainees were being held incommunicado, "not permitted to communicate with the outside world through correspondence. They may not receive or send out letters." In this context, "The Letter" is the kind of text that the state would hope to make unwritable, undeliverable, as international and domestic correspondence.

Just as the story does not reveal how her husband's letter led to the woman's detention, it does not detail how a woman in detention is telling her story to another, nor do we even know whether the "telling" is oral or written. In leaving the "you" of the story ambiguous, Dangarembga implicates both "foreign audiences" and white South Africans as potential narratees. The plural first-person of the final sentence recalls the other families in the village waiting for letters, but it might also reach for a broader, more complex and subversive national solidarity between narrator and narratee. The woman's description of her daily life in a homeland village creates a context for her story that would be nearly as necessary for a white South African narratee as for someone not of "our country," implicating the "you" as both ignorant agent and complicit victim of "what is happening to us in our country." "The Letter" tears down—through its insistence on imaginative correspondence—borders such as those that aimed to separate the homelands from South Africa. As a Zimbabwean writer, from "across one of our borders," Dangarembga's assumption of a black South African woman's voice is another kind of narrative border-crossing, a ventriloquism and sympathetic sight facilitated by her access to international outlets such as the Swedish International Development Cooperation Agency (SIDA), for whom she edited the anthology in which "The Letter" appears.

If the salutation of a letter can constitute identity by demarcating relationships—" 'My dear wife' " means "I am still his wife!"—then what does the story's implication of its narratee, or its reader, do? What does the narrative smuggling of an unsent, undeliverable letter like "The Letter" do? Twelve years after the SADF raided Sebokeng township in 1984—through the efforts of "political people" within the country, and pressure brought to bear by those outside who had been implicated with "knowledge" the state had hoped to keep undeliverable—South Africa had adopted a democratic constitution and Nelson Mandela had been president for two and a half years. "The Letter," which narrates a day twelve years after her husband left Sebokeng, on which a woman receives both a letter and a visit from an army jeep, has participated in eliminating its own historical possibility. The letter's postmark was for a day that didn't happen.

The Costs of Forgetting

Like the women in "The Open Letter" and "The Letter," the main character in Janette Turner Hospital's "Dear Amnesty" is a woman who receives and writes letters. In response to the Urgent Action Bulletins she receives "once or twice a week" from Amnesty International, Sarah writes letters to government officials on behalf of detainees and torture victims around the world. In the eyes of her two adult children, Sarah's letter-writing is "obsessive"; her son Richard, a medical student who "liked to draw short straight lines between cause and effect," asks whether " 'all this [is] because of Dad,' " whether the recent break-up of Sarah's marriage has precipitated the "snowstorm" of letters she writes. Confronted with her son's hypothesis that her activism is a "displacement" of marital anguish, Sarah remarks that it is odd "how people only *comment* when the private and the public . . . when outer politics and inner politics, I suppose I should say . . . at those brief interludes, you know, when they become *congruent*." (ellipses in original). Instead of locating politics solely in the public realm, Sarah recognizes the ubiquity and correspondence of inner and outer politics.

The story concerns a "brief interlude" in which Sarah's familial and activist commitments correspond and collide, a time when "things got out of hand." Although Sarah writes on behalf of many prisoners, "they had all come to look like Rosita." In the words of one of the Urgent Action Bulletins that Sarah receives, *"Rosita Romero, factory worker,"* is detained and tortured *"for circulating a petition requesting better conditions at the factory where she works."* We learn, through an Amnesty bulletin at the end of the story, that Rosita is released *"after a worldwide barrage of letters."* While this narrative trajectory endorses the efficacy of human rights letter-writing, the story's examination of the outer and inner politics of Sarah's family and her psyche measures its costs as well.

Just as Sarah reshapes a public-private opposition, the narrative involves multiple layers of discourse. The story opens with a description of an activist genre that Sarah has mastered: "All the letters—they would have made a snowstorm—began with *Your Excellency.*" Throughout the story, italic type demarcates activist documents, including Sarah's letters and Amnesty's Urgent Action Bulletins; ellipses appear with unusual frequency and generally indicate incomplete or interrupted, rather than excised, statements. (In order to accommodate this narrative strategy in our own discussion, we indicate our own omissions from quotations with ellipses inside brackets.) Sarah's daughter Katy admonishes her mother, " 'There's such a thing as knowing your own limits,' " proposing a division of human rights labor in which some people, including Sarah, should " 'just give money and leave the letters' " to " 'people who can handle this.' " The ellipses in "Dear Amnesty" demarcate such "limits," pointing in dialogue to the limits of what can be said, and in interior narration to the limits of what can be thought. These modulations between dialogue and thought are a narrative device that, by revealing the gulf between what Sarah says and what she thinks, suggests that her family life, no less than her human rights letter-writing, is a conflict among politics ranging from outer to inner. Here Sarah responds to Richard's diagnosis that her letter-writing is a "displacement" of her feelings about the divorce: " 'Yes,' Sarah said, 'but the thing is . . .' The thing was, she was one of them now; no outer casing, naked, exposed, waiting for blows. 'I know how she feels, so I *have* to help.' " Richard is "disturbed" by his mother's comments, despite the fact that her statement of analogic empathy aims to mask a more radical, unvoiced claim of identification with Rosita that compels her to write.

In the innermost layer of its "politics," the story examines what it means to "know how she feels," a project neither antithetical nor unrelated to Katy's encouragement to "know your own limits." Sarah literally knows how Rosita feels, a knowledge which reshapes the limits of her own body. Their menstrual cycles are aligned, and when she is stricken one night with acute uterine pain that a well-meaning neighbor, Mrs. Donovan, identifies as a miscarriage, Sarah insists, " 'It's not a baby, it's Rosita.' " The neighbor, who accompanies Sarah to the emergency room, warns Sarah not to expect doctors to understand "women's problems," and her doctor's ultimate diagnosis of "hysteria" is etymologically not so different from Mrs. Donovan's. Dr. Fisher initially suspects that a desire for "some physical bond" between her and her husband has generated a hysterical pregnancy, until the Urgent Action Bulletins that Katy gives him lead him to modify his diagnosis and identify Rosita as the source of Sarah's hysteria: " 'You believe that if you suffer with her, it will help. You believe you are, as it were, draining off some of her pain into your own body.' " Echoing her son's earlier displacement diagnosis, Dr. Fisher concludes, " 'It's not Rosita Romero's problems you have to work on [. . .] You have to stop avoiding your own.' "

Sarah effectively accepts Dr. Fisher's diagnosis but not his conclusion, and the narrative, too, validates the import of what Dr. Fisher says if not his motivation, for Dr. Fisher proceeds to read aloud, from an Urgent Action Bulletin, details of Rosita's vaginal torture that account for Sarah's pain. She knows "it would not be a good idea to admit" to Dr. Fisher that she does believe that she can bear some of Rosita's pain for her, just as she is "deeply embarrassed" that her children notice that she shivers uncontrollably when she writes for Amnesty. Sarah would prefer to conceal the external signs of her knowledge of Rosita's condition, a knowledge—like that questioned in Araujo's "The Open Letter" and invited in Dangarembga's "The Letter"—that is formed through imagination of another's physical sensation. We see Sarah's hyperliteral response to Amnesty's appeals as Dr. Fisher reads, *"Letters should be sent"* and she interjects, " 'I know [. . . .] I did' "; when he reads about Rosita's torture, Sarah folds in pain and says, " 'I know [. . . .] You don't have to tell me, I know.' "

Although Sarah laments early in the story that "she and Rosita lived parallel lives and could not hold hands," in the narrative's climax she again "wakes in agony [. . .] as though she is giving birth to a wombful of razor blades"; in this state Sarah finds Rosita, also in pain, bloodied and beaten, and not only "cradles," "rocks," and "sings to" her, but also "braces her legs against the wall" and "clasps Rosita's hands and hangs on," as "guards appear, swinging their truncheons" and try to pull Rosita away by the ankles. Even Rosita begs her to let go, but Sarah "wakes exhausted" in the morning and thinks, "I did not let go." Sarah's nightmare implies that solidarity means not letting go even when victims have lost their will to resist or survive. After the nightmare, the narrative moves toward resolution of Sarah's conflict with her children and revelation of Rosita's release.

The dream-state correspondence that Sarah experiences with Rosita revolves around entangled images of motherhood: Rosita's torture (and Sarah's pain) targets reproductive organs, even as Sarah comforts her as she would an infant, and, indeed, that potential relationship is perhaps overdetermined by the affectionate, but diminutive, form of Rosita for Rosa. Earlier in the story, Sarah thinks of Rosita's ten children, imagines her "brushing their hair and singing to them" while Sarah's daughter Katy is brushing Sarah's hair. Having her hair brushed evokes a constellation of thoughts and memories for Sarah; acknowledging her pleasure, she remembers (and asks Katy if she remembers) brushing her young daughter's "black ringlets [. . .] one by one, wrapping each around her index finger like a tendril, stroking it with the bristles." The sensuousness of an index finger repetitively engaged with spirals resonates with the description of Sarah writing letters "by hand, with a fountain pen, taking particular care with the flourishes: "the sensuous f's, the loopy l's, the trailing lace flounces on the y's." The pleasure Sarah takes in writing the letters, like the pain that compels her to write them, is bound up in her correspondence with Rosita as mothers who brush daughters' hair; Sarah also thinks of combing Rosita's matted hair, "untangling the wrongs, smoothing out the day's cruelties."

But Rosita's detention means that neither woman is able to brush her daughter's hair; Katy's and Sarah's roles have been reversed, suggesting that in her maternal concern for Rosita, Sarah has lost her ability to care for herself and her children. Discovering letters hidden in a pillowcase, Katy fumes, " 'these people you write letters for . . . I don't see where they get the right to swallow up our lives.' " Thus the story's final scene, which follows Sarah's nightmare, suggests a restoration of the normalcy of an adult mother-daughter relationship as Sarah brushes Katy's hair while she is "visiting for Sunday dinner." When Sarah asks whether Katy remembers a boy who had teased her as a child, Katy laughs and says, " 'I'd completely forgotten. I used to have *nightmares* about that boy.' " This exchange suggests the ironies of confronting forgotten trauma: Sarah is unlikely to forget Rosita completely, but she is already unable to remember precisely when ("oh, two months ago?" she asks herself casually) she received the Amnesty bulletin that noted Rosita's release.

This final scene aims to resolve the correspondences of pleasure and pain, family and activism, memory and forgetting. Rosita's condition is "*stable*"; Katy muses, " 'We're not doing so badly, are we?' " The narrative discloses the news of Rosita's release because Katy asks Sarah whether she is still writing letters and whether she thinks—or hears—that " 'it accomplishes anything.' " Sarah responds noncommittally and continues brushing Katy's hair; Katy says, " 'Don't stop,' " and Sarah replies, " 'I had no

intention of stopping.' " Whether this final exchange refers to hair brushing or letter writing is nearly immaterial, given their association in the
narrative. More important, however, is that Sarah has forgotten some of
the extremity of her correspondence with Rosita, which led her to become
dependent on her children; when they had forced her to promise to stop
writing letters, Sarah had admitted to herself that she "wanted to stop.
But she couldn't [. . .] it was not within her power to stop." Sarah's final
statement revises her earlier relationship to writing, suggesting that the
price of resolution is forgetting the intensity, and the felt powerlessness, of
her own experience.

Sarah writes not *to* Amnesty but *for* Amnesty, on behalf of a woman herself detained for the sake of a petition: "Dear Amnesty" is not the salutation of a letter but rather a suggestion of the dearness—the cost—of
forgetting. Amnesty International's message to prisoners of conscience
and their jailers alike is "You are not forgotten," at the same time that the
organization works to secure amnesty—due process, release, pardon, and
most literally, forgetting of alleged offenses—for political prisoners. Rosita
is released, but the fate of her own petition is one of the things consigned
to oblivion in the story.

In its update on Rosita, Amnesty notes that pressure from "*political figures in the U.S., Canada, Australia, and Europe* [. . . who were] *themselves a
target of our letter writing campaign*" had preceded her release; the bulletin
also includes "news of fresh arrests in South Korea [. . .] and reports of torture in Iran" with generic appeals for letters. These are the only geopolit-
ical references in the story; Sarah interrupts Dr. Fisher before he reads
Rosita's nationality, as she is consistently less interested in details that in-
dividuate Rosita than in experiences in their lives that correspond. The
story (published in Janette Turner Hospital's native Australia in the late
1980s, and in the United States in 1991) presumes an absolute geographic division between the perpetrators and protesters of human rights
violations that allows its settings to remain unspecified.

Sarah, too, relies presumptuously on this division, as she tells Katy
while thinking of Rosita and her daughters, " 'You're so *unharmed*.' " Katy
makes clear that she is not *unharmed* by the divorce, nor by Sarah's correspondence with and for Rosita. In the crucial scenes where Sarah and Katy
brush each other's hair, Hospital seems to be devising a trope on the logo
that appears on Amnesty's letters, "a candle in a cage of barbed wire": they
sit in "a bay window that looked out on the horsechestnut tree," whose
large flowers resemble, and are referred to in the story as, "candles." Not
wrapped in barbed wire, but instead separated from the women through
the "cage" of a bay window, the recurring image of the candle emphasizes
that Sarah's house is indeed not a prison, at the same time that it

foregrounds her children's ability to conceive of human rights as either a cause worth donating money to or a distraction not suitably "upbeat" for their mother in a difficult time.

Although Amnesty International is careful not to credit its campaigns for the release of prisoners, in the logic of the story both Sarah's letters and her not letting go of Rosita precede and perhaps predicate Rosita's release; yet her "brief interlude" of total correspondence with and for Rosita nearly reduces her to helplessness. In the same vein, Sarah does not deny the repeated insinuation that the dissolution of her marriage has some relationship to her immersion in letter-writing; indeed, Sarah writes her letters in what was once her marriage bed. The most private room of the house has become the center of Sarah's activism; she uses the bed not only as a desk, but also as a hiding place. Under the mattress, where the woman in Dangarembga's story concealed her letters, where Rosita might have concealed the petition, Sarah hides her fountain pen. It is fitting, then, given the ways in which letters bring Sarah so close to a woman half a world away, at the same time that they alienate her own children, that Sarah hides her letter-writing from her children by "huddl[ing] under the quilt, pretending to read," presumably novels whose vicarious experience her children would find less disturbing.

Questions of Closure: Writing Beyond Consummation and Death

The three stories discussed here draw on, and yet violate, some of the generic conventions that Ruth Perry and others identify for epistolary fiction. One reason for this generic transgression may well be our selection of short stories rather than novels; but that explanation begs the question of closure, for it is the very activity of letter-writing, of petitioning, in these stories that forecloses the possibility of extending the plot to novel length. In this regard, a comment made by the South African writer Njabulo Ndebele in his review of the prose production of black South African writers seems especially poignant: "For a long time South Africa has been known in Africa as the land of the short story" (1989, p. 27). Acknowledging not only the historical circumstances of black South Africans under apartheid, Ndebele's observation also characterizes the literary limitations of the novel when it is tied to an Enlightenment notion of the "development of full personality." Reviewing the impact on the development of South African intellectual life under apartheid of such specific factors as access to education, leisure, publishing outlets, reading material, and means of information retrieval, Ndebele goes on to observe: "It is clear . . . that the history of prose is inseparable from the history of society and the manner of its organization" (p. 30). In this context, it becomes clear that

Ruth Perry's confident allusion in *Women, Letters, and the Novel* to the "purposes of novels as we know them, providing a coherent world to experience and permitting readers to live vicariously in the borrowed emotional lives of the characters," presupposes the plausibility of a "coherent world" and a reading audience interested in vicarious emotional experience for its own sake.

We would not want to suggest that human rights stories are, by some sad fact of history, necessarily short or uninterested in connections among reader, character, and imagined worlds. Instead, the stories we have examined here suggest the personal, and therefore political, costs of profound and sustained correspondence. As literary lessons in letter writing, the three stories resist the temptation to configure writing and activism as simple matters of empathy or "borrowed experience." Instead, these stories suggest some of the risks entailed in any "housebreaking," in the establishment of a radical correspondence between one who suffers and one who is implicated by knowledge of that suffering. Of course, a correspondence predicated on suffering is itself somewhat at odds with the conventions of epistolary literature.

Perry identifies the conventions that determine relationships between correspondents in the epistolary novel: "Epistolary fiction always works according to a formula: two or more people, separated by an obstruction which can take a number of forms, are forced to maintain their relationship through letters. . . . The characters are prevented from acting directly and can only respond to their difficulties by writing about them and hoping for a solution which will bring them together" (p. 93). Given the structural dynamics of the relationship between the subjects of epistolary fiction, only two conclusions, Perry argues, are available for the literary correspondents: consummation or death. "These alternatives of sexual union or death make sense within the paradigm of the letter novel, for either [alternative] puts a stop to the letter writing and resolves the separation which the characters spend their fictional lives trying to overcome" (p. 95). Both of these endings signal the return of the letter writers to the privacy of the world.

It might be tempting to account for the "failure" of the stories we read here to end in marriage or death by noting their historical distance from the age of the epistolary novel, when, as Perry says, "literate women [were] dispossessed of all meaningful activity save marrying or breeding." However, despite the fact that the women in these stories are engaged in other kinds of activities and activisms, we have been concerned throughout to consider how the concerns of marriage and children cannot easily be separated, by means of a stable public-private divide, from the "meaningfulness" of what the women do, read, and write. Thus, while the plots of each of the stories involve the dissolution or effective termination of a marriage, more significant is the fact that the women's letters are aimed not to maintain interrupted relationships in an interim of separation but rather to create relationships whose trajectories are not so easily mapped in terms of "consummation." At the same time, the stories not only decisively reject death as the alternative ending for epistolary plots; they reject the entire logic—the need to cease letter-writing activity—of the resolution of the conventional narratives. Sarah's final words in "Dear Amnesty," " 'I had no intention of stopping,' " convey the sense of continued correspondence implicit in the three stories; even in Dangarembga's "The Letter," the woman's interrupted life and letter-writing are transformed and mobilized by her very act of narration and her faith in its economy of knowledge.

The exchange of letters, the dissemination of literary information, and the vicarious pleasure of the "borrowed lives" of these women, themselves "borrowing lives," make extraliterary demands on a reader, demands that exact a cost for entering the narrative bargain and receiving the letter. That is, the ways in which these stories reconceive individual identity, particularly female identity, in relation to writing, rights, and other people relies upon and resists the expectations a reader might normally bring to a work of epistolary fiction. It is in the imaginative correspondence between the narrator and the narratee, between the writer and the reader, that these stories re-letter the world, the individual, and solidarity.

NOTE
*Kathleen McKenzie's invitation to us to participate with her on a panel on women's rights and the international novel inspired our thinking about the ideas elaborated in this article.

WORKS CITED
Amnesty International. "Detentions Under the State of Emergency." 6 August 1985. Reprinted in *The Anti-Apartheid Reader: South Africa and the Struggle against White Racist Rule,* edited by David Mermelstein. New York, 1987.

Araujo, Helena. "The Open Letter." Translated by Nancy Saporta Sternbach. In *Landscapes of a New Land,* edited by Marjorie Agosín. Buffalo, N.Y., 1989.

Dangarembga, Tsitsi. "The Letter." In *Whispering Land: An Anthology of Stories by African Women,* edited by Tsitsi Dangarembga and Swedish International Development Agency. Stockholm, 1985.

Hospital, Janette Turner. "Dear Amnesty." In *Isobars: Stories by Janette Turner Hospital.* Baton Rouge, La., 1991.

Marcus, Gilbert. "Civil Liberties under Emergency Rule." In *The Last Years of Apartheid: Civil Liberties in South Africa,* edited by John Dugard. New York, Ford Foundation Foreign Policy Association (South Africa UPDATE Series), 1992.

Ndebele, Njabulo. "The Challenges of the Written Word." In *Culture in Another South Africa,* edited by Willem Campschreur and Joost Divendal. New York, 1989.

Perry, Ruth. *Women, Letters, and the Novel.* New York, 1980.

Rao, Arati. "The Politics of Gender and Culture in International Human Rights Discourse." In *Women's Rights, Human Rights: International Feminist Perspectives,* edited by Julie Peters and Andrea Wolper. New York, 1995.

Staves, Susan. " 'The Liberty of a She-Subject of England': Rights Rhetoric and the Female Thucydides." *Cardozo Studies in Law and Literature* 1, no. 1 (1989): 161–183.

Sullivan, Donna. "The Public/Private Distinction in International Human Rights Law." In *Women's Rights, Human Rights: International Feminist Perspectives,* edited by Julie Peters and Andrea Wolper. New York, 1995.

Tutu, Desmond. "The Question of South Africa." *Africa Report* 30 (January-February 1985): 50–52. Originally a statement to the United Nations Security Council, 23 October 1984.

Watt, Ian. *The Rise of the Novel.* Berkeley, Calif., 1965 (1957).

Before the Mirror
Christopher Merrill

⚭ IT is burned into our collective imagination: the confrontation in the opening lines of the *Iliad,* between Agamemnon and Chryses, a priest of Apollo who has come to ransom his daughter Chryseis. But the priest's offer brings "no joy to the heart of Agamemnon." The king tells the priest the girl will die "far from her fatherland, slaving back and forth at the loom, forced to share my bed," and then dismisses him with a threat on his life. Accordingly, Chryses prays to Apollo to send a plague down on the Achaeans, and the ensuing slaughter leads the chieftains to convene an assembly to implore the king to let the girl go. But Agamemnon will part with his war booty only if Achilles gives up his share, a girl named Briseis, the loss of whom sparks Achilles' rage, the theme of Homer's epic, which is also the founding document of the Western literary tradition. The literature of women as war booty, which begins with Briseis and Chryseis, is thus as old as epic poetry itself.

No doubt this is one reason why Simone Weil suggested, in an essay dating from the first year of World War II, that the true hero, subject, and center of the *Iliad* was force:

> Force employed by nature, force that enslaves man, force before which man's flesh shrinks away. . . . For those dreamers that considered that force, thanks to progress would soon be a thing of the past, the *Iliad* could appear as an historical document; for others, whose powers of recognition are more acute and who perceive force, today as yesterday, at the very center of human history, the *Iliad* is the purest and the loveliest of mirrors.

I wish to hang this lovely mirror in front of the following portraits from my travels, from 1992 to 2000, through the war zones of the former Yugoslavia, which I hope will illustrate not only the centrality of force in human history but also the force of the imagination—the poetry, if you will—displayed by some courageous women in bearing witness to the central tragedy of post–cold war Europe.

"It was strange, it was heart-rending," Rebecca West wrote of Sarajevo, "to stray into a world where men are still men and women still women." Women went to great lengths during the siege to keep up their appearance. Beauty parlors thrived, and with little water Sarajevans prided themselves on wearing clean clothes whenever possible. Applying makeup, said Ljiljana Sulentić, an architect, is how we tell the primitives we will not surrender. Ljiljana needed no makeup to stand out, even in Sarajevo. Tall and slender, with shoulder-length auburn hair and deep brown eyes and flushed cheeks, she always looked as if she had just returned from a long walk. Her suits came from Italy—she had studied and worked in Rome— and it was her passion, as the head of a household of women (her mother, her aunt, a younger cousin), to explain why the women of Sarajevo were so attractive.

"Mixing the races is what makes the richest and most beautiful people," she told me one overcast afternoon as we walked to her apartment. "It's the nature of life to mix."

Ljiljana was a fine illustration of her thesis. Her father, who died in the first winter of the war, was Croatian, her mother was Serbian, and in her extended family were Muslim, British, and French relatives. Her best friend, a Montenegrin woman, was killed in Serbian-occupied Grbavica, when she sneaked across the river to bring a packet of food to her parents. It was a Bosnian sniper who shot her. Most of the mourners at her funeral were Muslim.

"It's so stupid, so primitive," said Ljiljana. "But I have decided to survive because I would like to go to concerts and travel again. For this someone has to be alive."

But she was tired, winter was coming, and she had not heard from her friends and colleagues in Belgrade and Zagreb. A thoroughgoing Sarajevan, she kept her distance from what she called the "half-people" destroying her city, the villagers who came here after World War II and during this war, some to fight on the Serbian side, some to occupy abandoned flats. Designing homes for refugees who would transform the city into a large village in which the arts had no place was the last thing she wanted to do, so she would probably have to leave Sarajevo when the war was over.

We climbed the stairs to what was left of her family's corner apartment. Ljiljana had prized its panoramic view of the mountains until it was struck by a pair of rocket-launched grenades. She thought she was prepared for the devastation, having already toured some 5,000 destroyed flats in her new job of estimating architectural damages. But this was the first set of ruins she visited in which she could not tell what had been there before the shells struck. Only her father's books and record albums survived; everything else was smashed under the falling walls.

"My friends think I have an American flat," she said with a bitter laugh, "because the walls are gone. But I don't think American flats have rain and snow coming into them."

A cold wind was blowing through the sheets of plastic covering the window frames; plaster and dust swirled on the floor. Ljiljana, who came from a family of engineers and urban planners, was now the architect in charge of demolishing Sarajevo's damaged buildings. Before we joined her mother and aunt for a cup of coffee she caught my arm.

"Silly job, silly people, silly country," she said.

Ferida Duraković was the young poet featured on an ABC *Nightline* special about Sarajevo. I recognized her at a meeting of the Writers' Association, and we had just begun to talk when she said, "They're all old men here!" Off we went to a café, where she announced that the literal meaning of Ferida was "unique," of Duraković, "foolish" or "durable." All three applied. She was a kind of holy fool who spoke outlandishly—for example, "happiness is the main task in this war"—and soon she was pressing on me a small painting by an artist friend. On one side of a shard of glass from a broken window was a hollow face on a green stem; on the other, a black figure, with two blank eyes, curling around the base of the stem and looming behind the head, like a three-cornered hat. My friend is painting the city, said Ferida. I can't accept this, I said. There's much more where that came from, she laughed, and led me outside. A firefight stopped us in our tracks. What was that about, I said when it was over. I don't know, she said. I don't know anything anymore.

Homeless for more than a year, somehow she retained her *joie de vivre.* Serbian shells had struck the bookstore she managed and burned it to the ground. Then her parents' flat was destroyed, and her personal library went up in flames. Usually we are just happy to be alive, she said when we walked on, sidestepping the so-called "Sarajevo roses," the marks left by mortar shells. Never have I been so happy to write, to live, to meet people, to eat. I don't have anything complicated in my life, just life and death. I have to choose, and I choose to write. She paused at a crosswalk we would have to sprint across to avoid a sniper. This is a war against civilians, she said, glancing at the houses on the hill, and calmly told me that 85 percent of the casualties in World War I were military, 15 percent civilian figures inverted in this war. The fate of the poet Georg Trakl was never far from her thoughts. After the battle of Grodek, in August 1914, Trakl, a pharmacist in the Austrian army, was put in charge of a barnful of seriously wounded men for whom he could do nothing. Outside in the trees were the convulsing bodies of hanged deserters. Inside, the poet, who saw one of the wounded shoot himself in the head, was also preparing to commit suicide, though not before writing for these men "the wild lament / of their broken mouths," the inspiration for Ferida's newest poem, "Georg Trakl on the Battlefield Again, 1993":

Our dear Lord dwells above the planes, in the highest Heaven.
His golden eyes settle on the dark, on blackened Sarajevo.
Blossoms and shells are falling outside my window.
Madness and me. We are alone, we are alone, alone.

Ferida looked at me. "Ready?" she said.

A visit to refugee camps on the outskirts of Zagreb, Croatia. My translator, Marina Pintarić, a student at the university, had postponed her exams in order to translate for a Spanish humanitarian organization; like many bright young people in the Balkans, she took advantage of her skills to earn much more money working for an international aid agency than she could hope to make otherwise. But this day she was reluctant to go to the first camp, a rehabilitation center located next to a hospital that had once served the Yugoslav National Army (JNA), because she used to visit a boy there who was afflicted with cerebral palsy. I don't like to be seen here now, she said at the door.

Many of these refugees were from Vukovar, the Croatian city which in the early days of the war had withstood some of the most intense bombardment in the history of modern warfare, with more shells landing per square meter than in the siege of Stalingrad. The night before our visit, Croatian television reported that nearly 1,200 people were still missing from the area; when the city fell in November 1991, the JNA had committed large-scale massacres, including the murder of some 300 patients taken from the hospital. Marina expected us to be greeted with bitterness at the center—only the year before, interviewing other refugees from Vukovar, I had been overwhelmed by their anger and despair—but these older men and women had apparently made peace with their strange turns of fate.

The first woman I met was so upbeat I grew suspicious. Živka Garbac was wearing a black skirt and a blue muscle T-shirt emblazoned with two palm trees and an English inscription: SUNDAY. She described her garden and the produce she shared with other refugees, her work in the kitchen, the cakes she baked for the children in the center; only the day before she had prepared a pig for her grandson's wedding. He had been wounded in the head and stomach, then imprisoned; upon his release, Croatian authorities gave him a house on the coast (which had probably once belonged to a Serbian family); now he was about to marry. Živka's husband and son had not fared so well. She had also lost her two houses and everything she owned except the clothes she was wearing. This she told me with a smile.

Her new boyfriend, a retired coal miner named Nikola Raković, said his entire family had fought in the war—men, women, children, grandchildren, and a great-grandchild. "When I retired, I spent my time farming," he said. "I had two horses, cows, pigs. I had my own forest and meadow. But I could see this coming. We had no weapons, and the Serbs were fully armed. They were bringing in guns for a long time—on helicopters and airplanes."

He showed me a photograph of his grandson in uniform; his son, he said with pride, had been on the front lines since the beginning of the war. "They burned my house and took all my animals. In my village they burned the church last. The only thing they can't take is the land."

Through the afternoon we listened to stories of destroyed houses and churches, ruined orchards and vineyards—one old Bosnian couple and their neighbors had even hid in their basement while the Serbs burned their house down. All had lost loved ones. And all wanted to return to their homes, even if it meant living in a tent, as one refugee said. Only the last old woman who talked to us, Katarina Gasparović, did not want to go back. She had thick arms and a heavily lined face; her red hair was balding at the top. She came from Rakovica, near Plitvica, once the most popular national park in Yugoslavia; before the war, 10,000 people a day had visited the region southwest of Zagreb, hiking to its lakes and in its deep forests, where bears, wolves, and wild boars lived. Katarina had been in the center for almost three years.

"Our village was attacked for months," she said, "but we kept working, going into the basements during the bombing. On November 15th eight tanks entered the village. People started to flee. I didn't want to leave my son, who was in the army. But he had a bad leg and couldn't go anywhere. And he trusted the Serbs. He was an electrician before the war, he wired all their houses. When he stayed behind, I went with a man on a tractor into the forest."

But the woods crackled with gunfire, and their tractor ran out of gas.

After three days and nights, a friend came and took them to another village, where they endured five weeks of intense fighting. At last she and other refugees boarded buses for Bosnia, which went only a few kilometers before being stopped by artillery fire.

"We had to walk forty kilometers through the woods," she said, "from four in the afternoon until sunrise. We came to a village in Bosnia, where we had tea and more buses came to take us away."

"Forty kilometers!" said Marina, shaking her head.

"Yes, I had a stroke," said the old woman. "I was five weeks in a hospital and five more in a spa. I knit when I can, but my hand is bad: it is often blocked. I'm the only one here from that region, because I'm the only one with family in Zagreb. My daughter works with the invalids, but I would like to go home. My son? They killed him. And then they burned my village down."

Tears welled in her eyes. "In World War II the Serbs killed my husband," she cried. "Now they have killed my son. I stayed alone with four children after the last war. My oldest daughter died seven years ago, and now they have killed my youngest son."

On our way out of the center we met Živka again. She showed us photographs of her son's wedding and funeral. "I was in an asylum during his funeral," she said, then gave me a gift, a hand-stitched doily. "I lost two brothers in World War II," she continued. "I lost a grandson in a car accident. I lost my husband and son in this war. I have some kind of curse on my family." Then she left.

Outside, Marina said, "When I was translating for the Spanish, we heard these stories all the time. 'I lost my father, my brother, my husband, my son,' they'd say. Then I'd have to ask, 'What are your needs? Five kilos of sugar?' It's crazy. What they need is what no one can give them: a father, a brother, a husband, a son."

We went on to another refugee camp, where more than a hundred Croats from central Bosnia were crammed into a converted barracks and ten huts fashioned out of sheet metal. In one hut the size of a small bedroom lived a family of nine. "My father," a little boy said proudly, pointing at the hut, "is an epileptic."

Relief workers from France Libertés had spent the last four days setting up an outdoor miniature circus. Actors taught the children to juggle; a film crew recorded the rehearsals; the next night there would be a performance, and then the humanitarians would pack up their masks, costumes, ring, curtains, and go home.

Raifa, a large woman who was in charge of the camp, led us into the barracks and assembled eight women in a space no bigger than a college dormitory room; a clothesline stretched from the only window to the door, and curtains hid her family's belongings. While the women, ranging in age from thirty to seventy, sat on a pair of beds and knitted, Raifa made strong Turkish coffee for Marina and me. In her village of Gracanica, she said, she had owned a three-story house with nine large rooms.

"If somebody had told me someday I would live, cook, and wash dishes in one room, I would have killed myself," she said with a laugh.

Their living conditions were abysmal: one washing machine (donated by a French relief organization), one ten-liter hot water heater, tiny tubs instead of showers in which to bathe. Families of six or seven people slept in a room. The unlighted hallway was lined with split wood, potatoes, onions, lockers, cardboard boxes, shoes. There were three toilets for the entire camp.

"We came in May 1992," said Ruza, a handsome woman dressed in red. "Only older women and children could go; the rest had to stay and fight. Our army fought the Serbs for three months and lost. Serbs occupy our village. We don't know what became of our houses. We came to Zagreb because before the war our husbands worked in a factory here. The factory turned this place into a camp."

"What do you miss most?" I asked the women.

"Everything," Iva, the youngest, said, laughing, "and the fact that our families are split up. My sister's in Germany, my brother's on the front—and that's typical."

Raifa took us on a brief tour of the camp. We began with the bathroom, where I was nearly overcome by the stench, and ended near the circus, where children wearing masks and costumes were playing. The air was filled with laughter. The French humanitarians eyed us suspiciously. Raifa's oldest son, dressed as a clown, asked me for sweets. She twisted his ear with a smile.

"The children go to school," she said, patting him on the head. "They have no problems with their classmates, but they have no books. And us? We get up in the morning, we take coffee, we talk, we knit. Winter is coming, so we have to make new socks."

"Do you have any hope of returning?" I said.

"Those who come from occupied villages have their doubts," she sighed. "We go to church every Sunday to meet the other Bosnians. Only God knows how long this will last. We never thought we would be here this long."

Marina and I left without a word. The sky was overcast. Rain was on its way. I recalled what her older sister, Jadranka, had said about refugees in Croatia: "They're like people who've lost a limb. Amputees. They can still feel their homeland, even though it's gone: it tingles. Subconsciously they know everything was destroyed, but as long as they're in a camp they can dream it's still there. Those who integrate into society know they'll never go back, those in camps all believe they'll return."

Marina led me through a vacant lot and soon we came to a wide thoroughfare. We walked past Croatia's only film studio, which on this day was deserted; in the parking lot were three rusted trucks and abandoned props. Marina let out a long sigh.

"Frightening," she said. "They've been there three years, and you see how they don't do anything to fix the place up? They could paint those rooms. They could pool their resources and buy some paint. Or ask the factory for money. And the smell in Raifa's room! It always smells like that. It comes from cooking with too much grease in a small place."

Marina's anger, I knew, was born of frustration. Rebel Serbs in Krajina held 30 percent of Croatia's territory, the tourist industry had collapsed in the wake of the fighting, hotels on the Dalmatian coast were filled with refugees. There were 14,000 UN peacekeepers in Croatia, and the economy was a shambles: the war had hindered the transition to a market economy (the government was in no hurry to privatize), and the refugees strained the country's ability to provide services to its own citizens. And nothing would change for years to come, was what many Croats believed. In such conditions it was easy to blame the refugees for Croatia's problems.

"Frightening," Marina repeated.

She had left Zagreb abruptly, without saying where she was going, and no one at the research institute could tell me when she might return. If you wait, said her assistant, perhaps she will call. I was more relieved than disappointed to lose out on an interview with the Bosnian lawyer: how to ask her about her internment in a rape camp. I knew only that in exile she was coordinating a study of Serbian propaganda, so I took a seat to listen to her colleagues describe Slobodan Milošević's mastery of the communist tactic known as "special war": inventing enemies, internal and external, in order to unite and discipline the people. Thus he painted a picture, through the media, of Croatian Ustaše and fundamentalist Muslims preparing to overrun the Serbs, and so on.

"Special war," it occurred to me, was what Serbian paramilitaries and soldiers waged when they began a systematic campaign to rape Muslim and Croatian women (as many as 20,000, the European Commission of Inquiry would conclude). What better way to ethnically cleanse a town or village than to subject its citizens to the most intimate, and heinous, crime short of murder? In *Rape Warfare: The Hidden Genocide in Bosnia-Herzegovina and Croatia* (1996), Beverly Allen unearthed an official document, from the army's special services, which suggests the Serbian rationale for raping, in public view, three-year-old girls and eighty-two-year-old women:

> Our analysis of the behavior of the Muslim communities demonstrates that
> the morale, will, and bellicose nature of their groups can be undermined only
> if we aim our action at the point where the religious and social structure is
> most fragile. We refer to the women, especially adolescents, and to the chil-
> dren.

"Genocidal rape" was the term coined by Allen for what Serbian forces did to Bosnian and Croatian women and girls, a new crime against humanity which generally took three forms. First, paramilitaries would enter a village, drag women from their homes, rape them, and leave, so terrifying the other villagers that when the regular army soon arrived they readily agreed to abandon their homes. Then there were concentration camps, where women were raped and often killed. Finally, the rape camps: the restaurants, hotels, hospitals, factories, schools, and stables in which women were impregnated (the raping continued until the pregnancies could not be terminated, resulting in the births of hundreds of unwanted babies) or executed. This was indeed a special war.

As for the Bosnian lawyer I had arranged to interview? She never called.

Perhaps I will never understand Ferida Duraković's decision to return to Sarajevo. In the winter of 1995, the poet had gone to an artist's colony in Oregon, where she could have stayed for the duration of the war. Yet in May, at the height of the Bosnian offensive, when the airlift was suspended indefinitely, she took a bus from Zagreb as far up Mount Igman as Serbian sniping and shelling would allow, then hiked for more than two hours, with four heavy pieces of luggage, through the forest until she came to a house in Hrasnica. There she waited until dark to risk going through the tunnel under the airport the day after Serbian gunners had shelled the entrance, killing ten. But first she and several others had to cross a corn-field and wait for an hour and a half outside the tunnel while Bosnian soldiers went through.

It was nearing curfew when Ferida, the last civilian in line, claustrophobic and struggling to catch her breath (she suffered from tachycardia), started down the stairs—and almost fainted. She went outside and sat down. She considered spending the night in Hrasnica, but her fear of dying before delivering to her family the presents she had brought from America persuaded her to try again. This time in the tunnel a draft of air caught her by surprise. I realized I could breathe, she said. It was marvelous. The tunnel was only wide enough for one, and Ferida had to stoop lower and lower until she was nearly crawling. "God is so near, so hard to grasp." She was reciting Hölderlin to keep up her courage. "But where danger lies, salvation also grows." Then she was in another cornfield, lugging her bags to Dobrinja, where she found a taxi driver who took her partway home, claiming to be out of gas; before the night was over she would walk another kilometer, then up fifteen flights of stairs to her brother's apartment. And within two weeks of her return, telling her boyfriend it was now or never (the Serbian shelling was continuous), Ferida was pregnant.

"Why did I do this?" she said. "I guess you could say it was the Grand Yes."

As for the peace accord?

"This could have happened two hundred thousand lives ago," she said.

It was the first warm day of the new millennium, and the streets of Podgorica, the Montenegrin capital, were filled with women clutching bouquets of flowers, celebrating International Women's Day. An eight-piece Gypsy band was heading for the center of town, where a Yugoslav army armored vehicle had taken up its position at a crosswalk. "I have learned over the years that when you feel the people growing quiet and cautious they are gearing up for the next blow," an American humanitarian told me soon after that telltale hush had descended over her Montenegrin friends. It was an explosive silence, and I felt it, too, wherever I went in the smallest republic of the former Yugoslavia.

Less than a year after enduring military defeat at the hands of NATO, Slobodan Milošević was taking steps to crush Montenegro's bid for independence. In the last year the indicted war criminal had infiltrated paramilitaries and special police units into the republic and closed the Serbian border, cutting off most of Montenegro's supply of food and medicine. During my travels in the war zones of Bosnia, Croatia, and Slovenia, in the thick of fighting and in its aftermath, I had often heard prophecies of Serbs fighting Serbs. And Montenegro, where the largely Slavic population is split between Serbs (who want to remain in Yugoslavia) and Montenegrins (who want to secede), though there is no ethnic or religious difference between the two, was on the verge of civil war. Miloševíc, who had lost four wars in the last decade while leading the Serbian people into economic ruin, resembled a wounded, cornered animal, probing his neighbors' defenses and the international community's resolve. French Foreign Minister Hubert Vedrine warned that invading Montenegro would be

"Slobodan Milošević's final mistake." But just before I arrived in Podgorica, Carl Bildt, the UN Special Representative to the Balkans, told the Security Council that Serbia and Montenegro are on a "slow collision course." And as a high-ranking Yugoslav army officer told an analyst for the Institute for Reporting on War and Peace, "For us war is a fait accompli, but we do not know exactly when it will break out."

I was crossing the bridge over the Moraca River when I heard shouting from a car on the opposite side of the road. Four young men had caught the attention of a woman walking ahead of me. She was dressed more provocatively than Montenegrin women, in her high heels, bright white pants, and a black blouse that left her midriff bare; and when she looked away from them the car cut across the traffic and sped up to the sidewalk. In English one man yelled, "I will kill you!" and spat at her again and again until she slapped his hand, her eyes wild with rage. Then the car drove off, but another one arrived with more young men shouting and spitting at her until she crossed the street and disappeared. I asked two teenage boys who had witnessed the event why the men were so angry. It occurred to me that the woman was a white slave (a Russian or Moldavian prostitute working, as a friend said, under strict passport control: the pimp keeps it). But all the boys would say was that she was crazy.

"What do you mean?" I said.

"Crazy," they repeated in unison.

NOTE

Portions of this essay originally appeared in *The Old Bridge: The Third Balkan War and the Age of the Refugee* (Minneapolis, Minn.: Milkweed Editions, 1995); *Only the Nails Remain: Scenes from the Balkan Wars* (Lanham, Md.: Rowman and Littlefield, 1999); and *Men's Journal* (April 2000).

About the Contributors

MAHNAZ AFKHAMI is president of Women's Learning Partnership and former Minister of State for Women's Affairs in Iran. She is the executive director of the Foundation for Iranian Studies and serves on advisory boards for a number of national and international organizations. She has also served as president of the Sisterhood Is Global Institute. Afkhami has been a leading advocate of women's rights internationally for the last three decades. She created the concept and mobilized support for the establishment of the Asian and Pacific Centre for Women and Development (APCWD) and the United Nations International Research and Training Institute for the Advancement of Women (INSTRAW). She has written and lectured extensively on women's human rights, women in leadership, and women, civil society, and democracy. Among her publications are *Women in the Law in Iran* (1993), *Women in Exile* (1994), *Faith and Freedom: Women's Human Rights in the Muslim World* (1995), *Claiming Our Rights: A Manual for Women's Human Rights Education in Muslim Societies* (1996), *Muslim Women and the Politics of Participation: Implementing the Beijing Platform* (1997), and *Safe and Secure: Eliminating Violence Against Women and Girls in Muslim Societies* (1998).

SUSAN C. BOURQUE is the Esther Booth Wiley Professor of Government at Smith College. Her books include *The Politics of Women's Education* (1993), *Learning about Women* (1989), *Women Living Change* (1985) and *Women of the Andes* (1981). She is at work on two volumes of essays: one on gender and race in Latin America and the second on women and leadership.

JULIA C. CHILL is director of administration for the Bioethics Institute at Johns Hopkins University. She currently serves as chair of the Children's Human Rights Network for Amnesty International-USA and on the steering committee for the U.S. Alliance for the Convention on the Rights of the Child. She has served in both an administrative and programmatic capacity at numerous organizations and is particularly concerned about human rights issues affecting children. Chill has written articles on children's rights and on health professionals' complicity in torture, as well as edited various publications on human rights issues. She holds a masters in public health from the School of Hygiene and Public Health at Johns Hopkins University and a bachelor of arts from the University of Chicago.

SHEILA DAUER is director of Amnesty International-USA's Women's Human Rights Program. She has developed several pivotal training and outreach programs as well as a campaign for indigenous rights. She is a charter member of an AI-USA Taskforce on Women's Human Rights, she has worked with both International and US AI staff, board and volunteer leaders to develop AI's mandate, action, and publications on women's human rights. In 1991, she prepared AI's first international report on women's human rights, Women in the Front Line. She has directed AI-USA's campaign on women's human rights concurrent with the UN 4th World Human Rights Program. Dauer received two research fellowships from the National Institute of Mental Health and a Ford Foundation Fellowship on Women's Studies.

ARVONNE S. FRASER is Senior Fellow Emerita, Humphrey Institute of Public Affairs, University of Minnesota and the former director of the International Women's Rights Action Watch (IWRAW) project, which focused on publicizing and monitoring the women's human rights treaty, the Convention on the Elimination of All Forms of Discrimination Against Women. She also organized and codirected the Center on Women and Public Policy at the Institute. In 1993–1994, she served as U.S. representative to the UN Commission on the Status of Women with the rank of Ambassador and was a U.S. delegate to the 1993 World Conference on Human Rights. In 1977–1978, she directed the Office of Women in Development at the United States Agency for International Development and was a U.S. delegate to the 1975 and 1980 UN World Conferences on Women. In the 1970s she was president and legislative director of the Women's Equity Action League (WEAL), an organization that focused on opening educational and employment opportunities for women.

FELICE GAER is a member of the Committee against Torture, a United Nations treaty monitoring body. She directs the Jacob Blaustein Institute for the Advancement of Human Rights of the American Jewish Committee. Gaer served as a public advisor to the United States delegation to the Beijing World Conference on Women. In 1995 she was awarded the Alumnae Achievement Award of Wellesley College.

MARY GESKE is an assistant professor of government at Smith College. Her work has appeared in *Alternatives* and *International Politics*. Her current research project focuses on sex tourism in Cuba.

BARBARA HARLOW teaches English at the University of Texas at Austin and has taught in Cairo, Galway (Ireland), and Pietermaritzburg (South Africa). She is the author of *Resistance Literature* (1987), *Barred: Women, Writing, and Political Detention* (1992), and *After Lives: Legacies of Revolutionary Writing* (1996), and coeditor, with Mia Carter, of *Imperialism and Orientalism: A Documentary Sourcebook* (1999). She is currently working on an intellectual biography of Ruth First.

TEMMA KAPLAN, an activist and a historian, has worked in grassroots movements of women dealing with civil rights, human rights, and social citizenship. A longtime scholar of women's studies, she has directed the Barnard Center for Research on Women and the Women's Studies Program at the State University of New York at Stony Brook. The author of three books, Temma Kaplan has combined her social and artistic commitments with her scholarship. Her most recent books are *Red City, Blue Period: Social Movements in Picasso's Barcelona* (1993); and *Crazy for Democracy: Women's Grassroots Movements* (1997). She is currently finishing a book entitled *Taking Back the Streets: Women, Popular Democracy, and Historical Memory* (forthcoming in 2002).

SUSAN KILBOURNE is the assistant director of Child Rights International Research Institute. She also serves on the steering committees of Amnesty International-

USA's Children's Human Rights Network and the U.S. Alliance for the Convention on the Rights of the Child, and as Director of Research for the Convention on the Rights of the Child Project of the American Bar Association Section of Individual Rights and Responsibilities. Kilbourne is the author of several law review articles and other publications on children's rights and has spoken on the subject of political opposition to U.S. ratification of the Convention on the Rights of the Child at many national conferences, law schools, and human rights events. She earned a J.D. degree from Georgetown University Law Center, an M.A. from George Washington University, and a B.S. from the University of Massachusetts.

JULIE H. LEVISON is a magna cum laude graduate of Wellesley College with a degree in history. As a Rhodes Scholar, Levison earned a M.Phil. degree in history at Oxford University, where she was awarded distinction for her thesis on the history of leprosy in Puerto Rico. Levison began her research in health and human rights while studying under the late Jonathan Mann, M.D., M.P.H., the first director of the World Health Organization's Global Programme on AIDS. A student at Harvard Medical School, Levison is coeditor, with Marjorie Agosín, of *Magical Sites: Women Travelers to Nineteenth-Century Latin America.*

SANDRA P. LEVISON, M.D., M.A.C.P., is a tenured professor of medicine at the MCP-Hahnemann University School of Medicine, where she is also chief of the division of nephrology and hypertension, nephrology fellowship program director, senior consultant to the Institute of Women's Health, and clinical service chief of medicine at the Medical College of Pennsylvania Hospital. Dr. Levison received her Bachelor of Arts degree, cum laude, from Hunter College in New York and her M.D. degree from New York University School of Medicine. For many years, she has supported women's health issues as cochair of the National Academy on Women's Health Medical Education. In 1993 she was awarded a U.S. Department of Education Fund for the Improvement of Post-Secondary Education (FIPSE) grant to implement a model medical student curriculum in women's health, which would serve as a template for medical student women's health teaching in the United States. Dr. Levison has written numerous articles on women's health both for professional and lay readers.

CHRISTOPHER MERRILL is a poet and critic and the author and translator of more than a dozen books, including the highly praised *The Old Bridge in the Third Balkan War* and the *Age of the Refugee.* His writings have appeared in such publications as the *Los Angeles Times,* the *San Francisco Chronicle, The Nation,* and *Paris Review.* He holds the William H. Jenks Chair in Contemporary Letters at the College of the Holy Cross.

SALLY ENGLE MERRY is professor of anthropology and codirector of the Peace and Justice Studies Program at Wellesley College. She is the author of four books and edited collections, including *Getting Justice and Getting Even: Legal Consciousness among Working Class Americans: The Possibility of Popular Justice,* coedited with Neil Milner and *Colonizing Hawai'i: The Cultural Power of Law.* She is currently engaged in research on the international movement combating violence against women. She is past president of the Law and Society Association and the Association for Political and Legal Anthropology.

AGATE NESAULE was born in Latvia and witnessed both Nazi and Soviet atrocities during World War II. Her memoir, *A Woman in Amber: Healing the Trauma of War and Exile,* won an American Book Award in 1996. A former professor of English and women's studies at the University of Wisconsin, Whitewater, she is currently at work on a novel.

JOSEPH SLAUGHTER completed his Ph.D. in ethnic and third-world literatures at the University of Texas at Austin in 1998. He has published articles on human rights and on African and Latin American literature. He is currently working on a book that explores the relationships between the development of human rights law and the international novel.

JANE STAPLETON, a teacher, writer, researcher, and community service provider, focuses on issues related to social justice and equity. She helped to establish and was a staff member of the Sexual Harassment and Rape Prevention Program (SHARPP), one of the first campus-based rape crisis centers in the United States, at the University of New Hampshire. She is a former member and secretary of the board of directors for the New Hampshire Coalition Against Domestic and Sexual Violence and has worked as an independent sexual harassment training consultant. Currently, at the University of New Hampshire Stapleton coordinates the President's Commission on the Status of People of Color and the President's Commission on the Status of Women and provides support to the President's Task Force on Gay, Lesbian, Bisexual and Transgender Issues. Appointed by the governor, she also serves as the treasurer of the New Hampshire Commission on the Status of Women.

CAROLA SUÁREZ-OROZCO is the codirector of the Harvard Immigration Project. She is also a Senior Research Associate and Lecturer in Human Development and Psychology at the Harvard Graduate School of Education. She coauthored, with Marcelo Suárez-Orozco, *Transformations: Migration, Family Life and Achievement Motivation Among Latino Adolescents,* the recipient of the 1995 Best Book Award from the Society on Research in Adolescence. The Suárez-Orozcos are also the authors of *Children of Immigration.* Currently they are editing a six-volume series on *The New Immigration* for Garland Press.

JEAN TROUNSTINE, a professor at Middlesex Community College in Massachusetts, worked at Framingham Women's Prison for ten years, where she directed eight plays with inmates and received awards for her work from the Massachusetts Humanities Foundation, Women in Philanthropy, and the Jewish Women's Archives. She has written extensively about her work with women offenders. Her books include *Changing Lives Through Literature* (Notre Dame Press, 1999) and *Shakespeare Behind Bars: The Power of Drama in a Women's Prison* (St. Martin's Press, 2001).

JENNIFER WENZEL teaches postcolonial literature in the English department at Stonehill College. She earned her Ph.D. in English, with a specialization in ethnic and third-world literatures, at the University of Texas at Austin. She has published articles on African and South Asian literature, and she is currently completing a manuscript on the Bengali writer and activist Mahasweta Devi and the South African novelist J. M. Coetzee.

Index

About the Editor

Marjorie Agosín is an award-winning poet and recipient of the United Nations Leadership Award for Human Rights and the Gabriella Mistral Medal of Honor. She is a professor of Spanish at Wellesley College. Among her most recent books are *A Map of Hope: Women's Writing on Human Rights—An International Literary Anthology* and the autobiographical *The Alphabet in My Hands*, both published by Rutgers University Press.